Proverbs Are Never Out of Season

PROVERBS ARE NEVER OUT OF SEASON

Popular Wisdom in the Modern Age

WOLFGANG MIEDER

OXFORD UNIVERSITY PRESS

New York   Oxford   1993

Oxford University Press

Oxford New York Toronto
Delhi Bombay Calcutta Madras Karachi
Kuala Lumpur Singapore Hong Kong Tokyo
Nairobi Dar es Salaam Cape Town
Melbourne Auckland Madrid

and associated companies in
Berlin Ibadan

Copyright © 1993 by Oxford University Press, Inc.

Published by Oxford University Press, Inc.
200 Madison Avenue, New York, New York 10016

Oxford is a registered trademark of Oxford University Press

Library of Congress Cataloging-in-Publication Data
Mieder, Wolfgang.
Proverbs are never out of season:
popular wisdom in the modern age / Wolfgang Mieder.
p. cm.   Includes bibliographical references and indexes.
ISBN 0-19-507728-8
1. Proverbs—History and criticism.   I. Title.
PN6401.M49 1993
398.9—dc20   92-25051

9 8 7 6 5 4 3 2 1

Printed in the United States of America
on acid-free paper

This book is dedicated to

TEUFEL

my Black Labrador who from 1980–1991
was the best of all proverbial friends

CONTENTS

INTRODUCTION

Even though some scholars and popular writers have claimed repeatedly that proverbial language has passed from usage in contemporary American culture, it remains an easily proven fact that proverbs are not passé and definitely not dead. They have not lost their well-established popularity, and they continue to be ever present, even in a modern technological society like that of the United States. This has recently been made abundantly clear by the thousands of proverbs registered in *A Dictionary of American Proverbs* (New York: Oxford University Press, 1992) edited by Stewart A. Kingsbury, Kelsie B. Harder, and myself. These texts were collected in this country from oral use during the forty-year span from 1945 to 1985, and they are ample proof of the vitality of proverbial wisdom in the twentieth century. It would be absurd to proclaim the twilight of the proverbs when they are in fact thriving in a manner that appears to match the frequent use of proverbial language during the sixteenth century. This golden age of the proverb abounded with traditional proverbs that continue to be in common use today.

Yet it would also be a mistake to assume that all proverbs in circulation at the present time must by definition be old bits of wisdom. Scholars have shown that the time of proverb creations is by no means over. While we continue to use many of the proverbs that can be traced back to classical times, the wisdom literature of the Jewish and Christian tradition, or the widely disseminated vernacular wisdom of the Middle Ages, we must not forget that new proverbs have been created at all times. This is also true for a modern society characterized by technology, mass culture, and rapid urbanization. Even the most sophisticated and best educated people appear to be in need of the pithy wisdom contained in metaphorical proverbs. While such old proverbs like "Hanging and wiving go by destiny" or "One knife whets another" might be dropping out, new ones have been and continue to be created to reflect our changing value system. Thus, the relatively recent proverb "Different strokes for different folks" from the mid-twentieth century is a truly new American proverb with wide currency. It expresses the liberating idea that people ought to have the opportunity to live their lives according to their own wishes. For once we have a proverb that is not prescriptive or blatantly didactic. Instead, it expresses the American worldview that individuals have the right to at least some free choice. Another example of a modern proverb would be "Garbage in, garbage out," indicating clearly its origin in the computer world. But of course this proverb does not have to be interpreted only literally as a comment on the frustrations that everybody has felt at times with computers. The text has long taken on the metaphorical meaning of cause and effect, that is, if you don't provide good information, the result will certainly be negative as well.

Proverbs, both old and new, continue to serve us well as concise statements of apparent truths. We might ridicule or parody them at times, but we are governed at least to some degree by their insights into human nature and the world as such. To be sure, some proverbs appear rather one-sided or even narrow-minded, but it must be remembered that proverbs are *not* absolute or universal truths. This is abundantly clear from such opposing proverb pairs as "Absence makes the heart grow fonder" and "Out of sight, out of mind." Proverbs only make sense in a given situation or context, and we will always choose that proverbial text that happens to suit us best. And if we can't find a particular proverb for the right occasion, it has become customary to simply change existing proverbs through additions or alterations of certain words. These manipulated proverbs might be called anti-proverbs, but such varied texts as "A new broom sweeps clean, but the old one knows the corners" or "You can't judge a car by its paint job" indicate a fascinating interplay of tradition and innovation in proverb use. Varying the common proverb "If the shoe fits, wear it," it could well be argued that we employ proverbs according to the maxim "If the proverb fits, use it." Proverbs are flexible and adaptable to ever new contexts and interpretations, because their metaphorical language is not limited to specific contexts. They contain plenty of truth, wisdom, and knowledge, which they express in a few colorful words. The message of the proverb is communicated quickly and to the point, making it a very useful tool in oral speech, political rhetoric, newspaper headlines, book titles, advertising slogans, cartoon captions, and so on. If used to manipulate people economically or politically, proverbs might even become dangerous weapons as expressions of stereotypical invectives or unfounded generalizations. But, for the most part, it can be said that if used consciously and perhaps somewhat sparingly, proverbs remain to the present day a most effective verbal tool. Proverbs are indeed very much in season in America today, and the statement "A proverb is worth a thousand words" will continue to be true for generations to come.

The ten chapters of this book all address the question of how proverbial wisdom survives in the modern age, that is, they deal with historical questions while at the same time emphasizing today's use and function of proverbs. While their titles and explanatory subtitles speak for themselves, the following paragraphs will serve as a short general overview of their content in order to introduce the reader to the specific issues addressed in them. The first four chapters range from definition problems, questions of form, structure, and content to considerations of how proverbs relate to cultural literacy and how they are used in the modern age. Next come two chapters that investigate the origin, history, and use of two specific proverbs, notably "Early to bed and early to rise, makes a man healthy, wealthy and wise" and "A picture is worth a thousand words." Two additional chapters discuss the subgenre of medical proverbs and regional Vermont proverbs. This is followed by a chapter showing how an old German proverb has become a very popular expression in the United States as "Don't throw the baby out with the bath water." Finally, there is the special chapter on "Proverbs in Nazi Germany" which is included to show the danger in the misuse of folklore in general and proverbs in particular. A detailed bibliography summarizes all publications on proverbs, both collections and studies, that are contained in the extensive notes to each chapter, and name, subject, and proverb indexes are also provided.

The first chapter on "The Wit of One, and the Wisdom of Many" presents a general discussion on the nature of the proverb. It is argued that proverbs are exactly not simple but rather complex verbal expressions. Several scholarly and popular definitions are analyzed, stressing the difficulty of establishing the traditionality and currency of proverbs that are definitely part of the characteristics of proverbiality. Some of the more easily recognizable markers of this proverbiality are certain structural aspects as well as external and internal markers. To the former belong such poetic and stylistic features as alliteration, rhyme, parallelism, ellipsis, and repetition, while the latter include personification, hyperbole, paradox, and metaphor. It is also pointed out that proverbs as metaphorical speech depend on the social context and function for their meaning. In fact, proverbs exhibit a kind of semantic indefiniteness because of their hetero-situationality, poly-functionality, and poly-semanticity. In addition to comments on various functions and the content of proverbs, this chapter also includes a detailed discussion on the origin of proverbs, that is, classical antiquity, Biblical wisdom literature, medieval Latin and vernacular proverbs, and so on. Above all, the point is made that proverbs always originate with an individual and there are usually variants until a standard form becomes traditional through a collective selection process. This is what Lord John Russell in the nineteenth century meant by defining the proverb as "The wit of one, and the wisdom of many."

While it is one thing for scholars to attempt an inclusive definition of the proverb, it is obviously also of interest to see what the actual folk thinks about proverbs. Thus, the second chapter with the popular definition of "A Proverb Is a Short Sentence of Wisdom" as its title deals with the popular views of the proverb. Fifty-five definitions formulated by students, friends, and acquaintances are analyzed and augmented by a discussion of what authors of general magazine and newspaper articles have had to say about proverbs. There is also a look at proverbs about proverbs, such as "Proverbs are the children of experience" and "All the good sense of the world runs into proverbs." In addition to registering and discussing many definition attempts, it is also shown that just because proverbs contradict each other, they cannot be dismissed as useless for people of the modern age. Proverbs have never claimed to be universally true, but they are correct in certain given contexts and situations. To argue that proverbs are passé because of such obvious limitations strikes us as uninformed intellectual snobbery. Imperfect as these bits of traditional wisdom might be, they continue to flow freely into our oral and written speech on all personal and professional levels. Lord Chesterfield's famous dictum that "A man of fashion never has recourse to proverbs and vulgar aphorisms" is as wrong today as it was in the year 1749 when he tried in a letter to dissuade his son from using proverbial wisdom.

The question of what proverbs have a particularly high frequency in American speech is answered in the third chapter on "Proverbs Everyone Ought to Know." Scholars throughout the world, but especially in the Soviet Union, Germany, and the United States, have attempted in the last twenty years to find out what the paremiological minimum for their respective languages might be. As folklorists, sociologists, psychologists, or psycholinguists, they have attempted to establish lists of those proverbs that have a high frequency or currency by using modern demographic methods including sophisticated questionnaires. We now know that proverbs like "Where there is a will, there's a way," "Practice makes perfect," "The early bird catches the worm," "If at first you don't succeed, try, try again," and "A bird in the hand is worth two in the bush" are especially well known in the United States. As such they make up part of the cultural literacy of English speakers, and the most common of them form a minimum of proverbial knowledge that one must have to communicate effectively in the English language. This fact is of great significance for lexicographers involved in writing foreign language dictionaries or for teachers who teach English as a second language. Realizing that there are so many non-native speakers in countries where English is the primary language, it is of much value to establish such meaningful paremiological minima so that we may assure meaningful metaphorical communication.

The fourth chapter on "Old Wisdom in New Clothing" is an attempt to show how traditional proverbs are used in an innovative fashion in modern communication. It is pointed out that seemingly antiquated proverbs can be adapted very well to new contexts by changing and twisting them to fit the modern age. The chapter is made up of four major sections, each treating a particular phenomenon of proverb use on a diachronic and synchronic level. The first part shows how traditional proverb illustrations can be traced from medieval woodcuts to Pieter Brueghel's famous oil painting of "Netherlandic

Proverbs" (1559) and on to modern cartoons, caricatures, and comic strips. At each given period in time these illustrations of proverbs reflect the mores and worldview of the people using them for serious or also humorous communication. The second section depicts how proverbs are often misogynous, expressing chauvinistic ideas and sexual stereotypes. Such proverbs as "Diamonds are a girl's best friend" or "A woman's place is in the home" still abound today, but there are now also noticeable liberating reactions against such sexual politics. Especially in some innovative advertisements and cartoons we can recognize conscious parodies of older proverbs, as for example "A Ms. is as good as a Male." The third part of this chapter deals with proverbs and their critical variations in lyrical poetry, citing poems by John Heywood, John Gay, Samuel Taylor Coleridge, Eliza Cook, Vincent Godfrey Burns, Arthur Guiterman, W. H. Auden, John Robert Colombo, Ambrose Bierce, and others. And the final section investigates the popularity of the originally German proverb "Who does not love wine, woman, and song, will remain a fool his whole life long" in the English language. It is shown that William Makepeace Thackeray around 1862 was instrumental in getting this proverb known among English speakers. By now it has become so popular that it is often used in the truncated form of "Wine, women, and song" in headlines, slogans, cartoons, and also on T-shirts. Many times proverbs continue to be used in their traditional wording, but quite often their wisdom is being questioned and they are parodied or perverted into anti-proverbs. Nevertheless, it must be remembered that such playing and punning with proverbs is only possible if the original texts are also somehow still known. The juxtaposition of traditional and innovative proverb texts is what makes the modern use of proverbs in the mass media, literature, and oral speech so fascinating and worthy of serious study.

There exists a long tradition of investigating the origin, history, and use of individual proverbs, and the fifth chapter of this book on the proverb "Early to bed and early to rise, makes a man healthy, wealthy and wise" follows this scholarly model. It is shown that Benjamin Franklin did *not* coin this particular proverb when he used it in his *Poor Richard's Almanack* in 1735 and again in 1758 as part of his famous essay on "The Way to Wealth." Early variants of this proverb go back to the fifteenth century, and it appeared as early as 1639 in exactly the wording that Franklin employed in John Clarke's bilingual proverb collection *Paroemiologia Anglo-Latina*. But Franklin helped to popularize the proverb, and so much so, that Mark Twain reacted to it with splendid irony and humor several times. Other parodies from George Ade, Groucho Marx, and literary authors from the nineteenth and twentieth centuries are reviewed, and the chapter also includes a whole list of humorous reactions to this deeply ethical proverb that appeared in newspapers, advertisements, cartoons, comic strips, and greeting cards. The chapter concludes with the observation that people today don't associate this proverb of rigid Puritan ethics very much with Benjamin Franklin anymore, thus returning the proverb to its proper folkloric anonymity.

The sixth chapter once again investigates one singular proverb, this time the frequently used text "A picture is worth a thousand words." Here we have the rare occasion when the originator of the proverb is indeed known. It was the advertising agent Fred R. Barnard who coined and used it for the first time as part of an advertisement on December 8, 1921, in the magazine *Printers' Ink*. He had realized that a predominance of visual communication was taking hold in the United States, and he argued convincingly that good advertising definitely needed pictures as much as or even more than words. His text now summarizes the so-called visualization of American culture, a worldview that is also expressed in the proverb "Seeing is believing." It should not be surprising that Barnard's proverb invention caught on quickly, gaining currency throughout the United States and by now in the other English-speaking countries as well. It has even been translated into other languages, having gained proverbial status in Germany, for example. The many textual references from the past decades all show how an invented text based on a proverbial structure can gain rather widespread currency in a short time through the incredible influence of the mass media. The acceptance of this thought and its subsequent elevation to true proverbiality were, of course, only possible since its message conformed to the actual worldview prevalent in modern society.

Proverbs have often been divided according to content or common themes, and we can even talk about weather, legal, and medical proverbs as actual subgenres. In the seventh chapter the traditional and modern aspects of medical proverbs are treated. Starting with the classical proverb "Mens sana in corpore sana" or its English translation "A sound mind in a sound body" from 1578, it is argued that common-sense attitudes about basic health matters have long been couched in easily recallable proverbs. While such medical proverbs can obviously not compete with modern medical science, they still communicate some general health rules that continue to be applicable in an age of medical specialization. This is especially true for the general medical advice contained in the proverb "Prevention is better than cure" from about 1618 and its longer variant of "An ounce of prevention is worth a pound of cure" that most likely was coined by Benjamin Franklin in 1735. The second example under discussion in this chapter is the proverb "Stuff (Feed) a cold and starve a fever," which actually gives rather precise medical advice since the middle of the nineteenth century. The proverb has come under attack at times by the medical profession, but once we add the word "moderately" to stuffing a cold or starving a fever it actually does make medical sense after all. The third example is a discussion of the proverb "An apple a day keeps the doctor away." It will be somewhat of a surprise to find out that this most popular medical proverb is traceable in print only to the year 1913. As with the other two examples, this proverb is quoted very frequently in its traditional wording, but there are also many modern variations of it in food advertisements, headlines, cartoons, and so on. While the medical wisdom of these proverbs is at best general, they do give valuable advice based on decades of everyday observation. As folk proverbs they are bound to continue competing favorably with the scientific medical language that common folk cannot possibly understand.

In the eighth chapter with the proverb variation "Good Proverbs Make Good Vermonters" as its title we look at the special flavor of one set of regional proverbs. Obviously there are such proverbs as "Time flies" or "Big fish eat little fish" that because of their classical origin have an international currency. There are also many English proverbs known throughout the English-speaking world and certainly also in the United States, for example, "Great oaks from little acorns grow" or "The grass is always greener on the other side of the fence." But there is also such a thing as regional proverbs, texts that refer especially to local aspects of life. It is, of course, difficult to prove for each local proverb that it is indeed restricted in its use to a certain area like the state of Vermont, for example. Care must also be taken that we do not deduce national or regional stereotypical characteristics from folklore in general or proverbs in particular. Nevertheless, the preponderance of proverbs in Vermont dealing with cows, rural life, farming, sugaring, and so on tells us something about the people who live there. Some of the more popular proverbs in Vermont do in fact express such Yankee virtues as ingenuity, perseverance, independence, and thriftiness. Texts like "You can't judge a cow by her looks," "Mud thrown is ground lost," and "The older the tree the sweeter the sap" all reflect the regional flavor of Vermont proverbs. It is also generally felt that the proverb "Good fences make good neighbors" which Robert Frost used in his famous poem "Mending Wall" (1914) is of Vermont if not Frost origin. But unfortunately it appeared as early as 1850 in this precise wording in a farmer's almanac of another state. Such are the pitfalls of regional proverb studies, which is not to say, of course, that the fence proverb is not one of the truly popular proverbs in the state of Vermont.

Since I live in Vermont, it was only natural to choose this state as an example for the flavor of regional proverbs. In the ninth chapter on the proverb or proverbial expression "(Don't) throw the baby out with the bath water" I was once again influenced by my own immigrant heritage. This chapter shows how a proverb that appeared in print for the first time in Germany in 1512 finally makes the jump across the English Channel and eventually to America as a loan translation. Thomas Carlyle used a bad translation of it already in 1849, but it was really only during the beginning of this century that the dramatist George Bernard Shaw popularized it in the English language. By now the proverb or in its wording "To throw the baby out with the bath water" as a proverbial expression have conquered the English-speaking world, as can be seen in headlines, cartoons, slogans, and so on. This chapter also shows what important role lexicographers of dictionaries of phraseology, quotation, or foreign languages play in disseminating proverbs from other languages. The difficulty faced by translators of works by Goethe and Günter Grass who both used the proverb is also discussed at length. Finally there are some comments on texts that were collected in oral use. The result is that the German proverb has become so internationalized by now that most people using it today do not know anymore that it originated in Germany.

As an excursus to the previous chapters and once again indicating my continued interest in German folklore, language, and culture as a German-American, I offer a final chapter on "Proverbs in Nazi Germany." This is a painful study of how such seemingly harmless bits of wisdom as proverbs were misused under the National Socialists to promulgate anti-Semitism and stereotypes. The chapter starts with a discussion of the perversion of the discipline of "Deutsche Volkskunde" (German folklore) under the Nazi regime. This is followed by an analysis of major Yiddish proverb collections from the nineteenth and early twentieth centuries, some of which eventually showed signs of anti-Semitism. But after Adolf Hitler's and Joseph Goebbels' blatant anti-Semitism in their speeches and publications, including the use of anti-Semitic proverbs, German folklorists and linguists started publishing articles and books on proverbial invectives against the Jewish population that are disgusting to a point of nausea. Whole books appeared in the late thirties and early forties that amassed in hundreds of pages anti-Semitic proverbs, at times including invented "proverbs" based on traditional proverbial structures. The discussion of this inhuman activity shows how the German society was infested by evil and unwarranted hate of the European Jews. The "scholarly" activities of these sick minds are a dark period in the study of proverbs, having played their part in bringing about the extermination of innocent people who were first reduced to thieves, liars, and even vermin by anti-Semitic proverbs. Most proverbs in themselves might be harmless pieces of folk wisdom, but when proverbial stereotypes become propagandistic tools in the hands of malicious persons, they can take on unexpected powers of authority, persuasion, and eventually cruelty. There are unfortunately still many regional, national, and international slurs in current use. It is my hope that this final chapter might serve as a warning that proverbs should never again be used to assist in bringing death to millions of innocent people.

Seen as a whole, the ten chapters of this book show how proverbs continue to play a significant role in our modern world. Obviously their misuse and perversion in Nazi Germany is a unique case of their manipulation to to serve certain evil ends, but that does not mean that proverbs in their more general use and function do not serve manipulative goals as well. Their frequent appearance in advertisements, headlines, or political speeches all indicate that proverbs have a highly valued communicative effect. When we use proverbs, we wish to strengthen our arguments or explanations with traditional wisdom that supposedly has withstood the test of time. We will always use those proverbs that fit our reasoning and wishes best, ignoring those that express a contradictory viewpoint. But that is human nature, for we don't live according to universal truths and unchallenged principles. Yet proverbs, those old gems of generationally tested wisdom, help us in our everyday life and communication to cope with the complexities of the modern human condition. The traditional proverbs and their value system give us some basic structure, and if their worldview does not fit a particular situation, they are quickly changed into revealing and liberating anti-proverbs. And there are, of course, also the new proverbs of our time, proverbs like "Different strokes for different folks" that express a more liberal worldview. Proverbs don't always have to be didactic and prescriptive; they can also be full of satire, irony, and humor. As such the thousands of proverbs that make up the stock of proverbial wisdom of all cultures represent not a universally valid but certainly a pragmatically useful treasure.

It is my pleasant duty to thank my many relatives, friends, colleagues, and students for their support and help. Among them are in alphabetical order Shirley L. Arora, Dan Ben-Amos, Janet Besserer, George B. Bryan, Lucille Busker, Walter and Lee Busker, William and Barbara Busker, Alan Dundes, Sandra Goldstein, Eva Maria Goy, Kathryn Henry, Henny Lewin, Kevin McKenna, Dennis Mahoney, Barbara Mieder, Horst and Elfriede Mieder, Kenneth Nalibow, Richard and Francine Page, Ann and Dick Park, Jack and Marlene Price, Veronica Richel, Lutz Röhrich, David Scrase, Helga Schreckenberger, Helmut Walther, and Beatrice Wood. Special thanks are due to the staff of the interlibrary loan office at the University of Vermont, notably Nancy Crane, Barbara Lambert, Patricia Mardeusz, Linda MacDonald, and Ruth Nolan. Our secretary Janet Sobieski of the Department of German and Russian was once again of invaluable help with the production of the manuscript, and I certainly appreciate her interest in my scholarly projects. The same appreciation and thanks are due all of the great people mentioned above and many more. I also want to thank Elizabeth Maguire and T. Susan Chang of the Oxford University Press for all their help in making this book become a reality.

The work on these ten chapters, of which eight have been published previously, spans about eleven years. During all this time I had the comforting company in my study and on walks through the woods of my wonderful

Black Labrador Teufel. He was always a good comrade and certainly a very special friend who invariably was at my side. Even though it might not be immediately noticeable, his spirit is present on many of these pages. A few days before finishing the work on this book, Teufel was tragically killed. How much I would like to exchange this book to have this great fellow back, but all that I can do is dedicate it to Teufel as an expression of my lasting love and enduring memory of him.

Proverbs Are Never
Out of Season

1

" The Wit of One, and the Wisdom of Many "

General Thoughts on the Nature of the Proverb

It is generally accepted that proverbs represent the smallest verbal folklore genre, and this fact might lead some people to the false conclusion that they must also be the simplest form of folklore. But nothing could be further from the truth. When we look at the massive scholarship that exists on the proverb in many national languages, we stand in awe of how such bits of traditional, plain, and obvious wisdom can have occupied so many scholarly minds from classical antiquity to the present. Even if we concern ourselves only with the proverb stock of the Anglo-American world, we are nevertheless literally overwhelmed by the richness of books, dissertations, and scholarly articles on these proverbs. Paremiographers of the English language have been extremely diligent in putting together superb historical and comparative proverb dictionaries, and the paremiologists who have dealt primarily with Anglo-American proverbs also belong to some of the very best. Such names as Richard C. Trench (1807–1886), Richard Jente (1888–1952), Archer Taylor (1890–1973), and others represent some of the finest paremiological work in the world.[1] Among the living proverb scholars who work primarily on English proverbs we mention in particular Roger D. Abrahams, Shirley Arora, Nigel Barley, David Cram, Robert W. Dent, Alan Dundes, Barbara Kirshenblatt-Gimblett, George Milner, Neal R. Norrick, Peter Seitel, and Bartlett Jere Whiting,[2] but there are also many others who have made major contributions to this fascinating field of study.[3] While we cannot possibly discuss all their achievements in these general remarks, we are including selected bibliographical references of the major paremiological scholarship that has appeared on the nature of the proverb in the English language. We will limit ourselves here to a short description of what proverbs are by referring to this scholarship and basing our arguments on Anglo-American proverb texts.

It would appear that nothing could be easier than writing down a precise proverb definition. Yet we can almost state that there are more definition attempts than there are proverbs. Obviously this is overstating matters a bit, but we do in fact have numerous proverb definitions right from Aristotle to the most recent linguistic description of what makes a proverb distinct from other short statements. Bartlett Jere Whiting has put together a fascinating historical list of such definitions in his article on "The Nature of the Proverb" (1932).[4] Whiting concludes his lengthy treatise with his own definition, which represents a conglomerate version of the many earlier definitions:

> A proverb is an expression which, owing its birth to the people, testifies to its origin in form and phrase. It expresses what is apparently a fundamental truth—that is, a truism—in homely language, often adorned, however, with alliteration and rhyme. It is usually short, but need not be; it is usually true, but need not be. Some proverbs have both a literal and a figurative meaning, either of which makes perfect sense; but more often they have but one of the two. A proverb must be venerable; it must bear the sign of antiquity, and, since such signs may be counterfeited by a clever literary man, it should be attested in different places at different times. This last requirement we must often waive in dealing with very early literature, where the material at our disposal is incomplete.[5]

In many ways Whiting's article and his own definition were a reaction to a statement his good friend Archer Taylor had made a year earlier in his famous book on *The Proverb* (Cambridge, Mass.: Harvard University Press, 1931). In the first paragraph of this classic study Taylor goes so far as to state that it is impossible to give *the* definition of a proverb, and it is precisely for this reason that he wrote his book, that is, his entire book became a definition attempt. But his pronouncement of the impossibility of defining proverbs has become proverbial in itself, and it is almost always cited whenever a scholar needs to deal with definition questions. Far be it from us to deny our readers the delight of reading how the world's greatest paremiologist tried to confront this insurmountable problem:

> The definition of a proverb is too difficult to repay the undertaking; and should we fortunately combine in a single definition all the essential elements and give each the proper emphasis, we should not even then have a touchstone. An incommunicable quality tells us this sentence is proverbial and that one is not. Hence no definition will enable us to identify positively a sentence as proverbial. Those who do not speak a

language can never recognize all its proverbs, and similarly much that is truly proverbial escapes us in Elizabethan and older English. Let us be content with recognizing that a proverb is a saying current among the folk. At least so much of a definition is indisputable, and we shall see and weigh the significance of other elements later.[6]

Judging by the fifty-five definitions we gathered from various people by simply asking them "How would you define a proverb?" we can basically agree with Archer Taylor that the "folk" seems to have a pretty good idea of what a proverb is. By analyzing the collected definitions according to the frequencies of certain words, we were able to formulate the following two definitions, the second being based on those words that were used in almost all definition attempts:

> "A proverb is a short, generally known sentence of the folk which contains wisdom, truth, morals and traditional views in a metaphorical, fixed and memorizable form and which is handed down from generation to generation" and "A proverb is a short sentence of wisdom."[7]

The longer version of this conglomerate definition resembles that formulated by B. J. Whiting, while the statement "A proverb is a short sentence of wisdom" based on the most frequent words reminds us of Taylor's short "definition." In this connection we should also mention some of the English proverbs about proverbs that in themselves are folk definitions of a sort: "All the good sense of the world runs into proverbs," "Proverbs are the children of experience," "Proverbs are the wisdom of the streets," "The wisdom of the proverb cannot be surpassed," "Common proverb seldom lies," "Every proverb is truth," and "Old proverbs are the children of truth." It appears that to the mind of proverb users, that is, the general population in all walks of life, proverbs contain a good dose of common sense, experience, wisdom, and above all truth.

While such proverbial or folk definitions suffice for the general public to know what a proverb is (i.e., sensing that incommunicable quality Taylor speaks of), scholars have not been satisfied with brushing aside the need for a precise and universal definition so quickly. In fact, we could argue that the last fifty or so years since the appearance of Taylor's often quoted passage have seen more and more complex definition attempts come into print, especially since the modern linguists have joined the search for a solution to this dilemma.[8] They all are looking for the key to unlock the secrets of "proverbiality"—what is it that makes a certain statement a proverb while a similar statement is judged not to be proverbial. Today we have dozens more proverb definitions, some so complex that a person without the knowledge of symbolic logic could not possibly understand them. Yet, whether we take the most complex or the simplest proverb definition, we remain basically unsatisfied with what scholars have stated.[9] The reason for not being able to formulate a universal proverb definition lies primarily in the central ingredient that must be part of any proverb definition—traditionality. The term "traditionality" includes both aspects of age and currency that a statement must have to be considered a proverb. But while we can describe the structure, style, form, and so on, of proverbs in great detail, we cannot determine whether a statement has a certain age or currency among the population by the text itself. It will always take external research work to establish the traditionality of a text, and this means that even the most precise definition attempt will always be incomplete. Our definition may include the aspect of traditionality, of course, but we cannot recognize it by looking at a particular text in isolation. This problem becomes immediately clear when we examine proverbs from a foreign culture. If someone were to write a statement on a piece of paper with many structural and stylistic features common to proverbs, we would not know whether the statement is in fact a proverb since we are not in a position to ascertain that it might have a certain age and currency in that foreign language.

The problem is exacerbated since we are only speaking of a relative age and currency. We can't even answer precisely how old a statement must be to qualify as a proverb. With modern mass media, any text might very quickly become known among a relatively large segment of the population. We need only to think of how quickly certain advertisement slogans become commonly recognized by all of us. What might have taken decades to spread from a few people to an entire city or country might today be accomplished in a few days. But how about the problem of currency? What do we really mean by that? Currency among how many people and for how long? The simple fact is that a text must exhibit at least some currency for an extended period of time. Our feeling tells us that a week would be too short, but perhaps a year would be long enough for a text to be considered a proverb. This must strike the reader as very ambiguous, and we are formulating our sentences purposely in this fashion to indicate how intangible a proverb really is. Currency basically means that a proverb must be repeated by members of a certain group of people. But again, even though we write currency into our definition statement, we cannot tell by looking at any text whether it has currency or not. All of this is complicated, of course, by the fact that some proverbs are known only regionally while others are internationally disseminated. We also must not forget that proverbs come and go, that is, not all proverbs are current for the same amount of time. Old proverbs remain or they are forgotten, new ones are created and forgotten, and so on. But this vexing problem of traditionality that includes the aspects of age and currency prevents us from determining whether a text is a proverb or not by means of a definition. Traditionality needs to be proven; it is not inherent in the text itself.

But obviously we do not need to do such painstaking research for every proverb. For the common proverbs of one's language the traditionality is obvious because of the steady repetition of them in various speech acts. It is only for the rarer proverbs or for those texts where we have some doubt concerning their traditionality where we must undertake such research. This is also the case for literary quotations that become proverbs. For example, is Theodore Roosevelt's (1858–1919) "Speak softly and carry a big stick" a quotation or a proverb? We would argue that it is both. It is a quotation to the person who cites it by referring directly to Roosevelt as the coiner of this statement, but it is a proverb because it has enjoyed high currency since it was first uttered on September 2, 1901. Most people also don't associate the statement with Roosevelt any more, and it is used as an anonymous proverb. Another problem are our newer proverbs. How do we know when a popular statement has become a proverb? How about those often repeated lines from songs everybody knows? Are we justified in calling "Garbage in, garbage out" a modern American proverb? We would argue yes, and we base our decision at least partly on the fact that we have noticed its currency among our population. The statement appears to us current enough to be called a proverb, just as we think that "It takes two to tango" or "Different strokes for different folks" are relatively new American proverbs. Eventually "proverbiality" boils down to a judgment call, of which traditionality is the most difficult and decisive element.

Luckily there are some other "markers" that will help us to decide whether a statement that we don't recognize as being proverbial might actually be a proverb. George Milner in particular and subsequently Alan Dundes have attempted to isolate certain structural characteristics of most proverbs. Milner showed that most proverbs are characterized by a quadripartite structure, for example, "A rolling stone gathers no moss." [10] We can divide this proverb into four parts and assign either negative or positive values to each of the four elements, thereby basically creating sixteen possible structural patterns. But a sentence like "A running chicken collects no flowers" would also exhibit a quadripartite structure without being a proverb. We encounter the same problem with Alan Dundes' definition that a proverb is a propositional statement consisting of at least a topic and a comment, for example, "Time flies." [11] This means that a proverb must have at least two words, and Dundes is also able to show that more complex proverbs are composed of an oppositional or non-oppositional structure, for example, "A bird in the hand is worth two in the bush." But what differentiates this statement from our made-up utterance "A chicken in the fist is worth two in the field"? Why is the first a proverb and the second text not? Dundes is well aware of this problem, and has added the adjective "traditional" to his definition: "The proverb appears to be a traditional propositional statement consisting of at least one descriptive element, a descriptive element consisting of a topic and a comment."[12] But this definition does not deal with the problem of "traditionality," that is, we can define and analyze only those texts with it where we already know we have a traditional proverb in front of us. Helpful as Milner's and especially Dundes' structural analyses are, they do not solve the traditionality problem.

In addition to these structural paradigms, we also have several other "markers" that enable us to characterize proverb texts. It is usually accepted that proverbs are relatively short or "pithy." We agree with Alan Dundes that a proverb must have at least two words, that is, a topic and a comment, as, for example, in "Money talks." But we also have proverbs that are considerably longer, as, for example, "Early to bed, and early to rise, makes a man healthy, wealthy and wise." Nevertheless, a proverb ought to be a relatively short and complete sentence. Perhaps it is fair to say that the shorter the better, since that also assures memorability and recognizability that enter into the actual use of proverbs in speech.[13] To maintain a maximum level of recognizability and memorability, the proverb is usually stated in a fixed form that is not changed. But newer research is showing more and more that proverbs are being changed for various reasons quite often. We don't always quote the entire proverb, since often a mere allusion to it suffices to communicate its message effectively. If we want to remind someone that "The early bird catches the worm," we might choose to simply state something like "You know 'the early bird' " or "Don't forget about 'the early bird.' " We might also vary the proverb for humor or irony or simply for the joy of punning. The key thing is that the fixed form of proverbs does not appear to be as sacrosanct anymore today as it might have once been. Neal R. Norrick has observed in this regard that "for well known proverbs, mention of one crucial recognizable phrase serves to call forth the entire proverb," and he has designated "this minimal recognizable unit as the *kernel* of the proverb."[14] Thus proverbs are not absolutely fixed or frozen, but they actually live by being varied to fit various situations and purposes.

It belongs to the tradition of proverb scholarship to enumerate the various poetic or stylistic features that characterize many proverbs. Lately Neal R. Norrick and Shirley L. Arora have dealt in much detail with these matters, and we also refer the reader to the inclusive statements by Archer Taylor and Beatrice Silverman-Weinreich.[15] Let us at least mention the following poetic aspects with a few examples: alliteration: "Many a little makes a mickle," "Live and let live," "Money makes the mare to go," and so on; rhyme: "Man proposes, God disposes," "No gain without pain," "Seeing is believing," and so on; parallelism: "Easy come, easy go," "A penny saved is a penny earned,"

Reprinted with special permission of King Features Syndicate.

"A little wood will heat a little oven," and so on; ellipsis: "Out of sight, out of mind," "Nothing ventured, nothing gained," "Sooner begun, sooner done," and so on.[16] We should also mention that certain fundamental proverb structures exist that have been the basis for dozens of proverbs, as, for example, "Where there's X, there's Y," "No X without Y," "Like X, like Y," "One X does not make a Y," and so on. Such patterns help us, of course, to recognize such texts as "Where there's smoke, there's fire," "No gain without pain," "Like father, like son," and "One swallow does not make a summer" as proverbs. But so do alliteration, rhyme, parallelism, ellipsis, and so on. These are all important markers, yet a proverb like "Love is never without jealousy" does not have any of the characteristics previously mentioned. We see once again that even a prosaic normal sentence might become a proverb, but we stress that the more "proverbial markers" a statement has, the greater its chance to become proverbial. That is certainly the reason why the relatively new American proverb "Different strokes for different folks" has become current and recognizable in this country. It has rhyme, repetition, parallelism, ellipsis, and it is short. Yet we doubt that "Different rights for different people" will or should become proverbial if we write it here as an example. Its idea is so alien to our worldview that this variation will not catch on despite its proverbial markers.

In addition to these external stylistic and structural markers we also find internal markers such as personification, hyperbole, paradox, metaphor. For personification we cite such popular proverbs as "Misery loves company," "Hunger is the best cook," and "Love laughs at locksmiths." For hyperbole the following proverb comes to mind: "It is easier for a camel to go through a needle's eye, than for a rich man to enter into the kingdom of God" (Matthew 19,24), and for paradox we cite "The nearer the church, the farther from God." As far as the metaphor is concerned, we should stress that some scholars want to count only metaphorical proverbs as *bona fide* proverbs. There is hardly any need for us to quote examples of proverbs containing metaphors, but here are some common ones: "A stitch in time saves nine," "New

brooms sweep clean," "All that glitters is not gold," "Don't look a gift horse in the mouth," "The pitcher goes to the well until it breaks at last," and so on. And yet plenty of common proverbs such as "Honesty is the best policy" or "A woman's work is never done" are not metaphorical. We can state, however, that metaphors constitute an important marker for many proverbs, and it is exactly this vivid imagery of most proverbs that makes them so appealing to us.[17]

Metaphorical proverbs also give us the opportunity to communicate in an indirect or figurative way rather than always calling a spade a spade, that is, stating everything in a direct way. By translating a realistic situation into a metaphorical proverb, we can generalize the unique problem and express it as a common phenomenon of life. Instead of scolding or reprimanding a child for being impatient about an upcoming surprise, we might simply say "A watched pot never boils." The proverb "The love of money is the root of all evil" is a fitting general statement to describe the greed of a person who might have embezzled money at a bank. And we might also use the proverb "Strike while the iron is hot" as an expression of encouragement for someone who needs to make a major decision. Kenneth Burke has described this use of metaphorical proverbs as follows: "Proverbs are strategies for dealing with situations. In so far as situations are typical and recurrent in a given social structure, people develop names for them and strategies for handling them. Another name for strategies might be attitudes."[18] Peter Seitel has expanded this important observation in his fundamental essay "Proverbs: A Social Use of Metaphor" (1969), and he stresses that proverbs in actual use always refer to social situations.[19] This social context gives meaning to a particular proverb, for a proverb in a collection that merely enumerates uncontextualized proverb texts is for all general purposes meaningless.

This leads us to the complex question of proverb meaning that must be seen in light of the manifold contexts in which every possible proverb might be used. Barbara Kirshenblatt-Gimblett has addressed this problem in her revealing article "Toward a Theory of Proverb Meaning" (1973) in which she explains the multiple meaning and usage of a number of common Anglo-American proverbs. Taking the proverb "A rolling stone gathers no moss" as an example, she asked about eighty Texas students the meaning of this common proverb and they came up with three possibilities: "(1) a rolling stone gathering no moss is like a machine that keeps running and never gets rusty and broken; (2) a rolling stone is like a person who keeps on moving, never settles down, and therefore never gets anywhere; (3) a rolling stone is like a person who keeps moving and is therefore free, not burdened with a family and material possessions and not likely to fall into a rut."[20] How is such a differentiated interpretation of a seemingly simple proverb possible? Kirshenblatt-Gimblett gives four sources for this proverb's multiple meaning: "(1) what is understood by the image presented in the metaphor (stone roller, stone in brook); (2) what is understood as the general principle expressed by the metaphor (movement promotes efficiency, stability promotes tangible gains); (3) how the general principle is evaluated (tangible gains are worthwhile, tangible gains are not worthwhile); (4) the requirements of the situation in which the proverb is used regardless of what one actually believes in principle (does one want to console or criticize the stable person; does one want to console or criticize the wanderer)."[21] From these possible interpretations it becomes clear that it is exactly the metaphor of the proverb that enables us to employ proverbs in so many different contexts. The Estonian paremiologist Arvo Krikmann has stressed repeatedly that we must consider the semantic indefiniteness of proverbs resulting from three major factors: (1) hetero-situationality of proverbs, (2) poly-functionality of proverbs, and (3) poly-semanticity.[22] What this comes down to is that the meaning of every proverb must be analyzed in each of its unique social contexts.[23]

We have already stated that proverbs name social situations, that is, they are used to communicate our general human concerns in traditional language. By employing proverbs in our speech we wish to strengthen our arguments, express certain generalizations, influence or manipulate other people, rationalize our own shortcomings, question certain behavioral patterns, satirize social ills, poke fun at ridiculous situations, and so on.[24] There are no limits to the use of proverbs, and each individual proverb may be employed in many different ways depending on its context. Realizing that there are thousands of proverbs to choose from, we should also not be surprised that their content fits every possible aspect of life. We could certainly group hundreds of proverbs into major categories such as proverbs dealing with the body, love, work, friendship, death, and so on. But by doing so, we should remember that the use of a proverb in any one of these groups would not be restricted to dealing just with that content. While the proverb "Two heads are better than one" clearly would belong to that group of proverbs whose content deals with the body, it obviously would be used to indicate that two people working together (pooling their intelligence) might be more successful than an individual doing things alone. It has become customary to talk of major proverb groups characterized by their content. Three of the more common groups mentioned are, for example, legal proverbs, medical proverbs, and weather proverbs. Some folklorists are now arguing that most weather proverbs are not proverbs at all but rather superstitions couched in proverbial language.[25] Nevertheless, we would still argue that such texts as "Lightning never strikes twice in the same place" or "Make hay while the sun shines" are proverbs, especially since they are usually used in a figurative and not a literal sense. However, those "weather proverbs" that are used as regional weather signs as, for example, "Red sky at night, sailor's delight" are in fact superstitions since they are always interpreted literally. As far as the legal proverbs are concerned, we might quote "Let the buyer beware," "Possession is nine points of the law," and "Silence gives consent."[26] From the medical profession we can cite "An apple a day keeps the doctor away," "Stuff a cold and starve a fever," and "An hour's sleep before midnight is worth two after." Yet such a statement as "A green winter makes a fat churchyard" is a superstition rather than a proverb.[27] Other professions obviously have "their" proverbs as well, but these examples suffice to show that various groups of people have had their influence on our proverb stock.

This leads us to a short discussion of the origin of proverbs about which Bartlett Jere Whiting published his richly documented article "The Origin of the Proverb" (1931).[28] There is no doubt that many of our proverbs originated in classical antiquity. A proverb like "Big fish eat little fish" can be traced back to the Greek author Hesiod, and we can also show how it reached the Roman world as a Latin loan translation. A large number of proverbs from various ancient languages and cultures entered the Latin language and eventually reached many of the vernacular languages when medieval Latin proverbs were being translated. Proverbs like "One hand washes the other," "Love is blind," and "A sound mind in a sound body" all followed this path and became translated proverbs in many languages. In fact, these classical proverbs are today some of the most widely disseminated proverbs, some of them enjoying international currency. Biblical proverbs went the same route, and such proverbs as "Man does not live by bread alone" (Matthew 4,4), "Pride goes before the fall" (Solomon 16,18), and "It is better to give than to receive" (Apostles 20,35) are known in dozens of languages. But the vernacular languages also developed their own proverbs, and the Anglo-American world is very rich in its particular proverb stock. Many proverbs were coined in the Middle Ages and throughout subsequent historical periods, with the sixteenth and seventeenth centuries being the golden age of the proverb in Europe in particular.

Proverbs always are "invented" by an individual at some time and at some given location, and if the particular statement exhibits at least one of the proverb markers previously discussed it might have caught on, that is, it might have gained some currency among a small circle of family members. Perhaps the budding proverb expressed an apparent truth in such a catchy fashion that people beyond this family adopted it into their proverb repertoire, and soon it became known in a village, then a city, an entire region, and finally a whole nation. On this path into general currency the proverb text might well have undergone some stylistic changes, which explains why we often find several variants of a given proverb once we study its origin and history.[29] Frequent use of a proverbial text will eventually result in such a statement whose "proverbiality" is acceptable to the largest group of people. When the proverb "Big fish eat little fish" entered the English language from the Latin version "In mari pisces maiores deuorant minores," it did so by the direct translation in the twelfth century by a monk as "The more fishes in the sea eten the lasse." Over the next centuries we find this proverb in such variants as "The more fishes the less frete," "The more fishes swelewen the lasse," "The great fish eat the small," "The great fish eat up the small," "The great fish devour the less," and finally the two most popular variants "Great fish eat little fish" and "Big fish eat little fish," where the parallel structure prevalent in so many proverbs is at its best.[30] Proverbs live in variants until the proper proverbial wording is found. Proverbs thus have their origin with an individual, but they are influenced by collective improvements over time. In this regard we can cite the famous proverb definition by Lord John Russell (1792–1878), which has become proverbial itself: "A proverb is the wit of one, and the wisdom of many."

Many other aspects of the proverb could be discussed here, above all its uses and functions in various contexts. But this will become clear in the following chapters. We simply wanted to give the reader an understanding at the outset of what a proverb is, how it derives its meaning, what its content is, and where it comes from. Our remarks have shown that the seemingly simple proverb is in fact a very complex verbal form of folklore that almost escapes definition. In fact, no definition has been found that would enable us to decide that this short statement is a proverb and that one is not. The aspect

of traditionality—a certain amount of currency during a certain time period—
is basically indefinable and must be established through research on individual proverbs. But we do have a good notion of what constitutes "proverbiality," and by studying various proverb markers we can actually reach sound
conclusions about what a proverb is. For the proverbs of our Anglo-American
world we can still agree with Archer Taylor's contention that an "incommunicable quality" helps us to decide what is a proverb and what is not. But the
many definition attempts all help us to understand proverbs even better, and
this intellectual process of zeroing in on an ever more precise definition will
doubtlessly continue. In the meantime we offer a work-definition by our former teacher Stuart A. Gallacher (1906–1977) who in 1959 stated that "A
proverb is a concise statement of an apparent truth which has [had, or will
have] currency among the people."[31] Our small addition of "had, or will
have" is meant to indicate that proverbs come and go, that is, antiquated
proverbs with messages and images we no longer relate to are dropped from
our proverb repertoire, while new proverbs are created to reflect the mores
and values of our time. An old English proverb like "Hanging and wiving
(wedding) go by destiny" has basically dropped out of use, and it continues
its existence only in literary documents and "dead" proverb collections. But
"Absence makes the heart grow fonder" is bound to be used for many more
centuries to come since people will always want to rationalize periods of sep-
aration from their loved ones. And such relatively new American proverbs as

Reprinted by permission of Universal Press Syndicate.

"Paddle your own canoe," "Different strokes for different folks," and "Garbage in, garbage out" (from our computer-run modern existence) have a good chance to survive for many years as well. Other new proverbs will doubtlessly follow,[32] and it will be up to the future paremiographers and paremiologists to show how Anglo-American proverbs live and enrich various modes of communication in America.

Notes

This chapter was first published in slightly different form in *Revista de etnografie si folclor,* 36 (1991), 151–164.

1. See Richard C. Trench, *On the Lessons in Proverbs.* New York: Redfield, 1853; Richard Jente, "The Untilled Field of Proverbs," in *Studies in Language and Literature,* ed. by George R. Coffman. Chapel Hill: University of North Carolina Press, 1945, pp. 112–119; and Archer Taylor, *The Proverb.* Cambridge, Mass.: Harvard University Press, 1931; rpt. Hatboro, Pa.: Folklore Associates, 1962; rpt. again with an introduction and bibliography by Wolfgang Mieder. Bern: Peter Lang, 1985.

2. For the many publications on proverbs by these scholars see Wolfgang Mieder, *International Proverb Scholarship: An Annotated Bibliography,* 2 vols. New York: Garland Publishing, 1982 and 1990. A number of specific references will be listed in the notes below.

3. In addition to the bibliography listed in note 2 see also Wolfgang Mieder's annual bibliographies entitled "International Bibliography of New and Reprinted Proverb Collections" and "International Proverb Scholarship: An Updated Bibliography" in *Proverbium: Yearbook of International Proverb Scholarship,* 1ff. (1984ff.).

4. See Bartlett Jere Whiting, "The Nature of the Proverb," *Harvard Studies and Notes in Philology and Literature*, 14 (1932), 273–307.

5. Whiting, p. 302.

6. Taylor (note 1), p. 3.

7. Wolfgang Mieder, "Popular Views of the Proverb," *Proverbium: Yearbook of International Proverb Scholarship*, 2 (1985), 119.

8. See especially David Cram, "Argumentum ad lunam: On the Folk Fallacy and the Nature of the Proverb," *Proverbium: Yearbook of International Proverb Scholarship*, 3 (1986), 9–31; Peter Grzybek, "Foundations of Semiotic Proverb Study," *Proverbium: Yearbook of International Proverb Scholarship*, 4 (1987), 39–85; and Richard Priebe, "The Horses of Speech: A Structural Analysis of the Proverb," *Folklore Annual of the University [of Texas] Folklore Association*, no. 3 (1971), 26–32.

9. See Nigel Barley, "A Structural Approach to the Proverb and Maxim with Special Reference to the Anglo-Saxon Corpus," *Proverbium*, no. 20 (1972), 737–750; Otto Blehr, "What Is a Proverb?" *Fabula*, 14 (1973), 243–246; and George B. Milner, "What Is a Proverb?" *New Society*, 332 (February 6, 1969), 199–202.

10. See George B. Milner, "The Quartered Shield: Outline of a Semantic Taxonomy [of Proverbs]," in *Social Anthropology and Language*, ed. by Edwin Ardener. London: Tavistock, 1971, pp. 243–269.

11. See Alan Dundes, "On the Structure of the Proverb," *Proverbium*, no. 25 (1975), 961–973; also in *The Wisdom of Many. Essays on the Proverb*, ed. by Wolfgang Mieder and A. Dundes. New York: Garland Publishing, 1981, pp. 43–64.

12. Dundes (note 11), p. 60.

13. See J. Kathryn Bock and William F. Brewer, "Comprehension and Memory of the Literal and Figurative Meaning of Proverbs," *Journal of Psycholinguistic Research*, 9 (1980), 59–72.

14. Neal R. Norrick, *How Proverbs Mean. Semantic Studies in English Proverbs*. Amsterdam: Mouton, 1985, p. 45.

15. See Shirley L. Arora, "The Perception of Proverbiality," *Proverbium: Yearbook of International Proverb Scholarship*, 1 (1984), 1–38; and Beatrice Silverman-Weinreich, "Towards a Structural Analysis of Yiddish Proverbs," *Yivo Annual of Jewish Social Science*, 17 (1978), 1–20; also in *The Wisdom of Many. Essays on the Proverb*, ed. by Wolfgang Mieder and Alan Dundes. New York: Garland Publishing, 1981, pp. 65–85.

16. See Ronald Grambo, "Paremiological Aspects," *Folklore Forum*, 5 (1972), 100–105; Bengt Holbek, "Proverb Style," *Proverbium*, no. 15 (1970), 470–472; Robert A. Rothstein, "The Poetics of Proverbs," in *Studies Presented to Professor Roman Jakobson by His Students*, ed. by Charles Gribble. Cambridge, Mass.: Slavica Publications, 1969, pp. 265–274; and Aleksandr K. Zholkovskii, "At the Intersection of Linguistics, Paremiology and Poetics: On the Literary Structure of Proverbs," *Poetics*, 7 (1978), 309–332.

17. See David Cram, "The Linguistic Status of the Proverb," *Cahiers de Lexicologie*, 43 (1983), 53–71; Paul D. Goodwin and Joseph W. Wenzel, "Proverbs and Practical Reasoning: A Study in Socio-Logic," *The Quarterly Journal of Speech*, 65 (1979), 289–302; also in *The Wisdom of Many. Essays on the Proverb*, ed. by Wolfgang Mieder and Alan Dundes. New York: Garland Publishing, 1981, pp. 140–160; Richard P. Honeck and Clare T. Kibler, "The Role of Imagery, Analogy, and Instantiation in Proverb Comprehension," *Journal of Psycholinguistic Research*, 13 (1984), 393–414; Susan Kemper, "Comprehension and the Interpretation of Proverbs," *Journal of Psycholinguistic Research*, 10 (1981), 179–198; and Judy Pasamanick, "Watched Pots Do Boil: Proverb Interpretation Through Contextual Illustration," *Proverbium: Yearbook of International Proverb Scholarship*, 2 (1985), 145–183.

18. Cited from the important essay by Kenneth Burke, "Literature as Equipment for Living," in K. Burke, *The Philosophy of Literary Form: Studies in Symbolic Action*. Baton Rouge: Louisiana University Press, 1941, p. 256.

19. See Peter Seitel, "Proverbs: A Social Use of Metaphor," *Genre*, 2 (1969), 143–161; also in *The Wisdom of Many. Essays on the Proverb*, ed. by Wolfgang Mieder and Alan Dundes. New York: Garland Publishing, 1981, pp. 122–139.

20. Barbara Kirshenblatt-Gimblett, "Toward a Theory of Proverb Meaning," *Proverbium*, no. 22 (1973), 821–827; also in *The Wisdom of Many. Essays on the Proverb*, ed. by Wolfgang Mieder and Alan Dundes. New York: Garland Publishing, 1981, p. 113.

21. Kirshenblatt-Gimblett (note 20), p. 113.

22. For semantic problems of proverbs see especially Arvo Krikmann, *On Denotative Indefiniteness of Proverbs*. Tallinn: Academy of Sciences of the Estonian SSR, Institute of Language and Literature, 1974; and A. Krikmann, *Some Additional Aspects of Semantic Indefiniteness of Proverbs*. Tallinn: Academy of Sciences of the Estonian SSR, Institute of Language and Literature, 1974. Both monographs have been reprinted in *Proverbium: Yearbook of International Proverb Scholarship*, 1 (1984), 47–91; and 2 (1985), 58–85.

23. See Galit Hasan-Rokem, "The Pragmatics of Proverbs: How the Proverb Gets Its Meaning," in *Exceptional Language and Linguistics*, ed. by Loraine K. Obler and Lise Menn. New York: Academic Press, 1982, pp. 169–173; Michael D. Lieber, "Analogic Ambiguity: A Paradox of Proverb Usage," *Journal of American Folklore*, 97 (1984), 423–441; and Kwesi Yankah, "Towards a Performance-Centered Theory of the Proverb," *Critical Arts*, 3 (1983), 29–43.

24. See Goodwin and Wenzel (note 17).

25. See Alan Dundes, "On Whether Weather 'Proverbs' Are Proverbs," *Proverbium: Yearbook of International Proverb Scholarship*, 1 (1984), 39–46. Shirley L. Arora takes the opposite view in her recent article on "Weather Proverbs: Some 'Folk' Views," *Proverbium: Yearbook of International Proverb Scholarship*, 8 (1991), 1–17.

26. See Donald Bond, "English Legal Proverbs," *Publications of the Modern Language Association*, 51 (1936), 921–935.

27. See Russell A. Elmquist, "English Medical Proverbs," *Modern Philology*, 32 (1934–1935), 75–84.

28. Bartlett Jere Whiting, "The Origin of the Proverb," *Harvard Studies and Notes in Philology and Literature*, 13 (1931), 47–80.

29. See Agnes Szemerkényi and Vilmos Voigt, "The Connection of Theme and Language in Proverb Transformations," *Acta Ethnographica Academiae Scientiarum Hungaricae*, 21 (1972), 95–108.

30. See Wolfgang Mieder, "History and Interpretation of a Proverb about Human Nature: 'Big Fish Eat Little Fish'," in W. Mieder, *Tradition and Innovation in Folk Literature*. Hanover, N.H.: University Press of New England, 1987, pp. 178–228 and pp. 259–268 (notes).

31. Stuart A. Gallacher, "Frauenlob's Bits of Wisdom: Fruits of His Environment," in *Middle Ages—Reformation—Volkskunde. Festschrift for John G. Kunstmann*, no editor given. Chapel Hill: University of North Carolina Press, 1959, p. 47.

32. See Wolfgang Mieder, *American Proverbs: A Study of Texts and Contexts*. Bern: Peter Lang, 1989; and the hundreds of examples in Wolfgang Mieder, Stewart Kingsbury, and Kelsie Harder, *A Dictionary of American Proverbs*. New York: Oxford University Press, 1992.

2

" A Proverb Is a Short Sentence of Wisdom "

Popular Views of the Proverb

The problem of defining a proverb appears to be as old as man's interest in them. People who consciously used them or began to collect them in antiquity obviously needed to differentiate proverbs from other gnomic devices such as apothegms, maxims, aphorisms, quotations, and so on. Not only did such great minds as Aristotle and Plato occupy themselves with the question of what constitutes a proverb, but early Greek paremiographers in particular wrestled with this seemingly insurmountable task as well. Jan Fredrik Kindstrand reviewed some of these early definition attempts in his fascinating paper on "The Greek Concept of Proverbs." [1] and Bartlett Jere Whiting had already in 1932 assembled dozens of definitions from ancient times to the modern age in his remarkable essay on "The Nature of the Proverb." [2] The last fifty years since Whiting's detailed study have witnessed highly scholarly articles, monographs, and even books which all seek to come to terms with a universal proverb definition. Scholars around the world continue to find their own so-called "working definitions," of which some of the most recent attempts in the English language are those by Shirley Arora, Nigel Barley, Otto Blehr, Margaret Bryant, David Cram, Alan Dundes, Galit Hasan-Rokem, George Milner, and Peter Seitel. [3] Yet, despite their erudite and important new definitions based on structural, semiotic, or linguistic insights, all must eventually agree with the contention of the old master proverb scholar Archer Taylor that "an incommunicable quality tells us this sentence is proverbial and that one is not." [4] The newer definitions might in fact fit those sentences that we *know* already to be proverbial, but, again in the words of the insightful Taylor, "no definition will enable us to identify positively a sentence as proverbial."[5] A definition cannot deal with such aspects as currency, traditionality, and familiarity which certainly are necessary ingredients for a true proverb.

But let us leave the world of the serious paremiologist for a moment and consider Taylor's "maxim" of the incommunicable quality that supposedly tells us what a proverb is. What do nonspecialists of proverbs think about them and what are proverbs to them? How do they in fact identify a statement as a proverb and what are the characteristic elements that constitute a proverb in their minds? In other words, what is a proverb today to the general public? In order to answer this question let us look at a sample of fifty-five proverb definitions that I collected from students, friends, and acquaintances in the past year or so. To my knowledge nobody has ever bothered to undertake such a survey, and, even though my sample is a relatively small one, it should still be able to give us a basic idea of what people today think a proverb to be. To this I will add an analysis of a number of popular articles on proverbs in magazines and newspapers that have also not been considered by proverb scholars. These essayistic treatments that appeared from 1877 to 1984 in such publications as *The New York Times, Saturday Review, Atlantic Monthly, Time, Newsday* and others will certainly help to come to terms with a general definition of the proverb as the "folk," and not the scholar, sees it.

Before starting this discussion, it might be wise to mention here at least some of the English proverbs about proverbs that in themselves are folk definitions of a sort: "A good maxim is never out of season"; "All the good sense of the world runs into proverbs"; "Proverbs are the children of experience"; "Proverbs are the wisdom of the streets"; "Nothing can beat a proverb"; "Proverbs cannot be contradicted"; "Though the old proverb be given up, it is none the less true"; "The old saying cannot be excelled"; "The wisdom of the proverb cannot be surpassed"; "Common proverb seldom lies"; "The old saying, long proved true, shall never be belied"; "Old saws speak truth"; "Every proverb is truth"; "Old proverbs are the children of truth"; "What everyone says is true"; and so on. It appears that to the mind of proverb users, that is, the general population in all walks of life, the proverb contains a good dose of common sense, experience, wisdom, and above all truth. Do such "definitions" still hold true today, or do modern adults in a technological society see proverbs in a much more critical light? Are proverbs still considered solid kernels of wisdom and truth, or are they laughed off as antiquated bits of moral teaching? The following fifty-five recent definitions of proverbs might include some surprises when one considers that they come from members of a sophisticated and highly educated society. The definitions were collected by merely asking various people to write their definition of a proverb on a piece of paper without any previous discussion of proverbs whatsoever. They represent spontaneous reactions to the simple isolated question "How would you define a proverb?" Here are the fascinating answers in alphabetical order:

1 A proverb consists of a short sentence which contains a general piece of wisdom.

2 A proverb contains wisdom which has been handed down from one generation to the next.

3 A proverb describes situations which happened before and which are repeated again and again.

4 A proverb expresses folk wisdom in formulaic, short and metaphorical language.

5 A proverb has been passed down through many generations. It sums up, in one short phrase, a general principle, or common situation, and when you say it, everyone knows exactly what you mean. It is often graphic, symbolic or rhyming, so that it is easily remembered.

6 A proverb is a common expression whose origin is not known or has been forgotten. It expresses wisdom concerning life.

7 A proverb is a common, repeated, and generally known phrase which expresses a general idea taken to be true. It usually draws upon everyday occurrences or events in nature which are easily understood.

8 A proverb is a commonly known, easily understandable example of descriptive, colorful, "folksy" wisdom, which, independent of the era, carries a lesson to and conveys a philosophy of life for the common man.

9 A proverb is a commonly known, often-quoted, concise saying which expresses a generalization concerning some aspect of everyday existence.

10 A proverb is a commonly used or known phrase, expressing knowledge, a conclusion, or an attitude about aspects of life that are universally familiar to mankind.

11 A proverb is a complete sentence which usually contains a moral or didactic "message."

12 A proverb is a condensed form of age-old folk sayings and biblical teachings. The proverb attempts to teach us, via the trials and tribulations of others who were not as fortunate as we. Proverbs can be positive or negative in nature; unfortunately, far too many of them are anti-women in their conclusions.

13 A proverb is a condensed version of basic opinions, prejudices, and beliefs common to a group of people. These are usually in the form of very short, easy-to-remember sentences or phrases.

14 A proverb is a fixed-phrase, metaphorical statement.

15 A proverb is a fixed phrase piece of folklore consisting of a comparison or analogy, applying one set of circumstances to a different but similar situation.

16 A proverb is a formulaic expression of a certain truth which is applicable only in a special situation. Used generally a proverb is only half a truth.

17 A proverb is a linguistic attempt to express a general truth or wisdom in a few words.

18 A proverb is a metaphorical statement that illustrates a lesson of behavior.

19 A proverb is a one-sentence statement which encapsulates an element of folk wisdom; a specific reference which applies to many generalized situations or meanings.

20 A proverb is a phrase or sentence, accepted and integrated into common verbal usage of the general population, although often regional in character, which is most likely generated by astute, humanistic, albeit didactic, assessment of the human experience, offering tidbits of wisdom applicable to these paradigms of existential encounter.

21 A proverb is a pictorial phrase in which a message is given, many times a picture of an oft done action.

22 A proverb is a pithy statement or comment usually involving advice or a moral.

23 A proverb is a saying or generalization often accepted as truth; it contains words of wisdom.

24 A proverb is a saying that is known to the public; sometimes a moral or a threat.

25 A proverb is a saying with which people often identify because it is universal and meaningful in some way or other.

26 A proverb is a sentence or phrase which expresses the generally accepted thought or belief of a group and which has, through use, become standardized in form.

27 A proverb is a sentence that has been developed orally and is still used by the people of a region. It has usually come about from experience and it is a statement that teaches the learning within an experience.

28 A proverb is a short and general statement which is handed down by tradition and which changes its meaning according to the speaker and the situation.

29 A proverb is a short and poetic statement used by the folk to express rules or wisdom concerning life.

30 A proverb is a short, concise, colloquial saying, easily memorized, and containing traditional beliefs taken to be true.

31 A proverb is a short, concise phrase which states a moral principle, bit of folk wisdom, or similar rule by which one should live.

32 A proverb is a short condensation of a piece of folk wisdom, formed in such a way that it will be memorable. Its main goal is thus to teach, whether it be a semi-scientific fact or a viewpoint.

33 A proverb is a short expression known by many people. It usually contains a commonly held view of life.

34 A proverb is a short phrase. It is used to convey a traditional bit of folk wisdom.

35 A proverb is a short saying which teaches a point or establishes a cultural norm based on the tradition of the people who use it. It is generally to be understood analogically—at least I have never heard of a proverb fundamentalist.

36 A proverb is a short sentence or phrase which capsulizes a thought about human nature, values or ideals, and is generally thought to be for instructive/exemplary purposes.

37 A proverb is a short sentence or saying which expresses a rather simple didactic concept, and which usually implies a right as opposed to a wrong action. Proverbs are brief, often not direct (metaphoric), and a great majority of the community will be familiar with the proverb and its meaning.

38 A proverb is a short, traditional statement which teaches or gives advice on a subject. Comparisons are often used to illustrate the point.

39 A proverb is a small saying that describes wisdom in a way that either teaches or makes fun of it.

40 A proverb is a statement often articulated in parallel or allegorical terms with the intent of expressing a general truth.

41 A proverb is a traditional, fixed-phrase saying, usually one sentence that expresses an opinion, often considered wisdom, on a subject or recommends a course of action.

42 A proverb is a traditional saying or sentence which summarizes an attitude toward something or describes a certain situation. It is an often used saying through which one learns. A "picture" or "image" accompanies, or is within the expression, which gives light to the lesson to be learned. This lesson is often referred to as a moral.

43 A proverb is a traditional wisdom, advice, or statement in a fixed phrase. It is short and precise, consists of at least two parts, and contains actor and verb.

44 A proverb is a well-known saying which belongs to folk poetry and which is used by everyone.

45 A proverb is a well-known saying without a known author, passed on from generation to generation, which gives advice, admonitions, or a moral lesson—usually a few words to not more than one sentence in length and stated in a manner that is easily remembered, that is, rhyme, workable language, alliteration, analogy, etc. It is related to man as a whole and often begins with "who."

46 A proverb is a witticism which combines clarity and precision of thought with brevity and profundity of word usage. The statement generally applies to a situation which is commonly understood and appreciated by all peoples of a given culture.

47 A proverb is an expression in colloquial or biblical terms which illustrates a moralistic point.

48 A proverb is an often repeated and metaphorical expression.

49 A proverb is generally used to provide "wisdom" in a concise way. It spares the speaker of the proverb the chore of being philosophically original.

50 A proverb is the wisdom of many, the wit of one. This is known as defining a proverb with a proverb. It doesn't hold up too well as a definition, but it sticks in my mind.

51 Certain principles and conditions of everyday life are expressed in proverbs, which in turn help people to understand the world and to learn from experience.

52 In a few words proverbs explain human problems and behavior.

53 Proverbs are general statements of truth which can apply to certain instances in a commentary fashion, and which can act as wise words for future actions.

54 Proverbs are golden words of folk wisdom that have been treasured from generation to generation.

55 Proverbs are short and aphoristic expressions of wisdom which reflect basic human situations and concerns.

A word analysis of these definitions results in an interesting composite of what a general definition of a proverb might look like. Taking the frequency of nouns first, the following picture emerges (the number in parentheses indicates how often a particular noun appears in the fifty-five definitions): wisdom (20); phrase (14); sentence, saying (13); statement (12); folk (10); situation (9); expression (7); life (6); truth, moral, people (5); generation, experience, advice, lesson, word (4); principle, analogy, belief, behavior, meaning, action (3); language, generalization, attitude, message, opinion, picture, comment, thought, comparison, tradition, rule, viewpoint (2); origin, idea, occurrence, philosophy, knowledge, conclusion, prejudice, folklore, paradigm, threat, form, norm, nature, value, ideal, image, poetry, author, admonition, rhyme, alliteration, witticism, brevity, profundity, clarity, precision, culture, condition, concern (1). From this it becomes clear that a proverb is commonly thought of as "a phrase, saying, sentence, statement, or expression of the folk which contains above all wisdom, truth, morals, experience, lessons, and advice concerning life and which has been handed down from generation to generation." This composite definition basically includes all those words that appear from four to twenty times in the collected definitions. But since the words phrase, saying, sentence, statement, and expression simply define a proverb as a basic sentence, it can certainly be stated that the shortest general definition of a proverb is simply "A proverb is wisdom expressed in a sentence."

Looking at modifying verbs, adjectives and adverbs in the fifty-five definitions, the following frequency picture arises: short (18); general (14); known (10); common, teach, traditional (6); metaphorical (5); concise, fixed (4); repeated, remembered, everyday, didactic (3); handed down, formulaic, true, understandable, often quoted, universal, moralistic, colloquial, memorizable, learned, familiar, biblical, human (2); sum up, graphic, symbolic, rhyming, colorful, descriptive, old, linguistic, regional, pictorial, pithy, standardized, accepted, oral, poetic, parallel, precise, aphorisitic, cultural, instructive, exemplary, small, allegorical (1). If one adds the eighteen occurrences of "short" together with the four of "concise," the one of "precise," and the one of "small" it is clear that twenty-four or almost half of the definitions stress the shortness of the proverb. Adding to this a few more of the frequent descriptive words, a composite definition could be something like "A proverb is a short, generally known sentence that expresses common, traditional and didactic views in a metaphorical and fixed form and which is easily remembered and repeated." But again, the shortest common denominator for this group of descriptive words would simply result in the definition "A proverb is a short sentence."

It is surprising that such nouns as meaning, message, comment, occurrence, paradigm, form (rhyme, alliteration, etc.) do not play much of a role in these definitions in light of the fact that scholarly definitions deal much more with them. This is also the case with the low frequency of such descriptive words as formulaic, universal, memorizable, symbolic, linguistic, and so on. There obviously exists a considerable difference between scholarly definition attempts and the common view of proverbs held by the folk. Taking the nouns and the other descriptive words with the highest frequencies together, we could attempt to formulate the following general definition of the proverb by people of the 1980s in an industrialized and progressive society: "A proverb is a short, generally known sentence of the folk which contains wisdom, truth, morals and traditional views in a metaphorical, fixed and memorizable form and which is handed down from generation to generation." Using only the truly high frequency words for the fifty-five definitions, one could also simply state that "A proverb is a short sentence of wisdom." That is a far cry away from modern scientific definitions, but it certainly indicates that the non-expert continues to define proverbs along those lines of the traditional proverbs about proverbs[6] cited above that also stressed in particular the wisdom and truth in proverbs.

Let us now in the second part of this chapter look at a number of popularly written articles on proverbs in magazines and newspapers in order to get an impression of how proverbs tend to be defined there. In 1877 a small editorial appeared on "The Influence of Proverbs" in *The New York Times* whose anonymous author did not at all share the positive feeling toward proverbs as they have been expressed in the definitions listed in this chapter thus far. The entire article is critical of proverbs and their users, and the value of traditional proverbs is severely questioned:

> They [the proverbs] are never quite true, though they are always plausible; they generally contain a fallacy of some sort, and one which it is pleasant to ignore. They are well qualified to deceive, and most of us are very willing to be deceived by them. . . . A proverb has been defined as the wit of one and the wisdom of many; it is oftener the sophistry of a few and the unreason of the multitude. The great trouble with a popular adage, or current phrase of any type, is, that it is commonly accepted as absolute truth. Hardly anyone thinks of examining or questioning it; for has it not already received the approval of thousands, if not of generations? It must be sound, especially if it fits our case. It commends itself, mainly by sparing us the trouble of reflection, which is always a relief, even to the most intelligent.[7]

The author chose Lord John Russell's "proverbial" definition that "a proverb is the wit of one, and the wisdom of many" (ca. 1850) and then proceeds to show that proverbs actually lack in wisdom, truth, and rationality. The attempt at discrediting proverbs is rather successful since the author presents a few isolated examples of proverbs out of context which appear to contain "seeds of deceit, injustice [and] falsehood," as, for example, "Silence gives consent," "Still waters run deep," "All is fair in love and war," and so on. Especially so-called contradictory proverbs are listed to support the fact that proverbs contain neither truths nor wisdom; notice, for example, such opposite pairs as "Two of a trade never agree" versus "Like pleases like"; "Delays are dangerous" versus "Wisdom lies in waiting"; "A little learning is a dangerous thing" versus "It is better to know something than nothing," and so on. Isolated proverbs as well as contradictory pairs have often been used to argue against the value of proverbs.[8] All that such proverb pairs show, however, is that proverbs are apparent truths about experiences and that each proverb does not have a universal applicability. In special situations, let's say where the shoe (the proverb) fits, proverbs do express wisdom of some sort

26

31
"All's fair in love and war,"
to him who believes
that the end justifies
the means.

as well as seeming truths. What is of importance is that proverbs are *not* universals, something that not even our general definitions have contended, for the word "universal" appears only two times in fifty-five definitions. Agreed, they often are cited as universals, but then it is the intent, be it malicious, manipulative, or destructive even, that makes them appear as absolute rules or laws. The folk seems to be perfectly aware of the fact that proverbs are anything but universal truths, and the anonymous author of this short newspaper account appears to be fighting against windmills with his "enlightening" comments on the dangers of proverbs. It is one thing to discuss the use and misuse of proverbs, but it is another to attempt to define them. Since proverbs reflect human experiences of all types, they are bound to contradict each other just as life is made up of a multitude of contradictions. Used in a very particular context any proverb will express some short wisdom of sorts that comments or reflects on a given situation, even though the truth of it could be put into question when looked at from a larger philosophical framework. Proverbs are context-bound and so is their wisdom, no matter how minute that kernel of truth might be.

Thirteen years later we find H. G. Keene's short article on "Conflicts of Experience" (1890) whose title already alludes to the problem of contradictory proverbs standing in striking conflict with each other. This author also refers to Lord John Russell's famous definition and adds many examples to the ones cited in the previous popular essay:

> Persons who accept Lord John Russell's definition of a proverb must sometimes be puzzled to find that one and the same community is in the habit of using adages which are diametrically opposed to one another. If it were true that a proverb is the wisdom of the many and the wit of one, we should surely be justified in expecting all accepted proverbs to resemble laws of nature or formulas of mathematics. But we see that this is far from being the case; and no sooner do we think we have obtained an irrefragable maxim from the crystallization of experience than another, equally authoritative, confronts us with an absolutely opposite direction.[9]

Later in his general discussion Keene points out correctly that proverbs "are not infallible weapons; when one [a proverb] breaks the combatants [people] have to betake themselves to another . . . a proverb will usually be merely a compendious expression of some principle, true or false, applicable or non-applicable, as the case may be in which it is employed."[10] It is the application of a proverb that really determines the sense or meaning of a proverb, that is, whether it is truth or wisdom in a particular situation or falsehood and folly. But again, the proverb in and of itself does express an observation that is at least to various degrees common to human experience.

In another short and anonymous article on "Proverbs as Literature" from 1900 proverbs are defined in a fashion which is very much congruent with the one that was stated as a summary of the 55 definitions listed above:

> It [the proverb] is artistic in form, it is a concentrated expression of worldly wisdom at least and very often of profound moral truth, it passes current everywhere, it formulates the universal ideas common to peasant and philosopher, it grows out of the general consciousness. Above all, it suggests to us that that which endures in human speech and writing is the happy phrase or sentence which aims not at preciseness of details, but at precision in the utterance of feeling, knowledge, or experience.[11]

The author once again stresses wisdom and truth in proverbs and only hints at the problem that at times they might be lacking in "preciseness of details," that is, in being universally true and applicable.

Vernon Rendall, on the other hand, a more intellectual writer, argues in his thoughts on "Proverbs and Popular Similes" (1929) that proverbs in the modern age are passé since they cannot comment on our complex life-styles any more:

> . . . the time has long gone by since a proverb could be regarded as an effective weapon. It is a broad generalization for a world which has be-

come far too subtle to believe in such things, knowing that circumstances alter cases, and that the infinite and mysterious complexity of
life cannot be circumscribed by any formula. A man of spirit, even if he
believe in proverbs for most people, will feel that he is above them himself, the bright exception to make the general experience look ridiculous.
. . . Whoever paused over the warning of a proverb? The next minute,
if he had a fairly good head, he might think of another that contradicted
it.[12]

Once again we are confronted with the problem of contradictory proverbs
plus a considerable dose of intellectual snobbery. The idea that intelligent and
sophisticated people do not believe in or use proverbs is an old one, as is
clearly illustrated in Lord Chesterfield's letter to his son in 1749: "A man of
fashion never has recourse to proverbs and vulgar aphorisms."[13] This is clearly
a statement of the age of enlightenment, but scholars of this century have
also made similar claims concerning the uselessness and invalidity of proverbs
in complex cultures. In *The New York Times,* for example, a one-paragraph
note appeared in 1930 proclaiming the "Twilight of the Proverbs," since they
obviously have been overtaken by new societal mores, as, for example, " 'Two's
company, three's a crowd.' There's a mid-Victorian for you! We moderns
recognize the triangle as part of the accepted order."[14] While this author
presents a few humorous comments on how some proverbs do not fit the
times anymore, the sociologist William Albig even concluded in 1931 that
"the proverb is a language form which has largely passed from usage in contemporary American culture,"[15] a view that has been proven absurd in more
recent research. Some of my own work on proverb usage in modern Germany and America represents ample proof that proverbs continue to survive
in complex societies even though they might also be intentionally varied or
parodied.[16] They are nevertheless current in their traditional wording as well,
and are thought of quite positively by members of such societies as all of the
definitions above have clearly shown. People in all walks of life continue to
use proverbs for different purposes in various situations, sometimes seriously
and then again also ironically or humorously, but to suggest that they are
"dying out" or that they are not used by intellectuals is certainly erroneous.
They might not use them intentionally or consciously, but even the finest
intellect does on occasion resort to fixed language forms such as the proverb.

One year after Rendall's condemnation of proverbs Ernest Weekley's
"Proverbs Considered" (1930) appeared which presents a general introduction to proverbs, their use in English literature, and a short survey of significant proverb collections. Weekley starts by quoting the proverb definition of
the *Oxford Dictionary* which states that a proverb is "a short pithy saying in
common and recognized use; a concise sentence, often metaphorical or alliterative in form, which is held to express some truth ascertained by experience

or observation familiar to all; an adage, a wise saw."[17] It should be noted how close this definition is in fact to the composite definition presented at the beginning of this chapter. Weekley suggests that the *Oxford Dictionary* should also have mentioned the rhyme of many proverbs and later suggests that:

> The true proverb is a condensed allegory. Though it may have literary record as far back as the Greeks, and may even be traceable in Hebrew and Sanskrit, it is rather the spontaneous product of human experience than the expression of the meditations of an individual sage. In its final form it is, in the words of Lord John Russell, "the wit of one man, the wisdom of many. . . ." The true proverb should suggest a little drama and express its meaning in metaphor.[18]

This definition is once again in agreement with what people in general conceive a proverb to be, even though it adds the obvious literary origin of some proverbs to the discussion. Proverbs are seen to be bits of wisdom concerning human experience that continue to be relevant in the modern age. Yet arguments still appear in the popular press that proverbs are things of the past. Scott Corbett labelled them "Our Toothless Old Saws" in 1954, claiming that "our old saws are fast disappearing under the impact of modern engineering magic. A lot of them don't cut much ice any more." In a humorous vein he brings a number of short reactions to proverbs that have seemingly outlived their usefulness, as for example this one:

> Another old saw which is definitely out of key with our present period of gracious living is the one which refers to "the pot calling the kettle black." Black pots and kettles are a thing of the past. Anyone who has seen five minutes of TV knows that. Just a touch with any of a dozen miracle cleaning pads assisted by one of the countless miracle cleaning powders carried by your friendly neighborhood grocer and all that unpleasant blackness is whisked away down the drain. Today's housewives would not put up with a black pot long enough for it to call anybody anything.[19]

This is clearly a humorous take-off on proverbs and the world of advertising as well, yet Corbett forgets in his zeal of uncovering outmoded proverbs that they are not necessarily to be taken literally but that their continuous significance lies, in fact, in their metaphorical nature. Were the United States to go over to the metric system, for example, such proverbs as "An ounce of prevention is worth a pound of cure" or "A miss is as good as a mile" would not be disregarded at all. The basic underlying thought of relating something small to something big would still be expressed even though we would measure with the metric system. There are plenty of German proverbs, for example, which still use medieval forms of measurement that have long fallen out of use and which most people could not identify precisely. But the met-

aphor is clear, and it is exactly the archaic imagery of certain proverbs contrasted with modern actuality that renders them especially effective today. Modern engineering magic might result in humorous parodies of proverbs, but it will hardly replace the general idea of a metaphorical proverb.

A more positive view of proverbs in the modern age was presented by Horace Reynolds in his short essay "A Proverb in the Hand—Is Often Worth a Thousand Words" (1959) which appeared in *The New York Times*. The varied proverb title which also combines the two proverbs "A bird in the hand is worth two in the bush" and "A picture is worth a thousand words" is ample proof that Reynolds considers proverbs to have continued value. As far as defining them is concerned, he seems to agree with Archer Taylor's view of the indefinability of a proverb and offers the following comments:

> Like poetry, the proverb is indefinable. There have been some good tries. Francis Bacon called proverbs: "The edged tools of speech." Lord John Russell in a much-quoted appraisal called a proverb "The wisdom of many and the wit of one." But the definition I like best comes from the good old *Encyclopaedia Britannica*: "A pungent criticism of life." That seems to fit the insight and compassion which mark the proverb at its best.[20]

Personally I like Reynolds's "title"-definition of his article, "A proverb in the hand is often worth a thousand words," since it stresses the practicality of proverbs which is augmented by being able to express much in a few words. This also agrees with the popular notions of the proverb, and the fact that Reynolds refers to Nikita Krushchev as a proverb user par excellence at the beginning of his essay indicates the effectiveness of these bits of wisdom even on the international political scene. Reynolds hastens to distinguish between national and international proverbs and warns that "everyone should be leery of attempting to discover national characteristics in a nation's proverbs," for many proverbs that seem indigenous prove to be on closer scrutiny "a kind of international fund of popular ideas" which "will last as long as human nature."[21] Regional, national, and international politics certainly remain a vital stamping ground for the proverb, and such international figures as Lenin, Krushchev, Churchill, Roosevelt, and Reagan knew or know how to use them for political argumentation. Even debates in the United Nations are often interspersed with proverbs which can become verbal weapons that are difficult to argue against. In such debates the proverbs take on serious meanings and are used by intelligent people to strengthen their arguments with the emotions and spice of traditional wisdom.[22]

"A bird in the hand, Julius. . . ."

Reproduced by special permission of *Playboy* magazine:
Copyright © 1969 by Playboy.

Another anonymous article with the questioning title "Can Anybody Compose a Proverb?" (1961) also presented a very positive picture of proverbs to thousands of readers of *The New York Times*. The author studies a few old proverbs like "Know thyself," "Festina lente," "Que sera, sera," "Qui s'excuse, s'accuse" and "Vox populi, vox Dei" and emphasizes in particular the shortness of these expressions:

> Many people have loved proverbs . . . for the wisdom embedded in them. Others have treasured proverbs for the vividness or earthiness of their imagery. But students of the subject are impressed by still another characteristic of the proverb: its verbal economy. Proverbs are rarely wordy. The usual proverb is spare and austere in expression, and some are marvels of compactness.[23]

Once again we have a view of proverbs in a major United States newspaper that resembles those of our composite definition at the beginning of this chapter. "Wisdom" and "shortness" doubtlessly belong to the popular notion of what makes up a proverb. Even when a scholar such as Mario Pei wrote a short piece on "Parallel Proverbs" (1964) for the *Saturday Review,* he basically adhered to this general view of the proverb in his article dealing with national and international proverbs, their cynicism, philosophy and humor, their obvious misogyny and their contradictory comments on life's experiences around the world:

> Proverbs are among the most ancient of human institutions. Criticism of life, in brief and pithy form, is characteristic of proverbs, while their popular philosophy is, indeed, proverbial. "Proverbs are the wisdom of peoples" goes an Italian saying. This is perhaps an exaggeration, but there is no doubt that much of a nation's folk-philosophy gets into proverbs, along with the spice of national customs and, above all, the peculiar flavor of the nation's language and phraseology. . . . Proverbs are generalizations of human experience, condensations of oft-repeated occurrences of the trial-and-error variety. Above all, they are the fruit of observation and inductive reasoning, two of the great faculties of the human mind. . . . A generalization . . . caught on, became popular, was passed from mouth to mouth, from generation to generation. Ultimately it became an integral part of the group's folklore, and was repeated whenever the situation it described recurred. . . . Every proverb tells a story and teaches a lesson.[24]

This lengthy discussion of the nature of the proverb by Pei reads almost as an attempt of summarizing the common understanding of proverbs. Many of the fifty-five definitions stated previously are similar to Pei's points, and it is amazing to notice how congruous these definitions are to those defining attempts printed in magazines and newspapers. There certainly is much agreement in the non-scholarly world of what a proverb is even if scholars seem to be unable to agree on a reasonable definition at all.

A similar article on "The Art of Proverbs" (1965) by F. L. Lucas followed Pei's article about a year and a half later. Here again we have a solid introductory view of the proverb written for general consumption. Lucas differentiates between proverbs and aphorisms;[25] he cites many examples from various national languages; he comments on their content as well as their contradictory nature; and he points in particular to their misanthropic and misogynous nature.[26] Even though Lucas states that "today proverbs appear to have lost their popularity" at the beginning of his essay, he presents argument after argument why proverbs are still useful today, for as the subtitle proclaims, proverbs are "an evaluation of the minds—wary and illusionless— that have created the world's wisdom." His definition attempt reads as follows:

> A proverb is by definition a popular maxim. . . . Proverbs are among the most ancient literary forms, and among the most universal. . . . Enough if it [the proverb] holds its measure of truth. . . . Proverbs are anonymous wisdom-literature of the common man in ages past. Yet they often bear the stamp of minds by no means common. They can throw fascinating light on human nature, on national character, on life itself. And even when we doubt their wisdom, we can still often admire their trenchancy, their brevity, their imaginative imagery. "A proverb," says the Arab, "is to speech as salt to food."[27]

We might choose to quibble with Lucas on whether proverbs do or do not reflect national character,[28] but altogether his definition encompasses once again wisdom and brevity as well as a number of other aspects that were also cited in our composite definition above. He certainly has given the general reader a good idea of what proverbs are, how they are used and what function they perform in human communication.

Reporting on George Milner's fascinating theoretical work on Samoan proverbs,[29] an anonymous reporter of *Time* labelled his account "The Wild Flowers of Thought" (1969), and as his poetic title already indicates, his entire essay is positively inclined toward proverbs. Despite having discussed proverbs with an important anthropologist and paremiologist, the reporter remains simple and general in his definition of the proverb, mentioning nothing of Milner's structural approach to the proverb for which he has become known in paremiological circles:

> These lean, didactic, aphoristic statements, so varied in their language, seem to distill a universal wisdom. . . . Can't it be that the proverb— literally, "before the word"—provides a clue to the common denominator of all human thought?[30]

Such fascination with newer proverb research was also expressed in Earl Lane's lengthy newspaper report on "A Proverbial Quest that Intrigues Scholars" (1975) which went through the national press via the wire services. Lane had studied Archer Taylor's book on *The Proverb* (Cambridge, Mass. 1931) and interviewed Matti Kuusi in Helsinki and myself here in Burlington, Vermont. The result was a fine account for the general public of what serious international proverb scholars do and how proverbs are and can be studied by scholars from various disciplines. As far as a definition is concerned, Lane simply quotes the three of us and leaves it with that:

> One problem has been simply trying to arrive at a good definition of what constitutes a proverb. "A proverb has a fixed form," Kuusi said recently, "but there are many thousands of definitions." The late Archer Taylor . . . shrewdly refused to be pinned down on a precise definition. "An incommunicable quality tells us that this sentence is proverbial and that one is not," Taylor once wrote. . . . Mieder defines a proverb as "a concise statement of an apparent truth which has currency."[31]

It should be added here that "my" definition which Lane is citing was first coined by my teacher Professor Stuart A. Gallacher, who stated more completely "A proverb must have two basic elements other than form, namely, it must be a concise statement of an apparent truth and have currency among the people. . . . The more the apparent truth is universally known and repeated, the better its chances of becoming accepted as an unquestioned proverb."[32] I have always enjoyed quoting Stuart Gallacher when asked to give a short and general definition of the proverb by people who are not experts in the field. I do this out of respect and admiration for the person who introduced me to paremiology and also because it appears to me to be an acceptable statement of what a proverb might be without going into great theoretical depth. I was obviously pleased to see Earl Lane pick this definition from the many that I had given to him as possibilities, and realizing the research this reporter had done to write his essay, Gallacher's definition obviously must have impressed him as a solid general definition for the layperson. And yet, the readers of Earl Lane's article most likely must have wondered why proverb scholars have such difficulty in defining the very matter they happen to know so much about. After all, the readers probably thought all along that proverbs are nothing more than short pieces of wisdom.

Two final articles from popular magazines need to be discussed; both are to a certain degree reactions to J. A. Simpson's *The Concise Oxford Dictionary of Proverbs* (London 1982) and John Gross's *The Oxford Book of Aphorisms* (London 1983). In his review article entitled "Wisdom of the Tribe. Why Proverbs Are Better than Aphorisms" Hugh Kenner defines proverbs in the following manner:

> Being recipes for managing our affairs, proverbs have been cherished likewise. . . . We say it [the proverb] now because it had seemed worth saying again and again, descending father to son, mother to daughter, mouth to mouth for centuries before. . . . It was useful because it touched on a general truth. . . . Proverbs use the experience people gain in skills to project what we're always wanting, some general guide for action. They did this for millennia before we'd acquired the habit of seeking guidance from something written. They were short and memorable and self-explanatory.[33]

It is interesting to note that Kenner sides decisively with the traditional proverbs over the "solitary ingenuity" of the aphorisms, for "what the aphorisms lack is the proverb's ability to generalize."[34] This is certainly a strong endorsement of the common wisdom or truth expressed in proverbs, and that in an age when the individual is supposed to reign supreme! For Kenner aphorisms "have the air of brittle special cases," whereas proverbs convey "a substantial portion of a philosophy of life."[35] And Kenner doesn't even stop here, but rather concludes his essay by making the remarkable statement that the genre of proverbs is *not* dead. He cites the example "If anything can go wrong, it will" (the so-called Murphy's Law from 1949) for a new proverb, and we could easily add such texts as "Different strokes for different folks," "It takes two to tango" and "A woman without a man is like a fish without a bicycle," which obviously should be counted as American proverbs by now.[36] The time of proverb creations is not over, for new proverbs are constantly coined through slogans, advertisements, and graffiti. The mass media are extremely important in establishing a quick and wide general acceptance and currency of such texts that are often structured on standard proverb patterns. Often these texts might be mere variations of existing proverbs, but they can also become proverbs in their own right. Doubtlessly modern-oriented proverb research needs to pay much more attention to such new proverbs.[37]

In a last essay based on Hugh Kenner's previous remarks Stefan Kanfer in *Time* queries once again "Proverbs or Aphorisms?" (1983). He presents short definitions for both genres and is in basic agreement with Kenner:

> The aphorism is a personal observation inflated into a universal truth, a private posing as a general. A proverb is anonymous human history compressed to the size of a seed.[38]

Kanfer, too, agrees that intellectual aphorisms have not replaced traditional proverbs: "Even now, proverb makers are at work. Traditions have to begin somewhere; today folk sayings arise from economics: 'There is no such thing as a free lunch,' from the comics: 'Keep on trucking,' and even from the computers: 'Garbage in, garbage out.' "[39] Kanfer has also chosen fitting examples to show that the age of proverb making is not over, and he decides that it is a toss-up whether proverbs or aphorisms have more applicability to modern life. Personally I would say that proverbs because of their memorability win this contest with ease, especially when one considers the frequency of usage of proverbs in contrast to aphorisms. It should be pointed out, however, that the proverbial aphorism, a more or less intellectual game in the form of parodies of traditional proverbs, appears to gain in popularity. They are used by intellectuals, the mass media, and also by the general population as a type of anti-proverb, varying existing proverb texts according to modern needs but at the same time retaining their linguistic structures in most cases. The tradition of proverbial aphorisms is not new; such relatively recent authors as Friedrich Nietzsche, Karl Kraus, Bertolt Brecht, and others were masters at this hybrid genre.[40] Many books of quips, quotes, aphorisms or other one-liners by lesser authors also abound in them, as for example:

> Like charity, obesity begins at home.
>
> Money may not be everything, but it's a pretty good cure for poverty.
>
> Castles in the air are all right until you try to move into them.
>
> When in doubt, tell the truth.
>
> It takes two to quarrel, but one gets the blame.
>
> An ounce of keep your mouth shut is worth a ton of explanation.
>
> Speech is silver, silence is golden, and oratory, at the moment, is mainly brass.[41]

But even such proverbial aphorisms will only seldomly become new proverbs, and actual proverbs will continue to flourish even in the most advanced societies since they do express still today basic human needs and concerns.

Matti Kuusi once defined proverbs simply as "monumenta humana,"[42] and this is exactly what they are to the general population. Our survey of fifty-five non-academic definitions has shown that proverbs are thought to express human wisdom and basic truths in a short sentence. Popular articles in magazines and newspapers tend to share this view of the proverb. Altogether proverbs are still seen as useful generalizations about life, even if at times their value of appropriateness in certain situations might be questioned. We can poke fun at proverbs, we can ridicule them, or we can parody them, but eventually we are all governed by their insights to some degree. Proverbs and their wisdom confront us daily, and modern people seem to have a clear idea of what proverbs are, what they express, and what they can do for us. Proverb scholars would do well to pay more attention to the present use of proverbs while obviously also continuing to tackle the frustrating question of whether a universal proverb definition can be found. But in their enduring

search for such an erudite definition, they can take solace in the fact that the people using proverbs do know in their minds what makes a good proverb— an incommunicable quality tells them that a short and repeated statement of wisdom, truth, and experience must be a proverb.

Notes

This chapter was first published in *Proverbium: Yearbook of International Proverb Scholarship,* 2 (1985), 109–143.

1. See Jan Frederik Kindstrand, "The Greek Concept of Proverbs," *Eranos,* 76 (1978), 71–85.

2. See Bartlett Jere Whiting, "The Nature of the Proverb," *Harvard Studies and Notes in Philology and Literature,* 14 (1932), 273–307.

3. See Shirley Arora, "The Perception of Proverbiality," *Proverbium: Yearbook of International Proverb Scholarship,* 1 (1984), 1–38; Nigel Barley, " 'The Proverb' and Related Problems of Genre Definition," *Proverbium,* no. 23 (1974), 880–884; Otto Blehr, "What Is a Proverb?" *Fabula,* 14 (1973), 243–246; Margaret Bryant, *Proverbs and How to Collect Them* (Greensboro, N.C.: American Dialect Society, 1945); David Cram, "The Linguistic Status of the Proverb," *Cahiers de Lexicologie,* 43 (1983), 53–71; Alan Dundes, "On the Structure of the Proverb," *Proverbium,* no. 25 (1975), 961–973 (also in: *The Wisdom of Many. Essays on the Proverb,* eds. Wolfgang Mieder and Alan Dundes [New York: Garland Publishing, 1981], pp. 43–64); Galit Hasan-Rokem, *Proverbs in Israeli Folk Narratives: A Structural Semantic Analysis*

(Helsinki: Suomalainen Tiedeakatemia, 1982); George Milner, "What Is a Proverb?" *New Society*, 332 (February 6, 1969), 199–202; Peter Seitel, "Proverbs: A Social Use of Metaphor," *Genre*, 2 (1969), 143–161 (also in: *The Wisdom of Many. Essays on the Proverb*, eds. Wolfgang Mieder and Alan Dundes [New York: Garland Publishing, 1981], pp 122–139).

    4. Archer Taylor, *The Proverb* (Cambridge, Mass.: Harvard University Press, 1931), p. 3.

    5. Taylor, p. 3.

    6. For a fair number of these proverbs about proverbs from many languages see Selwyn Gurney Champion, *Racial Proverbs* (London: George Routledge & Sons, 1938), pp. 3–9.

    7. See Anonymous, "Influence of Proverbs," *The New York Times* (April 29, 1877), p. 6, cols. 5–6.

    8. Most major books on the proverb deal with contradictory proverbs, but see also in particular Kenneth Burke, "Literature as Equipment for Living," in K. Burke, *The Philosophy of Literary Form. Studies in Symbolic Action* (Baton Rouge, Louisiana: Louisiana University Press, 1941), pp. 253–262; Oskar Cöster, "Maulschellen für den 'Volksmund.' Epigramme zur Dialektik des Sprichworts," in *Projekt Deutschunterricht 12. Kommunikationsanalyse II— Sprachkritik*, ed. Bodo Lecke (Stuttgart: Metzler, 1977), pp. 131–147; Willy Kramp, "Sind Sprichwörter wahr?" *Die Furche*, 23 (1937), 135–140; Wallace H. Maw and Ethel W. Maw, "Contrasting Proverbs as a Measure of Attitudes of College Students Toward Curiosity-Related Behaviors," *Psychological Reports*, 37 (1975), 1085–1086; and Wolfgang Mieder, *Antisprichwörter* (Wiesbaden: Verlag für deutsche Sprache, 1982).

    9. H. G. Keene, "Conflicts of Experience," *The Living Age*, 185 (May 24, 1890), 483–486 (here p. 483).

    10. Keene, p. 486.

    11. Anonymous, "Proverbs as Literature," *The Living Age*, 226 (September 22, 1900), 785–787 (here p. 785).

    12. Vernon Rendall, "Proverbs and Popular Similes," *The Saturday Review*, 148 (October 19, 1929), 443.

    13. See *Letters to His Son by the Earl of Chesterfield*, ed. Oliver H. Leigh (New York: Tudor Publishing, n.d.), p. 218 (the letter was written on October 2, 1749).

    14. Anonymous, "Twilight of the Proverbs," *The New York Times* (May 3, 1930), p. 18, col. 6.

    15. See William Albig, "Proverbs and Social Control," *Sociology and Social Research*, 15 (1931), 527 (the whole article on pp. 527–535).

    16. See for example, Wolfgang Mieder, *Das Sprichwort in unserer Zeit* (Frauenfeld: Huber, 1975) and *Deutsche Sprichwörter in Literatur, Politik, Presse und Werbung* (Hamburg: Helmut Buske, 1983). See also Barbara and Wolfgang Mieder, "Tradition and Innovation: Proverbs in Advertising," *Journal of Popular Culture*, 11 (1977), 308–319 (also in: *The Wisdom of Many. Essays on the Proverb*, eds. Wolfgang Mieder and Alan Dundes [New York: Garland Publishing, 1981], pp. 309–322).

    17. Ernest Weekley, "Proverbs Considered," *Atlantic Monthly*, 145 (April 1930), 504–512 (here p. 504).

    18. Weekley, p. 507.

    19. See Scott Corbett, "Our Toothless Old Saws," *Atlantic Monthly*, 193 (March 1954), 92.

    20. Horace Reynolds, "A Proverb in the Hand—Is Often Worth a Thousand Words," *The New York Times Magazine* (September 13, 1959), p. 74.

    21. Reynolds, p. 74.

    22. See, for example, Lt. Colonel Victor S. M. de Guinzbourg, *Wit and Wisdom of the United Nations. Proverbs and Apothegms on Diplomacy* (New York: Privately printed, 1961); R. D. Hogg, "Proverbs," *Secretariat News*, 14 (1960), 5–7; Joseph Raymond, "Tensions in Proverbs: More Light on International Understanding," *Western Folklore*, 15 (1956), 153–158 (also in: *The Wisdom of Many. Essays on the Proverb*, eds. Wolfgang Mieder and Alan Dundes

[New York: Garland Publishing, 1981], pp. 300–308); L. A. Morozova, "Upotreblenie V. I. Leninym poslovits," *Russkaia Rech'*, no. 2 (1979), 10–14; Edd Miller and Jesse J. Villarreal, "The Use of Clichés by Four Contemporary Speakers [Churchill, Eden, Roosevelt, Wallace]," *Quarterly Journal of Speech*, 31 (1945), 151–155. Concerning the perverted use of proverbs by Hitler and the National Socialists see Wolfgang Mieder, "Proverbs in Nazi Germany. The Promulgation of Anti-Semitism and Stereotypes through Folklore," *Journal of American Folklore*, 95 (1982), 435–464; a similar German version of this paper was published as "Sprichwörter unterm Hakenkreuz," *Muttersprache*, 93 (1983), 1–30.

23. Anonymous, "Can Anybody Compose a Proverb?" *The New York Times* (November 12, 1961), Section IV, p. 8, col. 3.

24. Mario Pei, "Parallel Proverbs," *Saturday Review*, 47 (May 2, 1964), 16–17 and p. 53 (here p. 16).

25. See Lutz Röhrich and Wolfgang Mieder, *Sprichwort* (Stuttgart: Metzler, 1977), pp. 4–6. For the subgenre of the "proverbial aphorism" see Wolfgang Mieder, "Karl Kraus und der sprichwörtliche Aphorismus," *Muttersprache*, 89 (1979), 97–115 (also in: W. Mieder, *Deutsche Sprichwörter in Literatur, Politik, Presse und Werbung* [Hamburg: Helmut Buske, 1983], pp. 113–131); and also W. Mieder, *Deutsche Sprichwörter und Redensarten* (Stuttgart: Reclam, 1979), pp. 144–152.

26. See for example, Richard Jente, " 'A Woman Conceals What She Knows Not,' " *Modern Language Notes*, 41 (1926), 253–254; Mary Ellen B. Lewis, "The Feminists Have Done It: Applied Folklore," *Journal of American Folklore*, 87 (1974), 85–87; and T. F. Thiselton-Dyer, *Folklore of Women* (London: Elliot Stock, 1905; rpt. Williamstown, Mass.: Corner House, 1975).

27. F. L. Lucas, "The Art of Proverbs," *Holiday*, 38 (September 1965), 8 and 10–13 (here pp. 10–11).

28. See, for example, Erich Berneker, "Das russische Volk in seinen Sprichwörtern," *Zeitschrift des Vereins für Volkskunde*, 14 (1904), 75–87 and 179–191; Alan Dundes, "Slurs International: Folk Comparisons of Ethnicity and National Character," *Southern Folklore Quarterly*, 39 (1975), 15–38; Alan Dundes, *Life is like a Chicken Coop Ladder. A Portrait of German Culture Through Folklore* (New York: Columbia University Press, 1984); Henri F. Muller, "The French Seen Through Their Proverbs and Proverbial Expressions," *French Review*, 17 (1943–1944), 4–8; Joseph Raymond, *Attitudes and Cultural Patterns in Spanish Proverbs* (Diss. Columbia University, 1951); F. N. Robinson, "Irish Proverbs and Irish National Character," *Modern Philology*, 43 (1945), 1–10 (also in: *The Wisdom of Many. Essays on the Proverb*, eds. Wolfgang Mieder and Alan Dundes [New York: Garland Publishing, 1981], pp. 284–299); Hans-Joachim Schoeps, "Völkerpsychologie im Sprichwort," in H. J. Schoeps, *Ungeflügelte Worte. Was nicht im Büchmann stehen kann* (Berlin: Haude & Spener 1971), pp. 162–171; Franz Thierfelder, "Sprich-und Schlagwörter zwischen den Völkern," *Welt und Wort*, 11 (1956), 369–370 and 373. Two important collections are Otto Freiherr von Reinsberg-Düringsfeld, *Internationale Titulaturen*, 2 vols. (Leipzig: Hermann Fries, 1863); and Abraham Roback, *A Dictionary of International Slurs* (Cambridge, Mass.: Sci-Art Publishers, 1944; rpt. Waukesha, Wis.: Maledicta Press, 1979).

29. See Milner (note 3). A longer version of this paper in French is "De l'armature des locutions proverbiales: Essai des taxonomie sémantique," *L'Homme*, 9 (1969), 49–70.

30. Anonymous, "The Wild Flowers of Thought," *Time* (March 14, 1969), 74–75.

31. Earl Lane, "A Proverbial Quest That Intrigues Scholars," *Newsday* (June 27, 1975), part II, pp. 4A–5A (here p. 5A). Lane's article was reprinted in other newspapers in various lengths as "Probing Perennial Proverbs," *The Montreal Star* (July 19, 1975), p. C1; "In the Proverbial Stew," *Boston Globe* (July 6, 1975), p. B1; "The Short, Salty Proverb is a Paroemiologist's Feast," *The Miami Herald* (July 9, 1975), p. F1; "Hot on the Trail of a Proverb," *San Francisco Sunday Examiner and Chronicle* (August 10, 1975), p. 5; "What's the Exchange Rate on a Bird in the Hand?" *The Milwaukee Journal* (August 1, 1975), p. B1; etc.

32. See Stuart A. Gallacher, "Frauenlob's Bits of Wisdom: Fruits of His Environment," in *Middle Ages—Reformation—Volkskunde. Festschrift for John G. Kunstmann,* no editor given (Chapel Hill: University of North Carolina Press, 1959), p. 47 (the entire article on pp. 45–58).

33. Hugh Kenner, "Wisdom of the Tribe. Why Proverbs are Better than Aphorisms," *Harper's* (May 6, 1983), 84–86 (here pp. 84–85).

34. Kenner, p. 86.

35. Kenner, p. 86.

36. For a discussion of such new proverbs see Wolfgang Mieder, " 'Eine Frau ohne Mann ist wie ein Fisch ohne Velo!' " *Sprachspiegel,* 38 (1982), 141–142; and Wolfgang Mieder and George Bryan, " 'Zum Tango gehören zwei,' " *Der Sprachdienst,* 27 (1983), 100–102.

37. See Barbara and Wolfgang Mieder (note 16); Wolfgang Mieder, "Proverbial Slogans are the Name of the Game," *Kentucky Folklore Record,* 24 (1978), 49–53; and Jess Nierenberg, "Proverbs in Graffiti. Taunting Traditional Wisdom," *Maledicta,* 7 (1983), 41–58.

38. Stefan Kanfer, "Proverbs or Aphorisms?" *Time* (July 11, 1983), 74.

39. Kanfer, p. 74.

40. See my collection of 4500 such German texts with the title *Antisprichwörter,* 3 vols. (Wiesbaden: Verlag für deutsche Sprache, 1982, 1985, and 1989). See also some English examples in my "A Sampler of Anglo-American Proverb Poetry," *Folklore Forum,* 13 (1980), 39–53.

41. Hundreds of such examples can be found in E. C. McKenzie, *Mac's Giant Book of Quips & Quotes* (Grand Rapids, Mich.: Baker Book House, 1980). The examples cited here appear on pp. 240, 344, 141, 140, 435, 467 (last two texts).

42. See Matti Kuusi, *Parömiologische Betrachtungen* (Helsinki: Suomalainen Tiedeakatemia, 1957), p. 52.

3

" Proverbs Everyone Ought to Know "

Paremiological Minimum and Cultural Literacy

Recent theoretical research on proverbs and proverbial expressions has been primarily linguistically oriented, emphasizing in particular structural and semiotic aspects of proverbs on a comparative basis. The Soviet linguist and folklorist Grigorii L'vovich Permiakov (1919–1983) published his now classic study *Ot pogovorki do skazki* in 1970 whose English translation with the title *From Proverb to Folk-Tale* from 1979 has had an invaluable influence on international paremiological scholarship. Matti Kuusi in Finland continues to work *Towards an International Type-System of Proverbs* (1972), and Alan Dundes' paper "On the Structure of the Proverbs" (1975) as well as Shirley L. Arora's article on "The Perception of Proverbiality" (1984) belong to the solid foundation of modern paremiology.[1] It must suffice to mention from among dozens of articles, dissertations, essay volumes, and books[2] only three additional studies, namely Zoltan Kanyo, *Sprichwörter—Analyse einer Einfachen Form* (1981), Peter Grzybek and Wolfgang Eismann (eds.), *Semiotische Studien zum Sprichwort* (1984), and Neal R. Norrick, *How Proverbs Mean: Semantic Studies in English Proverbs* (1985).[3]

While these contributions represent major advances concerning the definition, language, structure, and meaning of proverbs, they fail for the most part to consider two extremely important questions that go beyond purely linguistic aspects of proverbial texts. The one deals with the diachronic problem of traditionality, i.e., the fact that any text to qualify as a proverb must have (or have had) some currency for a period of time. Related to this is the synchronic question of frequency of occurrence or familiarity of a given text at a certain time. None of the dozens of proverb definitions can answer these questions, and yet any proverb must "prove" a certain traditionality and frequency to be considered verbal folklore. As far as proverbs from past generations are concerned, questions as to their true proverbiality can be and have been ascertained by historical proverb dictionaries that amass references and variants for particular proverbs from written sources. Paremiographers around the world have assembled superb diachronic collections, the model being the massive collections of the Anglo-American language that Bartlett Jere Whiting has painstakingly put together.[4] With the use of modern computers such historically oriented volumes will obviously continue to be published for various national languages, but this type of paremiographical work usually stops short of answering some extremely important questions: How about the proverbs right now? Which texts from former generations are still current today? What are the truly new proverbs of the modern age? How familiar are people with proverbs today, and so on?

These questions are not new, but they need to be addressed in a more scientific fashion using modern means of statistical research. The American sociologist William Albig was one of the first scholars to use demographic methods with proverbs. While his conclusion that proverbs have little use in complex cultures with rapid social change is not valid in light of newer research, he did include a list of the 13 most popular proverbs around 1930 based on the answers of 68 university students who were asked to list all the proverbs they could think of during a thirty-minute period. A total of 1443 proverbs or 21.2 proverbs per student were written down. Of these 442 were different proverbs, and the most frequently cited proverb was "A stitch in time saves nine" with 47 of the 68 students referring to it. The following table shows the frequency for the top 13 proverbs.[5]

Times Mentioned	*Proverb*
47	A stitch in time saves nine.
40	A rolling stone gathers no moss.
39	A bird in the hand is worth two in the bush.
37	Early to bed and early to rise, makes a man healthy, wealthy, and wise.
30	Never put off till tomorrow what you can do today.
27	Haste makes waste.
26	An apple a day keeps the doctor away.
23	All that glitters is not gold.
23	Do unto others as you would have them do unto you.
21	Laugh and the world laughs with you.
21	Birds of a feather flock together.
20	There's no fool like an old fool.
20	Make hay while the sun shines.

A Stitch in time, saves nine.

The house-wife plies her needle and her thread,
Long after idle people are in bed ;
The rent is small, but she full well doth know,
That little rents to larger ones will grow.

Eight years later yet another American sociologist, Read Bain, reached quite similar results using almost twice the number of students. He asked 133 first-year college students to write down all the proverbs they could. A total of 3654 proverbs or 27.5 texts per student were listed.[6] Unfortunately Bain did not cite any of the proverbs, but we may assume that they included those found by Albig to be known among American university students a few years earlier. What is of special interest, however, is that on the average students could cite *only* between 21.2 and 27.5 proverbs in the 1930s. Admittedly, the sample was relatively small, and we know today that it is difficult to quote proverbs out of context, but this number is nevertheless surprisingly low from a cultural literacy let alone a folkloric point of view.

Unfortunately this type of research was not expanded. It took some thirty years until the Soviet folklorist and paremiologist Isidor Levin called for detailed demographic research by paremiologists, especially if they wanted to reach conclusions about the national character or worldview of certain people via proverbs. He refers to a survey that a German Institute of Demography undertook in 1968 that included a list of 24 German proverbs, asking the informants to indicate whether they totally agree with their wisdom. The highest agreement of 69% fell on the proverb "Es ist nicht alles Gold, was glänzt" (All that glitters is not gold). "Reden ist Silber, Schweigen ist Gold" (Speech is silver, silence is gold) received 61%, and "Gut Ding will Weile haben" (A good thing needs time, i.e., Haste makes waste) only 36%.[7] To Levin this showed that much more demographic research is needed about the popularity and acceptance of certain proverbs before they can be interpreted as indicators of commonly held attitudes.

Levin's short two-part essay appeared in the international journal *Proverbium* (1968/69), and it is surely for that reason that other paremiologists began to heed his advice. The same journal published only one year later a minute but significant study by the Swedish folklorist Carl-Herman Tillhagen in which he discusses in three pages the proverb repertoire of a number of inhabitants of a small Swedish village in the 1930s. From his field research with informants he was able to conclude that a good elderly informant has knowledge of about 1000 proverbs, proverbial expressions, proverbial comparisons and other phraseological units. In an accompanying statistical table representing the frequency of the different genres of these fixed phrases Tillhagen shows that his informants vary in the knowledge of proverbs as such from a mere 21 texts all the way to 575 proverbs.[8] Again it must be remembered that these texts were collected out of context, but this rural population of retirement age certainly "knew" its proverbs (an average of about 134 proverbs per informant) better than their American college counterparts.

It is to be assumed that these two articles influenced G. L. Permiakov as an ardent reader of and contributor to *Proverbium* to conduct a major paremiological experiment with the help of folklore students in Moscow. They presented 300 Muscovites with a large list of proverbs, proverbial expressions, proverbial comparisons, and other types of fixed phrases. The informants were asked to mark those texts they knew, and the result was that all informants were acquainted with about 1000 of the texts. Permiakov considered them the basic stock of fixed phrases among native Russian speakers, referring to the texts as a paremiological minimum in his short monograph on this experiment.[9] This was followed by a short summary statement "On the Paremiological Level and Paremiological Minimum of Language" in English in *Proverbium* (1973) that was not published in Russian until eleven years later.[10] A list of seventy-five of the most frequent Russian proverbial comparisons also appeared in *Proverbium* (1975) to which Matti Kuusi added an appendix of English, French, and Finnish equivalents, showing that many of these common comparisons have general currency throughout Europe.[11] Permiakov's most complete essay on his idea of a paremiological minimum appeared in Russian in 1982, and its English translation by Kevin J. McKenna has recently been published with the title "On the Question of a Russian Paremiological Minimum" in the international yearbook *Proverbium*.[12] Since the short English note from 1973 on the need for establishing paremiological minima for Russian and other languages in the old *Proverbium* journal did not draw the desired scholarly reaction, it is now hoped that this longer English essay in the new *Proverbium* yearbook will encourage scholars to begin working on the establishment of paremiological minima for other national languages.

Permiakov's aim of establishing the Russian paremiological minimum was anything but merely academic. He had definite pragmatic ideas in mind and discussed them in the publications mentioned above. On the one hand he was very interested in the lexicographical problem of getting the most frequent phraseological units into foreign language dictionaries, and on the other he was committed to the idea that the paremiological minimum was of important consequence in the instruction and learning of foreign languages.[13] Toward the end of his life he finished the manuscript for a small book that combines these two interests for 300 of the most well-known Russian proverbs and proverbial expressions. The book appeared posthumously with a splendid introduction and the 300 texts with variants and cultural notes in Russian as *300 obshcheupotrebitel'nykh russkikh poslovits i pogovorok (dlia govoriashchikh na nemetskom iazyke)* (1985). For German students studying Russian as a foreign language a German edition appeared in the same year, and a Bulgarian edition came out one year later.[14] It was Permiakov's wish that this book would be translated into many other languages to help those studying the Russian language to gain the knowledge of the Russian paremiological minimum, to become proverbially literate in the foreign language as it were. With the resurgence in studying Russian in the Anglo-American world, it is indeed high time that an English version of this standard work be made available to students of Russian. As Permiakov would have argued, no speaker of a foreign language can hope to gain cultural literacy in the target language without the knowledge of its paremiological minimum.

Two friends of G. L. Permiakov are keeping his insistence on demographic research toward paremiological minima alive. Matti Kuusi in a short laudatory essay about Permiakov stressed the fact that he was the first to do systematic frequency analysis in order to establish the Russian paremiological minimum.[15] And the German linguist and paremiologist Peter Grzybek published a longer paper on Permiakov's accomplishments in this vein with the bilingual title "How to Do Things with Some Proverbs: Zur Frage eines parömischen Minimums."[16] Three additional German papers have also touched on the importance of such paremiological or phraseological minima for foreign language instruction and dictionaries.[17] But this is not to say that other scholars have not pursued questions of frequency and currency of proverbs in their societies using statistical research methods. The American psychologist Stanley S. Marzolf, for example, presented 159 college students with a list of 55 "common sayings" (i.e., proverbs), asking them which of the texts were familiar. The proverb most frequently reported (by 87.4%) was "If at first you don't succeed, try, try again." Next in familiarity were "Where there's a will, there's a way" (73.0%) and "Actions speak louder than words" (69.2%).

Unfortunately Marzolf did not include his list of proverbs, but if the above percentages seem already a bit alarming, then what follows indicates indeed a rather low familiarity with proverbs by American students: "Only 16 of the 55 sayings were familiar to more than 50%, 6 were familiar to less than 10%. 'Act in haste, repent at leisure' (6.3%) and 'One bad apple spoils the whole bushel' (5.0%) were least familiar."[18]

Another psychological study used a standard psychological proverbs test to ascertain the familiarity that 278 Afro-American students had with its 40 proverbs.[19] The following table shows the five most familiar and most unfamiliar proverbs with percentages of respondents.[20]

Five Most Familiar Proverbs	*Known by (%)*
Where there's a will there's a way	90
Don't judge a book by its cover	89
Quickly come, quickly go	89
When the cat's away the mice will play	86
All's well that ends well	86
Five Least Familiar Proverbs	*Known by (%)*
One swallow doesn't make a summer	12
A golden hammer breaks an iron door	14
The used key is always bright	15
The hot coal burns, the cold one blackens	17
The good is the enemy of the best	18

A larger familiarity test based on 203 "sayings" (i.e., proverbs) given to 50 students who were asked to rate the proverbs on a 7-point scale ranging from low familiarity (1, defined as "sayings that you have never heard or read") to high familiarity (7, defined as "sayings that you have heard or read many times") also showed that there was not one proverb very well known to all students while others, like "One swallow does not make a summer," have a very low level of familiarity. Listed here are the 15 most familiar and the 15 most unfamiliar texts with their average scores.[21]

Most Familiar	*Mean value*
Practice makes perfect	6.92
Better late than never	6.90
If at first you don't succeed, try, try, again	6.88
Like father, like son	6.84
A place for everything and everything in its place	6.76
Two wrongs do not make a right	6.76
Two's company, three's a crowd	6.72
Where there's a will, there's a way	6.72
All's well that ends well	6.70
Don't count your chickens before they're hatched	6.70

Most Familiar	Mean value
Easier said than done	6.70
Practice what you preach	6.70
An apple a day keeps the doctor away	6.68
You can't tell a book by its cover	6.68
A penny saved is a penny earned	6.64

Most Unfamiliar	Mean value
One swallow does not make a summer	1.22
Little pitchers have big ears	1.32
It's better to be right than president	1.44
Vows made in storms are forgotten in calms	1.50
It's an ill wind that blows nobody good	1.54
There's many a slip twixt the cup and the lip	1.68
A drowning man will clutch at a straw	1.74
Beware of Greeks bearing gifts	1.78
Make haste slowly	1.78
Brevity is the soul of wit	1.82
Rats desert a sinking ship	1.90
He who pays the piper can call the tune	1.94
Hope springs eternal	2.00
Handsome is as handsome does	2.04
Make hay while the sun shines	2.06

These findings certainly show that some of the old proverbial standbys as "One swallow does not make a summer" and even "Make hay while the sun shines" have a surprisingly low familiarity level among today's college students. While it is perhaps understandable that such "literary" proverbs as "Beware of Greeks bearing gifts" or "Brevity is the soul of wit" are less known due to the steady decline of cultural literacy, it is amazing to see such "simple" proverbs as "Hope springs eternal" or "Handsome is as handsome does" fall by the wayside. One thing is for sure—these small psychological tests on the familiarity of proverbs are clear indicators that some of the hitherto commonly known proverbs are definitely declining in popularity and currency. This in itself is nothing new. Proverbs have always come and gone with some of them hanging on steadily, but we appear to live in an age where even the paremiological minimum looks as if it is shrinking.

But then again perhaps this is not happening as much as one might at first think. How about the new proverbs of our age that might be replacing some of the overused and outdated proverbs of times long passed? Have the psychologists listed such new twentieth-century proverbs as "Different strokes for different folks," "It takes two to tango," "A picture is worth a thousand words," or "Garbage in, garbage out"? Of course not, for they have for the most part simply compiled their lists of texts from standard proverb collections that contain plenty of items whose currency is to be questioned today. A German survey of the familiarity of modern slogans, graffiti, and certain anti-proverbs by young students revealed astonishingly high ratings for some

Where there's a will, there's a way!

Transplant

of them. Even the English language slogan "Make love—not war!" reached a familiarity rating of 85% among young Germans, a clear sign that such subcultures have their own repertoire of very frequent fixed phrases.[22] The fact that the previous familiarity tests by psychologists were based on only a limited sample of young college students renders them somewhat invalid as far as the actual familiarity of proverbs is concerned among a cross section, both in education and age, of the American population. There is no doubt in my mind that the familiarity ratings of some standard proverbs used in these psychological tests would be considerably higher if they would be addressed to the total spectrum of American society.

There exists a fascinating study of 198 pages by the German pollster company Intermarket (Düsseldorf) that reports in dozens of statistical tables about the familiarity and use of proverbs by 404 informants (203 males, 201 females) of all walks of life, ages, and professions.[23] It was based on a large questionnaire that contained 27 questions, among them "Which proverb do you use quite frequently?," "How often do you use proverbs?," "What kind of people use proverbs a lot?," "When do you use proverbs in particular?," "Do proverbs help to cope with certain difficult situations?," "Do proverbs contain a lot of practical wisdom?," "Do you think that men or women use

Practice
your Canadian,
because
practice makes
perfect.

more proverbs?," "How did you learn most of your proverbs?," "What is the educational level of people who use a lot of proverbs?," and so on.[24] Permiakov's pioneering paremiological experiment didn't include such questions, but this German study contains truly invaluable statistical information concerning the attitude toward, familiarity with, and use of proverbs by native speakers of a modern technological society. Of interest for the discussion at hand are the responses to the first question: "Which proverb do you use quite frequently?" Of the 404 subjects 363 answered this question. The answers contained 167 different proverbs, of which 114 texts were mentioned only once, while the other 53 texts were recorded between 2 and 26 times for a total of 249 citations. The most frequent and by implication the most popular German proverb was "Morgenstund hat Gold im Mund" (The morning hour has gold in the mouth, i.e., The early bird catches the worm) with 26 informants citing it as their most commonly used proverb.[25] Next comes the Biblical proverb "Wer andern eine Grube gräbt, fällt selbst hinein" (He who digs a pit for others falls in himself) with 21 references, followed by 16 recordings of "Zeit ist Geld" (Time is money). These three texts are then the most popular German proverbs, and they certainly belong to the German paremiological minimum.[26] What is now needed is that a team of scholars from such disciplines as folklore, linguistics, sociology, psychology, anthropology, paremiology, and demography works out an even more elaborate questionnaire to be used with several thousand German citizens. The result of such an integrated study would in turn give us a very precise idea of how proverbs are used and viewed today and which proverbs belong to the German paremiological minimum, or any other nationality for that matter. Once such national paremiological minima are established, we will also be able to determine the most frequently used international proverb types through comparative proverb collections.[27] Such work will eventually lead to an international paremiological minimum of the world's proverbial wisdom.

Much work is required before this scholarly dream becomes reality. After all, we are only at the very early stages of establishing paremiological minima for some national languages. Returning to the Anglo-American scene, it must be stated that the few psychological studies already mentioned represent but a meager beginning. Their purpose never was to establish a paremiological minimum, and in order to accomplish that task major cross-cultural demographic research will be necessary. But what can be said today at least speculatively about the Anglo-American paremiological minimum? Ever since E. D. Hirsch published his best-selling book *Cultural Literacy: What Every American Needs to Know* (1987) educators, intellectuals, and citizens at large have in fact been discussing a kind of minimum of cultural knowledge for the average educated person. With the help of Joseph Kett and James Trefil, the author added a controversial appendix of "What Literate Americans Know: A Preliminary List."[28] Among this list are plenty of references to folklore in general and proverbs in particular. Just under the letter "A" alone appear the proverbs "Absence makes the heart grow fonder," "Actions speak louder than words," "All roads lead to Rome," "All's fair in love and war," "All's well that ends well," "All that glitters is not gold," "Any port in a storm," "April showers bring May flowers," and "As you make your bed so must you lie in it."[29] In other words, proverbs figure prominently in what Hirsch and his co-authors consider to be part of American cultural literacy. In the meantime the three authors have published their massive annotated *Dictionary of Cultural Literacy: What Every American Needs to Know* (1988) which, after chapters on "The Bible" and "Mythology and Folklore," contains as the third chapter a major list of approximately 265 "Proverbs."[30] Hirsch takes credit for this chapter at the end of a short introduction (p. 46) that unfortunately does not give away the secret of how he came up with this list of Anglo-American proverbs that every American should know. He also is not sure about the difference between a proverb and a proverbial expression. Thus his "Don't throw out the baby with the bath water" (p. 56) would surely be better placed in the following chapter on "Idioms"[31] which contains numerous proverbial expressions like "To throw out the baby with the bath water." Every paremiologist would obviously disagree with Hirsch for including "Carpe diem" (p. 48) or "Yes, Virginia, there is a Santa Claus" (p. 57) in a chapter on proverbs. Another problem is, of course, the alphabetical arrangement of the texts according to the first significant word, which is rather arbitrary to say the least. Hirsch might have been much more consistent by alphabetizing his texts by the subject nouns of the proverbs. But leaving these quibbles aside, the fundamental criticism is the fact that Hirsch does not reveal how he came up with his list. In the introduction to the entire book it is merely stated that entries were tested "to determine how widely known an item is in our culture. Only those items that are likely to be known by a broad majority of literate Americans ought to appear in this dictionary. Therefore, in selecting entries, we drew upon a wide range of national periodicals. We reasoned that if a major daily newspaper refers to an event, person, or thing without defining it, we assume that the majority of the readers of that periodical will know what that item is. If this is true, that event, person, or thing is probably part of our common knowledge, and therefore part of our cultural literacy."[32] Perhaps proverbs fall under "things" in this statement, but I doubt that Hirsch got all these texts out of newspapers or magazines. Besides, this statement says nothing about the general frequency of appearance that was necessary for any item to have been included in this dictionary. It is my feeling that a dictionary of cultural literacy ought to be based on frequency analyses. In any case, Hirsch most likely gleaned his list from one or more of the standard Anglo-American proverb dictionaries and perhaps discussed a somewhat longer list with friends and colleagues before deciding on these particular texts. Realizing that no studies on the Anglo-American paremiological minimum exist, Hirsch really had not much of a choice but to compile this "unscientific" list.

Lest my statements are interpreted to be too harsh, permit me to admit that I was faced with very much the same problem at the same time that Hirsch worked on his proverb list. I had been asked by the Philipp Reclam publishing house in Germany to put together a collection of *English Proverbs* (1988) and was given enough space to include 1200 texts with English-German vocabulary and some annotations at the bottom of each page. How else was I to come up with these 1200 texts but to go to some of the historical English and Anglo-American proverb collections and letting my scholarly knowledge of proverbs together with my subjective feeling be the guide to decide whether any given text had enough currency (frequency, traditionality, familiarity, etc.) to be included. And my task was to a certain degree easier than Hirsch's for my chance to include most of the texts of a paremiological minimum of let's say 300 proverbs (to match that established by Permiakov for the Russian language) was far better than that of Hirsch and his much shorter list. I stuck out my proverbial neck at times and marked some proverbs in the notes as being particularly "popular," but I remember a certain scholarly unease since I was not really basing this judgment on demographic research.[33]

So much for scholarly honesty. Were I today in a position of having to reduce my list of 1200 proverbs to Permiakov's 300 or even Hirsch's 265 texts, and were I to be restricted to listing texts that have proven familiarity among Anglo-American speakers of the twentieth century, I would now be able to enlist Bartlett Jere Whiting's large new collection of *Modern Proverbs and Proverbial Sayings* (1989). This book contains 5567 main entries based on the proverbial materials that the avid reader Whiting discovered in over 6000 books and countless magazines and newspapers published in this century. Of special importance is that these publications range from serious literary works to mysteries and even light reading that represent a true cross section of written communication in the twentieth century of the Anglo-American world. Under each entry, the proverbs and their many variants are listed in chronological order, with some entries of the more popular proverbs amounting to short monographs of references. Those entries with the most texts obviously also represent the proverbs with high frequency and they belong by implication to the paremiological minimum of the Anglo-American language. What follows is a list of such high frequency proverbs having key-words that start with the letters A, B, or C and listing thirteen or more references.[34]

Whiting's Number	Proverb Text	Number of References
C257	Every *Cloud* has a silver lining	28
B229	A *Bird* in the hand is worth two in the bush	26
B291	*Blood* is thicker than water	24
B236	The early *Bird* catches the worm	23
C164	*Chickens* come home to roost	22
B136	One had made his *Bed* and must lie on it	21
C11	One cannot have his *Cake* and eat it	21
C141	*Charity* begins at home	21
C318	Too many *Cooks* spoil the broth	21
C236	*Cleanliness* is next to godliness	20
A99	*Appearances* are deceitful	19
B235	*Birds* of a feather flock together	19
C42	Unlucky at *Cards*, lucky in love	19
B432	New *Brooms* sweep clean	18
C302	Easy *Come*, easy go	18
C404	*Crime* does not pay	17
B135	Early to *Bed* and early to rise, makes a man healthy, wealthy and wise	16
C115	When the *Cat's* away the mice will play	16

Whiting's Number	Proverb Text	Number of References
B234	It's an ill *Bird* that fouls its own nest	15
B488	*Business* before pleasure	15
C180	*Children* should be seen and not heard	15
C275	Let the *Cobbler* stick to his last	15
C318	*Confession* is good for the soul	15
C360	The *Course* of true love never did run smoothly	15
C449	*Curiosity* killed the cat	15
C82	A *Cat* has nine lives	14
A12	*Absence* makes the heart grow fonder	13
A110	One rotten *Apple* can spoil the whole barrel	13
B162	*Beggars* cannot be choosers	13
B206	The *Bigger* they are, the harder they fall	13
B525	Let *Bygones* be bygones	13
C175	The *Child* is father to the man	13
C218	*Circumstances* alter cases	13

Both Hirsch and I missed "Crime does not pay"; I also somehow failed to register "Let bygones be bygones"; and Hirsch also does not include "Charity begins at home," "Appearances are deceitful," "Unlucky at cards, lucky in love," "It's an ill bird that fouls its own nest," and "Children should be seen and not heard." Alas, Whiting is not foolproof either. It is amazing that he did not come across the American proverb "One picture is worth a thousand words" that originated in 1921 and which both Hirsch and I have included in our lists.[35] And how about the quite modern, but nevertheless very common, American proverb "Different strokes for different folks" that was coined in the South around 1950? Neither Whiting nor Hirsch have registered it—I was lucky since at the time of putting my 1200 texts together I had just completed a chapter on this particular proverb in my book *American Proverbs: A Study of Texts and Contexts* (1989).[36]

What this short comparison of Hirsch, Whiting, and Mieder has shown is, of course, that the study of the larger idea of cultural literacy and the narrower concept of a paremiological minimum of any group of people must be based on scientific demographic research. Especially for the Anglo-American language it is of utmost importance that today's paremiological minimum of native speakers be ascertained through a widely distributed questionnaire. While such a study has its obvious benefits for national and international paremiographers and paremiologists, it will also assure that the most frequently used proverbs of the modern age will be included in foreign language dictionaries and textbooks. This in turn will enable new immigrants and for-

54

eign visitors to communicate effectively with Anglo-American native speakers. Proverbs continue to be effective verbal devices and culturally literate persons, both native and foreign, must have a certain paremiological minimum at their disposal in order to participate in meaningful oral and written communication.

Notes

This chapter was first published in slightly different form in *Creativity and Tradition in Folklore: Essays in Honor of Wilhelm Nicolaisen,* ed. by Simon J. Bronner. Logan/Utah: Utah State University Press, 1992, pp. 185–203.

1. See Grigorii L'vovich Permiakov, *Ot pogovorki do skazki (Zametki po obshchei teorii klishe).* Moskva: Nauka, 1970; English translation by Y. N. Filippov with the title *From Proverb to Folk-Tale (Notes on the General Theory of Cliché).* Moscow: Nauka, 1979; Matti Kuusi, *Towards an International Type-System of Proverbs.* Helsinki: Suomalainen Tiedeakatemia, 1972; also in *Proverbium,* no. 19 (1972), 699–736; Alan Dundes, "On the Structure of the Proverb," *Proverbium,* no. 25 (1975), 961–973; also in *The Wisdom of Many. Essays on the Proverb,* ed. by Wolfgang Mieder and A. Dundes. New York: Garland Publishing, 1981, pp. 43–64; and Shirley L. Arora, "The Perception of Proverbiality," *Proverbium: Yearbook of International Proverb Scholarship,* 1 (1984), 1–38.

2. For bibliographical references see Wolfgang Mieder, *International Proverb Scholarship: An Annotated Bibliography.* 2 vols. New York: Garland Publishing, 1982 and 1990. See also Wolfgang Mieder's annual bibliographies entitled "International Bibliography of New and

Reprinted Proverb Collections" and "International Proverb Scholarship: An Updated Bibliography" in *Proverbium: Yearbook of International Proverb Scholarship*, 1ff. (1984ff.).

3. See Zoltan Kanyo, *Sprichwörter—Analyse einer Einfachen Form. Ein Beitrag zur generativen Poetik*. The Hague: Mouton, 1981; Peter Grzybek and Wolfgang Eismann (eds.), *Semiotische Studien zum Sprichwort. Simple Forms Reconsidered I*. Tübingen: Gunter Narr, 1984; and Neal R. Norrick, *How Proverbs Mean: Semantic Studies in English Proverbs*. Amsterdam: Mouton, 1985.

4. See Bartlett Jere Whiting's three superb collections *Proverbs, Sentences, and Proverbial Phrases from English Writings Mainly Before 1500*. Cambridge, Mass.: Harvard University Press, 1968; *Early American Proverbs and Proverbial Phrases*. Cambridge, Mass.: Harvard University Press, 1977; and *Modern Proverbs and Proverbial Sayings*. Cambridge, Mass.: Harvard University Press, 1989.

5. William Albig, "Proverbs and Social Control," *Sociology and Social Research*, 15 (1931), 532.

6. Read Bain, "Verbal Stereotypes and Social Control," *Sociology and Social Research*, 23 (1939), 436.

7. Isidor Levin, "Überlegungen zur demoskopischen Parömiologie," *Proverbium*, no. 11 (1968), 291.

8. Carl-Herman Tillhagen, "Die Sprichwörterfrequenz in einigen nordschwedischen Dörfern," *Proverbium*, no. 15 (1970), 539.

9. See Grigorii L'vovich Permiakov, *Paremiologicheskii eksperiment. Materialy dlia paremiologicheskogo minimuma*. Moskva: Nauka, 1971.

10. See Grigorii L'vovich Permiakov, "On the Paremiological Level and Paremiological Minimum of Language," *Proverbium*, no. 22 (1973), 862–863; published in Russian as "O paremiologicheskom urovne iazyka i russkom paremiologicheskom minimume" in *Paremiologicheskie issledovaniia. Sbornik statei*, ed. by G. L. Permiakov. Moskva: Nauka, 1984, pp. 262–263; rpt. in G. L. Permiakov, *Osnovy strukturnoi paremiologii*, ed. by I. L. Elevich. Moskva: Nauka, 1988, pp. 143–144.

11. See Grigorii L'vovich Permiakov, "75 naibolee upotrebitel'nykh russkikh sravnitel'nikh oborotov," *Proverbium*, no. 25 (1975), 974–975; and Matti Kuusi, "Nachtrag [to Permiakov: 75 naibolee . . .]," *Proverbium*, no. 25 (1975), 975–978.

12. See Grigorii L'vovich Permiakov, "K voprosu o russkom paremiologicheskom minimume," in *Slovari i lingvostranovedenie*, ed. by E. M. Vereshchagina. Moskva: Russkii iazyk, 1982, pp. 131–137; English translation by Kevin J. McKenna with the title "On the Question of a Russian Paremiological Minimum" in *Proverbium: Yearbook of International Proverb Scholarship*, 6 (1989), 91–102. A shortened version of the Russian text with the same title has been reprinted twice in G. L. Permiakov's two essay volumes (see note 10) from 1984 (pp. 265–268) and 1988 (pp. 145–149).

13. A colleague of Permiakov, A. Barulin, also delivered a lecture in 1973 in Varna (Bulgaria) with the title "Russkii paremiologicheskii minimum i ego rol' v prepodavanii russkogo iazyka" of which a summary has subsequently been published in Permiakov's 1984 (pp. 264–265) essay volume (see note 10). Following Permiakov, Barulin stresses the importance of teaching proverbs, proverbial expressions, and other phraseological units to students studying Russian as a foreign language. He refers to Permiakov's paremiological minimum of about 1000 texts and argues that the learning and active oral and written use of proverbial materials should be part of all foreign language instruction.

14. The complete titles for the three editions of this book in Russian, German and Bulgarian are as follows: *300 obshcheupotrebitel'nykh russkikh poslovits i pogovorok (dlia govoriashchikh na nemetskom iazyke)*. Moskva: Nauka, 1985; *300 allgemeingebräuchliche russische Sprichwörter und sprichwörtliche Redensarten (Ein illustriertes Nachschlagewerk für Deutschsprechende)*. Leipzig: VEB Verlag Enzyklopädie, 1985; and *300 obshcheupotrebitel'nykh russkikh poslovits i pogovorok (dlia govoriashchikh na bolgarskom iazyke)*. Sofiia: Narodna prosveta, 1986. It should

be noted that A. M. Bushui from Samarkand quite independently from G. L. Permiakov published an article in 1979 on the minimum of German proverbs that should be part of the curriculum of secondary schools in the Soviet Union: "Paremiologicheskii minimum po nemetskomu iazyku dlia srednei shkoly," in *Problemy metodiki prepodavaniia razlichnykh distsiplin v shkole i vuze,* ed. by Kh. M. Ikramova. Samarkand: Samarkandskii gosudarstvennyi universitet, 1979, pp. 4–28. The major part of the article (pp. 9–28) presents a bilingual list of German proverbs in alphabetical order according to the first word with Russian translations. Comments on the frequency and linguistic level of these proverbs as well as important considerations for the teaching of folk speech in foreign language classes are included.

15. See Matti Kuusi, "Zur Frequenzanalyse," *Proverbium Paratum,* 2 (1981), 119–120.

16. See Grzybek (note 3), pp. 351–358.

17. See Karlheinz Daniels, " 'Idiomatische Kompetenz' in der Zielsprache Deutsch. Voraussetzungen, Möglichkeiten, Folgerungen," *Wirkendes Wort,* 35 (1985), 145–157; Ingrid Schellbach-Kopra, "Parömisches Minimum und Phraseodidaktik im finnisch-deutschen Bereich," in *Beiträge zur allgemeinen und germanistischen Phraseologieforschung,* ed. by Jarmo Korhonen. Oulu: Oulun Yliopisto, 1987, pp. 245–255; and Hans Ruef, "Zusatzsprichwörter und das Problem des parömischen Minimums," in *Europhras 88. Phraséologie contrastive. Actes du Colloque International Klingenthal—Strasbourg, 12–16 mai 1988,* ed. by Gertrud Gréciano. Strasbourg: Université des Sciences Humaines, 1989, pp. 379–385.

18. Stanley S. Marzolf, "Common Sayings and 16PF [Personality Factor] Traits," *Journal of Clinical Psychology,* 30 (1974), 202.

19. For a review of the use of proverbs tests by psychologists see Wolfgang Mieder, "The Use of Proverbs in Psychological Testing," *Journal of the Folklore Institute,* 15 (1978), 45–55.

20. Nolan E. Penn, Teresa C. Jacob, and Malrie Brown, "Familiarity with Proverbs and Performance of a Black Population on Gorham's Proverbs Test," *Perceptual and Motor Skills,* 66 (1988), 852.

21. Kenneth L. Higbee and Richard J. Millard, "Visual Imagery and Familiarity Ratings for 203 Sayings," *American Journal of Psychology,* 96 (1983), 216–219.

22. See Jürgen Zinnecker, "Wandsprüche," in *Jugend '81. Lebensentwürfe, Alltagskulturen, Zukunftsbilder,* ed. by Arthur Fischer. Hamburg: Jugendwerk der Deutschen Shell, 1981, vol. 1, pp. 430–476.

23. See K. Hattemer and E. K. Scheuch, *Sprichwörter: Einstellung und Verwendung.* Düsseldorf: Intermarket. Gesellschaft für internationale Markt- und Meinungsforschung, 1983.

24. For a detailed analysis of this publication see Wolfgang Mieder, "Neues zur demoskopischen Sprichwörterkunde," *Proverbium: Yearbook of International Proverb Scholarship,* 2 (1985), 307–328; and W. Mieder, "Moderne Sprichwörterkunde zwischen Mündlichkeit und Schriftlichkeit," in *Volksdichtung zwischen Mündlichkeit und Schriftlichkeit,* ed. by Lutz Röhrich und Erika Lindig. Tübingen: Gunter Narr, 1989, pp. 187–208 (esp. pp. 189–194).

25. For a discussion of this German proverb see Wolfgang Mieder, *Deutsche Sprichwörter in Literatur, Politik, Presse und Werbung.* Hamburg: Helmut Buske, 1983, pp. 105–112.

26. For a list of all the proverbs see Hattemer and Scheuch (note 23), pp. 161–175.

27. See Matti Kuusi et al., *Proverbia septentrionalia. 900 Balto-Finnic Proverb Types with Russian, Baltic, German and Scandinavian Parallels.* Helsinki: Suomalainen Tiedeakatemia, 1985, pp. 22–28.

28. See E. D. Hirsch, *Cultural Literacy. What Every American Needs to Know. With an Appendix "What Literate Americans Know."* Boston: Houghton Mifflin Co., 1987, pp. 146–215.

29. Hirsch (see note 28), pp. 152–156.

30. E. D. Hirsch, Joseph Klett, and James Trefil, *The Dictionary of Cultural Literacy: What Every American Needs to Know.* Boston: Houghton Mifflin Co., 1988, pp. 46–57.

31. Hirsch et al. (note 30), pp. 58–80.

32. Hirsch et al. (note 30), p. ix.

33. See the introductory remarks in Wolfgang Mieder, *English Proverbs*. Stuttgart: Philipp Reclam, 1988, pp. 3–19.

34. See Whiting (note 4), pp. 1–146. I thank Janet Sobieski for her help in putting together these statistics by counting the references in Whiting's 1989 collection.

35. For a discussion of this proverb see Wolfgang Mieder, " 'Ein Bild sagt mehr als tausend Worte': Ursprung und Überlieferung eines amerikanischen Lehnsprichworts," *Proverbium: Yearbook of International Proverb Scholarship*, 6 (1989), 25–37.

36. See Wolfgang Mieder, *American Proverbs: A Study of Texts and Contexts*. Bern: Peter Lang, 1989, pp. 317–332.

4

" Old Wisdom in New Clothing "

The Proverb in the Modern Age

The traditional proverb has been studied in a multitude of ways by folklorists, literary and cultural historians, philologists, social scientists, and many more.[1] Numerous large collections have been published over the centuries for the major national languages and dialects,[2] and a vast amount of secondary literature on the fascinating subject of proverbs also exists.[3] Yet, we can generalize and claim that most scholarly publications on the proverb have been historically oriented, searching for the origin and dissemination of various proverb texts or looking for the proverbs among so-called primitive tribes. Lately, however, proverb scholars have also become aware of the use and function of traditional proverbs in modern technological and sophisticated societies, and we now have important studies of proverbs in modern literature, in psychological testing, and in the various forms of mass media such as newspapers, magazines, and advertisements.[4]

The following remarks will present a picture of precisely how traditional proverbial wisdom continues to live and function in modern communication. Doubtlessly traditional proverbs still play a significant role in today's speech, where they continue to be used to moralize, to instruct, to advise, and to reflect on everyday occurrences. But perhaps more often than not proverbs now are used in an innovative way, that is, they are changed and twisted until they fit the demands of our modern age. Changing times and situations require forms of expression that the traditional proverbs can no longer supply. However, it often suffices to adapt an antiquated proverb to the modern context. This process of innovation on the basis of tradition becomes proof of the continuity of such traditional forms as proverbs, and it is this "constancy in change" that makes modern-oriented proverb studies such a challenging field of investigation for interdisciplinary and comparatively oriented researchers.

In order to present as complete a picture as possible of the way proverbs survive in the modern age, we will address four major aspects of the traditional and innovative use of proverbs: first, there will be a general analysis of proverb illustrations from the Middle Ages to modern cartoons and caricatures; second, we will deal with the more specific problem of misogynous proverbs and their role in modern sexual politics; third, we will demonstrate ways well-known proverbs or their critical variations are used in lyrical poetry; and, finally and more specifically, we will discuss a case study of one proverb, "Wine, Women and Song," from its origin to its appearance in modern cartoons and on T-shirts. Throughout the pages of this chapter examples will be cited from literary sources, art, and the mass media, indicating that proverbs belong to all types of communication and that they distinguish themselves through an unlimited adaptability to ever new contexts. Proverbs in collections might appear to be trite remnants of the wisdom of times past, but when contextualized in their original wording or in telling variations they become a most effective verbalization of human and societal concerns.

Turning now to our first concern, proverbs in various forms of art from medieval times to the present, we will see that proverb illustrations traditionally represent an attempt to depict basic human problems, usually in a satirical and moralistic manner. Proverb pictures can be traced from the Middle Ages to the twentieth century,[5] but it is without doubt Pieter Brueghel's celebrated picture "Netherlandic Proverbs" (1559) that is best known.[6] It has long been established that Brueghel illustrates proverbial expressions or phrases and not proverbs, but the more than forty extant investigations, ranging from shorter notes on particular expressions to the book-length studies by Wilhelm Fraenger, Jan Grauls, Franz Roh, and recently Alan Dundes and Claudia Stibbe[7] have not been able to isolate all the expressions in the picture. The entire picture contains about 115 illustrations of standard European and Dutch proverbs and proverbial expressions. A detail of the left bottom corner[8] exemplifies the complexity of this proverbial review of the follies and vices of the world. With great artistic skill Brueghel has been able to illustrate fifteen expressions in this section alone, among them "To bang one's head against the wall," "To bell the cat," and "To be as patient as a lamb." Each individual scene is an intrinsic part of the larger satirical mosaic of everyday life in the sixteenth century.

Surely Brueghel's colorful picture has the greatest artistic value of all proverb pictures, but there were many other pictures that showed multiple proverb scenes before and after him. Franz Hogenberg, for example, made an

etching in 1558 that contains twenty-one proverbs,[9] and Jan van Doetinchem
followed in 1577 with a series of four etchings depicting eighty-eight proverbs
and proverbial expressions.[10] Yet another print from around 1633 by Johannes Galle assembles seventy expressions with captions,[11] attesting that this art
form survived well into the baroque age. What differentiates these prints from
Brueghel's oil painting is that each proverbial scene has a caption, and it
might be added here that these captions have been of great value in determining the proverbial expressions in Brueghel's picture. The proverb illustration together with the proverbial caption satirizes standard human behavior
and fulfills a didactic purpose similar to that of much of the popular literature
of the sixteenth and seventeenth centuries. While Brueghel's famous picture
continues to fascinate viewers in the Berlin art museum or as a reproduction
in art books, on posters, or even a large jigsaw puzzle,[12] there are also two
modern posters that attempt to continue this tradition of illustrating numerous proverbs and proverbial expressions. In 1975 T. E. Breitenbach published
his poster entitled "Proverbidioms,"[13] which is an attempt to illustrate approximately three hundred phrases and idioms. While he depicts a more recent village scene, the picture is definitely a variation of Brueghel's earlier
picture. Many expressions from the Brueghel picture are included, but there
are also illustrations of such newer expressions as "To be off one's rocker,"
"To have a screw loose," and "To be a self-made man." As in the painting

by Brueghel so in this modern poster we find the proverbial expressions interpreted literally, which adds to the humor and satire of the picture. The verbal metaphor is illustrated in a realistic sense, thereby giving at times grotesque new meanings to common expressions. Two years earlier William Belder had already printed his similar poster "As the Saying Goes" (1973), which illustrates fifty-one proverbs and sayings with captions.[14] Here the human figures are humorous drawings, and most of the poster basically attempts to translate proverbs such as "A bird in the hand is worth two in the bush" or "Many hands make light work" into literal illustrations. Despite the humor, the poster has a definite didactic character and would probably be a good addition to a child's room. The game of identifying the various proverb scenes on these posters has most likely entertained many viewers just as generations of people have been intrigued by the more famous Brueghel picture.

Besides these pictures with multiple proverb scenes—called "Wimmelbilder" or "De blauwe huyck" (The blue cloak) after the central proverb scene in Brueghel's picture depicting the expression "To hang the blue cloak on the husband" (i.e., to commit adultery)—there also developed a tradition of painting twenty to thirty-six individually framed proverb scenes onto one page, with each scene carrying a proverbial caption and once again basically illustrating in a satirical manner the shortcomings of the world. Many examples of these prints can be found from the sixteenth to nineteenth centuries, attesting to the popularity of proverb illustrations as a satirical tool. Most of them carry the general title "De verkeerde wereld" (The absurd world, or The world upside-down), a name also given at times to the multiple-scene pictures mentioned above. A fine example of such a framed proverb print containing thirty-two illustrations and captions was printed in Amsterdam in the sixteenth century.[15] Another Dutch print with the title "Spreekwoordenprent" (proverb print) from the eighteenth century illustrates thirty similar expressions,[16] while a print with "Gewoonelijke Spreekwoorden in figuren afgebeeld" (common proverbs in pictures) from the beginning of the nineteenth century assembles twenty frames.[17] Toward the end of that century we have a print entitled "De verkeerde wereld" with thirty-six illustrations,[18] showing the popularity of this traditional satirical medium. Many expressions such as "To throw pearls before swine," "To hang one's coat to the wind," and the popular "To shit on the world" appear again and again in these prints as well as in the "Wimmelbilder," indicating a certain stock of about one hundred favored expressions.

Paralleling the two multiple-scene-oriented proverb illustrations there exists a third form of proverb picture where one picture depicts only one proverb or proverbial expression. Of particular interest is a fifteenth-century collection of 182 woodcuts, each illustrating a proverb with a French verse caption, appropriately called *Proverbes en rimes* by its two twentieth-century editors.[19]

Among others we find illustrations of the proverbs "Who keeps company with the wolf must learn to howl,"[20] and "Let sleeping dogs lie,"[21] as well as the proverbial expression "To beat the dog before the lion."[22] In each case the verse caption includes the proverb, whose basic underlying didactic content is enhanced by the satirical and moralistic lines of the verse.

Woodcuts illustrating proverbs can also be found in many books, especially of the sixteenth century, as, for example, "Das Kind mit dem Bade ausschütten"[23] (To pour the baby out with the bath water) and "Sein Stekkenpferd reiten"[24] (To ride one's hobby-horse) in Thomas Murner's *Narrenbeschwörung* (1512), or "Zwischen die Mühlsteine geraten"[25] (To get between two millstones) in Sebastian Brant's *Narrenschiff* (1494). Pieter Brueghel also drew single proverb scenes, especially in the well-known series of twelve round proverb pictures from 1558. In his drawing of the Dutch proverb "With no other guide the two blind men fall into a ditch full of water"[26] it is clear that Brueghel has the biblical proverb "The blind leading the blind" in mind, a motif that he repeated in a more artistic oil picture in 1568.[27] A systematic search through illustrated books and large collections of woodcuts and etchings would yield more examples. They would help to bring to light a definite chain of proverb motifs that have fascinated illustrators over the centuries with their satirical view of the world.

It is especially the modern cartoonists who are keeping the tradition of satirical illustrations alive. Proverbs like "Don't look a gift horse in the mouth," "To buy a pig in a poke," and "Strike while the iron is hot" can, for example, all be traced from the aforementioned French manuscript *Proverbes en rimes* of the fifteenth century to cartoons of the present day. The woodcut illustrating the gift-horse proverb[28] reappeared in 1919 as a caricatuare showing Woodrow Wilson's problems with the Senate of the United States over the conception of the League of Nations.[29] Similarly, the woodcut of "To buy a pig in a poke"[30] finds its 1880 counterpart in a caricature satirically commenting on the shady dealings that went into the building of the Canadian Pacific Railway.[31] And the effectiveness of a third woodcut, depicting the proverb "Strike while the iron is hot,"[32] has lost nothing of its satirical and didactic persuasiveness in a modern German caricature, showing former Chancellor Helmut Schmidt as a blacksmith decisively striking the spreading terrorism in Germany with a large hammer.[33]

For the proverbial expression "To bell the cat" we have been able to collect five illustrations ranging from the fifteenth century to the present day. There is first of all a woodcut from 1494 in Sebastian Brant's *Narrenschiff.*[34] Brueghel also included the expression in his "Netherlandic Proverbs" picture.[35] This expression was also very popular on prints with multiple-framed proverb illustrations, as, for example, in the upper left corner of an eighteenth-century proverb print.[36] Changing the expression from a mere "Belling the cat" to a provocative "Who will bell the elephant?" Francisco Goya included in his collection of twenty-two grotesque etchings called *Los Proverbios* from before 1824 one in which several men are trying to fasten bells onto a large elephant.[37] The intriguing illustration brings to mind the military occupation of Spain by Napoleon, and perhaps one could interpret this etching as a precursor of modern political caricatures. Such a political cartoon appeared in *Time* in 1975 showing the former Secretary of State Henry Kissinger as the political cat that needs to be belled.[38] Just as in the Brueghel and Goya pictures this caricature does not need a caption, since it is clear that the roaming political cat should be watched with care.

In modern cartoons, proverbs and proverbial expressions continue to play a significant role.[39] Often the cartoonist simply draws a humorous sketch of the literally interpreted expression, as, for example, for "To drink like a fish,"[40] "To lose one's marbles,"[41] "To be out of one's gourd,"[42] and "That's the way the ball bounces."[43] But the images and captions of more serious cartoons depict in a satirical tone the wide range of problems of modern life. For example there appeared a cartoon of a customer in a bakery store being forced to ask, "Since when is a baker's dozen eleven?"[44] And the same satirical view of spiraling inflation was expressed in another cartoon with the caption, "It used to be that a fool and his money were soon parted—now it happens to everybody."[45] In another cartoon the proverb "To err is human, to forgive divine" is drastically altered to read "To err is unlikely, to forgive unnecessary"[46] in light of our computer-run lives. Very effective and to the point was a caricature of oil sheiks who summed up their advantageous position in controlling the flow and price of oil with the gloating statement, "Hate to admit it,

Whatsoever a man soweth

but I don't think we've a better expression in Arabic than having 'em over a barrel."[47] A sad commentary on today's employment problems is expressed in the next two cartoons and their altered proverb captions: "If at first you don't succeed, you're fired,"[48] and "Now Ted says if we can't beat the unemployment figures we can join them."[49] And to turn to a timely political problem, we have a British cartoon from 1954 about the growing racial hatred and prejudice in South Africa, which carried the appropriate biblical proverb caption "Whatsoever a man soweth,"[50] whose bitter conclusion, "he must reap," we can see in present-day South Africa.

Most of the examples presented thus far have rather explicit proverbial captions, either stating the expressions in their original wording or varying them to fit a certain satirical purpose. Often, however, cartoonists use captions that merely allude to a proverb, but the illustration makes it perfectly clear which proverb is meant. This is the case with a humorous drawing of some beavers at work with the caption "Just because we're beavers, I don't see why we can't goof off like other animals once in a while."[51] Obviously this is an allusion to the common expression, "To work like a beaver." In the following three examples the proverbial statement is truly kept to a mere allusion, but the illustrated birds permit the actual expression to come to the viewer's mind immediately: "It's time you know about the bees and us"[52] hints at the expression "To know about the birds and the bees," while the cartoons with the caption "Good Lord! How early do you have to be around here?"[53] and "Good morning"[54] obviously allude to the well-known proverb "The early bird catches the worm," especially in light of the fact that birds and worms are being illustrated.

These final examples show a tendency to return to Brueghel's famous "Netherlandic Proverbs" picture. The modern cartoonist, just like Brueghel in the sixteenth century, assumes that the viewer knows the proverb or proverbial expression that is being illustrated. However, although Brueghel needed no captions for his proverbial scenes, the modern cartoonist seems to prefer a simple verbal allusion to insure meaningful communication. At times these proverbial cartoons are nothing more than humorous play, but more often they become pointed satirical commentaries on human problems and concerns, especially with the altered proverb texts as captions. Since metaphorical proverbs could in fact be defined as verbalized pictures, it is not surprising that illustrators since the Middle Ages have felt compelled to translate the traditional proverb texts into pertinent pictures depicting the values of their time.

That proverbs contain the value system of the time of their origin leads us to our second point, the traditionally misogynous proverb in confrontation with the modern concerns of sexual politics. A cursory glance at any major proverb collection reveals the obvious antifeminism prevalent in proverbs. Almost every proverb that touches on women contains a severe negation of the value of women in society. This is easily illustrated by such proverbs as "A woman is the weaker vessel," "A woman's answer is never to seek," "A woman's tongue wags like a lamb's tail," "All women may be won," "Women are as wavering as the wind," "Women naturally deceive, weep, and spin," "Women in state affairs are like monkeys in glass houses," and, of course, the often quoted "Women are necessary evils."[55] These examples amply show that the proverb makers of past centuries were misogynists, who in the bitterness of old age and regret could seemingly think of nothing better to do than to discredit with proverbial invectives the women who most likely had served them very well. Yet these unflattering expressions of folk wisdom have been handed down to us from generation to generation, and it will obviously take time to break down the barriers of tradition in these antifeminist slurs.

These proverbs reflect male chauvinistic ideas in an easily repeatable formulaic structure greatly enhanced by metaphorical images. It is not surprising, therefore, that male artists from the Middle Ages to the present day have drawn on this type of proverb to express their own stereotypical views of women as malicious, deceitful, vain, irritable, and so on. For example, we have an engraving by Pieter Brueghel from the year 1558 that illustrates a variant of the internationally disseminated proverb about the great house plagues, "Three things drive a man out of his house: smoke, rain, and a scolding wife."[56] Brueghel also included several other sketches of antifeminist proverbial expressions in his already mentioned "Netherlandic Proverbs" picture. In addition to the young adultress hanging a blue cloak over her cuckolded husband we have, for example, a quarrelsome and cunning woman tying the devil onto a pillow, illustrating the Dutch expression "Zij zou de duivel op het (en) kussen binden"[57] (She would bind the devil himself to a pillow). This expression about a strong and shrewish woman was very popular in the late Middle Ages, as a Flemish misericorde depicting it indicates.[58] Such a woman would, of course, also insist on wearing the breeches (pants) in the house, and there exist many broadsheets of the "De verkeerde wereld" type mentioned above that illustrate such a domineering woman.[59] The remedy for this type of aggressive woman is drastically indicated in a misericorde from the sixteenth century that depicts the most antifeminist proverb of them all, "A good woman must be beaten."[60]

These quarrels between husband and wife are, perhaps not surprisingly, still the subject matter of many modern proverbial cartoons that delight in showing the battle of the sexes. In one caricature, a husband attempts to maintain his special position in the office with the proverbial argument "How many times must I tell you, Mildred? A man's office is his castle!"[61] But in another illustration of the same proverb we can see a liberated wife denying her spouse his lordship in the house, and his proverbial argument, "But, dear, a man's castle is supposed to be his home" does not appear to hold water anymore.[62] Even when the husband might be sick and wants to be waited on, the woman counters with the spiteful answer "Sick my eye . . . you just like the idea of 'feed a cold.' "[63] And in another caricature it is once again the woman who degrades her partner in a sarcastic fashion with the statement "I'll tell you what makes him tick. Booze makes him tick."[64] But it is not surprising for wives to act this way when their husbands throw such proverbial statements as the following at their heads: "In this house, only ONE cook spoils the broth."[65] The woman has stood in the kitchen as usual, and all that the spouse can do is complain or ignore her completely, as another delightful but telling caricature shows: A minister and his wife are sitting at the breakfast table. He is reading the newspaper and pouring his own cup of coffee, while his wife sits there neglected and bored. Her appropriate comment in the caption reads, "Careful, dear, your cup runneth over."[66] But even this biblical comment does not awaken her husband from his morning routine.

The quibbling between spouses also often results from sexually oriented comments, as is the case with a cartoon showing a couple watching the evening news with Harry Reasoner and Barbara Walters. In the caption the wife asks disgustedly: "Can't you just watch the news without speculating on whether he's getting into her pants?"[67] Very typical without doubt is the proverbial scene in which a man observes a beautiful woman at the beach. His wife has just pointed out to him that beauty isn't everything and he snaps, "All right, so you can't judge a book by its cover!"[68] Another wife in a second cartoon reacts to this situation with a similar proverbial remark concerning her husband's weaker moments: "That's Harold for you—other pastures always look greener."[69] That a woman might finally be fed up with her spouse's lack of interest in her is shown in a cartoon where a woman is about to leave

"*All right, so you can't judge a book by its cover!*"

Drawing by Richter; © 1960. The New Yorker Magazine, Inc.

her surprised husband with the short proverbial and therefore only too human statement, ''To make a long story short, goodbye.''[70] In another cartoon it's the husband who has left, as his wife relates to a friend, ''And then one day I told him to shape up or ship out, and he shipped out.''[71] These scenes from a marriage seem to be final stages, yet there is always that modern wisdom expressed by a young woman in love with a handsome man, ''I've been told, Adam, that two can live as cheaply as one,''[72] which will lead people into marriage and its proverbial quarrels. And altered or unaltered proverbs and proverbial expressions will continue to express such basic sexual household politics in a most telling manner.[73]

But proverbial illustrations of our day are not always reflections of basic human problems. On the contrary, modern cartoonists and commercial advertising artists do their very best (or worst) to continue sexual stereotyping. It is amazing how many advertisements still use proverbial headlines (often altered) with appropriate pictures to keep alive the image of woman as being inferior to man, capable only of cooking and being man's ever-ready pretty little servant and sex object. Taking the well-known proverb ''Four things drive a man out of his house: too much smoke, a dripping roof, filthy air, and a scolding wife'' as a basis, a plumbing business varied its content but kept the basic structure of the saying for the following chauvinistic customer handout:

Four Things a Woman Should Know
  How to look like a girl
  How to act like a lady
  How to think like a man
  And how to work like a dog.[74]

The idea that a woman should work like a dog is also picked up in a disgusting advertisement varying the proverb "A dog is man's best friend." The picture shows a dog and a water softener with the proverbial slogan: "One is man's best friend. The other is a woman's,"[75] which is to say that man and dog belong together while woman and such household chores as dishes and laundry are equally natural friends. And even the postscript, "after diamonds, that is," on the bottom left makes matters only worse, for it hints at the slanderous proverb that "Diamonds are a girl's best friend," which implies that the materialistic value system is inherent in women. Such sexual stereotyping is also obvious in the next two advertisements for Dole bananas: "If the dress no longer fits, peel it,"[76] and "Waist not, want not."[77] Yes, the copywriters have performed impressive linguistic tricks on existing proverbs to create catchy headlines that will most certainly get the reader's attention. Yet why do they address themselves only to women in the illustration? Do men not equally suffer from weight problems so that at least in one example an overweight male might have been included?

The opposite of such stereotyping of female obesity is, of course, the illustration and exploitation of the beautiful female for sales purposes.[78] Why, one asks, are "sexy" women shown in the following advertisements, which clearly address themselves to men: "Winchester separates the men from the boys"[79] is the proverbial headline for a Winchester cigars ad that pictures a cigar-smoking man with an attractive woman; "Smart as a whip"[80] attempts to sell fashionable male shirts and includes a female model with a whip; and "Our suit is known by the company it keeps"[81] is a headline based on a proverb used to sell elegant suits. The man modeling such a suit is accompanied by yet another striking woman. The women are clearly reduced to attention-getting sex objects, which is obviously also the fact with the advertising slogan "Beautiful hindsight"[82] for women's jeans, recalling the proverb "Hindsight is better than foresight."

To get away from the obvious sexist examples we could turn to the seemingly proper biblical proverb "Man does not live by bread alone" (Matthew 4:4) and the interesting piece of graffiti that states "Man cannot live by sex alone."[83] The word "man" is most likely meant to refer to humans of both sexes. Nevertheless, in the advertisement slogan "Traveling man does not live by bed alone"[84] one definitely gets the feeling that the male-dominated advertising world is addressing only male hotel customers. The word "woman" would fit equally well into this headline, and if the copy writers do not want to use the lengthy "man and woman" formula, why don't they simply say "People do not live by bed alone"? The proverbial ring would be kept alive, and we are sure that the effectiveness of the slogan would also be assured. Why talk about "traveling man" when many women are very active in various professions that include travel? That the business world is still very much a man's world is also illustrated by the way Japan Air Lines tried to sell its service with the headline "One man's sushi is another man's steak."[85] Once again we have the basic linguistic problem of the traditional proverb "One man's meat is another man's poison," but is it not nevertheless fair to ask where the woman is in the accompanying picture? And take this advertisement by PPG Industries with the proverbial question "If man believed in leaving well enough alone, where would we be?"[86] This example is clearly chauvinistic because the expression "To leave well enough alone" is in itself absolutely free from any gender identification. But the copywriter chose to stress the man's world. There is no reason whatsoever why this headline could not have read "If people believed in leaving well enough alone, where would we be?"

Problematic also is the popular proverb "Behind every great man, there is a woman," which, to be sure, implies a positive influence of the woman on the man but without placing her on his level of success. A florist's advertisement for national secretaries' week used the modified headline "Behind every great man . . . are the great women who helped you make it,"[87] but one wonders how seriously the statement of "the great women" was meant. Much more realistic perhaps was a caricature showing one of those successful males who tries by shrewd proverbial reasoning to take advantage of just such a hard working and supportive secretary by stating "They say behind every successful man, Miss Ashton, there's a woman. Will you be that woman to me?"[88] However, Pierre Cardin has come out with a proverbial slogan for its perfume advertisements, namely "Behind every great woman, there's a man."[89] In a modern world that starts to emphasize equality of the sexes, the old proverb "Behind every great man, there is a woman" should most certainly be reversible. Both forms of the proverb, original and variation, stress the teamwork of the sexes and illustrate how a new version of a proverb can complement the old one.

Many other national advertisements attempt to overcome the male-oriented proverb slogan by changing the original proverb ever so slightly. The First National Bank of Boston, for example, chose the headline: "If you're disappointed with your pension plan's performance . . . how do you think Tom, Dick and Mary feel?"[90] The familiar expression "Every Tom, Dick, and Harry" is quickly changed to include at least one woman, and good old Mary is even in a picture with the two men. Yet one senses a certain amount of lip-service to the women's liberation movement in this advertisement, for, after all, how long will it take until the picture will show two women and only one man? But it is a start, and because of the feminist movement there does in fact seem to be an attack against the traditionally misogynous proverbial wisdom. At least some newer advertisements and cartoons try to rectify false beliefs about women by drawing on traditional proverbs and effectively changing them or even by creating new ones. Already in 1957 the *New York Times* dared an advertisement like "Their work is never done,"[91] explicitly showing women as professionals and not doing house chores. Twenty years later we find the delightful advertisement "A woman's work is never done,"[92] showing a businesswoman hard at work in a plane while a man is fast asleep next to her. Obviously this woman is taking care of business matters, and perhaps she even uses a briefcase that was advertised with the headline "For women who mind their business,"[93] again meaning professional activities and not the timid role-playing at home. Perhaps she even works for Sears, where "They don't separate the women from the men"[94] in the hiring process, or she might also be employed with an insurance company, for "A woman's place may be with New York Life"[95] and not at home. While the basic structure of the proverb is maintained in these innovative headlines, the small verbal changes create a new slogan that is a true reflection of modern societal needs and concerns.

One of these concerns is the role that the modern woman ought to play on the political scene. Let us return once more to the old proverb "A woman's place is in the home" and notice how it can suddenly take on a very relevant meaning, one that is politically of great importance. Junior House fashions used the following advertisement: "A woman's place is in the House."[96] A basically chauvinistic proverb is here given an entirely new meaning, by changing the original text from "home" to "house," thereby referring to the White House and House of Representatives. Of course, this country needs more female politicians, and the day will come when a woman will finally occupy the White House itself. In the meantime one can purchase T-shirts with the expanded inscription "A woman's place is in the House . . . and in the Senate!"[97] Because of the effects such advertisements have on all of us, it becomes more and more conceivable that some of the old prejudices will be destroyed and that some of these feminist T-shirt slogans might be the proverbs of tomorrow.

In this regard notice this advertisement for T-shirts with three splendid slogans:

1. A woman's place is in the House . . . and in the Senate!

2. A woman without a man is like a fish without a bicycle.

3. The best man for the job . . . may be a woman.[98]

While the women express their independence and liberation by wearing T-shirts with inscriptions such as "A woman without a man is like a fish without a bicycle"[99] or even "A man's house is his castle—let him clean it,"[100] men perhaps wonder where all of this will lead, although they basically agree that the following proverbial slogan should characterize modern women: "Out of the frying pan and into the future!"[101]

Such examples of "liberated" proverb usage and proverb alteration are still relatively rare. Unfortunately, people are much too quick to continue to accept the stereotypical proverbs as ultimate truths without analyzing their texts properly. Modern mass media helps in keeping many of the one-sided views concerning women alive by not discriminating more carefully in their slogan choice. But by shrewdly varying existing proverbs some advertisers and cartoonists have in fact created proverbial slogans that are more befitting to the modern age. In such a fashion the misogyny of the old proverbial statements is revealed while at the same time effective new expressions of emancipatory ideas and concerns are found, indicating the proverbs' continued relevance even for modern aspects of sexuality and sexual politics. Verbal stereotypes have done and still do much damage to the relationship between the sexes, and much time will still have to pass until all people realize that the proverbial quotation "All men are created equal" should in fact say "All *people* are created equal." In the meantime we have at least the appropriately transfigured proverb: "A Ms. is as good as a Male."[102]

Modern literary authors have also reacted in a critical fashion to traditional proverbs. While proverbs in older literature usually served didactic and moralistic purposes, they are now often employed for expressions of parody, irony, or satire. Even more important, the texts are manipulated to express novel ideas for which the originals are no longer fitting. The use and function of proverbs in literature have been the subject of numerous scholarly investigations, ranging from collections and interpretative remarks concerning proverbial materials in the works of such world-renowned authors as William Shakespeare, François Villon, or Johann Wolfgang von Goethe to analyses of proverbs in lesser known regional writers.[103] Such studies have always concentrated on prose and dramatic literature, while lyrical poetry (including folksongs and ballads) has been neglected for an apparently obvious reason. Somehow lyrical verses seem not to be suitable for bits of prosaic wisdom, yet there does exist a considerable amount of proverbial poetry, or paremiological verse, to use a more technical term, in Anglo-American,[104] French, German,[105] and other languages.

François Villon's fifteenth-century *Ballade des proverbes* is an early French example. Similar didactic proverb poetry was also well established in late medieval England and Germany. John Heywood assembled the largest number of short, rhymed proverb poems (two to forty lines) in his six hundred *Epigrams upon Proverbs* (1556–1562), usually elaborating on a proverb in a didactic and yet at times humorous fashion, as the following two examples make clear:

Of Wits

So many heads, so many wits: nay, nay!
We see many heads and no wits, some day.[106]

Praise of a Man above a Horse

A man may well lead a horse to the water
But he cannot make him drink, without he list.
I praise thee above the horse, in this matter;
For I, leading thee to drink, thou hast not missed
Alway to be ready, without resistance,
Both to drink, and be drunk, ere thou were led thence.[107]

The creation of epigrams or short poems around proverbs continued well into the eighteenth century and is occasionally still practiced today. Samuel Taylor Coleridge, for example, did not consider it beneath his dignity to write a poem elaborating on the proverb "Love is blind," entitled "Reason for Love's Blindness":

I have heard of reasons manifold
  Why Love must needs be blind,
But this the best of all I hold—
  His eyes are in his hand.

What outward form and feature are
  He guesseth but in part;
But that within is good and fair
  He seeth with the heart.[108]

Certainly better known and doubtlessly of much greater poetic value is Robert Frost's somewhat longer poem "Mending Wall" (1914) reflecting on the traditional wisdom expressed in the proverb "Good fences make good neighbors."[109]

A more complex type of proverb poem is represented by those three to seven-stanza poems in which the proverb title is repeated at the end of each stanza as a leitmotif. This repetitive use of the proverb is congruous with the unquestioning didactic use of proverbs that we have already observed above. The following anonymous, sixteenth-century, five-stanza poem is based on the proverb "Wedding and hanging is destiny," and the proverbial leitmotif becomes an ironic expression of the frustrated husband's all-too-human problems with his wife:

> I am a poor tiler in simple array,
> And get a poor living, but eightpence a day,
> My wife as I get it doth spend it away,
>   And I cannot help it, she saith; wot we why?
>   *For wedding and hanging is destiny.*
>
> I thought, when I wed her, she had been a sheep,
> At board to be friendly, to sleep when I sleep;
> She loves so unkindly, she makes me to weep;
>   But I dare say nothing, God wot! wot ye why?
>   *For wedding and hanging is destiny.*
>
> Besides this unkindness whereof my grief grows,
> I think few tilers are matched with such shrows:
> Before she leaves brawling, she falls to deal blows
>   Which, early and late, doth cause me cry
>   *That wedding and hanging is destiny.*
>
> The more that I please her, the worse she doth like me;
> The more I forbear her, the more she doth strike me;
> The more that I get her, the more she doth glike [mock] me;
>   Woe worth this ill fortune that maketh me cry
>   *That wedding and hanging is destiny.*
>
> If I had been hanged when I had been married,
> My torments had ended, though I had miscarried;
> If I had been warned, then would I have tarried;
>   But now all too lately I feel and cry
>   *That wedding and hanging is destiny.*[110]

In the nineteenth century Eliza Cook wrote a wholesome poem interpreting the world as a glorious place since "There's a Silver Lining to Every Cloud," as the title and the end of each of the six stanzas—of which the fourth serves as an example here—declare.

> Let us not cast out mercy and truth,
>   When guilt is before us in chains and shame.

When passion and vice have cankered youth,
    And age lives on with a branded name;
Something of good may still be there,
    Though its voice may never be heard aloud,
For while black with the vapors of pestilent air,
    "There's a silver lining to every cloud."[111]

Another poet, Alice Cary, quite shrewdly uses the proverb "Hoe your own row" (1849) repeatedly to teach young people the necessity and value of good solid work. Even the slowest learner will have gotten the message that untiring personal effort will lead to a successful life when reaching the seventh and last stanza:

I've known too, a good many
    Idlers, who said,
"I've right to my living,
    The world owes me bread!"
A *right!* lazy lubber!
    A thousand times No!
'Tis his, and his only
    Who hoes his own row.[112]

Equally didactic is the following poem by Vincent Godfrey Burns whose title, "Man Does Not Live by Bread Alone" (1952) makes clear from the start that it is a poetic examination of the basic truth of the biblical proverb (Matthew 4:4). Each of the three stanzas is enclosed by this proverb and this six-time repetition of the same proverb makes the intention of the author very obvious. Between the proverb texts, he explains such spiritual matters as thought, truth, and love, by which man lives in addition to his materialistic need for bread.

Man doth not live by bread alone
But by each elevating thought
By which his ship of life is wrought;
Each harbor light however dim
That makes life's broad sea plain to him
Is like a searchlight from the throne—
Man doth not live by bread alone.

Man doth not live by bread alone
But by those truths which greatly feed
His hungering soul's deep spirit-need,
By inward music sweet and clear
That tunes with joy his inner ear;
Give man the food of soul, not stone—
He doth not live by bread alone.

Man doth not live by bread alone,
He hath a hunger of the heart

And cannot walk from man apart;
No living human long can stand
Without the grasp of friendly hand,
The touch, the fellowship, the voice
That make the lonely heart rejoice;
Love all our sorrows can atone—
Man doth not live by bread alone.[113]

While the poems mentioned thus far function as clear and straightforward reaffirmations of the basic wisdom of traditional proverbs, there exists also an interesting modern exception to this use of proverbial leitmotifs. W. H. Auden wrote a poem based on a highly didactic proverb, but he reversed the text from "Look before you leap" to the provocative new title "Leap Before You Look" (1940), thereby pointing to an existential philosophy that entails and accepts danger and chance. The important thing is no longer the careful looking advised by the old proverb, but rather the need for leaping into an active and committed life.

The sense of danger must not disappear:
The way is certainly both short and steep,
However gradual it looks from here;
Look if you like, but you will have to leap.

Tough-minded men get mushy in their sleep
And break the by-laws any fool can keep;
It is not the convention but the fear
That has a tendency to disappear.

The worried efforts of the busy heap,
The dirt, the imprecision, and the beer
Produce a few smart wisecracks every year;
Laugh if you can, but you will have to leap.

The clothes that are considered right to wear
Will not be either sensible or cheap,
So long as we consent to live like sheep
And never mention those who disappear.

Much can be said for social savoir-faire,
But to rejoice when no one else is there
Is even harder than it is to weep;
No one is watching, but you have to leap.

A solitude ten thousand fathoms deep
Sustains the bed on which we lie, my dear:
Although I love you, you will have to leap;
Our dream of safety has to disappear.[114]

Notice also a poem, "I Built Myself a House of Glass" (ca. 1910), by Edward Thomas, who chose the proverb "People in glass houses should not throw stones" to allude to his isolated way of living, which seems to lack the acceptance of risk and danger called for in W. H. Auden's poem.

> I built myself a house of glass:
> It took me years to make it:
> And I was proud. But now, alas!
> Would God someone would break it.
>
> But it looks too magnificent.
> No neighbour casts a stone
> From where he dwells, in tenement
> Or palace of glass, alone.[115]

It is this indirect quotation and critical reflection on standard proverbs that characterize the use of proverbs in modern lyrical poetry—traits that can also be noticed in the use of proverbs in other forms of literature and in the mass media of advertisements and cartoons as we have discussed above.

Thus far every poem that has been mentioned centers on the interpretation of but one proverb, and the question naturally arises whether there exist also poems in which several proverbs or proverbial expressions are combined to give the resulting poem meaning. François Villon's already mentioned "Ballade des proverbes" merely lists twenty-eight proverbs, and, since they are not contextually linked, it is actually more a small proverb collection than a poem with meaningful content. However, there does exist quite a tradition of poems incorporating numerous expressions. One of the finest examples is the anonymous "Ballad of Old Proverbs" (1707), which contains twenty-seven proverbs and proverbial expressions. The eight stanzas are a humorous and somewhat sarcastic defense of a rebuffed lover, and they gain their effectiveness by the many earthy and partially lewd folk expressions they use, as the following stanza shows:

> Alas, no Enjoyments, nor Comfort I can take,
>   In her that regards not the worth of a Lover;
> A Turd is as good for a Sow, as a Pancake:
>   Swallow that Gudgeon, I'll Fish for another,
> She ne'er regards my aking Heart,
>   Tell a Mare a Tale, she'll let a Fart.[116]

John Gay wrote a similar poem entitled "A New Song of New Similes," which puts dozens of proverbial comparisons into the mouth of another rejected lover, and which most likely was directly influenced by the previous poem. The poem starts with the lover describing the effects of his ill-fated love affair in most vivid comparisons:

> My passion is as mustard strong;
>   I sit, all sober sad;

> Drunk as a piper all day long,
>   Or like a March hare mad.

This lamentation carries over to several stanzas praising the beauty of his love Molly in such phrases as:

> Brisk as a body-louse she trips,
>   Clean as a penny dressed;
> Sweet as a rose her breath and lips,
>   Round as the globe her breast.

And the last stanza paints a gloomy picture of possible death by employing proverbial comparisons:

> Sure as a gun, she'll drop a tear
>   And sigh perhaps, and wish,
> When I am rotten as a pear,
>   And mute as any fish.[117]

This playful manipulation of proverbial expressions also found its way to the United States, where a similar poem dealing with a problematic love affair was published under the title "Yankee Phrases" in 1803. This one stanza suffices to draw the by-now-familiar picture:

> But now to my sorrow I find,
>   Her heart is as hard as a brick;
> To my passion forever unkind,
>   Though of love I am full as a tick.[118]

But perhaps more interesting and an even greater tour de force, literally consisting of nothing but proverbs, proverbial expressions, and allusions, is the following poem by the twentieth-century American poet Arthur Guiterman, entitled "A Proverbial Tragedy" (1915):

> The Rolling Stone and the Turning Worm
>   And the Cat that Looked at a King
> Set forth on the Road that Leads to Rome—
>   For Youth will have its Fling,
> The Goose will lay the Golden Eggs,
>   The Dog must have his Day,
> And Nobody locks the Stable Door
>   Till the Horse is stol'n away.
>
> But the Rolling Stone, that was never known
>   To Look before the Leap
> Plunged down the hill to the Waters Still
>   That run so dark, so deep;
> And the leaves were stirred by the Early Bird

> Who sought his breakfast where
> He marked the squirm of the Turning Worm—
> And the Cat was Killed by Care![119]

Guiterman succeeds in twisting and changing proverbs in such a fashion that they take on new meanings without becoming unrecognizable by the reader. The proverbial "rolling stone" even becomes a sort of a character whose life path is described in laconic expressions to its tragic end. And his fellow travelers, the equally proverbial worm and cat, also find their destruction in a proverbially predestined fashion. The poem thus mirrors the pessimistic worldview inherent in so many proverbs, and on a more philosophical level becomes an expression of the tragic beginning of World War I. The metaphorical apocalypse expressed in the poem is, therefore, much more than a playful linguistic trick.

Proverb poems of such depth are obviously rare and the Guiterman poem most likely will remain the proverb poem par excellence. One need only compare this poem with the following collage text, "Proverbial Ruth" (1974), by the Canadian poet John Robert Colombo, who has done nothing else but take about two dozen proverbs of parallel structure and link them by replacing key words with the name Ruth, in the following manner:

> A good archer is known by his Ruth, not his arrows.
> A good Ruth makes a good ending.
> A good cause makes a stout heart and a strong Ruth.
> A good Ruth makes good company.
> A good Ruth needs never sneak.
> A good Ruth deserves a good bone.
> A good Ruth is the best sermon.
> A good Ruth needs no paint.
> A good fellow lights his Ruth at both ends.
> A good Ruth is one-half of a man's life, and bed is the other half.
> A good garden may have some Ruth.
> A good Ruth is better than a bad possession.
> A good Ruth should be seldom spurred.
> A good Jack makes a good Ruth.
> A good key is necessary to enter Ruth.
> A good Ruth keeps off wrinkles.
> A good Ruth is no more to be feared than a sheep.
> A good Ruth is never out of season.
> A good Ruth is better than gold.
> A good Ruth keeps its lustre in the dark.
> A good Ruth never wants workmen.
> A good Ruth makes a good master.
> A good Ruth is the best sauce.
> A good Ruth is none the worse for being twice told.
> A good tongue has seldom need to beg Ruth.
> A good Ruth and health are a man's best wealth.
> A good Ruth brings a good summer.

> A good Ruth makes a good husband.
> A good Ruth for a bad one is worth much, and costs little.[120]

Some sentences like "A good Ruth makes good company" and "A good Ruth is better than gold" make sense, but how about such antifeminist slurs as "A good Ruth deserves a good bone" and "A good Ruth is never out of season"? The author has added a postscript to his "poem" stating that he sees it "as an ironic, playful love poem." In this light some of the altered proverbs suddenly take on meanings, and at least parts of the poem become commentaries on modern sexual politics.

If the poem by John Colombo is an ironic reflection about love in our time, then the following text of forcefully changed proverbs by Ambrose Bierce may be looked at as a satirical interpretation of man's condition as he is faced with ever more insurmountable obstacles and problems. The title, "Wise Saws and Modern Instances, or Poor Richard in Reverse" (1911), clearly illustrates the point Bierce wants to make:

> Saw, *n.* A trite popular saying, or proverb. (Figurative and colloquial.) So called because it makes its way into a wooden head. Following are examples of old saws fitted with new teeth.
>
> A penny saved is a penny to squander.
> A man is known by the company that he organizes.
> A bad workman quarrels with the man who calls him that.
> A bird in the hand is worth what it will bring.
> Better late than before anybody has invited you.
> Example is better than following it.
> Half a loaf is better than a whole one if there is much else.
> Think twice before you speak to a friend in need.
> What is worth doing is worth the trouble of asking somebody to do it.
> Least said is soonest disavowed.
> He laughs best who laughs least.
> Speak of the Devil and he will hear about it.
> Of two evils choose to be the least.
> Strike while your employer has a big contract.
> Where there's a will there's a won't.[121]

The shortness and conciseness of Bierce's proverb variations might in fact lead to new proverbs, for innovations such as "A man is known by the company he organizes" and "Where there's a will there's a won't" do contain a good amount of wisdom meriting proverbial status. But the mere enumeration of intellectual proverb variations can hardly be considered lyrical poetry, since it fits better under the rubric of the laconic aphorism.

From some of the examples cited it has become clear that a definite tradition of paremiological verse exists in which proverbs are quoted in their traditional wording, but there are also those poets who tend to tamper with the old texts. This difference shows the changed attitude toward proverbial wisdom of modern mankind. In an ever-more-sophisticated and learned society, proverbs are critically questioned about their validity. This questioning of the absolute truth of proverbs can already be seen at times in the epigrams of John Heywood and his followers, but man's dissatisfaction with the one-sidedness and apparent narrow-mindedness of certain proverbs is expressed to a much greater extent in the modern intellectual proverb poems. Even though the proverbial texts are more often than not changed to fit modern needs, the proverbial structure of the original proverb is maintained, and such altered proverbs are also a definite indication that modern humans depend on the formulaic proverb patterns for communicating effectively their concerns and thoughts. Even if many proverb poems over the centuries have dealt critically with the proverbs, they are nevertheless a solid proof that proverbs were and continue to be important linguistic and philosophical statements.

This is also true for such a seemingly lighthearted proverb as "Who does not love wine, women, and song, will remain a fool his whole life long," to which we direct our final remarks in this chapter. This individual proverb had a serious and didactic start; but it has not only been shortened to "Wine, women, and song," it has also become an expression of the carefree lifestyle of modern mankind.[122] By tracing this one proverb from its origin to modern cartoons and even inscriptions on T-shirts, we will once again notice how traditional proverbial wisdom is being manipulated to fit more modern social mores. But here too the variations gain in expressive value if they are put in contrast with the original text. Tradition and innovation are complementary forces, which together assure meaningful communication in proverb usage.

There exists a long tradition claiming that Martin Luther coined the common proverb, "Who loves not wine, women, and song, remains a fool his whole life long." Even though the proverb appeared in print for the first time in the year 1775 in Germany, scholars and others have continued to attribute it to Luther.[123] But nobody has been able to locate this epicurean proverb anywhere in Luther's voluminous works. The closest statement that Luther ever made was in one of his so-called "Table-Talks," which was recorded between 28 October and 12 December 1536. Here Luther discusses the over-indulgence of the Germans in drinking and concludes his macaronic German and Latin comments with "wie wollt ir jetzt anders einen Deudschen vor-thuen, denn ebrietate, praesertim talem, qui non diligit musicam et mulieres"[124] (how else would you characterize the German, who in his drunkenness does not choose music and women). The reference to drinking, music, and women is somewhat reminiscent of the proverb, but it is still a far cry from the actual proverb text.

Besides, Luther might only be alluding to one of the many classical and medieval Latin or German proverbs that follow the basic triadic structure of "Wine, women, and X" in various sequences, as for example:

> Nox, mulier, vinum homini adulescentulo.[125] (classical Latin)
> (Night, women, wine are for the adolescent man)
>
> Alea, vina, venus tribus his sum factus egenus.[126] (medieval Latin)
> (Dice, wine, love are three things that have made me destitute)
>
> Drei Dinge machen der Freuden viel:
> Wein, Weib und Saitenspiel.[127] (German)
> (Three things make much joy:
> Wine, woman, and strumming)

The many variants of such proverbs in Latin and German are clear indications that "Wine, women, and X" was a very popular proverbial formula, and one that was doubtlessly known to Martin Luther. Considering his detailed knowledge, appreciation, and use of German folk speech, which led him to put together his own proverb collection around 1536,[128] it would not be at all surprising if this skillful linguist and poet had coined the rhyming German proverb, "Wer nicht liebt Wein, Weib und Gesang, der bleibt ein Narr sein Leben lang" (Who does not love wine, women, and song, remains a fool his whole life long). But then the proverb might also have been current already in his time as only one further variant of the many texts based on the well-known triad of "Wine, women, and X." Alas, since the proverb appears nowhere in Luther's works, it is impossible to ascertain his possible authorship and, as Archer Taylor points out in regard to this proverb, "all ascriptions [of a proverb] to definite persons must be looked upon with suspicion."[129] There is, however, no doubt that folk tradition has declared the down-to-earth reformer to be its author, and to this day books of quotations, proverbs, and phrases continue to associate this proverb with Luther, making it his most famous apocryphal statement.

In print the proverb appeared for the first time in Germany on 12 May 1775 as part of an anonymous small poem ascribed to the poet Johann Heinrich Voss:

> Wer nicht liebt Wein, Weib und Gesang,
> Der bleibt ein Narr sein Lebelang,
> Sagt Doctor Martin Luther.[130]
>
> (Who does not love wine, woman and song,
> Remains a fool his whole life long,
> Says Doctor Martin Luther.)

The same author included the proverb again as a small epigram in a thin volume of poetry that he edited in 1777,[131] and he cites it in his own longer poem "An Luther" (To Luther), which he wrote on 4 March 1777.[132] This has led some scholars to consider Voss as the originator of the proverb,[133] but once again there is no certain proof. Voss never admitted to having written the short poem or the epigram, and in his own longer poem he quotes the proverb as having been already used by Martin Luther, as do the anonymous authors of the two shorter texts. Considering also the great popularity of the triad "Wein, Weib, und Gesang," which appeared in print for the first time in a German folk song recorded in 1602,[134] we cannot help questioning Voss's authorship. Most likely he is only quoting a proverb that had already been current for a considerable period of time, possibly since or even before Luther.

After the proverb's first appearance in 1775, German folk songs, particularly drinking songs, lighthearted love poems, folk literature, and serious literary works (including one by none less than Thomas Mann) abound with references to it and to Martin Luther. The proverb and Luther seem to be permanently coupled to each other in the German language, even though the longer proverb text is of late often reduced to a mere "Wein, Weib, und Gesang." This truncated version is applicable to numerous situations; it satisfies modern people's desire for short statements; it is based on the popular number three; and it has dropped the archaic relative clause about the "Narr" (fool). Nevertheless there is hardly a German native speaker who will not connect this sensuous triad with the reformer, who, as legend has it, was quite a lover of the good life himself.

How, then, did this very German "Luther-proverb" enter the Anglo-American realm? Just as in German, there were early English proverbs of the sixteenth century and later that are vernacular versions of the classical and medieval Latin originals: "Weemen, dise, and drinke, lets him nothing" (1576),[135] "Play, women, and wine undo men laughing" (1660),[136] "Women, wine, and dice will bring a man to lice" (1732).[137] Such gloomy proverbial pessimism is surely alluded to by Robert Burton in a chapter concerning the dangers of Epicureanism in his *The Anatomy of Melancholy* (1621): "Who wastes his health with drink, his wealth with play, / The same with womenfolk shall rot away."[138] How much more does the "carpe diem" mood of a short song out of John Gay's *The Beggar's Opera* (1728) remind us of the pleasure-seeking German proverb:

> Fill ev'ry glass, for wine inspires us,
>   And fires us
> With courage, love, and joy.
> Women and wine should life employ.
> Is there aught else on earth desirous?
> Fill ev'ry glass [etc.][139]

Another hundred years later we find a similar short poem by John Keats with the title "Give Me Women, Wine, and Snuff" (1817), which is certainly but another variation of the triad of "Wine, women, and X":

> Give me women, wine, and snuff
> Untill I cry out "hold, enough!"
> You may do sans objection
> Till the day of resurrection;
> For, bless my beard, they aye shall be
> My beloved Trinity.[140]

And finally Byron wrote the following verses in his *Don Juan* (1819) in which he expands the triad by a fourth element:

> Few things surpass old wine; and they may preach
> Who please,—the more because they preach in vain,—
> Let us have Wine and Women, Mirth and Laughter,
> Sermons and soda-water the day after.[141]

None of these proverbs and literary texts contains as a third element "Gesang" (song), but they are ample proof that triads of the pattern "Wine, women, and X" were indeed popular in England as well. It took, however, until the year 1857 for the German proverb to appear in print in English. Henry Bohn, one of England's greatest paremiographers, discovered it in Karl Simrock's proverb collection *Die deutschen Sprichwörter* (1846) and printed it in German with an English translation in his valuable collection *A Polyglot of Foreign Proverbs* (1857):

> Wer nicht liebt Wein, Weib und Gesang, der bleibt ein Narr sein Lebelang. Who loves not women, wine, and song, remains a fool his whole life long.[142]

With this entry the proverb found its way into English paremiography, even though Bohn erroneously reversed the order of "wine" and "women" and also changed "woman" to the plural "women." Such variants exist in German as well, but the normal sequence is in both languages today "Wine, woman [women], and song" (Wein, Weib [Weiber] und Gesang).

Yet a scholarly proverb collection is hardly the medium to help a foreign proverb gain currency in another culture. Who, after all, reads proverb collections and tries to remember hundreds of translated proverbs as assembled in Bohn's book of Danish, Dutch, French, German, Italian, Portuguese, and Spanish proverbs? Much more important is that William Makepeace Thackeray was in Germany from 1830 to 1831, where he came in contact with

German literary figures and works, possibly even with Voss's poem "An Luther." He subsequently translated four poems by German romanticists, which appeared in his works under the collective title of "Five German Ditties."[143] The fifth poem, entitled "A Credo" is no translation but rather a poem written by Thackeray himself, which also appeared in slightly different form with the title "Doctor Luther" in his novel *The Adventures of Philip* (1862).

> For the soul's edification
> Of this decent congregation,
> Worthy people! by your grant,
> I will sing a holy chant.
>   I will sing a holy chant.
> If the ditty sound but oddly,
> 'Twas a father wise and godly,
> Sang it so long ago.
>   Then sing as Doctor Luther sang,
>   As Doctor Luther sang,
>   Who loves not wine, woman, and song,
>   He is a fool his whole life long.
>
> He, by custom patriarchal,
> Loved to see the beaker sparkle,
> And he thought the wine improved,
> Tasted by the wife he loved,
>   By the kindly lips he loved.
> Friends! I wish this custom pious
> Duly were adopted by us,
> To combine love, song, wine;
>   And sing as Doctor Luther sang,
>   As Doctor Luther sang,
>   Who loves not wine, woman, and song,
>   He is a fool his whole life long.
>
> Who refuses this our credo,
> And demurs to drink as we do,
> Were he holy as John Knox,
> I'd pronounce him heterodox,
>   I'd pronounce him heterodox.
> And from out this congregation,
> With a solemn commination,
> Banish quick the heretic.
>   Who would not sing as Luther sang,
>   As Doctor Luther sang,
>   Who loves not wine, woman, and song,
>   He is a fool his whole life long.[144]

Before quoting this poem Thackeray gives a hint of where he got the idea for its composition: "Then politeness demanded that our host should sing one of his songs, and as I have heard him perform it many times, I have the privilege of here reprinting it: premising that the tune and chorus were taken from a

German song-book, which used to delight us melodious youth in bygone days." Thackeray must be referring to a song that he heard and perhaps sang as a student in Cambridge or while he was in Germany, and he now quotes the chorus from memory while writing his own poem.

After much searching we have been able to locate the "German songbook" that Thackeray mentions. It is Albert Methfessel's *Allgemeines Commers- und Liederbuch* (1818), which contains a student song by L. von Lichtenstein and music by Methfessel, with the predictable title "Wein, Weib und Gesang":

> Wo der geistge Freudenbringer,
> Wo der starke Grillenzwinger,
> Wo der Wein mit Götterkraft
> Jugendliches Leben schafft;
> Wo die vollen Becher schäumen,
> Wo die Dichter trunken reimen,
>   Fühlt die Brust
>   Lebenslust!
> Drum singt wie Doctor Luther sang,
> Wie Doctor Luther sang:
> Wer nicht liebt Wein, Weib und Gesang,
> Der bleibt ein Narr sein Leben lang!
>
> Wo ein Weib mit süßem Triebe
> Liebe tauscht um Gegenliebe,
> Wo die Höchste gern gewährt,
> Uns der Minne Glück beschert,
> Strahlt aus verklärten Blicken
> Vollgelohnter Lieb' Entzücken,
>   Wallt im Blut
>   Wonn' und Glut;
> Drum singt [etc.]
>
> Wo des Weins, der Liebe Leben
> Im Gesang wird kund gegeben,
> Blüht der köstlichste Verein,
> Leben, Brüder! Denn, wo Wein,
> Wo Gesang und Liebe thronen,
> Müssen gute Menschen wohnen,
>   Füllt das Herz
>   Glück und Scherz;
> Drum singt [etc.] [145]

(Where the spiritual bringer of joy,
Where the powerful banisher of bad moods,
Where the wine with its divine power
Creates youthful vitality;
Where the full mugs foam,
Where the poets drunkenly rhyme,
    There the breast
    Feels the joy of life!
Therefore sing as Doctor Luther sang,
As Doctor Luther sang:

Who does not love wine, woman, and song,
Remains a fool his whole life long!

Where a woman with sweet desires
Exchanges love for love,
Where the noblest love glady grants
And presents us with love's fortunes,
The delight of fully requited love
Shines forth from the transfigured gaze,
  There seethes in the blood
  Rapture and passion;
Therefore sing [etc.]

Whereever the vitality of wine and love
Is proclaimed in song,
There blossoms the most agreeable company,
Let's live, Brothers! Because, where wine,
Where song and love hold sway,
There good people must reside,
  There the heart is filled
  With happiness and jest;
Therefore sing [etc.])

Thackeray's chorus is a precise translation of the German original, while his three stanzas are a free rendition for English readers (see, for example, his reference to John Knox). Thackeray's poem is also more a statement about Luther while the German poem is a drinking song that has as its motto "Wine, women, and song." But the fact that Thackeray brings Luther in connection with the joyful attitude of life helped to associate Luther with this proverb in the Anglo-American world (Bohn made no reference to Luther in his proverb collection!). And since the triad "Wine, women, and X" already existed in a number of English proverbs and literary texts, this translation of a German proverb fell on receptive ears and was easily acceptable as just another variant, this time one that stresses the enjoyable aspects of life to boot.

Thackeray's poem was clearly more influential in spreading this new proverb among English speakers than was Bohn's slightly earlier translation. But there was also the famous waltz "Wein, Weib und Gesang," which Johann Strauss composed in 1869 and which conquered London, then England, and eventually the entire United States with the English title "Wine, Women, and Song." By the end of the nineteenth century this waltz title had become so popular that the American author Eugene Field used it as a fitting title for an ironic love and drinking song (1892):

O Varus mine,
Plant thou the vine
Within this kindly soil of Tibur;
Nor temporal woes,
Nor spiritual, knows

The man who's a discreet imbiber.
  For who doth croak
  Of being broke,
Or who of warfare, after drinking?
  With bowl atween us,
  Of smiling Venus
And Bacchus shall we sing, I'm thinking.

  Of symptoms fell
  Which brawls impel,
Historic data give us warning;
  The wretch who fights
  When full, of nights,
Is bound to have a head next morning.
  I do not scorn
  A friendly horn,
But noisy toots, I can't abide 'em!
  Your howling bat
  Is stale and flat
To one who knows, because he's tried 'em!

  The secrets of
  The life I love
(Companionship with girls and toddy)
  I would not drag
  With drunken brag
Into the ken of everybody;
  But in the shade
  Let some coy maid
With smilax wreathe my flagon's nozzle,
  Then all day long,
  With mirth and song,
Shall I enjoy a quiet sozzle![146]

Only seven years later John Addington Symonds published a collection of translated student songs with the title *Wine, Women and Song: Medieval Latin Student Songs* (1899), which also helped to popularize the proverb since the entire proverb, with reference to Luther, is placed as a motto at the beginning of the collection. Many songs deal with wine, women, and song, but only the one that contains the triad "wine and love and lyre"[147] comes close to the words of the proverb. Surely this book, Thackeray's poem, and Strauss's waltz were influential in getting people acquainted with the actual proverb, but one must also consider the many German immigrants who translated their proverbs into English, of which some were obviously picked up by English speakers in due time.[148]

By the end of the nineteenth century the short version of the proverb and the proverb itself were equally current in England as can be seen from the poem "Villanelle of the Poet's Road" (1899) by Ernest Christopher Dowson. Almost every stanza contains the "wine and woman and song" motif whose pleasureable and sensuous tendency is, however, negated by a second leitmotif of "Yet is day over long." Thus the poet contrasts the "carpe diem" and the "memento mori" throughout his short stanzas:

> Wine and woman and song,
>   Three things garnish our way:
> Yet is day over long.
>
> Lest we do our youth wrong,
>   Gather them while we may:
> Wine and woman and song.
>
> Three things render us strong,
>   Vine leaves, kisses and bay;
> Yet is day over long.
>
> Unto us they belong,
>   Us the bitter and gay,
> Wine and woman and song.
>
> We, as we pass along,
>   Are sad that they will not stay;
> Yet is day over long.
>
> Fruits and flowers among,
>   What is better than they:
> Wine and woman and song?
>   Yet is day over long.[149]

The reduction of the proverb text to a mere "Wine, women, and song" appears to be even more prevalent in modern-day Anglo-American usage than in German. A 1938 book was entitled *Wine, Women and Song*, for example, but it was nothing but a trick by members of the temperance movement to get people to read their tirades against alcoholism. One of the chapters is appropriately called "Wine, Women, Irreverence and Ruin,"[150] and it depicts a not-at-all positive image of "Wine, women, and song." A convincing indication of how the short triad is preferred to the longer proverb text is Helen T. Lowe-Porter's 1948 translation of a passage in Thomas Mann's *Doctor Faustus*. While the German original has the complete proverb "Wer nicht liebt Wein, Weib und Gesang, der bleibt ein Narr sein Leben lang,"[151] Lowe-Porter renders it by a mere "Wine, Women, and Song."[152] Obviously the translator was of the opinion that this shortened form was more acceptable to the Anglo-American reader, even though a more direct translation of the entire proverb would have been no serious problem.

The shortened expression "Wine, women, and song" has become so common that it has replaced the longer and somewhat awkward older version, which never gained a large currency in the English language. Because of its popularity it is often parodied in caricatures, headlines, slogans, or on T-shirts. From the American journalist and humorist Franklin Pierce Adams stems, for

"For this I gave up a lifetime of wine, women, and song?"

Drawing by Ed Arno; © 1980. The New Yorker Magazine, Inc.

example, the funny statement, "In the order named, these are the hardest to control: Wine, Women, and Song."[153] Perhaps President Harry S. Truman also alluded to this epicurean motto when he exclaimed: "Three things can ruin a man—money, power, and women. I never had any money, I never wanted power, and the only woman in my life is up at the house right now."[154] As a third and considerably earlier American bon mot we can add J. A. McDougall's quadruple alliterative remark from his Senate speech in February 1861: "I believe in women, wine, whiskey and war."[155]

But finally a few truly modern references. *Playboy* magazine printed the following party joke in the sixties: "Advice to the exhausted: When wine, women, and song become too much for you, give up singing."[156] The same magazine included in 1977 a caricature in which a doctor gives the following advice to a homosexual: "All right, then, you'll have to give up wine, men, and song for a while."[157] Also on this sexual plane is a caricature from the *New Yorker*. It depicts a gentleman getting out of a limousine about to enter an establishment on whose marquee are inscribed the suggestive words "Wine, Women & Song."[158] Another cartoon from the same magazine shows two deceased men as angels on a cloud in heaven who are obviously bored with their life after death. The accompanying caption asks ironically, "For this I gave up a lifetime of wine, women, and song?"[159] The use of the word "lifetime" permits the assumption that the cartoon also refers to the second part of the actual proverb, namely "remains a fool his whole life long." And finally the famous triad appears on a T-shirt, where "wine and women" are, however, brought into connection with a materialistic goal: "Wine, Women & Porsche, not necessarily in that order."[160]

Further references could certainly be found, and many will continue to appear in literature, magazines, advertisements, and caricatures. The proverb also continues to be popular in oral speech, and there can be no doubt that the shortened version of this German loan proverb will survive in modern Anglo-American language usage. The longer original proverb with its association with Martin Luther will, however, most likely fall more and more into disuse, while the triad of "Wine, women, and song" will remain an often-cited expression in our modern pleasure-seeking society.

Other proverbs continue to be equally popular, as the many examples discussed here have amply shown. It would indeed be a serious mistake to think that proverbs do not fulfill an important function in modern society any longer.[161] No matter how sophisticated and technologically advanced our society might become, traditional proverbs will always summarize in colorful metaphors basic and universal human experiences. There are plenty of occasions in oral and written speech of all modes to use proverbs in their original wording to strengthen an argument, to make a particular point, to summarize a discussion, or to interpret a situation. Proverbs belong to our common stock of ready-made linguistic formulas that will come to mind as part of our thinking process, just as the Bible and literary quotations or certain modern political and advertising slogans might. But what our discussion has shown is that the old and familiar proverb is consciously manipulated in innovative fashions to create new formulaic expressions that might fit certain aspects of modern life more precisely. This deliberate play with traditional proverbial formulas can be noticed in modern literature, in journalistic writing, in advertisements or blurbs of caricatures, cartoons, comic strips, greeting cards, graffiti,[162] and T-shirts. These alterations of existing proverbs might be mere humorous wordplay, but more often than not such anti-proverbs represent a critical reaction to the worldview expressed in seemingly antiquated proverbs. It is important to notice that proverbs are no longer sacrosanct bits of wisdom laying out a course of action that must be adhered to blindly. Instead proverbs are considered as questionable and at best apparent truths that are called on if the shoe (proverb) happens to fit. When that is not the case, they are freely changed to express opposite points of view. The juxtaposition of the traditional proverb text with an innovative variation forces the reader into a more critical thought process. Whereas the old proverbs acted as preconceived rules, the modern anti-proverbs are intended to activate us into overcoming the naive acceptance of traditional wisdom. But both the traditional proverb and the innovative manipulation of it belong to our stock of formulaic expressions on which we will continue to draw for meaningful and comprehensible communication. Proverbs and anti-proverbs are here to stay, since they are both part of our modern life, which also oscillates between the accepted values of tradition and the new mores of an existence characterized by innovation.

Notes

This chapter was first published with different illustrations in Wolfgang Mieder, *Tradition and Innovation in Folk Literature.* Hanover, N.H.: University Press of New England, 1987, pp. 118–156 and pp. 248–255 (notes).

1. See, for example, the representative essay collection edited by Wolfgang Mieder and Alan Dundes, *The Wisdom of Many: Essays on the Proverb.* New York: Garland Publishing, 1981. Other such essay volumes include W. Mieder (ed.), *Ergebnisse der Sprichwörterforschung.* Bern: Peter Lang, 1978; François Suard and Claude Buridant (eds.), *Richesse du proverbe,* 2 vols. Lille: Université de Lille III, 1984; Naiade Anido (ed.), *Des proverbes . . . à l'affût.* Paris: Publications Langues'O, 1983; and Peter Grzybek and Wolfgang Eismann (eds.), *Semiotische Studien zum Sprichwort: Simple Forms Reconsidered I.* Tübingen: Gunter Narr, 1984.

2. See above all the two bibliographies by Wilfrid Bonser, *Proverb Literature: A Bibliography of Works Relating to Proverbs.* London: William Glaisher, 1930; rpt. Nendeln, Liechtenstein: Kraus Reprint, 1967; and Otto Moll, *Sprichwörterbibliographie.* Frankfurt: Vittorio Klostermann, 1958.

3. Over two thousand books, dissertations, and articles are critically evaluated in Wolfgang Mieder, *International Proverb Scholarship: An Annotated Bibliography.* New York: Garland Publishing, 1982. See also the many bibliographical references in Lutz Röhrich and W. Mieder, *Sprichwort.* Stuttgart: Metzler, 1977; as well as the yearly bibliographical updates prepared by W. Mieder in *Proverbium: Yearbook of International Proverb Scholarship.*

4. For the German proverb see Wolfgang Mieder, *Das Sprichwort in unserer Zeit.* Frauenfeld: Huber, 1975; W. Mieder, *Deutsche Sprichwörter in Literatur, Politik, Presse und Werbung.* Hamburg: Helmut Buske, 1983; and W. Mieder, *Sprichwort, Redensart, Zitat: Tradierte Formelsprache in der Moderne.* Bern: Peter Lang, 1985. See also the two large collections of modern proverb variations edited by W. Mieder, *Antisprichwörter,* 2 vols. Wiesbaden: Verlag für deutsche Sprache, 1982 and 1985.

5. For a bibliographical review of the scholarship on proverbs in art see Wolfgang Mieder, "Bibliographischer Abriß zur bildlichen Darstellung von Sprichwörtern und Redensarten," *Forschungen und Berichte zur Volkskunde in Baden-Württemberg 1974–1977,* ed. by Irmgard Hampp and Peter Assion. Stuttgart: Müller & Gräff, 1977, vol. 3, pp. 229–239.

6. A good reproduction of the picture is included in Christopher Brown, *Bruegel.* New York: Crescent Books, 1975, p. 11.

7. See Wilhelm Fraenger, *Der Bauern-Bruegel und das deutsche Sprichwort.* Erlenbach-Zürich: Eugen Rentsch, 1923; Jan Grauls, *Volkstaal en volksleven in het werk van Pieter Bruegel.* Antwerpen: N. V. Standaard-Boekhandel, 1957; Franz Roh, *Pieter Bruegel d. Ä. Die niederländischen Sprichwörter.* Stuttgart: Philipp Reclam, 1960; and Alan Dundes and Claudia A. Stibbe, *The Art of Mixing Metaphors: A Folkloristic Interpretation of the "Netherlandish Proverbs" by Pieter Bruegel the Elder.* Helsinki: Suomalainen Tiedeakatemia, 1981.

8. For this detail see Timothy Foote, *The World of Bruegel, c. 1525–1569.* New York: Time-Life Books, 1968, pp. 154–155.

9. Louis Lebeer, "De blauwe huyck," *Gentsche Bijdragen tot de Kunstgeschiedenis,* 6 (1939/1940), 167 (the entire article pp. 161–229).

10. Maurits de Meyer, " 'De Blauwe Huyck' van Jan van Doetinchem, 1577," *Volkskunde,* 71 (1970), 334–343. In French translation published as " 'De Blauwe Huyck': La Cape Bleue de Jean van Doetinchem, datée 1577," *Proverbium,* no. 16 (1971), 564–575.

11. See Lebeer (note 9), p. 176.

12. The German Ravensburger Puzzle Company produced a large puzzle with three thousand pieces of this picture with a list of the proverbial expressions.

13. The poster "Proverbidioms" by T. E. Breitenbach appeared in 1975 in Altamont, New York. I found it in 1985 in a bookstore in Cambridge, Massachusetts.

14. The poster "As the Saying Goes" by William Belder was published in 1973 by the James Galt Company in London. My student Lori Greener located it in a Boston bookstore.

15. See Maurits de Meyer, *De volks- en kinderprent in de Nederlanden van de 15e tot de 20e eeuw*. Antwerpen: Standaard Boekhandel, 1962, p. 32 (ill. 12). See also pp. 427–432 and 440–451 for other prints.

16. Ibid., p. 444 (ill. 135).

17. Ibid., p. 94 (ill. 40).

18. Ibid., p. 426 (ill. 131).

19. Grace Frank and Dorothy Miner, *Proverbes en rimes: Text and Illustrations of the Fifteenth Century from a French Manuscript in the Walters Art Gallery, Baltimore*. Baltimore, Md.: The Johns Hopkins Press, 1937.

20. Ibid. plate 48.

21. Ibid. plate 135.

22. Ibid., plate 162.

23. The woodcut is reprinted in Lutz Röhrich, *Lexikon der sprichwörtlichen Redensarten*. Freiburg: Herder, 1973, vol. 1, p. 91.

24. Ibid., vol. 2, p. 1001.

25. Ibid., p. 1011.

26. Jacques Lavalleye, *Pieter Bruegel the Elder and Lucas van Leyden: The Complete Engravings, Etchings, and Woodcuts*. New York: Harry N. Abrams, 1967 plate 158. See also Jozef de Coo, "Twaalf spreuken op borden van Pieter Bruegel de Oude," *Bulletin des Musées royaux des Beaux-Arts*, 14 (1965), 83–104.

27. Brown (note 6), p. 92.

28. Frank and Miner (note 19), plate 34.

29. See A. T. Reid, *Selections of the Current Cartoons Drawn by Albert T. Reid Bearing upon Issues of the Day 1919*. New York: W. A. Grant, 1920, no pp. given.

30. Frank and Miner (note 19), plate 2.

31. J. W. Bengough, *A Caricature History of Canadian Politics*. Toronto: Grip Printing Co., 1886; rpt. Toronto: Peter Martin, 1974, p. 231.

32. Frank and Miner (note 19), plate 109.

33. *Die Zeit*, no. 19 (9 May 1975), p. 1. All references from this German weekly newspaper refer to the American edition.

34. Röhrich (note 23), vol. 1, p. 496.

35. Ibid.

36. Louis Maeterlinck, *Le Genre satirique dans la sculpture flamande et wallone*. Paris: Jean Schemit, 1910, p. 289 (ill. 196).

37. Enrique Lafuente Ferrari, *Goya: His Complete Etchings, Aquatints, and Lithographs*. New York: Harry N. Abrams, 1962, p. 236. See also George Levitine, "The Elephant of Goya," *Art Journal*, 20 (1961), 145–147.

38. *Time* (1 December 1975), pp. 8–9.

39. See the excellent paper with many examples by Lutz Röhrich, "Die Bildwelt von Sprichwort und Redensart in der Sprache der politischen Karikatur," *Kontakte und Grenzen: Probleme der Volks-, Kultur- und Sozialforschung: Festschrift für Gerhard Heilfurth*, ed. by Hans Friedrich Foltin. Göttingen: Otto Schwarz, 1969, pp. 175–207.

40. *Playboy* (July 1974), p. 165.

41. *Playboy* (November 1974), p. 176.

42. *Playboy* (October 1974), p. 172.

43. *New Yorker* (6 July 1957), p. 65.

44. *New Yorker* (28 April 1975), p. 46.

45. *St. Louis Post-Dispatch* (19 January 1975), p. 12D.

46. *New Yorker* (14 August 1965), p. 24.

47. *Punch* (2 May 1973), p. 602.

48. *St. Louis Post-Dispatch* (31 January 1975), p. 12D.

49. *Punch* (3 November 1971), p. 589.

50. Michael Wynn Jones, *The Cartoon History of Britain.* New York: Macmillan, 1971, p. 270.

51. *New Yorker* (21 July 1962), p. 18.

52. *New Yorker* (16 May 1959), p. 39.

53. *New Yorker* (20 June 1964), p. 39.

54. *New Yorker* (3 May 1958), p. 43.

55. See, for example, *The Oxford Dictionary of English Proverbs,* ed. by F. P. Wilson. Oxford: Clarendon Press, 3d ed. 1970; and Wolfgang Mieder, *The Prentice-Hall Encyclopedia of World Proverbs.* Englewood Cliffs, N.J.: Prentice-Hall, 1986.

56. Lavalleye (note 26), plate 151. See also the international study of this proverb by Archer Taylor, " 'Sunt tria damna domus,' " *Hessische Blätter für Volkskunde,* 24 (1926), 130–146; reprinted in *Selected Writings on Proverbs by Archer Taylor,* ed. by Wolfgang Mieder. Helsinki: Suomalainen Tiedeakatemia, 1975, pp. 133–151.

57. A detail in Röhrich (note 23), vol. 2, p. 1072.

58. Maeterlinck (note 36), p. 255 (ill. 164).

59. For a detail illustration from about 1700 see Röhrich (note 23), vol. 1, p. 440.

60. Maeterlinck (note 36), p. 201 (ill. 123).

61. *New Yorker* (30 March 1963), p. 34.

62. *New Yorker* (15 November 1958), p. 59.

63. *St. Louis Post-Dispatch* (22 August 1974), p. 9D.

64. *New Yorker* (18 November 1974), 47.

65. *St. Louis Post-Dispatch* (29 November 1975), p. 4B.

66. *New Yorker* (17 March 1956), p. 37.

67. *Playboy* (January 1978), p. 279. For sexual matters in proverbs see also Wolfgang Mieder, "Sexual Content of German Wellerisms," *Maledicta,* 6 (1982), 215–223.

68. *New Yorker* (27 August 1960), p. 45.

69. *New Yorker* (21 March 1959), p. 45.

70. *New Woman* (November/December 1977), p. 26.

71. *New Yorker* (21 July 1975), p. 33.

72. *New Yorker* (12 December 1964), p. 235.

73. See the fascinating paper by Frank A. Salamone on how proverbs are used in a traditional society to solve marriage problems, "The Arrow and the Bird: Proverbs in the Solution of Hausa Conjugal-Conflicts," *Journal of Anthropological Research,* 32 (1976), 358–371. See also Martine Segalen, "Le mariage, l'amour et les femmes dans les proverbes populaires français," *Ethnologie Française,* 5 (1975), 119–160 and 6 (1976), 33–88.

74. *Ms.* (May 1976), p. 91.

75. *New Yorker* (26 September 1964), p. 35.

76. *Woman's Day* (May 1975), p. 57. The actual proverb is, of course, "If the shoe fits, wear it."

77. *Better Homes and Gardens* (April 1977), p. 165.

78. For the use of proverbs in advertising see Barbara and Wolfgang Mieder, "Tradition and Innovation: Proverbs in Advertising," *Journal of Popular Culture,* 11 (1977), 308–319; reprinted in Mieder and Dundes (note 1), pp. 309–322.

79. *Playboy* (September 1973), p. 48.

80. *Penthouse* (April 1975), p. 99.

81. *New York Times Magazine* (19 September 1976), p. 13.

82. *Playgirl* (October 1977), p. 3.

83. *Punch* (17 November 1971), p. 684.

84. *Flightime* (June 1978), p. 51.

85. *Gourmet* (September 1974), p. 69.

86. *Time* (25 November 1974), p. 76.

87. *Time* (25 April 1977), p. 5.

88. Included in *The New Yorker: Album of Drawings 1925–1975*. New York: Viking Press, 1975, no pp. given.

89. *New Yorker* (20 September 1976), p. 58.

90. *Financial Executive* (April 1974), p. 87. See also Archer Taylor, " 'Tom, Dick, and Harry,' " *Names*, 6 (1958), 51–54.

91. *New Yorker* (20 July 1957), p. 47.

92. *Ms.* (May 1977), p. 49.

93. *New Yorker* (4 October 1976), p. 21.

94. *Ms.* (February 1975), p. 1.

95. *Time* (5 December 1947), p. 35.

96. *New York Times Magazine* (22 September 1974), p. 34.

97. *Ms.* (March 1976), p. 119.

98. *Ms.* (October 1977), p. 109.

99. *Ms.* (March 1978), p. 101.

100. *Ms.* (March 1978), p. 100.

101. *Ms.* (June 1976), p. 46.

102. Bob Abel (ed.), *The American Cartoon Album*. New York: Dodd, Mead, & Co., 1974, no pp. given.

103. See Wolfgang Mieder, *Proverbs in Literature: An International Bibliography*. Bern: Peter Lang, 1978.

104. This part of the present chapter was previously published as "Traditional and Innovative Proverb Use in Lyric Poetry" in *Proverbium Paratum*, 1 (1980), 16–27; a longer version with the title "A Sampler of Anglo-American Proverb Poetry" appeared in *Folklore Forum*, 13 (1980), 39–53.

105. See Wolfgang Mieder, "Moderne deutsche Sprichwortgedichte," *Fabula*, 21 (1980), 247–260; reprinted in Mieder, *Sprichwort, Redensart, Zitat* (note 4), pp. 73–90.

106. John S. Farmer (ed.), *The Proverbs, Epigrams, and Miscellanies of John Heywood*. London: Early English Drama Society, 1906; rpt. New York: Barnes & Noble, 1966, p. 168.

107. Farmer, p. 175.

108. E. H. Coleridge (ed.), *The Poems of Samuel Taylor Coleridge*. London: Oxford University Press, 1912, p. 418.

109. See George Monteiro, " 'Good Fences Make Good Neighbors.' A Proverb and a Poem," *Revista de Etnografia*, 16, no. 31 (1972), 83–88.

110. Robert Whitney Bolwell (ed.), *The Renaissance*. New York: Charles Scribner's Sons, 1920, pp. 269–270.

111. Phineas Garrett (ed.), *One Hundred Choice Selections, No. 9*. Freeport, New York: Books for Libraries Press, 1874, pp. 53–54.

112. Alice and Phoebe Cary, *Ballads for Little Folk*, ed. by Mary Clemmer Ames. Freeport, New York: Books for Libraries Press, 1873, pp. 81–83. A similar poem in this collection is "Keep a Stiff Upper Lip," pp. 174–175.

113. Vincent Godfrey Burns, *Redwood and other Poems*. Washington D.C.: New World Books, 1952, p. 114. See also a similar poem entitled "By Bread Alone" by Edna Jaques, *The Best of Edna Jaques*. Saskatoon, Saskatchewan: Modern Press, 1966, p. 50.

114. W. H. Auden, *The Collected Poems of W. H. Auden.* New York: Random House, 1941, pp. 123–124.

115. Harold Monro (ed.), *Twentieth Century Poetry.* London: Chatto, 1950, p. 79.

116. See Charles Clay Doyle, "On Some Paremiological Verses," *Proverbium,* no. 25 (1975), 979–982.

117. Kingsley Amis (ed.), *The New Oxford Book of English Light Verse.* New York: Oxford University Press, 1978, pp. 33–35.

118. Quoted from Bartlett Jere Whiting, *Early American Proverbs and Proverbial Phrases.* Cambridge, Mass.: Harvard University Press, 1977, pp. 511–512.

119. Arthur Guiterman, *The Laughing Muse.* New York: Harper & Brothers, 1915, p. 16.

120. John Robert Colombo, *Translations from the English.* Toronto: Peter Martin, 1974, p. 27.

121. Robert P. Falk (ed.), *American Literature in Parody.* New York: Twayne Publishers, 1955, p. 27.

122. This section has previously been published with the title " 'Wine, Women and Song': From Martin Luther to American T-Shirts," *Kentucky Folklore Record,* 29 (1983), 89–101.

123. For a review of the German literature on this proverb see Wolfgang Mieder, " 'Wer nicht liebt Wein, Weib und Gesang, der bleibt ein Narr sein Leben lang': Zur Herkunft, Überlieferung und Verwendung eines angeblichen Luther-Spruches," *Muttersprache,* 94 (special issue, 1983–1984), 68–103. See also W. Mieder, " 'Wine, Women and Song': Zur anglo-amerikanischen Überlieferung eines angeblichen Lutherspruches," *Germanisch-Romanische Monatsschrift,* 65, new series 34 (1984), 385–403.

124. Ernst Kroker (ed.), *D. Martin Luthers Werke: Kritische Gesamtausgabe.* Weimar: Hermann Böhlau, 1914. *Tischreden,* vol. 3, p. 344 (no. 3476).

125. August Otto, *Die Sprichwörter und sprichwörtlichen Redensarten der Römer.* Leipzig: Teubner, 1890; rpt. Hildesheim: Georg Olms, 1971, p. 372. With further examples of proverbs based on the triad "nox, amor, vinum."

126. Hans Walther, *Proverbia Sententiaeque Latinitatis Medii Aevi: Lateinische Sprichwörter und Sentenzen des Mittelalters.* Göttingen: Vandenhoeck & Ruprecht, 1965, vol. 1, p. 88 (no. 72). See also nos. 64, 71, and 73.

127. Karl Friedrich Wilhelm Wander, *Deutsches Sprichwörter-Lexikon.* Leipzig: F. A. Brockhaus, 1867; rpt. Darmstadt: Wissenschaftliche Buchgesellschaft, 1964, vol. 1, col. 616 (no. 322). Wander lists literally dozens of such proverbs attesting to the popularity of expanding the alliterative binary formula of "wine and woman" by a third element, many of them also starting with a *w.*

128. For a critical edition of this proverb collection see *Luthers Sprichwörtersammlung: Nach seiner Handschrift herausgegeben und mit Anmerkungen versehen,* ed. by Ernst Thiele. Weimar: Hermann Böhlau, 1900.

129. See Archer Taylor, *The Proverb.* Cambridge, Massachusetts: Harvard University Press, 1931; rpt. Hatboro, Pennsylvania: Folklore Associates, 1962, rpt. with an introduction and bibliography by Wolfgang Mieder, Bern: Peter Lang, 1985, p. 38.

130. Matthias Claudius (ed.), *Wandsbecker Bothe* (Friday, 12 May 1775), no. 75.

131. Johann Heinrich Voss (ed.), *Musen Almanach für 1777.* Hamburg: L. E. Böhn, 1777, p. 107.

132. Johann Heinrich Voss, *Sämtliche Gedichte.* Königsberg: Friedrich Nicolovius, 1802; rpt. Bern: Peter Lang, 1969, vol. 4, pp. 58–60.

133. See for example Bernard Darwin, *The Oxford Dictionary of Quotations.* Oxford: Oxford University Press, 1953, p. 321; Burton Stevenson, *The Macmillan Book of Proverbs, Maxims, and Famous Phrases.* New York: Macmillan, 1948; 7th ed. 1968, p. 2526 (no. 4); and John Bartlett, *Familiar Quotations.* Boston: Little, Brown and Co., 15th ed. 1980, p. 399.

134. The song is included in *Herders sämtliche Werke,* ed. by Carl Redlich. Berlin: Weidmann, 1885, vol. 25, pp. 21–22.

135. Wilson (note 55), p. 296.

136. Morris Palmer Tilley, *Elizabethan Proverb Lore in Lyly's "Euphues" and in Pettie's "Petite Pallace" with Parallels from Shakespeare.* New York: Macmillan, 1926, p. 248 (no. 491).

137. G. L. Apperson, *English Proverbs and Proverbial Phrases: A Historical Dictionary.* London: J. M. Dent, 1929, rpt. Detroit: Gale Research Co., 1969, p. 706 (no. 43).

138. Robert Burton, *The Anatomy of Melancholy,* ed. by Holbrook Jackson. London: J. M. Dent, 1972, p. 291.

139. John Gay, *The Beggar's Opera,* ed. by Edgar V. Roberts. Lincoln, Nebraska: University of Nebraska Press, 1969, p. 32.

140. *The Poems of John Keats,* ed. by Jack Stillinger. Cambridge, Massachusetts: Harvard University Press, 1978, p. 47.

141. *The Works of Lord Byron,* ed. by Ernest Hartley Coleridge. London: John Murray, 1903, vol. 6, p. 132, verse 178.

142. Henry G. Bohn, *A Polyglot of Foreign Proverbs.* London: Henry G. Bohn, 1857; rpt. Detroit: Gale Research Co., 1968, p. 184.

143. See *The Complete Works of William Makepeace Thackeray.* Boston: Houghton, Mifflin and Co., 1895, vol. 20, pp. 297–299. None of the editions gives a date for these translations.

144. Ibid., vol. 17, part 1, pp. 199–200.

145. Albert Methfessel, *Allgemeines Commers- und Liederbuch enthaltend ältere und neuere Burschenlieder, Trinklieder, Vaterlandsgesänge, Volks- und Kriegslieder, mit mehrstimmigen Melodien und beigefügter Klavierbegleitung.* Rudolstadt: Hof-, Buch- und Kunsthandlung, 1818; 3d ed. 1823, pp. 102–104. The translation is my own.

146. *The Poems of Eugene Field.* New York: Charles Scribner's Sons, 1912, pp. 390–391.

147. See John Addington Symonds, *Wine, Women and Song: Medieval Latin Student Songs. Now First Translated into English Verse with an Essay.* Portland, Maine: Thomas B. Mosher, 1899, pp. 147–148.

148. See as an example Wolfgang Mieder, " 'Der Apfel fällt weit von Deutschland': Zur amerikanischen Entlehnung eines deutschen Sprichwortes," *Der Sprachdienst,* 25 (1981), 89–93.

149. *The Poems of Ernest Christopher Dowson,* ed. by Mark Longaker. Philadelphia: University of Pennsylvania Press, 1962, p. 110. A villanelle is a short poem of French origin consisting usually of five stanzas of three lines each and a final stanza of four lines. It has only two rhymes throughout.

150. See Sam Morris, *Wine, Women and Song.* Del Rio, Texas: William McNitzy, 1938, pp. 58–69.

151. See Thomas Mann, *Doktor Faustus.* Frankfurt: S. Fischer, 1947, p. 149.

152. See Thomas Mann, *Doctor Faustus,* translated from the German by Helen T. Lowe-Porter. New York: Alfred A. Knopf, 1948, p. 97.

153. Franklin Pierce Adams, *Book of Quotations.* New York: Funk & Wagnalls, 1952, p. 848.

154. Leo Rosten, *Infinite Riches: Gems from a Lifetime of Reading.* New York: McGraw-Hill, 1979, p. 510.

155. See H. L. Mencken, *A New Dictionary of Quotations on Historical Principles from Ancient and Modern Sources.* New York: Alfred A. Knopf, 1942; 2d ed. 1960, p. 1303.

156. Quoted from A. K. Adams, *The House Book of Humorous Quotations.* New York: Dodd, Mead & Co., 1969, p. 331.

157. *Playboy* (September 1977), p. 234.

158. *New Yorker* (8 August 1983), p. 62. I owe this reference to my graduate student Leesa Guay.

159. *New Yorker* (4 February 1980), p. 58.

160. *Der Stern,* no. 39 (17 September 1981), p. 142.

161. Some scholars have attempted to argue that proverbs have little use if any in complex cultures with rapid social change. See for example William Albig, "Proverbs and Social Control," *Sociology and Social Research,* 15 (1931), 527–535.

162. See Jess Nierenberg, "Proverbs in Graffiti: Taunting Traditional Wisdom," *Maledicta,* 7 (1983), 41–58.

5

" Early to Bed and Early to Rise "

From Proverb to Benjamin Franklin and Back

In a short essay entitled "The Truth and Myths about Benjamin Franklin" that appeared in the 1990 issue of *The Old Farmer's Almanac* commemorating the bicentennial of Benjamin Franklin's (1706–1790) death, David Lord repeats the often stated claim that "Franklin coined countless catch phrases of morality and wisdom in his peerless *Poor Richard's Almanac.*"[1] In an accompanying box listing twenty of "Franklin's Famous Phrases" and a few examples of phrases that "Franklin didn't mint," he seriously misleads his readers by this juxtaposition of "true" and "false" Franklin proverbs into believing that this great American printer, writer, publisher, scientist, inventor, businessman, and diplomat was in fact also the originator of numerous new proverbs. Yet nothing could be further from the truth, as Robert Newcomb, in particular, has shown in his study *The Sources of Benjamin Franklin's Sayings of Poor Richard* (Diss. University of Maryland, 1957). Among Franklin and proverb scholars it is now generally known that this pragmatist of common-sense philosophy relied heavily on various proverb collections for the numerous proverbial texts he included in his instructive and entertaining *Poor Richard's Almanack* that he published for twenty-five years from 1733 to 1758.[2] Many of these proverbs he integrated verbatim into the almanacs, but as an acute "proverb stylist" he also reformulated some of them in his own wording. Many of these became current due to the unrivaled popularity of the almanacs, of which about 10,000 copies were sold every year. A very few of his own creations, at most 5% of the total of 1044 proverbial texts that appeared in the almanacs, did become proverbs in their own right, notably "Three

98

removes is as bad as a fire," "Laziness travels so slowly, that poverty soon overtakes it," and "There will be sleeping enough in the grave."[3]

It should, therefore, not be surprising that the extremely popular proverb "Early to bed and early to rise, makes a man healthy wealthy and wise" [sic] which Franklin cites in this precise wording as a bit of proverbial wisdom and advice for the month of October in his *Poor Richard's Almanack for the Year 1735* does *not* stem from him at all.[4] That does not, of course, prevent such popular writers as David Lord from continuing the "myth" that Franklin did originate this favorite Anglo-American saying. On a more official level E. D. Hirsch and his co-compilers of the best-selling *Dictionary of Cultural Literacy* (1988) claimed with equal conviction at the end of the eighties that this is "a saying of Benjamin Franklin in *Poor Richard's Almanack.*"[5] The same is true for the widely disseminated fifteenth edition of John Bartlett's *Familiar Quotations* (1980),[6] whose modern editor Emily Morison Beck should have known better. After all, previous editions including the centennial thirteenth edition of 1955 referred quite correctly to John Clarke's (d. 1658) *Paroemiologia Anglo-Latina [. . .] or Proverbs English, and Latine* (1639) where the proverb is cited almost one hundred years before Franklin used it.[7] It is not at all clear why Beck dropped this extremely important source reference that even includes a very early quite similar variant from 1598 in the fourteenth and fifteenth edition of this major reference work. This unfortunate exclusion should certainly be rectified in the next edition.

While it is one thing to criticize a scholarly publication as Bartlett's *Familiar Quotations*, it is quite another matter with the misconception that the general folk might have regarding the origin of this particular proverb. To this day people use such introductory formulas as "Benjamin Franklin said" or even more frequently "as Poor Richard says," a formula Franklin himself had employed so often in his almanacs. There can be no doubt that Franklin played a major role in spreading and popularizing traditional proverbs among his compatriots. They read them daily in his almanacs, they heard them on Sunday in church, and clearly they used them in all public encounters and at home in the family. People got so used to citing proverbs with reference to the almanacs that proverbs which were long in use in England since the Middle Ages became looked at as American proverbs originating with Benjamin Franklin. That is still the case at the present time, as field research by folklore students of the University of California at Berkeley shows. One of these students reports what her grandfather used to say to her when at the age of seven she wanted to stay up and watch TV: "You know what Ben Franklin always said? Early to bed and early to rise, makes a man healthy, wealthy, and wise."[8] Another student recorded that her informant "thinks that this saying originated with Benjamin Franklin,"[9] while a third collector quotes his informant to have "remembered that Ben Franklin said this."[10]

The informants are not always that certain about Franklin's authorship, one reporting "that it was possibly Benjamin Franklin who first said it"[11] and another stating that "she believes that her father learned it as something that Benjamin Franklin once said. She was not certain that he did state this proverb but she said it is a good example to follow."[12] Whether assertively or with some doubt, many if not most current speakers of the proverb will refer to or think of Benjamin Franklin or his *Poor Richard's Almanack* when citing this proverb. In the folk's mind this proverb and many others that appear in the almanacs and continue to be favorites in the United States today were created by Benjamin Franklin when, in fact, he merely stated or slightly re-stated old proverbs. As a scholar, one can point out this descrepancy, but it is part of folklore that these texts are often regarded as Benjamin Franklin's "proverbs."

Nothing could, however, be further from the truth, and it is important to note that Franklin himself tried to rectify this popular error during his life-time. As a didactic writer and as a printer and shrewd businessman with the desire of spreading high moral and practical wisdom among his readers, he must have been very pleased about the success of his little almanacs that averaged only thirty-six pages per issue. Obviously he was excited to read and hear how people were quoting "his" proverbs in written and oral com-munication. Yet he knew only too well that most of the proverbs and maxims were not at all his own. In his autobiography he wrote in 1788 that the proverbs he cited in the almanacs "contained the wisdom of many ages and nations."[13] But this was by no means a belated admission on Franklin's part that he had actually been copying the proverbial wisdom from various sources throughout the many years that he acted as the compiler of the almanacs. He had been honest about this fact before, especially at the end of his famous preface to the almanac of 1758 which he wrote in the summer of 1757 and which became an international best-seller essay with the title "The Way to Wealth." At the end of this masterful treatise on virtue, prosperity, prudence and above all economic and monetary common sense, he openly admitted the following: "my vanity was wonderfully delighted with it [that people quote "his" proverbs by adding the formula "as Poor Richard says"], though I was conscious that not a tenth part of the wisdom was my own . . . but rather the gleanings that I made of the sense of all ages and nations."[14] There was thus no intentional deception on Franklin's part, but in keeping with the spirit of the time he certainly didn't mind copying proverbs and maxims out of books without citing his sources and taking a bit of credit where he could.

But what is the origin and history of the proverb "Early to bed and early to rise, makes a man healthy, wealthy and wise" for which Benjamin Frank-lin appears to have been but an intermediate popularizer and at best an apoc-ryphal source? The first recorded reference of this proverb in the English language is an early variant that appeared in *A Treatyse of Fysshynge wyth an Angle* dating from 1496:

> Also who soo woll vse the game of anglynge: he must ryse erly. Whiche thyng is prouffrable to man in this wyse / That is to wyte: moost to the heele of his soule. For it shall cause hym to be hole. Also to the encrease of his goodys. For it shall make hym ryche. As the olde englysshe prouverbe sayth in this wyse. Who soo woll ryse erly shall be holy helthy & zely.[15]

This proverb does not yet talk about "going to bed early" and the triad of "holy helthy & zely" (i.e., happy, fortunate) does not yet completely agree with the proverb as it is cited later, but this variant is clearly a precursor. The statement that early rising will "encrease [. . .] goodys" already alludes to the later idea of becoming "wealthy." And that the author introduces the text with the introductory formula "as the olde englysshe prouverbe sayth in this wyse" is, of course, of great importance in establishing the fact that the proverb might be considerably older than 1496, dating perhaps from the middle or even the beginning of the fifteenth century.

The second historical reference stems from *The Book of Husbandry* (1523) by Anthony Fitzherbert (1470–1538) that contains a half-page paragraph entitled "A shorte lesson for the husbande":

> One thinge I wyl aduise the to remembre, and specially in wynter-tyme, wha*n* thou sytteste by the fyre, and hast supped, to consyder in thy mynde, whether the warkes, that thou, thy wyfe, & thy seruauntes shall do, be more auauntage to the than the fyre, and candell-lyghte, meate and drynke that they shall spende, and if it be more auantage, than syt styll: and if it be not, than go to thy bedde and slepe, and be vppe betyme, and breake thy faste before day, that thou mayste be all the shorte wynters day about thy busynes. At grammer-scole I lerned a verse, that is this, *Sanat, sanctificat, et ditat surgere mane.* That is to say, Erly rysyng maketh a man hole in body, holer in soule, and rycher in goodes. And this me semeth shuld be sufficie*n*t instruction for the husbande to kepe measure.[16]

Fitzherbert talks about going to bed and rising early before citing the proverb first in Latin and then in English. He also argues that he learned the Latin verse "Sanat, sanctificat, et ditat surgere mane" in grammar school and cites the English version as its translation. This naturally leads to the important question of what came first—the Latin or the English proverb? Realizing that Fitzherbert must have been in grammar school around 1480, this Latin text is certainly older than the English variant from the 1496 treatise on fishing. The British scholars F. C. Birkbeck Terry, Ed Marshall, and Robert Pierpoint attempted to find the earliest reference of this Latin proverb at the end of the nineteenth century, but the best they could do is to locate "Sanat, sanctificat, ditat te [not: et ditat] surgere mane" in the rather popular Latin proverb collection *Carminum proverbialium loci communes* that was published in Basel in 1576 (London 1579) with numerous later editions.[17] Hans Walther in his multi-volume *Proverbia sententiaeque latinitatis medii aevi* (1963–1969) was not able to find any earlier published citations of this Latin proverb,[18] but he does state that "fast alle Sprüche [sind] in ma. Hss. nachweisbar", that is, that almost all proverbs registered in the *Carminum proverbialium* are traceable to earlier unpublished medieval manuscripts.[19] The medieval Latin proverb appears after 1576 in many Latin proverb collections throughout Europe, but not in Erasmus of Rotterdam's (1469–1536) famous *Adagia* (1500ff.). Since it can not be traced to any of the classical Latin proverb collections either, it appears to belong to the group of common medieval Latin proverbs that were used in European schools for language instruction.[20] It thus is probably justified to conjecture that the English proverb "Early to bed and early to rise, makes a man healthy, wealthy and wise" has its roots in the Latin language of the Middle Ages.

By about 1545 when Hugh Rhodes (fl. 1550) wrote his *Boke of Nurture* (published 1577) to teach young people good manners by interweaving his didactic verses with practical proverbial wisdom, he cites the proverb in plain English without the Latin:

> Ryse you earely in the morning,
>   for it hath propertyes three:
> Holynesse, health, and happy welth,
>   as my Father taught mee.[21]

Of importance is here that Rhodes does not quote a Latin school grammar as the source of this wisdom any longer. Instead he uses the standard formula "as my Father taught mee" to stress the general folk wisdom of the saying. However, by changing the three adjectives to nouns he appears to create a more poetic variant of this fledgling English proverb that did not gain any particular currency.

But just because a number of English variants were current in the sixteenth century does not mean that the Latin original dropped out immediately. Among educated people Latin remained an important language that certainly was integrated liberally into English texts. Thus an anonymous author of that century states somewhat haughtily that "it is an infallible Rule, 'Sanat, sanctificat, et ditat, surgere mane' " in his *Health to the Gentlemanly Profession of Servingmen* (1598).[22] Of considerable surprise is, however, that William Shakespeare (1564–1616) has made no use of either the English or

Latin proverb in his works, which might be an indication that the English translation was still not very current and that the Latin original was not in much use anymore. In a scene between Sir Toby and Sir Andrew in *Twelfth Night* (1599) Shakespeare had ample opportunity to cite either text but instead introduces yet another common Latin proverb of the Middle Ages that states merely that to rise early is very healthy:

> *Sir To.* Approach, Sir Andrew; not to be abed after midnight, is to be up betimes; and *diluculo surgere*, thou know'st—
> *Sir And.* Nay, by my troth, I know not: but I know, to be up late, is to be up late.
> *Sir To.* A false conclusion: I hate it as an unfilled can. To be up after midnight, and to go to bed then, is early: so that to go to bed after midnight, is to go to bed betimes. Does not our life consist of the four elements?
> *Sir And.* Faith, so they say, but I think it rather consists of eating and drinking.
> *Sir To.* Th'art a scholar; let us therefore eat and drink. Marian, I say! a stoup of wine![23]

The entire Latin proverb that Shakespeare assumes his audience does know is "Diluculo surgere saluberrimum est," and it appears as early as 1513 in William Lily's (c. 1468–1522) *Latin Grammar* that was still in common use in Shakespeare's time.[24] The proverb appears about three years later again only in Latin in Thomas Heywood's (1574–1641) play *How a Man May Choose a Good Wife from a Bad* (1602):

> But Mistris *Virga*, Ladie *Willowby*,
> Shall teach him that *Diluculo surgere*,
> *Est saluberrimum*, here comes the knaue.[25]

In a second play entitled *The Royall King, and the Loyall Subject* (1637) Heywood uses the proverb in a scene between the Prince and Katherine, but this time only in English translation:

> *Kath.* So early up! how did you like your rest?
> *Prince.* I found my most rest in my most unrest:
> A little sleep serves a new married man,
> The first night of his bridals. I have made you
> A woman of a maid.
> *Kath.* You were up both late and early.
> *Prince.* Why, you were abroad
> Before the sun was up; and the most wise
> Do say 'tis healthful still betimes to rise.—
> Good day.[26]

Yet this English rendition of a Latin proverb that was also used repeatedly for translation exercises in the sixteenth century did not become proverbial as did "Sanat, sanctificat, et ditat surgere mane" and its English adaptations.

It is interesting to note that Thomas Draxe (d. 1618) in his *Bibliotheca scholastica instructissima* (1616) actually listed both of these Latin proverbs under the key-word of "morning":

> *He shal be healthfull that riseth in the morning.*
> Diluculo surgere saluberrimum est.
> Sanat, sanctificat, ditat te, surgere mane.[27]

Clearly the English statement is more a translation of the first text, perhaps indicating that the longer proverb with the triad of "healthy, wealthy, and wise" had not yet gained absolute currency in the early seventeenth century. But by 1639, when John Clarke published his bilingual proverb collection *Paroemiologia Anglo-Latina*, the English proverb had found its final wording in print that Franklin used some one hundred years later and which is still the most common form today. Under the key-word "diligentia" Clarke juxtaposes the English and Latin texts:

> *Earely to bed and earely to rise,*   Sanat, sanctificat, ditat quoque
> *makes a man healthy, wealthy, and*   surgere mane.[28]
> *wise.*

Twenty years later the proverb appears in this exact wording and the more modern spelling of "early" in James Howell's (1593–1666) important polyglot collection *Paroimiografia. Proverbs, or, Old Sayed Savves & Adages in English (or the Saxon Toung) Italian, French and Spanish* (1659) as a *bona fide* English proverb: "Early to bed, and early to rise, / Makes a man healthy, wealthy and wise."[29] And according to Robert Newcomb's careful analysis of Benjamin Franklin's sources for the proverbs in his *Poor Richard's Almanacks*, this American friend of old proverbs excerpted about 150 proverbs from Howell's collection and integrated them into his almanacs that appeared between 1733 and 1742. In fact, "for the *Almanack* of 1735, 1736 and 1737 Franklin relied almost exclusively on Howell,"[30] and he clearly found this proverb there—a fact that does not, of course, preclude the possibility that Franklin knew the proverb from oral tradition as well. Newcomb was also able to prove that Franklin found almost 200 texts in Thomas Fuller's (1654–1734) *Gnomologia: Adagies and Proverbs* that he integrated into the almanacs between 1745 and 1751. He clearly came across the proverb again at that time in the slightly different wording of "Early to go to Bed, and early to rise, / Will make a Man Healthy, Wealthy and Wise,"[31] but he himself stuck to the wording that he had used initially in 1735 when, as will be shown later, he repeated the proverb two more times in 1758 and 1779.

Even though it is a fact that Franklin definitely was using Howell's *Paroimiografia* when he wrote *Poor Richard's Almanack* for 1735, and even though he most likely had not come across Fuller's *Gnomologia* yet at that time, he almost doubtlessly had also occasion to use John Ray's (1627–1705) well-known *Compleat Collection of English Proverbs* (1670) which includes the proverb in the variant formulation of "Early to go to bed and early to rise, makes a man healthy, wealthy, and wise."[32] Perhaps he might also have had access to Robert Codrington's (d. 1665) *Collection of Many Select, and Excellent Proverbs out of Several Languages* (1664) that lists the slight variant "Early to Bed, and early to Rise, makes a Man healthful, wealthy, and wise."[33]

By the time the flood of modern proverb collections begins in the middle of the nineteenth century, the variant of "Early to bed and early to rise, makes a man healthy, wealthy and wise," as it was recorded by Clarke in 1639, Howell in 1659, and Franklin in 1735 (and again in 1758 and 1779), had emerged as *the* traditional text. Only Henry G. Bohn (1796–1884) looked at the first part of the proverb as a plural subject in his very popular *Hand-Book of Proverbs* (1855), thus using the verb form "make" instead of "makes": "Early to bed, and early to rise, make a man healthy, wealthy, and wise."[34] But only two years later he too switched to "makes" in his *Polyglot of Foreign Proverbs* (1857), where he cites the proverb as an English equivalent of a similar German proverb: "Früh zu Bett und früh wieder auf, macht gesund und reich in Kauf. / Early to bed and early to rise, makes a man healthy, wealthy, and wise."[35] In this precise form the proverb reappears, often with quite detailed historical annotations (see the accompanying notes), in the following major proverb collections: John W. Barber, *Hand Book of Illustrated Proverbs* (1856),[36] William Carew Hazlitt, *English Proverbs and Proverbial Phrases* (1869),[37] Vincent S. Lean, *Lean's Collectanea* (1903),[38] Dwight E. Marvin, *Curiosities in Proverbs* (1916),[39] G. L. Apperson, *English Proverbs and Proverbial Phrases* (1929),[40] Burton Stevenson, *The Home Book of Proverbs, Maxims, and Famous Phrases* (1948),[41] Morris Palmer Tilley, *A Dictionary of the Proverbs in England in the Sixteenth and Seventeenth Centuries* (1950),[42] Archer Taylor and Bartlett Jere Whiting, *A Dictionary of American Proverbs and Proverbial Phrases, 1820–1880* (1958),[43] Bartlett Jere Whiting, *Proverbs, Sentences, and Proverbial Phrases from English Writings Mainly Before 1500* (1968),[44] F. P. Wilson, *The Oxford Dictionary of English Proverbs* (1970),[45] Bartlett Jere Whiting, *Early American Proverbs and Proverbial Phrases* (1977),[46] John A. Simpson, *The Concise Oxford Dictionary of Proverbs* (1982),[47] Wolfgang Mieder, *Encyclopedia of World Proverbs* (1986),[48] Bartlett Jere Whiting, *Modern Proverbs and Proverbial Sayings* (1989),[49] and Wolfgang Mieder, Stewart Kingsbury, and Kelsie Harder, *A Dictionary of American Proverbs* (1992).[50]

There are only a few amateur paremiographers who have bothered to check any of these scholarly collections to establish that Benjamin Franklin was not the originator of the phrase. Thus J. Gilchrist identifies the proverb in his popular collection of *The World's Best Proverbs and Maxims* (1926)[51] as having been coined by Franklin. Ronald Ridout and Clifford Witting in their *English Proverbs Explained* (1967) even go so far as to state that "we owe this admirable precept to that great and versatile American Benjamin Franklin,"[52] and Maryjane Tonn also cites the proverb as belonging to Franklin in her small collection *Proverbs to Live By* (1977).[53] And there is, finally, the anonymously produced, hardcover little book by the Peter Pauper Press with quaint woodcuts by Joseph Crawhall and the befitting title *Ben Franklin's Wit and Wisdom* (1960) that lists the proverb with a befitting illustration as one of the many gems of Benjamin Franklin. This popular gift-book has done its share more than any other printed publication save the actual *Poor Richard's Almanacks* to perpetuate the myth that Franklin actually coined these proverbs. In all fairness it must be stated that the Pauper Press has included the short disclaimer that "Of course not all the sayings here are original with old Ben, for he included in *Poor Richard,* along with his own, proverbs copied or adapted from other collections—but he usually gave to them a flavor of his own."[54] But of course there are no annotations in this unscholarly and randomly assembled collection to indicate which proverbs Franklin coined himself, which he adapted, and which he copied directly from earlier sources.

The misinformation regarding this proverb presented in most books of quotations is much more prevalent and perhaps more serious, since most people will go to such compilations to establish the sources of famous sayings. John Bartlett (1820–1905) himself started attributing the phrase "Early to bed, and early to rise, / Makes a man healthy, wealthy and wise" in the first edition of his renowned *Familiar Quotations* from 1855 to Benjamin Franklin by including it among six quotations from *Poor Richard.*[55] It is, however, to his scholarly credit that he removed this particular proverb from the "new [i.e., second] edition" of his book that was published only one year later, obviously a clear indication that Bartlett had realized that this was in fact a traditional proverb and not a newly coined phrase by Franklin.[56] Later editions up through the thirteenth edition of 1955 include the proverb with the correct annotation of its early appearance in John Clarke's *Paroemiologia Anglo-Latina* (1639) as well as Franklin's almanac.[57] But unfortunately, as has already been pointed out, Emily Morison Beck as the editor of the two most recent editions of *Familiar Quotations* (fourteenth ed. 1968; fifteenth ed. 1980) has returned to the misinformation of Bartlett's first edition from 1855 by giving only Benjamin Franklin credit for having invented this proverb.

This unfortunate situation is reflected in almost all quotation collections of lesser reputation and quality than Bartlett's *Familiar Quotations.* Listing only

Franklin as the source and thus misleading readers into thinking that he originated the proverb is the case in the following collections: John Keitges, *Proverbs and Quotations* (1905),[58] Marshall Brown, *Sayings that Never Grow Old* (1918),[59] Tryon Edwards, *Useful Quotations* (1936),[60] Theodore Backer, *A Compact Anthology of Bartlett's Quotations* (1974),[61] and Gorton Carruth and Eugene Ehrlich, *American Quotations* (1988).[62]

Two quotation dictionaries parallel the way proverb collections have dealt with this saying by referring both to John Clarke's early reference and Franklin's use of it—namely Burton Stevenson, *The Home Book of Quotations* (1934),[63] and Bergen Evans, *Dictionary of Quotations* (1968).[64] The entry by the latter compiler is of special interest since it attempts to explain the reason for the common practice of crediting Franklin with the origin of the proverb: "The proverb, in slightly different forms, is very old. Franklin copied Clarke's wording in *Poor Richard's Almanack* (1735) and repeated it in 1758, and most Americans simply ascribe the saying to Franklin." The only change in this statement that one might want to insist on is that, as Robert Newcomb has shown so clearly, Franklin copied the proverb from Howell's *Paroimiografia* (1659) that appeared twenty years after Clarke's *Paroemiologia*.

Regarding Clarke it should be mentioned that two editors of quotation books list only him as the first person to have used the proverb in the wording that is still current today. This is, of course, correct scholarship, but readers should nevertheless be informed that Franklin did his share in maintaining its popularity in later centuries. The two authors and books that treat the proverb in this somewhat truncated fashion are D. C. Browning, *Dictionary of Quotations and Proverbs* (1951),[65] and H. L. Mencken, *A New Dictionary of Quotations* (1960).[66] One editor refers only to John Ray's inclusion of the proverb in his English proverb collection from 1670, namely W. Gurney Benham, *Complete Book of Quotations* (1926).[67] And, as to be expected, there is also the recent *Macmillan Dictionary of Quotations* (1987), whose multiple editors simply list the text as an anonymous proverb.[68] One might well wonder why the editors included this text at all in a quotation dictionary if they are not aware of any sources. In this regard the compilers of the various editions of *The Oxford Dictionary of Quotations* (1941, 1953, and 1979) appear to be more consistent—they simply have excluded the proverb from appearing in their massive volume altogether. Compilers of such dictionaries have to draw the line somewhere. Yet it would seem that this proverb should have been included if not merely for the reason to dispel the commonly held notion that Benjamin Franklin coined it.

It is now high time to consider that Franklin's first use of the proverb in his *Poor Richard's Almanack* for the year 1735 might by itself not have been able to attach his name so lastingly to it. The credit for accomplishing this feat belongs more appropriately to Franklin's stroke of genius in preparing *Poor Richard's Almanack* for 1758 in the summer of 1757. For its introduction Franklin composed his famous essay "The Way to Wealth" which could be considered as the manifesto of Puritan ethics based on 105 proverbs that he excerpted from the previous twenty-four almanacs. Toward the beginning of this didactic and pragmatic rhetorical masterpiece Franklin talks about the value of time and industry and concludes his ethical paragraph very appropriately with the proverb that instructs people to adhere to solid work ethics:

> If Time be of all Things the most precious, *wasting Time must be,* as *Poor Richard* says, *the greatest Prodigality,* since, as he elsewhere tells us, *Lost Time is never found again;* and what we call *Time enough, always proves little enough:* Let us then up and be doing, and doing to the Purpose; so by Diligence shall we do more with less Perplexity. *Sloth makes all Things difficult, but Industry all easy,* as *Poor Richard* says; and *He that riseth late, must trot all Day, and shall scarce overtake his Business at Night.* While *Laziness travels so slowly, that Poverty soon overtakes him,* as we read in *Poor Richard,* who adds, *Drive thy Business, let not that drive thee;* and *Early to Bed, and early to rise, makes a Man healthy, wealthy and wise.*[69]

Proverb follows proverb instructing the average Colonial American that industry and frugality will eventually lead to economic and personal independence.[70] There is no doubt that this "proverb essay" became a sort of "national orthodoxy"[71] whose proverbs were cited *ad infinitum* if not *ad nauseum* at every conceivable opportunity. The essay has been republished dozens of times to the present day, and it has also been translated into many foreign languages. Early translations of it caused some of its proverbs to become current outside of the Anglo-American world. The German paremiographer Karl Friedrich Wilhelm Wander (1803–1879), for example, included this proverb in the first volume of his massive *Deutsches Sprichwörter-Lexikon* (1867) with a correct reference to Franklin's use of it in *Poor Richard's Almanack* and "The Way to Wealth":

> Früh zu Bette und auf zu früher Stund', macht den Menschen glücklich, reich, gesund.
>> Dieser Spruch scheint aus B. Franklin's *Kalender des armen Richard* oder aus dessen *Weg zum Reichthum* in unsere Sprache übergegangen zu sein: Early to bed and early to rise, makes a man healthy, wealthy and wise.[72]

The German translation did, however, not gain much currency due to its length and the fact that Germany's most popular proverb "Morgenstunde hat Gold im Munde" (The morning hour has gold [i.e., success, money, wealth] in its mouth) already expresses the basic thought of the Anglo-American proverb in a much shorter and colloquial fashion.[73]

Franklin himself certainly must have valued the proverb about early rising a great deal, as can be seen from a letter dated October 2, 1779. In it he discusses the possibility of producing copper coins "that may not only be useful as small change, but serve other purposes"—and those would, of course, have been didactic in nature. Reading this letter makes clear that early Americans might well have had various types of proverbial wisdom on their coins and just imagine what that would have done for spreading "Poor Richard's" proverbs among the people:

> Instead of repeating continually upon every halfpenny the dull story that everybody knows (and what it would have been no loss to mankind if nobody had ever known) that Geo. III is King of Great Britain, France, and Ireland, &c. &c., to put on one side, some important Proverb of Solomon, some pious moral, prudential or economical Precept, the frequent Inculcation of which, by seeing it every time one receives a piece of Money, might make an impression upon the mind, especially of young Persons, and tend to regulate the Conduct; such as, on some, *The fear of the Lord is the beginning of Wisdom;* on others, *Honesty is the best Policy;* on others, *He that by the Plow would thrive, himself must either hold or drive;* on others, *Keep thy Shop, and thy Shop will keep thee;* on others, *A penny saved is a penny got;* on others, *He that buys what he has no need of, will soon be forced to sell his necessaries;* on others, *Early to bed and early to rise, will make a man healthy, wealthy, and wise;* and so on, to a great variety.
>
> The other side it was proposed to fill with good Designs, drawn and engraved by the best artists in France, of all the different Species of Barbarity with which the English have carried on the War in America, expressing every abominable circumstance of their Cruelty and Inhumanity, that figures can express, to make an Impression on the minds of Posterity as strong and durable as that on the Copper.[74]

Listing the proverb in this short enumeration some twenty years after using it in "The Way to Wealth" is ample proof that Franklin continued to believe in its basic wisdom and apparent truth. And doubtlessly he would have been delighted to know that to this very day his original use of the proverb in *Poor Richard's Almanack* remains its first documented reference in an American publication. There is, to be sure, John Saffin's (1632–1710) earlier American epigram from about 1700, but it represents at best a poetic allusion, if that, to the actual proverb:

> He that to [sic] much loves his bed
> Will surely scratch a poor man's head
> But he that Early doth arise:
> Is in a way to win the prise.[75]

Yet the fact that the proverb was indeed well known toward the end of the eighteenth century can be seen from a diary entry from January 9, 1782, by a loyalist contemporary of Benjamin Franklin, in which Samuel Curwen (1715–1802) cites part of the proverb not so much in its economic but rather medical sense:

> At 5 o'clock Doctor Jeffries called and abode ½ hour, on my request he gave me his opinion, that considering my advanced age and past state of body, I should use warming and best dry wines, most excellent and prize in their kinds as Madiera, sherry, dry mountain, avoid the lean meagre and red of all productions; spirits as rum brandy and gin, Hollands in water, unsweetened. Choisest flesh, roast, baked or boiled only, without butter fat or sauces, of vegetables, turnips, carrots, onions, potatoes and no other, but above all in moderate quantitys. Tea very sparingly, not to suffer stomach to be a long time empty, nor go to bed on a full one. Early to bed, early to rise, moderate exercise. No other malt liquor but mild porter. Keep fresh air as much as possible.[76]

The good doctor obviously realized that the proverb "Early to bed, early to rise, makes a man healthy, wealthy and wise" is clearly sound advice from a medical point of view, telling people that they need a proper amount of sleep.[77] Whether that will also translate into wealth and wisdom is not necessarily a solid guarantee, but it stands to reason that a well-rested person might also learn and work better, which should lead to increased knowledge and financial well-being. In any case, the paragraph cited reads almost like a statement out of a popular magazine article on diet and exercise, and it is quite conceivable that the proverb variation "Early to bed, early to rise, moderate exercise" might reappear any day as a ready-made slogan for yet another health program.

But the proverb contains clearly more than common-sense medical advice. Its main purpose is doubtlessly to get people, especially children, to adhere to rigid work ethics. As one of several folklore students reports in 1974 from California, his informant stated "that this is probably one of the most commonly quoted proverbs by parents to their children."[78] Field research has also shown that parents employ the proverb especially "when the children didn't want to go to bed."[79] But many informants also stress repeatedly that the proverb "relates to our [American] society and how capitalistic and geared toward money everything is,"[80] that the proverb's "idea is typical of the American work ethic that if you work hard you can be as rich as anybody,"[81] and that the "American culture stresses good health, money and intelligence in this proverb."[82] Such views are naturally not limited to today's American society, especially if one considers that the proverb was current in England several centuries before these recent interpretations were recorded from informants in California. As early as 1766 one finds the instructional statement that "every little good Boy and Girl should get by Heart [the proverb] 'Early to Bed, and early to rise, Is the Way to be healthy, and wealthy, and wise" in the anonymously published little children's book *Goody Two-Shoes*.[83] And the following verse from the early nineteenth century has become part of the *Mother Goose* nursery rhymes, teaching thousands of children to follow a life of solid work ethics:

> The cock crows in the morn
> To tell us to rise,
> And he that lies late
> Will never be wise:
> For early to bed,
> And early to rise,
> Is the way to be healthy
> And wealthy and wise.[84]

It must not be forgotten that books like *Mother Goose* had a sizable influence on the dissemination of verbal folklore, assuring a certain folkloric cultural literacy among the entire population. Just as certain nursery rhymes became deeply instilled in the psyche of people, common proverbs also maintained their general currency at least in part through various types of children's books, including school readers.

It should, therefore, not be surprising to see the old favorite of "Early to bed and early to rise" appear again and again in written sources of the nineteenth and twentieth centuries. Thus Herman Melville (1819–1891) includes in his mid-nineteenth-century *Moby Dick* (1851) an allusion to the proverb while at the same time linking it with the equally well-known proverb "The early bird catches the worm": "Generally he's [the harponeer] an early bird—airley to bed and airley to rise—yes, he's the bird that catches the worm."[85] Another such shortened allusion to the proverb appears two years later at the beginning of a chapter in Robert Smith Surtees' (1805–1864) novel *Mr. Sponge's Sporting Tour* (1853): "Early to bed and early to rise being among Mr. Sponge's maxims, he was enjoying the view of the pantiles at the back of his hotel shortly after daylight the next morning, a time about as difficult to fix in a November day as the age of a lady of a 'certain age'."[86] A third reference that once again merely alludes to the first part of the proverb is included in an 1854 didactic etiquette book by Cedric Oldacre (John W. Warter, 1806–1878) entitled *The Last of the Old Squires*, whose main character in Franklin-like fashion "taught all the younger Tenants upon the Estate that if they would thrive they must be 'early to Bed and early to rise,'—that the Labours of the Day must precede the Pleasures—that the Money they had to spend must be well earned—that Nothing must be spent which would not properly be spared."[87] Quoting only the first half of this proverb for brevity's sake and because the entire text is perfectly well known in any case is even more prevalent today, especially in fast oral communication. In a recent *Dictionary of Proverbs* (1988) put together by Kam Chuam Aik for the thousands of people around the world learning English as a foreign language, this common proverb is very appropriately treated in the following fashion:

> **Early to bed and early to rise, makes a man healthy, wealthy and wise**
>
> A person who wants to be happy and successful in life should always go to bed early and also wake up early. If you want to be successful and healthy, you must live sensibly and not have too much of any activity or enjoyment (e.g. too much work or too much drink).
> *1. Mr A: Jack goes out drinking night after night. He's seldom home before 3 a.m. Mr B: No wonder he looks so worn out and pathetic nowadays. Someone must remind him of the age-old wisdom of early to bed and early to rise. 2. I'm an early-to-bed-and-early-to-rise type. I'm certainly healthy and, perhaps, also wise. But I still don't have the money to be wealthy.*[88]

As will be shown later in the modern use of the proverb in newspapers, advertisements, and comics, the shortened piece of wisdom of "early to bed and early to rise" has taken on a certain proverbiality of its own.

Yet that is not to say that the longer proverb has not been equally often cited as an unshakable truism throughout the nineteenth century and the modern age. Quite often Franklin or his "Poor Richard" are mentioned right along with it, giving the proverb additional credence and also maintaining the myth that he was the coiner of the saying. This can be seen quite well from an essay entitled "A Gallimaufry" that was included in Thomas Chandler Haliburton's (1796–1865) book *The Season-Ticket* (1860):

> Travellers are generally early risers. In many countries it is absolutely necessary to be up long before sunrise, in order to finish a journey ere the heat of the day becomes insupportable. In towns, and on shipboard, this habit is rendered inconvenient either by the dusters and brooms of housemaids, or the holy stones and swabs of sailors; but wherever practicable, it is a most healthy as well as agreeable custom. Indeed, I have heard it asserted of those who have attained to great longevity, that nine out of ten of them have been distinguished as 'peep-o'-day boys.' Poor Richard has given us his experience in rhyme, to impress it more easily on the memory:
>
> 'Early to bed and early to rise,
> Makes a man healthy, wealthy, and wise.'
>
> I cannot say that I have always strictly complied with the first part of the advice (which, to a certain extent, is rendered necessary by the latter), because the artificial state of society in which we live, interferes most inconveniently with its observance; but the early morning ought to be at our own disposal, and with the exception of the two impediments

I have named (which are by no means insurmountable) it is our own fault, if we do not derive all the advantages resulting from it.[89]

From Eliza Cook (1818–1889) stems an even more didactic ten-stanza poem from about 1868 with the title "Early to Bed and Early to Rise" which discusses in typically moralistic fashion the value of this proverbial advice for a proper life of health, wealth, and wisdom:

Early to Bed and Early to Rise

"EARLY to bed and early to rise."
    Ay! note it down in your brain,
For it helpeth to make the foolish wise,
    And uproots the weeds of pain.

Ye who are walking on thorns of care,
    Who sigh for a softer bower;
Try what can be done in the morning sun,
    And make use of the early hour.

Full many a day for ever is lost,
    By delaying its work till to-morrow;
The minutes of sloth have often cost
    Long years of bootless sorrow.

And ye who would win the lasting wealth
    Of content and peaceful power;
Ye who would couple Labour and Health,
    Must begin at the early hour.

We make bold promises to Time,
    Yet, alas! too often break them;
We mock at the wings of the King of kings,
    And think we can overtake them.

But why loiter away the prime of the day,
    Knowing that clouds may lower;
Is it not safer to make Life's hay
    In the beam of the early hour?

Nature herself e'er shows her best
    Of gems to the gaze of the lark,
When the spangles of light on earth's green breast
    Put out the stars of the dark.

If we love the purest pearl of the dew,
    And the richest breath of the flower,
If our spirits would greet the fresh and the sweet,
    Go forth in the early hour.

Oh! pleasure and rest are more easily found
    When we start through Morning's gate,
To sum up our figures or plough up our ground,
    And weave out the threads of Fate.

The eye looketh bright and the heart keepeth light,
    And Man holdeth the conqueror's power,
When ready and brave, he chains Time as his slave,
    By the help of the early hour.[90]

This almost pious interpretation of a proverb preaching rigorous Protestant ethics deserves to be contrasted with a more liberal view. Benjamin Franklin and his proverbial wisdom had reached such heights of adoration and adherence that Mark Twain (1835–1910) saw fit to react humorously and ironically to it several times during his life. In a relatively early sketch on "Early Rising as Regards Excursions to the Cliff House" that appeared in the *Golden Era* on July 3, 1864, Twain takes Benjamin Franklin and "his" proverb to task in a wonderfully humorous way. And while doing so, he discredits or "disproves" the other popular proverb about early rising, namely "The early bird catches the worm," right along with it.

Early Rising
AS REGARDS
EXCURSIONS TO THE CLIFF HOUSE

Early to bed, and early to rise,
Makes a man healthy, wealthy and wise.—Benjamin Franklin.

I don't see it—George Washington.

Now both of these are high authorities—very high and respectable authorities—but I am with General Washington first, last, and all the time on this proposition.
    Because I don't see it, either.
    I have tried getting up early, and I have tried getting up late—and the latter agrees with me best. As for a man's growing any wiser, or any richer, or any healthier, by getting up early, I know it is not so; because I have got up early in the station-house many and many a time, and got poorer and poorer for the next half a day, in consequence, instead of richer and richer. And sometimes, on the same terms, I have seen the sun rise four times a week up there at Virginia, and so far from my growing healthier on account of it, I got to looking blue, and pulpy, and swelled, like a drowned man, and my relations grew alarmed and thought they were going to lose me. They entirely despaired of my recovery, at one time, and began to grieve for me as one whose days were numbered—whose fate was sealed—who was soon to pass away from them forever, and from the glad sunshine, and the birds, and the odorous flowers, and murmuring brooks, and whispering winds, and all the cheerful scenes of life, and go down into the dark and silent tomb—and they went forth sorrowing, and jumped a lot in the graveyard, and made up their minds to grin and bear it with that fortitude which is the true Christian's brightest ornament.
    You observe that I have put a stronger test on the matter than even Benjamin Franklin contemplated, and yet it would not work. Therefore, how is a man to grow healthier, and wealthier, and wiser by going to bed early and getting up early, when he fails to accomplish these things even when he does not go to bed at all? And as far as becoming wiser

is concerned, you might put all the wisdom I acquired in these experiments in your eye, without obstructing your vision any to speak of.

As I said before, my voice is with George Washington's on this question.

Another philosopher encourages the world to get up at sunrise because "it is the early bird that catches the worm."

It is a seductive proposition, and well calculated to trap the unsuspecting. But its attractions are all wasted on me, because I have no use for the worm. If I had, I would adopt the Unreliable's plan. He was much interested in this quaint proverb, and directed the powers of his great mind to its consideration for three or four consecutive hours. He was supposing a case. He was supposing, for instance, that he really wanted the worm—that the possession of the worm was actually necessary to his happiness—that he yearned for it and hankered after it, therefore, as much as a man *could* yearn for and hanker after a worm under such circumstances—and he was supposing, further, that he was opposed to getting up early in order to catch it (which was much the more plausible of the two suppositions). Well, at the end of three or four hours' profound meditation upon the subject, the Unreliable rose up and said: "If he were so anxious about the worm, and he couldn't get along without him, and he didn't want to get up early in the morning to catch him—why then, by George, he would just lay for him the night before." I never would have thought of that. I looked at the youth, and said to myself, he is malicious, and dishonest, and unhandsome, and does not smell good—yet how quickly do these trivial demerits disappear in the shadow, when the glare from this great intellect shines out above them![91]

About 1870 Mark Twain dealt once again with this "objectionable" proverb in a short essay with the ironic title "The Late Benjamin Franklin." Here he attacks Franklin for having "prostituted his talents to the invention of maxims and aphorisms calculated to inflict suffering upon the rising generation of all subsequent ages." Remembering his own childhood and how his father, and probably most parents, quoted "Poor Richard's" proverbs *ad nauseam,* Twain makes the following humorous yet telling remarks:

His maxims were full of animosity toward boys. Nowadays a boy cannot follow out a single natural instinct without tumbling over some of those everlasting aphorisms and hearing from Franklin on the spot. If he buys two cents' worth of peanuts, his father says, "Remember what Franklin has said, my son—'A groat a day's a penny a year' "; and the comfort is all gone out of those peanuts. If he wants to spin his top when he has done work, his father quotes, "Procrastination is the thief of time." If he does a virtuous action, he never gets anything for it, because "Virtue is its own reward." And that boy is hounded to death and robbed of his natural rest, because Franklin said once, in one of his inspired flights of malignity:

Early to bed and early to rise
Makes a man healthy and wealthy and wise.

As if it were any object to a boy to be healthy and wealthy and wise on such terms. The sorrow that that maxim has cost me, through my parents, experimenting on me with it, tongue cannot tell. The legitimate result is my present state of general debility, indigence, and mental aberration. My parents used to have me up before nine o'clock in the morning sometimes when I was a boy. If they had let me take my natural rest where would I have been now? Keeping store, no doubt, and respected by all.[92]

Twain makes plain here that proverbs can indeed have their negative side if they are applied as universal rules in an excessive fashion. Even a health proverb can lead to illness if adhered to too strictly. The proverb "Moderation in all things" obviously also applies to the use of proverbs.

Twain definitely had a dislike for this particular proverb. In his *A Tramp Abroad* (1880) he alludes to it again in connection with a humorous description of how tourist excursions to the Mont Blanc are organized: "The time employed is usually three days, and there is enough early rising in it to make a man far more 'healthy and wealthy and wise' than any one man has any right to be."[93] And two years later in a lecture on "Advice to Youth" delivered on April 15, 1882, in Boston he cites part of the proverb again and also plays ironically with the related proverb "Go to bed with the lamb, and rise with the lark":

> Go to bed early, get up early—this is wise. Some authorities say get up with the sun; some others say get up with one thing, some with another. But a lark is really the best thing to get up with. It gives you a splendid reputation with everybody to know that you get up with the lark; and if you get the right kind of a lark, and work at him right, you can easily train him to get up at half past nine, every time—it is no trick at all.[94]

There is no doubt that Mark Twain despised this proverb which he quite clearly thought to be Benjamin Franklin's own invention. His humorous paragraphs about the "ills" of early rising thus helped to keep Franklin's name attached to a proverb that actually predates him by at least one hundred years.

Turning to more modern literary references of the twentieth century, it will be noticed that the proverb appears quite often in its truncated form of "early to bed and early to rise," but the full-length text is also cited with some references to Franklin. A passage from George Dyre Eldridge's (1848–1928) detective novel *The Millbank Case* (1905) is in fact quite reminiscent of Twain's feeling about this proverb:

> On the night of the 10th of May, 1880, the light burned late in Lawyer Wing's library. It was the scandal of Millbank that this occurred often. The village was given to regarding the night as a time when no man should work. "Early to bed and early to rise" was its motto, and though an opposite practice had left Theodore Wing with more of health, wealth,

and wisdom than most Millbankians possessed, he had never succeeded in reconciling his townsmen to his methods. But to-night conditions were more outrageous than usual.[95]

In Mary N. Murfree's (1850–1922) novel *The Fair Mississippian* (1908) is yet another example of how this proverb does not have universal support or appeal. Here a rural character exclaims that " 'we don't keep reg'lar hours in the swamp, you see, like you cits do in Memphis,—early to bed and early to rise makes you-al so all-fired healthy, wealthy, and wise'."[96] Yet in the mystery novel *Suspected* (1920) by George Dilnot (1883–1951) one of the characters says in taking leave late in the evening: " 'Well, I must be off, Jack. Early to bed and early to rise, you know—well, so long'."[97] This formulaic "you know" identifies the statement as commonly shared proverbial wisdom, and it also explains why the speaker does not utter the entire proverb. Its general knowledge is simply and correctly assumed and thus makes the quotation of the entire lengthy proverb unnecessary.

Of special interest is the following reference from Joseph S. Fletcher's (1863–1935) mystery novel *Ravensdene Court* (1922) which, just as Mark Twain almost sixty years previously, connects the two proverbs "Early to bed and early to rise . . ." and "The early bird catches the worm." But there is, to be sure, quite a difference here since both proverbs are merely alluded to, leaving it up to the reader to fill in the actual proverbial texts:

> "Wise lad!" he said. "That's another reason why I'm what I am. Don't let any mistake be made about it!—the old saw, much despised and laughed at though it is, has more in it than anybody thinks for. Get to your pillow early, and leave it early!—that's the sure thing."
> "I don't think I should like to get up as early as you do, though," remarked Mr. Raven. "You certainly don't give the worms much chance!"
> "Aye, and I've caught a few in my time," assented the old gentleman, complacently. "And I hope to catch a few more yet. You folk who don't get up till the morning's half over don't know what you miss."[98]

One year later, in his *The Markenmore Mystery* (1923), Fletcher does use "the old saying" in its entirety but connects it, again as Twain had done about forty years earlier, with the proverb "Go to bed with the lamb, and rise with the lark":

> There was, indeed, an air of perpetual youth and freshness about Mr. Fransemmery: each spring seemed to find him younger than the last. People chaffed him about his juvenility; if he ever troubled himself to explain it, he did so by solemnly repeating the old saying—"Early to bed and early to rise makes a man healthy, wealthy, and wise." Mr. Fransemmery, since his arrival at The Warren, and his beginning of a truly rural existence, had always gone to bed at half-past nine o'clock and risen with the lark.[99]

Here the basic truth of the proverb is seriously maintained, and the same is true in Sinclair Lewis' (1885–1951) account of *The Man Who Knew Coolidge* (1917), where the narrator asserts the following: "I tell you there never was a truer saying than 'Early to bed, early to rise, makes a man healthy, wealthy, and wise'—I have certainly found it true in my own case."[100] The positive evaluation of the proverb is also evident in the short statement " 'Ah, my boy. Early to bed and early to rise! That's right. Good morning, good morning' "[101] in Henry C. Bailey's (1878–1961) *The Red Castle Mystery* (1932). The same is true with the observation that "All was very quiet. Hardly a soul was to be seen. Early to bed and early to rise was still a maxim generally observed in that part of England"[102] in *The Golf House Murder* (1933) by Herbert Adams (1874–1952). In Val Gielgud's (1900–1981) detective novel *The Ruse of the Vanished Women* (1934) there is a quite similar passage that has reduced the long proverb to a mere "early to bed," but the introductory formula identifying this mere remnant as an "old adage" assures its recognition as proverbial wisdom: "We drove into the village of Ilkley a little after ten o'clock. It was evident that its few inhabitants believed firmly in the old adage of early to bed, for it was dark and deserted."[103]

Such positive reaction to the old proverb, maxim, or adage is, however, by no means universal, and Mark Twain would certainly have agreed completely with some of the following "sacriligious" reinterpretations of master Franklin's proverb. The most famous one-liner parodies of the proverb are George Ade's (1866–1944) "Early to bed and early to rise and you won't meet many prominent people" and "Early to bed and early to rise / Will make you miss all the regular guys"[104] from around 1900. The former was included in slightly varied form as "Early to bed and early to rise and you never meet any prominent people"[105] in the poem "Good Morning, America" (1928) by Carl Sandburg (1878–1967), in which the author characterizes the American people of the twenties by their slang and proverbial language. In 1948 Cleveland Amory (b. 1917) cites the second slight variant "Early to bed and early to rise and you meet few prominent people" in his novel *The Last Resort,* attesting that Ade's "saying" had taken on a proverbial nature of itself.[106] The basic idea of Ade's proverb parody or anti-proverb is marvellously present in Groucho Marx's (1895–1977) autobiography *Groucho and Me* (1959) some fifty years later:

> They say that every man has a book in him. This is about as accurate as most generalizations. Take, for example, "Early to bed, early to rise, makes a man you-know-what." This is a lot of hoopla. Most wealthy people I know like to sleep late, and will fire the help if they are disturbed before three in the afternoon. Pray tell (I cribbed that from *Little Women*), who are the people who get up at the crack of dawn? Policemen, firemen, garbage collectors, bus drivers, department store clerks and others in the

lower income bracket. You don't see Marilyn Monroe getting up at six in the morning. The truth is, I don't see Marilyn Monroe getting up at any hour, more's the pity. I'm sure if you had your choice, you would rather watch Miss Monroe rise at three in the afternoon than watch the most efficient garbage collector in your town hop out of bed at six.[107]

Yet George Ade and Groucho Marx are not alone in their parodistic reaction to the rigid proverb. In one of his modern fables entitled "The Shrike and the Chipmunks" (1939), James Thurber (1894–1961) has two husband and wife chipmunks killed by a shrike. The end of this anti-fable states in typically proverbial fashion the newly found insight: "Moral: Early to rise and early to bed makes a male healthy and wealthy and dead."[108] Dorothy Parker (1893–1967) had already in 1936 played with the substitution of "wise" with "dead" in her humorous essay "The Little Hours." Following a short paragraph describing the fact that she has just woken up in the middle of the night and being upset about lying there awake, she goes into a proverbial tirade, twisting around also the well-known weather proverbs "Rain before seven, dry before eleven" and "Red sky at night, sailors' delight; Red sky at morning, sailors take warning":

> Yes, and you want to know what got me into this mess? Going to bed at ten o'clock, that's what. That spells ruin. T-e-n-space-o-apostrophe-c-l-o-c-k: ruin. Early to bed, and you'll wish you were dead. Bed before eleven, nuts before seven. Bed before morning, sailors give warning.[109]

Eugene Healy (b. 1912) in his mystery novel *Mr. Sandeman Loses His Life* (1940) has a character connect the first part of the proverb with the second part of another Anglo-American favorite, namely "All work and no play makes Jack a dull boy". The resulting text is a bit of innovative and funny "wisdom":

> Rocheleau strode across the room, shut the windows and turned the radiator valve.
> "You ought to be ashamed of yourself," he said, "lying in bed on a beautiful morning like this. Come on, get up out of there. You're disgusting. It's after eight."
> "Nonsense," Paul said, yawning luxuriously. "Do you think I'd be mad enough to get out of my warm bed at this cold, early hour just for the sake of a principle? Nope. I'm going to stay here till eleven, or twelve—or one, if I feel like it. Early to bed and early to rise makes Jack a dull boy." He pulled the covers snugly up about his chin and settled himself shamelessly in the bed's warmth.[110]

Throughout these proverb parodies one senses an obvious dislike of getting up early or going to bed at an early hour. It should, of course, also not be surprising to see people react critically to the time change that they have to deal with twice a year that appears to throw off their daily routine for a few days. Robertson Davies (b. 1913) wrote the following remarks concerning Daylight Saving Time in his *Diary of Samuel Marchbanks* (1947) that are once again reminiscent of Mark Twain's reaction to the proverb:

> Went cheerfully through the whole day without realizing that the usual haphazard tinkering with the clocks was in progress, and that I should have been enjoying the benefits of Daylight Saving Time. I don't really care how time is reckoned so long as there is some agreement about it, but I object to being told that I am saving daylight when my reason tells me that I am doing nothing of the kind. I even object to the implication that I am wasting something valuable if I stay in bed after the sun has risen. As an admirer of moonlight I resent the bossy insistence of those who want to reduce my time for enjoying it. At the back of the Daylight Saving scheme I detect the boney, blue-fingered hand of Puritanism, eager to push people into bed earlier, and get them up earlier, to make them healthy, wealthy and wise in spite of themselves.[111]

This concern over time changes is still an issue today, as can be seen from an article in the *Burlington Free Press* from January 5, 1974, with the appropriate headline "Early-bird Vermonters to Rise in Darkness as DST Resumes". While the headline clearly alludes to the proverb "The early bird catches the worm," the article itself cites the "early-to-bed, early-to-rise" proverb by also mentioning Franklin:

> Nobody was more serious about DST than Ben Franklin back in 1784. As U.S. ambassador to France, he was shocked by Paris shopkeepers' habit of opening late in the morning and staying open until long after dark.
>
> He calculated the French burned 96 million unnecessary candles, costing more than $1 million francs, in a year.
>
> His solution: a daily sunrise serenade of clanging church bells and booming cannons to "wake the sluggards and make them open their eyes."
>
> The French managed to survive without adopting Franklin's early-to-bed, early-to-rise advice.
>
> Now, almost 200 years later, Franklin's advice is heeded as a means of saving electric power. But nobody is that sure that it will.[112]

About a dozen years later a small report in *Time* from June 2, 1986, again described Franklin's thoughts concerning DST with its own very appropriate headline and clear reference to Benjamin Franklin:

> **Early to Bed, Early to Rise**
>
> Daylight saving time, first suggested by Benjamin Franklin in 1784 as a means of cutting down on candle consumption, is a proven conservator of another of Franklin's tinkering projects, namely electricity. But the

system also forces some early risers in the springtime to start their day in the dark: When best to make the twice-yearly time change?[113]

Such a statement in a national news magazine once again did its share in keeping Franklin's name attached to the proverb, even though the actual text does it in a rather indirect way. But there are, of course, much more direct modern references as, for example, Robert L. Fish's (b. 1912) mystery novel *Rub-a-dub-dub* (1971). Here one of the characters refuses to play a game of bridge due to the lateness of the hour: "I'm afraid that after dinner I'm scarcely at my best. Getting on, you know. Early to bed and early to rise, has some salubrious effect on a man, if I recall my Franklin correctly."[114]

Realizing that everybody knows the complete proverb in any case, Homer Nearing (b. 1915) reduced it to a lengthy hyphenated adjective in his description of a person as "an early-to-bed-early-to-rise guy"[115] in his novel *The Sinister Researches of C. P. Ransom* (1954). Margaret Scherf (1908–1979) in her novel *The Cautious Overshoes* (1956) describes someone by stating "you know how Harvey is—early to bed and early to rise gets the worm,"[116] thus once again linking these two popular proverbs into a statement that might just have the possibility to become a new proverb. Surprisingly enough there appears a character in Harry Carmichael's (Leopold Ognall, 1908–1979) novel *Too Late for Tears* (1975) who for once does not seem to know the proverb which is, however, also only being alluded to:

> Piper said, 'You should go to bed earlier and you wouldn't need to sleep during the day.'
> 'I was in bed last night earlier than I've been for months,' Quinn said. 'What's more, I was up early this morning. And it only succeeded in disproving the old adage.'
> 'Which one?'
> 'About early to bed and early to rise. With me it works in reverse. I feel lousy, I'm flat broke—and I'm no wiser about the Whittle affair than I was when I started.'[117]

Mere proverb allusions run the risk of not being understood, even if they refer to very common proverbs. Nevertheless, such lack of communication is rather rare among native speakers, and there certainly was no confusion possible in the case of a short gossipy column by Stanton Delaplane (1907–1988) in the *San Francisco Chronicle* of March 12, 1980, that mentions only part of the proverb in the title and more of it plus Benjamin Franklin in the text itself:

> **'And Early to Rise'**
>
> "Plough deep while sluggards sleep," said Benjamin Franklin. "Early to bed and early to rise."

> Ran into some of Ben's personal history the other night. He was in
> France doing a little work for the U.S. government. He was quite a dude
> with the Paris girls. "Early to bed and as often as possible," was Ben's
> motto.
> How he managed to get up early—with the routine he had going—is
> beyond me. He certainly gave the mademoiselles a vote of confidence.
> Didn't find out how well he did for the U.S.A.
> "Early to bed and early to rise" doesn't give you much leisure time.
> But some smart fellow has discovered that the "leisure class" no longer
> exists. The more money you have, the harder you have to work.
> I never figured to get out of work and into the leisure class. Now it
> seems I did the right thing. If I had made it, there's no leisure left.[118]

And nothing seems to have changed as far as the lack of leisure time is concerned in the capitalistic societies. A headline in the *Wall Street Journal* of
March 20, 1987, proves that Franklin's apocryphal proverb is as true for today's business executives as it was two hundred fifty years ago when Franklin
preached its wisdom to his contemporaries for their economic well-being:
"Early to Bed . . . The motto of Ben Franklin has become the M. O. of many
a chief executive."[119] More than ever before, serious business people must
make sure that they get a good night's rest by going to bed early and then
being true "early birds" in the morning to stay ahead of the competition. The
thrifty and industrious Benjamin Franklin would surely have been pleased to
see "his" motto of "Early to bed and early to rise, makes a man healthy,
wealthy and wise" become a treasured slogan of the business elite of the
United States. There must be some deep-rooted truth in this common-sense
proverb after all if business executives make its traditional wisdom their *mo-
dus operandi*.

In this respect it is of interest that the business world already in 1898
created the following slogan from the proverb to encourage merchants to
advertise their products:

To Succeed
Early to bed, early to rise,
Never get tight, and—advertise.[120]

This advertising slogan was also recorded a few years later as "Early to bed
and early to rise / Is no good unless you advertise."[121] Recently, on June 17,
1991, the magazine *Money* and the cereal producer *General Mills* joined forces
in an advertising page that included the large headline "Healthy, wealthy and
wise."[122] Eating whole grain "total" cereal and reading *Money* will obviously
make you healthy and wealthy, and you will also gain in wisdom about food
and prosperity. That at least must have been the thoughts of the advertisers
when they put this particular advertisement together. The modern world would,

"Remember this: early to bed, early to rise, work like hell and computerise."

of course, not argue that advertising is the only way to have success in business. It would also push the computer on people, since it facilitates accounting procedures. One might even argue that today's work ethic is best expressed in the way a father lectures his son in a *Punch* cartoon from 1989: "Remember this: early to bed, early to rise, work like hell and computerise."[123] The modern term "computerize" does not only end with the same sound as the old "wise," thus clearly indicating that this is an effective adaptation of the traditional proverb, it also equates the technological computer with wisdom. One only wonders what will become of the important aspect of health in a world of stress and competition! In any case, imagine being awakened in the morning by the chambermaid exclaiming, "Early to bed and early to rise—or the boss'll promote the other guys . . . ,"[124] which was the caption of a 1959 cartoon in *The Boston Herald?*

What follows is a small sample of other parodies of this traditional proverb that have been collected over the years. The frequent quotation of this proverb has led people to react with humor or satire to its solid-work-ethics ideal, and these parodies or anti-proverbs[125] clearly express some sort of wisdom as well:

1927   Late to bed and late to rise,
      That's the way of the college guys.

1935   Early to bed, early to rise
      And your girl goes out with the other guys.

1942   Late to bed, late to rise,
      who in the hell wants to be wise? [126]

1943   Early to bed and early to rise
      makes a man a farmer. [127]

1955   Early to bed, early to rise,
      makes a man healthy, wealthy, and horny. [128]

1958   Early to bed, early to rise,
      While your date goes out with the other guys. [129]

1965   Early to bed, early to rise:
      dull isn't it? [130]

1966   Early to bed and early to rise
      makes a man tired.

1966   Early to bed and early to rise
      makes a man not watch TV. [131]

1967   Early to bed and early to rise
      —and your gal goes out with other guys.
      —doesn't make a girl a friend of the guys.
      —and it probably means your TV set is being repaired.
      —and it's a sure sign that you don't care for the Late, Late Shows.
      —and your neighbors will wonder why you can't get a job with better hours.
      —and you'll miss some of the most interesting people.
      —and you'll remain an unskilled employee.
      —and you'll never see red in the whites of your eyes.
      —makes you healthy, but socially a washout. [132]

1967   Late to bed and early to rise,
      —and you'll have dark rings under your eyes.
      —and your head will feel five times its size. [133]

1967   Early to bed and early to rise
      makes a poor bridge player. [134]

1969   Early to bed and early to rise,
      And you wake up with a family of a pretty big size. [135]

1974   Late to bed and early to rise
      makes a man tired by afternoon. [136]

1976   Early to bed and early to rise
      makes sure you get out before her husband arrives. [137]

1976   Early to bed and early to rise
      gives a guy reason for hiding his eyes. [138]

1980   If you're not interested in being healthy, wealthy, and wise—how
        about early to bed?[139]

Some of these parodies, including the last one which served as a suggestive
birthday card message, are clearly sexual and at times chauvinistic. Considering the linguistic awareness of sexism in everyday language, it should not
be surprising that there is some objection to the gender-specific noun "man"
in the traditional proverb. Women have reacted to the male dominance and
the misogyny in proverbs in recent years,[140] but it might come as a pleasant
surprise to find the "man" replaced by "woman" as early as 1880 in a short
humorous verse:

> Early to bed and early to rise
> Makes *woman* healthy, wealthy, and wise.
> Live while you live, and live to grow old,
> And so keep the doctor from getting your gold,
> And the sexton from putting you under the mould.[141]

From 1969 stems the variant "Early to bed, early to rise, makes a girl healthy,
wealthy and wise,"[142] yet the term "girl" is not at all acceptable to feminists
at the present time. The way to go is without doubt to cite the old proverb
as "Early to bed and early to rise, makes you healthy, wealthy and wise"[143]
as Stephen Vizinczey (b. 1933) did in his book *In Praise of Older Women* (1965).

Another gender-free possibility would be to replace "man" by "person," as it was recorded from an informant in 1986 in California: "Early to bed, early to rise, makes a person healthy, wealthy, and wise."[144]

But it will take time until these changes will in fact be accepted by large numbers of the population in the English-speaking world. Most of the parodies cited, perhaps with the exception of George Ade's "Early to bed and early to rise and you won't meet many prominent people," will certainly not become proverbial in their own right. The fact that such parodies in the form of anti-proverbs[145] exist at all is ample proof that the traditional proverb is still very much present and valid. A wonderful example of how people to this day are surrounded by this proverbial wisdom can be seen from a Hager comic strip from 1985 that presents a number of proverbs that argue for getting up early and then creates a new text in order to avoid rising that early: " 'Up and at 'em, Tiger'—'The early bird gets the worm'—'Up sluggard, and waste not life'—'Early to bed and early to rise makes a man healthy, wealthy and wise'—'He who gets up early is a blooming fool'—'I knew if I tried long enough I'd find one I liked'."[146] That last self-rationalizing invented pseudo-proverb won't do the "trick" unfortunately—everybody confronted by this comic strip knows that. There is not much or at least only a temporary chance of escaping the inevitability of proverbs. It is one thing to poke fun of proverbs, to parody them or to argue against them with biting satire, but a complete escape from or utter denunciation of the age-old wisdom expressed in them is simply not possible. Benjamin Franklin knew this only too well when he drew on the traditional proverb stock of the English language to instruct his colonial Americans with their wisdom in his many volumes of *Poor Richard's Almanack*. He invented or coined barely any proverbs, but he popularized them to such an extent that some of them, notably the proverb "Early to bed and early to rise, makes a man healthy, wealthy and wise," came to

Reprinted with special permission of King Features Syndicate.

be attached to his name especially in the mind of Americans.[147] Yet even this apocryphal identification of the proverb with Benjamin Franklin is starting to be forgotten as the general level of cultural literacy appears to be declining, and the proverb is once again becoming a piece of true folk wisdom attached to no individual person. Benjamin Franklin as "coiner" of the proverb was thus but a mere interlude in the history of this proverb about health, wealth, and wisdom. It was, therefore, quite appropriate that a traditional embroidery sampler[148] of the proverb from 1977 did not attach the name of Benjamin Franklin to it but rather let the proverb speak for itself with proper anonymity:

> Early to Bed,
> Early to Rise,
>   Makes a Man
> Healthy, Wealthy
>   and Wise.

Notes

1. David Lord, "The Truths and the Myths about Ben Franklin," *The Old Farmer's Almanac for the Year 1990,* ed. by Robert B. Thomas. Dublin, N.H.: Yankee Publishing Inc., 1989, pp. 44–47.

2. See Thomas Herbert Russell (ed.), *The Sayings of Poor Richard. Wit, Wisdom, and Humor of Benjamin Franklin in the Proverbs and Maxims of Poor Richard's Almanacks for 1733 to 1758*. Chicago: Veterans of Foreign Wars of the United States, 1926; Carl van Doren, *Benjamin Franklin*. New York: The Viking Press, 1938, esp. pp. 106–115, 149–150, and 266–268; Richard E. Amacher, " 'Poor Richard's Almanack'," in R. E. Amacher, *Benjamin Franklin*. New York: Twayne Publishers, 1962, pp. 51–66; and James A. Sappenfield, " 'Poor Richard's Almanac [sic]," in J. A. Sappenfield, *A Sweet Instruction. Franklin's Journalism as a Literay Apprenticeship*. Carbondale: Southern Illinois University Press, 1973, pp. 121–177 and 221–223 (notes).

3. See F. Edward Hulme, *Proverb Lore*. London: Elliot Stock, 1902; rpt. Detroit: Gale Research Co., 1968, pp. 62–64; Charles Meister, "Franklin as a Proverb Stylist," *American Literature*, 24 (1952–1953), 157–166; Frances M. Barbour, *A Concordance to the Sayings in Franklin's "Poor Richard."* Detroit: Gale Research Co., 1974; and Wolfgang Mieder, "Benjamin Franklin's 'Proverbs'," in W. Mieder, *American Proverbs: A Study of Texts and Contexts*. Bern: Peter Lang, 1989, pp. 129–142.

4. *The Complete Poor Richard Almanacks published by Benjamin Franklin*. Reproduced in facsimile with an introduction by Whitfield J. Bell. Barre, Mass.: Imprint Society, 1970, vol. 1, p. 64.

5. See E. D. Hirsch, Joseph F. Kett, and James Trefil (eds.), *The Dictionary of Cultural Literacy*. Boston: Houghton Mifflin Co., 1988, p. 49.

6. See John Bartlett, *Familiar Quotations*, ed. by Emily Morison Beck. 15th ed. Boston: Little, Brown and Co., 1980, p. 347.

7. See John Bartlett, *Familiar Quotations*, no eds. given. 13th ed. Boston: Little, Brown and Co., 1955, p. 330. See also p. 421 of the 14th ed. from 1968, where Emily Morison Beck as editor must have made the decision to drop the significant reference to John Clarke.

8. The student collector was Lorrie Behrhorst, who remembered her grandfather Paul Schorr making this statement to her in 1967. She recorded it for the Berkeley Folklore Archive on November 13, 1979, in Berkeley, California. I would like to thank Alan Dundes from the University of California at Berkeley for making these archival materials available to me.

9. Melissa Davis collected this statement from her husband Richard Davis on October 30, 1977, in Albany, California.

10. Michael Lobo collected the proverb and this comment from Krista Lobo on November 26, 1976, in Oakland, California.

11. Jane Franklin collected this statement from Susan Belloni on March 8, 1969, in Berkeley, California.

12. Kathleen Mossi collected the proverb from Kathleen St. John who had heard it spoken by her father on November 7, 1978, in Berkeley, California.

13. Cited from *The Works of Benjamin Franklin*, ed. by Jared Sparks. Philadelphia: Childs & Peterson, 1840, vol. 2, p. 92.

14. *Ibid.*, p. 103.

15. *A Treatyse of Fysshynge wyth an Angle*, by Dame Juliana Berners. Being a Facsimile reproduction of the first book on the subject of fishing printed in England by Wynkyn de Worde at Westminster in 1496. With an introduction by M. G. Watkins. London: Elliot Stock, 1880, p. hi[a].

16. Anthony Fitzherbert, *The Book of Husbandry*. Reprinted from the edition of 1534 (1st ed. 1523) and edited by Walter W. Skeat. London: Trübner & Co., 1882, p. 101 (no. 149).

17. See F. C. Birkbeck Terry, " 'Early to bed'," *Notes and Queries*, 6th series, 7 (February 17, 1883), 128; Ed. Marshall, " 'Early to bed'," *Notes and Queries*, 6th series, 7 (June 2, 1883), 438; Robert Pierpoint, "Latin Quotation," 8th series, 12 (September 25, 1897), 248; and Terry and Marshall, "Latin Quotation," *Notes and Queries*, 8th series, 12 (October 23, 1897), 336.

18. See Hans Walther, *Proverbia sententiaeque latinitatis medii aevis.* Göttingen: Vandenhoeck & Ruprecht, 1966, vol. 4, p. 706 (no. 27470). See also vol. 1 (1963), p. 743 (no. 6031).

19. *Ibid.,* vol. 1, p. xxx.

20. See Archer Taylor, *The Proverb.* Cambridge: Harvard University Press, 1931; rpt. with an introduction and bibliography by Wolfgang Mieder. Bern: Peter Lang, 1985, pp. 43–52.

21. Cited out of *The Babees Book,* ed. by Frederick J. Furnivall. London: N. Trübner & Co., 1868, p. 72 (lines 57–60).

22. Cited from William Carew Hazlitt (ed.), *Inedited Tracts: Illustrating the Manners, Opinions, and Occupations of Englishmen during the Sixteenth and Seventeenth Centuries.* London: Roxburghe Library, 1868, p. 121.

23. William Shakespeare, *Twelfth Night,* ed. by J. M. Lothian and T. W. Craik. London: Methuen & Co., 1975, pp. 42–43 (Act II, scene 3).

24. *Ibid.,* p. 43 (note). See also Walther (note 18 above), vol. 7 (1982), p. 599 (no. 34318). The proverb is also included as " 'Diluculo surgere saluberrimum est'.—Early rising is most conducive to health" in Alfred Henderson, *Latin Proverbs and Quotations.* London: Sampson Low, Son, and Marston, 1869, p. 86. Henderson also cites the proverb "Early to bed, and early to rise, / Make a man healthy, wealthy, and wise" in this connection but without giving its Latin source. The same type of reference can be found in Sir John Sinclair, *The Code of Health and Longevity.* Edinburgh: Constable & Co., 1807, vol. 1, p. 732 (note).

25. Thomas Heywood, *How a Man May Choose a Good Wife from a Bad.* Facsimile edition. Edinburgh: Tudor Facsimile Texts, 1912, no pp. given.

26. Thomas Heywood, *The Royal King, and Loyal Subject / A Woman Killed with Kindness. Two Plays,* ed. by J. Payne Collier. London: Shakespeare Society, 1850, pp. 76–77 (Act V).

27. Thomas Draxe, *Bibliotheca Scholastica Instructissima.* London: Ioann Billius, 1616; rpt. Norwood, N.J.: Walter J. Johnson, 1976, p. 134.

28. John Clarke, *Paroemiologia Anglo-Latina in usum scholarum concinnata. Or Proverbs English, and Latine.* London: Felix Kyngston, 1639, p. 91.

29. James Howell, *Paroimiografia. Proverbs, or, Old Sayed Savves & Adages in English (or the Saxon Toung) Italian, French and Spanish wereunto the British, for their great Antiquity, and weight are added.* London: J. G., 1659, p. 4. In the French section "Proverbes et dictons en la langue françoise / Proverbs and common Sayings in the French Toung" Howell also cites "Homme matineux sain & soigneux / An early riser is healthy and careful" (p. 12). The similar text based on a triadic enumeration "Homme matineux sain, alaigre, & soigneux / An earlie man is buxome, healthfull, carefull" had previously been included in Randle Cotgrave, *A Dictionarie of the French and English Tongves.* London: Adam Flip, 1611; rpt. New York: Da Capo Press, 1971, p. Fffiv[a].

30. Robert Newcomb, *The Sources of Benjamin Franklin's Sayings of Poor Richard.* Diss. University of Maryland, 1957, pp. 52–53. Franklin's indebtedness to Howell is discussed on pp. 50–65. This valuable dissertation includes an annotated list of all the proverbs contained in the almanacs.

31. Thomas Fuller, *Gnomologia: Adagies and Proverbs; Wise Sentences and Witty Sayings, Ancient and Modern, Foreign and British.* London: B. Barker, 1732, no. 6080. For a discussion of Franklin's use of Fuller see Newcomb (note 30), pp. 65–80. For the proverb "Early to bed . . ." see p. 262.

32. John Ray, *A Compleat Collection of English Proverbs.* 4th ed. London: W. Otridge, 1768, p. 30.

33. Robert Codrington, *A Collection of Many Select, and Excellent Proverbs out of Several Languages.* London: S. and B. Griffin, 1672 (1st ed. London: W. Lee, 1664), p. 13 (no. 273).

34. Henry G. Bohn, *A Hand-Book of Proverbs.* London: H. G. Bohn, 1855, p. 29 (same wording in index on p. 347).

35. Henry G. Bohn, *A Polyglot of Foreign Proverbs*. London: H. G. Bohn, 1857; rpt. Detroit: Gale Research Co., 1968, p. 148. The German paremiographers have also added the English text as a parallel to this German proverb; see Wilhelm Körte, *Die Sprichwörter und sprichwörtlichen Redensarten der Deutschen*. Leipzig: F. A. Brockhaus, 1837; rpt. Hildesheim: Georg Olms, 1974, p. 44 (no. 577) and p. 121 (no. 1635); and Karl Friedrich Wilhelm Wander, *Deutsches Sprichwörter-Lexikon*. Leipzig: F. A. Brockhaus, 1867; rpt. Darmstadt: Wissenschaftliche Buchgesellschaft, 1974, vol. 1, col. 1237 (no. 12).

36. John W. Barber, *The Hand Book of Illustrated Proverbs*. New York: George F. Tuttle, 1856, p. 158.

37. William Carew Hazlitt, *English Proverbs and Proverbial Phrases*. London: Reeves and Turner, 1869; rpt. Detroit: Gale Research Co., 1969, p. 135. Citing *Health of Servingmen* (1598) and Clarke as the earliest sources.

38. Vincent Stuckey Lean, *Lean's Collectanea*. Bristol: J. W. Arrowsmith, 1903; rpt. Detroit: Gale Research Co., 1969, vol. 2, p. 733. Also citing Fitzherbert and Clarke.

39. Dwight Edwards Marvin, *Curiosities in Proverbs*. New York: G. P. Putnam's Sons, 1916; rpt. Darby, Pa.: Folcroft Library Editions, 1980, vol. 2, p. 221. Referring especially to Benjamin Franklin but pointing to the sixteenth century as the first source.

40. G. L. Apperson, *English Proverbs and Proverbial Phrases. A Historical Dictionary*. London: J. M. Dent, 1929; rpt. Detroit: Gale Research Co., 1969, p. 173. Referring to Fitzherbert, Rhodes, Ray, and Franklin.

41. Burton Stevenson, *The Home Book of Proverbs, Maxims, & Famous Phrases*. New York: Macmillan, 1948, p. 1995 (no. 7). References from Fitzherbert, Clarke, Ray, and Franklin. Stevenson also cites a few modern variants and parodies.

42. Morris Palmer Tilley, *A Dictionary of the Proverbs in England in the Sixteenth and Seventeenth Centuries*. Ann Arbor/Michigan: University of Michigan Press, 1950, p. 36 (B184). Valuable citations from Fitzherbert, Rhodes, Berners, Heywood, Cotgrave, Draxe, Clarke, Howell, Codrington, Ray, Fuller, and Franklin.

43. Archer Taylor and Bartlett Jere Whiting, *A Dictionary of American Proverbs and Proverbial Phrases, 1820–1880*. Cambridge, Mass.: Harvard University Press, 1958, p. 21 (no. 1). Literary references from Cooper, Porter, Haliburton, Melville, and Twain.

44. Bartlett Jere Whiting, *Proverbs, Sentences, and Proverbial Phrases from English Writings Mainly before 1500*. Cambridge, Mass.: Harvard University Press, 1968, p. 489 (R143). Early reference from Berners.

45. F. P. Wilson, *The Oxford Dictionary of English Proverbs*. 3rd ed. Oxford: Clarendon Press, 1970, p. 211. With citations from Berners, Fitzherbert, Shakespeare, Heywood, Clarke. *Goody Two-Shoes*, and Surtees.

46. Bartlett Jere Whiting, *Early American Proverbs and Proverbial Phrases*. Cambridge: Harvard University Press, 1977, p. 24 (B98). Citations from Saffin, Franklin, and Curwen.

47. John A. Simpson, *The Concise Oxford Dictionary of Proverbs*. Oxford: Oxford University Press, 1982, p. 62. Citing references from Berners, Fitzherbert, Clarke, Surtees, and Wiseman.

48. Wolfgang Mieder, *The Prentice-Hall Encyclopedia of World Proverbs*. Englewood Cliffs, N. J.: Prentice-Hall, 1986, p. 24 (no. 744). Registering the proverb as being of English origin.

49. Bartlett Jere Whiting, *Modern Proverbs and Proverbial Sayings*. Cambridge: Harvard University Press, 1989, p. 37 (B135). Twentieth-century literary references from Eldridge, Dilnot, Fletcher, Adams, Gielgud, Healy, Davies, Amory, Nearing, Scherf, Marx, Vizinczey, Fish, and Carmichael.

50. Wolfgang Mieder, Stewart Kingsbury, and Kelsie Harder (eds.), *A Dictionary of American Proverbs*. New York: Oxford University Press, 1992, p. 42 (no. 3). Citing Berners and Saffin as earliest English and American sources respectively.

51. J. Gilchrist Lawson, *The World's Best Proverbs and Maxims*. New York: Grosset & Dunlap, 1926, p. 97.

52. Ronald Ridout and Clifford Witting, *English Proverbs Explained.* London: Heinemann Educational Books, 1967, p. 57.

53. Maryjane Hooper Tonn (ed.), *Proverbs to Live By.* Milwaukee, Wis.: Ideals Publishing Corp., 1977, p. 64.

54. Anonymous, *Ben Franklin's Wit & Wisdom.* White Plains, N.Y.: Peter Pauper Press, 1960, p. 41.

55. See John Bartlett, *A Collection of Familiar Quotations.* Cambridge, Mass.: John Bartlett, 1855. Facsimile edition. New York: Philosophical Library, 1958, p. 252.

56. See John Bartlett, *A Collection of Familiar Quotations.* New edition [i.e., 2nd ed.]. Cambridge, Mass.: John Bartlett, 1856, p. 298.

57. The third to sixth editions of Bartlett's *Familiar Quotations* were not available to me. However, the seventh edition of 1879 clearly cites Clarke and Franklin as references (see p. 667).

58. John Keitges, *Proverbs and Quotations for School and Home.* Chicago: A. Flanagan, 1905, p. 47.

59. Marshall Brown, *Sayings that Never Grow Old. Wit and Humor of Well-Known Quotations.* Boston: Small, Maynard & Co., 1918, p. 94.

60. Tryon Edwards, *Useful Quotations. A Cyclopedia of Quotations.* New York: Grosset & Dunlap, 1936, p. 41.

61. Theodore B. Backer, *A Compact Anthology of Bartlett's Quotations.* Middle Village, N.Y.: Jonathan David Publishers, 1974, p. 53. It is, of course, exactly such a popularized collection of quotations that reaches the average reader.

62. Gorton Carruth and Eugene Ehrlich, *The Harper Book of American Quotations.* New York: Harper & Row, 1988, p. 31.

63. Burton Stevenson, *The Home Book of Quotations.* 5th ed. New York: Dodd, Mead & Co., 1947 (1st ed. 1934), p. 872 (no. 4). For a much more detailed and scholarly treatise of this proverb by Stevenson see note 41.

64. Bergen Evans, *Dictionary of Quotations.* New York: Avenel Books, 1968, p. 51 (no. 21).

65. David C. Browning, *Dictionary of Quotations and Proverbs.* London: Dent, 1951; rpt. London: Octopus Books, 1982, p. 367 (no. 83).

66. H. L. Mencken, *A New Dictionary of Quotations on Historical Principles.* New York: Alfred A. Knopf, 1960, p. 1045.

67. W. Gurney Benham, *Putnam's Complete Book of Quotations.* New York: G. P. Putnam's Sons, 1926, p. 754.

68. John Daintith et al., *The Macmillan Dictionary of Quotations.* New York: Macmillan, 1987, p. 40 (no. 1).

69. The proverb appears on one of the pages for the month of February 1758. See Bell (note 4), vol. 2, p. 367 and p. 369.

70. For a detailed analysis of the source of each proverb in this essay see Stuart A. Gallacher, "Franklin's 'Way to Wealth': A Florilegium of Proverbs and Wise Sayings," *Journal of English and Germanic Philology,* 48 (1949), 229–251.

71. See Patrick Sullivan, "Benjamin Franklin, the Inveterate (and Crafty) Public Instructor: Instruction on Two Levels in 'The Way to Wealth'," *Early American Literature,* 21 (1986–1987), 250 (the whole essay on pp. 248–259). See also Edward J. Gallagher, "The Rhetorical Strategy of Franklin's 'Way to Wealth'," *Eighteenth-Century Studies,* 6 (1973), 475–485; and Thomas J. Steele, "Orality and Literacy in Matter and Form: Ben Franklin's 'Way to Wealth'," *Oral Tradition,* 2 (1987), 273–285.

72. Wander (see note 35), vol. 1, col. 1237 (no. 14). A number of German variants of this proverb were also listed together with an English reference from Franklin's "Way to Wealth" in the "Bartlett" of the German language; see Georg Büchmann, *Geflügelte Worte.* 5th ed. Berlin: Haude & Spener, 1868, p. 110. It was dropped from inclusion as of the 28th ed. (1937).

73. For studies on this proverb see Richard Jente, " 'Morgenstunde hat Gold im Munde'," *Publications of the Modern Language Association*, 42 (1927), 865–872; and Wolfgang Mieder, "Rund um das Sprichwort 'Morgenstunde hat Gold im Munde'," *Muttersprache*, 88 (1978), 378–385.

74. Cited from *The Writings of Benjamin Franklin*, ed. by Albert Henry Smyth. New York: Macmillan, 1906, vol. 7, pp. 381–382 (letter no. 1043 to Edward Bridgen).

75. John Saffin, *His Book (1665–1708)*, ed. by Caroline Hazard. New York: Harbor Press, 1928, p. 187.

76. *The Journal of Samuel Curwen, Loyalist*, ed. by Andrew Oliver. Cambridge: Harvard University Press, 1972, vol. 2, p. 804.

77. Regarding the interpretation of this saying as a medical proverb see Helmut A. Seidl, "Health Proverbs in Britain and Bavaria: A Sampling of Parallels," in *Bavarica Anglica. A Cross-Cultural Miscellany Presented to Tom Fletcher*, ed. by Otto Hietsch. Bern: Peter Lang, 1979, pp. 71–97 (esp. pp. 82–83); H. Seidl, *Medizinische Sprichwörter im Englischen und Deutschen*. Bern: Peter Lang, 1982, esp. pp. 145–148; and Wolfgang Mieder, " 'An Apple a Day Keeps the Doctor Away': Traditional and Modern Aspects of English Medical Proverbs," *Proverbium: Yearbook of International Proverb Scholarship*, 8 (1991), 77–106 (esp. pp. 85–92).

78. Paula Beatty collected this statement from Gordon Ansley on February 29, 1974, in Mountain View, California.

79. Meredith Pike recorded this information from her mother Jane Pike on March 8, 1969, in Kentfield, California.

80. Ida Nishimura solicited this information from Jane Tsujimoto on November 18, 1974, in Berkeley, California.

81. Mary L. von Rotz recorded these personal thoughts on October 1, 1984, in Walnut Creek, California.

82. Dawn Ide expressed this interpretation of the proverb on July 6, 1971, in Lafayette, California.

83. *Goody Two-Shoes*. A facsimile reproduction of the edition of 1766, ed. by Charles Welsh. London: Griffith & Farran, 1881, p. 76.

84. *The Annotated Mother Goose*, ed. by William and Ceil Baring-Gould. New York: Bramhall, 1962, pp. 290–291 (no. 780).

85. Herman Melville, *Moby Dick or, The Whale*, ed. by Luther S. Mansfield and Howard P. Vincent. New York: Hendricks House, 1962, p. 17 (chapter III: "The Spouter-Inn").

86. Robert Smith Surtees, *Mr. Sponge's Sporting Tour*. London: Bradbury, Agnew & Co., 1892, p. 41.

87. Cedric Oldacre (John W. Warter), *The Last of the Old Squires*. London: Longman, Brown, Green, and Longmans, 1854, p. 60.

88. Kam Chuam Aik, *Dictionary of Proverbs*. Singapore: Federal Publications, 1988, p. 60.

89. Thomas Chandler Haliburton, *The Season-Ticket*. London: Richard Bentley, 1860; rpt. Toronto: University of Toronto Press, 1978, p. 187. A "gallimaufry" is a "stew of various kinds of edibles, fish, flesh, fowl, and vegetables" (p. 186).

90. Eliza Cook, *The Poetical Works of Eliza Cook*. London: Frederick Warne, 1869, pp. 451–452.

91. Quoted from Mark Twain, *The Washoe Giant in San Francisco Being Heretofore Uncollected Sketches*, ed. by Franklin Waller. Norwood, Pa.: Norwood Editions, 1976, pp. 83–85.

92. Mark Twain, *Sketches New and Old*. New York: Harper & Brothers, 1917, pp. 188–190.

93. Mark Twain, *A Tramp Abroad*. New York: Harper & Brothers, 1907, vol. 2, p. 171.

94. Cited from *The Complete Essays of Mark Twain*, ed. by Charles Neider. Garden City, N.Y.: Doubleday 7 Co., 1963, p. 564.

95. George Dyre Eldridge, *The Millbank Case*. New York: Henry Holt and Co., 1905, p. 8.

96. Charles Egbert Craddock (pseud. Mary N. Murfree), *The Fair Mississippian*. Boston: Houghton Mifflin Co., 1908, p. 387.

97. George Dilnot, *Suspected*. New York: Edward J. Clode, 1920, pp. 153–154.

98. Joseph S. Fletcher, *Ravensdene Court*. New York: Alfred A. Knopf, 1922, p. 42.

99. Joseph S. Fletcher, *The Markenmore Mystery*. New York: Alfred A. Knopf, 1923, p. 47.

100. Sinclair Lewis, *The Man Who Knew Coolidge*. Freeport, N.Y.: Books for Libraries Press, 1971, pp. 51–52.

101. Henry C. Bailey, *The Red Castle Mystery*. Garden City, N.Y.: Doubleday, Doran & Co., 1932, p. 273. I thank my wife Dr. Barbara Mieder for locating this reference for me.

102. Herbert Adams, *The Golf House Murder*. New York: Walter J. Black, 1933, p. 276.

103. Val Gielgud, *The Ruse of the Vanished Women*. Garden City, N.Y.: Doubleday, Doran & Co., 1934, p. 155.

104. Cited from Evans (see note 64), p. 51 and p. 190. See also Stevenson (note 41), p. 1995 (no. 7). Despite much effort I have not been able to find their original publications and exact dates.

105. Carl Sandburg, *Complete Poems*. New York: Harcourt Brace Jovanovich, 1970, p. 330. See also Wolfgang Mieder, " 'Behold the Proverbs of a People': A Florilegium of Proverbs in Carl Sandburg's Poem 'Good Morning, America'," *Southern Folklore Quarterly*, 35 (1971), 160–168. There is a reference to George Ade in a footnote.

106. Cleveland Amory, *The Last Resort*. New York: Harper & Brothers, 1948, p. 475.

107. Groucho Marx, *Groucho and Me*. New York: Random House, 1959, p. 9.

108. James Thurber, *The Thurber Carnival*. New York: The Modern Library, 1945, pp. 254–255.

109. *The Portable Dorothy Parker*, ed. by Brendan Gill. New York: The Viking Press, 1973, p. 254.

110. Eugene Healy, *Mr. Sandeman Loses His Life*. New York: Henry Holt and Co., 1940, pp. 22–23.

111. Robertson Davies, *The Diary of Samuel Marchbanks*. Toronto: Clarke, Irwin & Co., 1947, p. 72.

112. *The Burlington Free Press* (January 5, 1974), p. 9.

113. *Time* (June 2, 1986), p. 27.

114. Robert L. Fish, *Rub-a-dub-dub. An Inner Sanction Mystery*. New York: Simon and Schuster, 1971, p. 41.

115. Homer Nearing, *The Sinister Researches of C. P. Ransom*. Garden City, N.Y.: Doubleday & Co., 1954, p. 188.

116. Margaret Scherf, *The Cautious Overshoes*. Garden City, N.Y.: Doubleday & Co., 1956, p. 29.

117. Harry Carmichael (Leopold H. Ognall), *Too Late for Tears*. New York: E. P. Dutton, 1975, p. 175.

118. *San Francisco Chronicle* (March 12, 1980), no pp. I owe this reference to Professor Alan Dundes.

119. *The Wall Street Journal* (March 20, 1987), p. 22D.

120. *Life*, 32, no. 833 (1898), p. 419.

121. Quotes from Lean (see note 38), vol. 2, p. 733.

122. Advertising insert in *The Burlington Free Press* from June 17, 1991. I owe this reference to my colleague Professor Dennis Mahoney.

123. *Punch* (January 13, 1989), p. 15.

124. *The Boston Herald* (January 2, 1959), p. 16.

125. See the chapter on "Proverb Parodies" in Mieder (note 3), pp. 239–275.

126. These three texts are cited from C. Grant Loomis, "Traditional American Wordplay: The Epigram and Perverted Proverb," *Western Folklore*, 8 (1949), 353.

127. Evan Esar, *Esar's Comic Dictionary*. New York: Harvest House, 1943, p. 88.

128. James G. Zander collected this from Thomas Nelson in July 1955 in Waubun, California. Nelson had heard this sexual parody as a student at the University of Minnesota.

129. Cited from a list of "Perverted Proverbs" from the UCLA Folklore Archives that were published anonymously in *Western Folklore*, 20 (1961), 200.

130. Cited from an anonymously published collection entitled "Parodied Proverbs from Idaho, *Western Folklore*, 24 (1965), 289–290.

131. These two texts are cited from George Monteiro, "Proverbs in the Re-Making," *Western Folklore*, 27 (1968), 128. These proverb parodies came about when the CBS television network program "Candid Camera" asked elementary school children from Long Island to complete proverbs to show that they really didn't know common proverbs. The children were given the truncated proverb "Early to bed and early to rise makes a man . . ."

132. This is an entire series of parodies that Louis A. Safian made up for his *Book of Updated Proverbs*. New York: Abelard-Schuman, 1967, pp. 32–33.

133. *Ibid.*, p. 33.

134. *Ibid.*, p. 46.

135. Kathleen Lorbier collected this sexual parody from Glen Seretan on March 9, 1969, in Berkeley, California.

136. Ann Patty collected this text from Patti Peterson on February 1, 1974, in Berkeley, California.

137. This parody is the caption of one of nine sexual cartoons by Rowland B. Wilson published with the title "Poor Rowland's Almanack. Proverbs for two hundred years after" in *Playboy* (July 1976), pp. 144–145.

138. This is the caption of a "B.C." cartoon that appeared in the *St. Louis Post Dispatch* (November 13, 1976), p. 4B.

139. This is the sexual message on a birthday card by Mark I Inc. (Chicago), purchased in November 1980 in Chicago.

140. See Wolfgang Mieder, "A Proverb a Day Keeps No Chauvinism Away," *Proverbium: Yearbook of International Proverb Scholarship*, 2 (1985), 273–277.

141. Quoted from R. H. Busk, "Early to Bed," *Notes and Queries*, 6th series, 8 (August 18, 1883), p. 136.

142. Marcia Mace collected this variant from Doris Petry on March 10, 1969, in Berkeley, California.

143. Stephen Vizinczey, *In Praise of Older Women*. London: Barrie and Rockliff, 1965, p. 107.

144. This variant was collected by Kenneth Israels from Robert Austin on November 27, 1986, in Antioch, California.

145. For a collection of 4500 such anti-proverbs in German see Wolfgang Mieder, *Antisprichwörter*. 3 vols. Wiesbaden: Gesellschaft für deutsche Sprache, 1982 and 1985; Wiesbaden: Quelle & Meyer, 1989.

146. *The Burlington Free Press* (June 9, 1985), comic section.

147. This false identification of the proverb with Benjamin Franklin was also carried on by folklore scholars. For example, Ray Browne in his article " 'The Wisdom of Many': Proverbs and Proverbial Expressions," in *Our Living Traditions. An Introduction to Folklore*, ed. by Tristram P. Coffin. New York: Basic Books, 1968, pp. 192–203, cites the proverb clearly as one "of Franklin's adages" (p. 200). Considering the popularity of this particular book, this statement did its share as well to spread misinformation among students of folklore. But Archer Taylor, the renowned American paremiologist, did point out in 1931 that the proverb goes back to a Latin proverb of the sixteenth century; see Taylor (note 20), p. 124.

148. The embroidery sampler is on the cover of my book on *American Proverbs* (see note 3) and was made by my wife Barbara Mieder in the summer of 1977.

6

"A Picture Is Worth a Thousand Words"

From Advertising Slogan to American Proverb

In Ivan Turgenev's (1818–1883) well-known novel *Otsy i deti* (*Fathers and Sons*, 1862) the geologist Eugenii Vasil'ich Bazarov is looking at a few drawings of the mountains in Saxony. When Anna Sergeevna Odintsova points out that he as a scientist could learn much more about these mountains from a book than these illustrations, Bazarov gives her the surprising answer "Risunok nagliado predstavit mne to, chto v knige izlozheno na tselykh desiati stranitsakh" (A picture shows me at a glance what it takes dozens of pages of a book to expound).[1] In other words, it is argued that a picture can in fact be worth more than numerous book pages. This is doubtlessly the case also for someone who has difficulty reading or who perhaps cannot read at all. An English proverb from around 1660 expresses this observation only too well as "Pictures are the books of the unlearned."[2] While these references claim that pictures can have a greater value than books, they can hardly be considered direct antecedents to the relatively new proverb "A (One) picture is worth a thousand words." Although the predominance of visual communication is stressed, the twentieth-century proverb does not contrast the picture with a book or the number of its pages. Instead it is based on an easily recognizable structure of one picture having the value of a thousand words, a typically proverbial exaggeration to emphasize the discrepancy between visual and verbal communication.

Modern psychological research on perception has shown that the message of this proverb is only too true in light of such visual mass media as television, videos, photographs, advertisements, cartoons, comics, and so on. We communicate more and more through pictures—a fine example being the signs in international airports for foreign travelers—and there is no doubt that imagery often precedes any verbal process.[3] Alan Dundes, in a fascinating study on this "primacy of vision in American culture,"[4] has argued convincingly that "Americans have a deep-seated penchant for the visual sense" since "for Americans the universe is essentially something they can draw a picture or diagram of."[5] Dundes supports this claim by referring to several proverbs and proverbial expressions that reflect this visual metaphorical attitude; his prime example is the proverb "Seeing is believing" that has a particularly high frequency in American speech.[6] While this proverb dates back to at least the year 1609 in England, it is surprising that Dundes does not cite the American proverb "A picture is worth a thousand words" to support his thesis of the visualization of American culture. Realizing the growing preference for visual communication in American society, a strong case could certainly be made that the proverb "A picture is worth a thousand words" had to originate in this country. The fact that it has gained considerable currency since about 1975 as a loan translation in the German language is yet another convincing indication of America's cultural predominance in the Western world where visual media are steadily gaining on the written and even oral word.[7]

The coiner of the proverb "A picture is worth a thousand words" certainly had an acute knowledge of this shift toward imagery of many kinds. But the insight needed a "catchy" wording and structure in order to gain proverbial currency. The actual structural pattern was definitely not invented by the person who so successfully formulated this new text. There exists a well defined international proverb structure of "a, one: hundred, thousand" as can be seen from such texts as "A friend is better than a thousand silver pieces" (Greek), "One good head is better than a hundred strong hands" (English), "A moment is worth a thousand gold pieces" (Korean), "A single penny fairly got is worth a thousand that are not" (German), and "Silence is worth a thousand pieces of silver" (Burmese).[8] Of particular significance might be the proverb "One deed is worth a thousand speeches" which Bartlett Jere Whiting includes in his important collection of *Early American Proverbs and Proverbial Phrases* with only one reference from the year 1767.[9] The "thousand speeches" could easily be changed into "thousand words" and the active "deed" became quite simply the visual "picture." However, the proverb was not included in a proverb collection until 1977, and by that time our proverb had already gained a considerable age itself. It is doubtful that this rather uncommon text served as a direct basis for the new proverb since it never achieved general currency.

To complicate matters a bit more, we must also mention such proverbs as "One laugh is worth a thousand groans," "One good deed is worth a hundred promises," "A smile is worth a million dollars," and "One smile is worth a thousand tears" that were all collected in oral use in the United States in the 1940s and 1950s and have recently been published in the *Dictionary of American Proverbs* edited by Stewart Kingsbury, Kelsie Harder, and Wolfgang Mieder.[10] No matter whether or not any of these texts were already current when "A picture is worth a thousand words" was formulated, they clearly illustrate the widespread use of the proverbial structure "a, one: hundred, thousand." That being the case, it only took a keen mind to come up with a new text (wording) that caught on quickly since it reflected the growing visualization of our culture and its worldview.

Although the actual coiner of a proverb is rarely known, in this case the lexicographer Burton Stevenson not only succeeded in 1948 in locating the individual himself, but also pinpointed the precise date of its first printed version.[11] He had discovered the original text "One look is worth a thousand words" in the American advertising journal *Printers' Ink* of 8 December 1921. There the National Advertising Manager Fred R. Barnard of the Street Railways Advertising Company had published a two-page advertisement with the headline "One Look Is Worth a Thousand Words." The dry explanatory text, *without* a picture, is an early plea for the desirability of including pictures in effective advertisements:

> ### *"One Look Is Worth a Thousand Words"*
>
> So said a famous Japanese philosopher, and he was right—nearly everyone likes to read pictures.
>
> "Buttersweet is Good to Eat" is a very short phrase but it will sell more goods if presented, with an appetizing picture of the product, to many people morning, noon and night, every day in the year, than a thousand word advertisement placed before the same number of people only a limited number of times during the year.
>
> Good advertising for a trade marked product is nothing more nor less than the delivery of favorable impressions [pictures] for it, and it does not make any difference whether they are delivered through newspapers, magazines or street car advertising. . . . It is simply the preponderance of favorable impressions [pictures] for a meritorious product that reminds the consumer to buy it again and again.[12]

From a modern point of view this advertisement is absolutely boring and the fact that a picture is missing makes matters even worse. But that is exactly the purpose of these two pages of text, for Barnard, the shrewd advertising executive, argues innovatively and convincingly that successful advertising is in fact only possible through pictures. How correct he was can be *seen* in almost all the advertisements that are produced today based on this marketing philosophy and surely also on yet another new American proverb "What you see is what you get."

About six years later Fred Barnard repeated his conviction in another two-page advertisement in *Printers' Ink* of 10 March 1927. This time, however, he also included a picture of the happy little boy Bobby, who is looking forward to a piece of cake his mother has baked with "Royal" baking powder. The picture of the boy, the cake and the can of baking powder result in an effective visual advertising message:

> **"Make a Cake for Bobby"**
> —that's what this car card said *every day* to many millions of women. It reminded all mothers *every day* of a sure way to give a treat to their own children. And hundreds of thousands got an extra thrill with their next cake making because of the happy expression of the boy on the car card.[13]

In addition Barnard also included a small illustration of six Chinese characters which represent a direct translation of the English caption that is provided: "Chinese Proverb: One picture is worth ten thousand words."

Quite obviously Barnard knew about the growing use of proverbs as advertising slogans since they express a message (or truth) with a certain claim of traditional authority and wisdom.[14] It is of interest that Barnard changed his earlier formulation "One look is worth a thousand words" to "One picture is worth ten thousand words." The use of the word "picture" expresses even more precisely the idea that the viewer of an advertisement should react with a mere "look" (glance) at a catchy and somewhat informative picture. The visualization of the advertising message is of utmost importance, and that is why Barnard changed his original text to the picture that is worth "ten thousand" words.

While Barnard referred to a fictitious "Japanese philosopher" as the originator of his first text he now claimed that his varied advertising slogan was in fact a Chinese proverb. This change of mind alone already indicates that Barnard simply invented the statement for his manipulative marketing purposes. The "Japanese philosopher" and the "Chinese proverb" were only added to increase the credibility and authority of the "proverbial" truth. American readers most likely thought of the sayings of Confucius (551–479 B.C.) when they read these references,[15] but Barnard's text is not to be found among his wisdom sayings nor in Asian proverb collections. Yet that has not stopped the editors of John Bartlett's standard collection of *Familiar Quotations* from including since the 1968 edition the slight variant "One picture is worth more than ten thousand words" as a "Chinese proverb."[16] The most recent edition from 1980 continues to label the proverb as being of Chinese origin but cites the more common variant "One picture is worth more than a thousand words."[17] This fallacious claim of a Chinese origin of the American advertising slogan-turned-proverb has become quite commonplace as can be seen from an entry in a fictitious diary from the year 1954: "I believe a sagacious Chinaman is credited with first having said, 'One picture speaks louder than ten thousand words.' Mr. Bovey repeated the adage this morning when, in answer to a telephone call, I went along to his Photographic Art Studio and he handed me my finished portrait. The amount of detail this brilliant man has concentrated into the artistic likeness of myself is quite remarkable."[18] It is of interest here that the author cites yet another variant in which the picture takes on anthropomorphic abilities (speaks louder than). But even more important, these variants become clear indications of how a new text is changed again and again until it reaches a certain standardized proverbial form. An oscillation between "ten thousand" and "thousand" is definitely noticeable, and the unnecessary comparative segment "more than" has occasionally been added. Well over sixty years after its origin the most general wording of the proverb today is the short form "A (One) picture is worth a thousand words."

In addition to borrowing an established proverb structure for his advertising slogan that in turn became a bona fide proverb, there might be yet another possible source that perhaps influenced Barnard's choice of words. It is generally known that copywriters of advertisements often use books of quotations or proverb collections for possible slogan ideas. In one of these books Barnard might just have come across a famous quotation from Christopher Marlowe's (1564–1593) *Doctor Faustus* (c. 1590) that in turn led him at least in part to his successful formulation: "Was this the face that launcht a thousand shippes?/And burnt the toplesse Towres of Ilium?/Sweete Helen, make me immortall with a kisse."[19]

In George Bernard Shaw's (1856–1950) play *The Admirable Bashville* (1926) is the similar line "This is the face that burnt a thousand boats."[20] This allusion to the beauty of Helen in Homer's *Iliad* is commonly quoted as "The face that launched a thousand ships," and it has been used repeatedly with appropriate alterations as an advertising slogan as well with an accompanying picture—for example, "This is the Eye-Fashion Collection that launched a thousand looks" (Du Barry Cosmetics),[21] "The face that launched a thousand quips" (Dick Cavett talk-show),[22] "The Tape that Launched a Thousand Hits" (Ampex Tapes),[23] and "The face [Khomeni] that launched a thousand car pools" (Paine Webber Consultants).[24] The beautiful "face" of Helen was changed by Barnard to "look" or "picture"—after all, Helen was pretty as a picture. The "thousand ships" that brought the Greeks to Troy to win Helen became the "thousand words" that couldn't possibly ("ten thousand words") do complete justice to her beauty. The appearance or the picture in this case is indeed worth a thousand words. This at least might have been Barnard's thought process if this classical allusion helped to formulate the proverbial slogan. That this conjecture is perhaps not too farfetched can be seen from the text of the popular song "If" written and composed by David Gates in 1971 that became a successful hit performed by the group "Bread." Here a stanza actually connects the proverb with the literary quotation: "If a picture paints a thousand words, / then why can't I paint you?/ . . . If a face could launch a thousand ships, / then where am I to go?"[25]

Be that as it may, Barnard's advertising slogan caught on quickly. In November 1934 the Lakeside Press advertising agency produced an advertisement based on the same reasoning that Barnard had used to create his slogan in the first place: A picture shows a pretty little girl helping her mother bake a cake. To this appealing illustration the copywriter has attached the varied headline "One *good* picture beats a thousand words" with the following text: "Everyone who has ever planned or published a *food* advertisement knows that while the copy-writer is struggling futilely for flavorous and aromatic adjectives to sell the product, the color photographer accomplishes the whole job with a single click of the shutter. It's a simple truth that *Pictures sell where words can't.*"[26] The last sentence, so appropriately called a "simple truth," has what it takes for a slogan to become a proverb—it is short and to the point, it contains a piece of wisdom, it is easily understandable, it uses everyday vocabulary, and it is memorable. However, I have located no other sources of this sentence. Hidden away in the copy of an advertisement it probably had no chance to catch on and become proverbial.

But advertisers have without doubt accepted the solid advice of the statement "Pictures sell where words can't" as can be seen in all types of advertising in the mass media. Barnard's slogan in its original wording or in varied form is heard frequently in oral communication, while at the same time it is effectively used in advertisements, cartoons, and literary works. In 1944 the DuMont Company of Precision Electronics and Television used the unchanged headline "One Picture Is Worth a Thousand Words" with the beginning of the text adding ". . . and each picture flashing across the screen of your DuMont Television-Radio Receiver will fill your home with a kind of delight you probably have dreamed of many times."[27] Abernathy's Department Store of Burlington, Vermont, quite literally printed only a picture of its establishment with just the caption "One picture is worth a thousand words,"[28] obviously taking the proverb at its face value. Fred Barnard would certainly have been pleased to see his advertising philosophy employed in this fashion. And his delight would surely have been at its pinnacle if he had had a chance to look at a newspaper advertisement depicting nothing but four roses and the headline "In whiskey, this picture is worth a thousand words."[29] The name of the distillery is not even mentioned, and the viewer must make the connection with Four Roses Whiskey by visual means alone. Here the picture truly is worth a lot for it must communicate the entire advertising message and the name of the whiskey.

The standard proverb has also been employed to advertise more serious matters. The people behind the Foster Parents' Plan program chose the caption "If one picture is worth more than ten thousand words, then what can we tell you of Viola?"[30] beneath a troublesome picture of an impoverished little girl. And the New England Anti-Vivisection Society placed an advertisement in a newspaper with the headline "This Picture Is Worth a Thousand Words"[31] that was accompanied by a picture of a sad looking Beagle. In an advertisement by the Kodak Company for using photographs for instructional purposes, the caption underneath the picture of two school children reads "Introducing the new 1000-word essay" which is followed by the explanation that "Sometimes, showing something once can be as meaningful as writing about it for two and a half pages. Photography lets students see and say things in a new way. And teachers can use it to make any subject more interesting." Only the very last line of the text about photographs as a teaching aid links the "1000-word" essay with the proverb by stating "You know what they say about one picture."[32] This is clearly an effective play with the proverbial text and solid proof that in 1975, when the advertisement was printed, the proverb "A (One) picture is worth a thousand words" was well enough established to be reduced to a mere allusion like this.

Equally intent on getting the advertising message across are colorful magazine pages promoting the sale of various types of electronic equipment. Panasonic used the paradoxical line "The picture says a thousand words but the sound will leave you speechless"[33] to stress the high visual and audio quality of its video recorder, and Intellevision placed a competitor's video picture next to its own product with the headline "Two pictures are worth a thousand words"[34] to show its higher visual quality without using much verbal text since "Nothing I (an Intellevision marketing expert) could say would be more persuasive than what your own two eyes will tell you." In other words, the proverb "Seeing is believing" might just as well have been added to strengthen the proverbial headline that already emphasizes the preoccupation with visual images.

The city of San Antonio did something unique to advertise its importance as a major place for conventions. The headline splits the proverb into two halves: "The Picture" (of a riverboat party) "The Thousand Words" (a picture and some text of a small brochure). And the short text promises that "when you receive our new packet (the brochure) you'll get considerably more than a thousand words. And many more pictures. All about the best San Antonio has to offer."[35] While the proverb "A picture is worth a thousand words" is expanded to many more pictures and words here to present an appealing image of San Antonio, the Frances Denny cosmetics company used a black and white picture of a partially shown female face and in a large empty area simply printed this short text: "Neither a picture nor a thousand words can adequately describe the magnetic radiance, the fascinating glow that is waiting for you in The Lustrous Make-up of Frances Denny."[36] In this case neither picture nor words are enough to describe the product's results so one must buy it and try it. The negation of the proverb thus becomes yet an even stronger advertising message to get the consumer to make a purchasing decision.

There are also a couple of comic strips that play on the standard form of the proverb. In a "Peanuts" comic strip Sally is confronted with the task of writing a 2000-word report. She wittily observes that "I have heard it said that one picture is worth a thousand words. . . ," quickly draws two pictures and smartly proclaims "What we have here is a couple of pictures."[37] This is pretty clever for a little girl, and it shouldn't surprise us that a youngster of our visual age should reach that literal interpretation of the proverb. Little wonder that Sally's cohort Billy from "The Family Circus" cartoons has quite a similar reaction to the proverb: "A picture is worth a thousand words. I guess Shakespeare should have learned to draw."[38] The latter example indeed indicates the unwillingness of the younger generation to read the classics; Shakespeare and other writers of world literature must today be presented in the form of comic strips, cartoons, videos, or major screen pictures to reach the young population at all. From a pedagogical and cultural literacy point of view the proverb "A picture is worth a thousand words" can take

on a rather depressing connotation since it helps to lessen the importance of the written word.

It should surprise no one that this often quoted proverb has by now been reduced to the formula "A (One) x is worth a thousand words" to express the importance that this society places on almost anything but the verbal message. Often the variable x reflects the materialism that people strive for so eagerly. As early as 1972 the British Jaguar automobile company advertised its luxury sedan with the slogan "One drive is worth a million words."[39] The advertising copy is accordingly very short indeed and merely states that the new model is yet further improved over the already previously perfect Jaguar. Why use a "million words" to inform the consumer properly when all that is needed is the experience of an actual ride? The Ford Motor Company eagerly followed suit in 1984 with an extensive advertising campaign for its classic Thunderbird. But predictably American, the advertisement only showed a picture of the car with the large headline "One drive is worth a thousand words."[40] There is no text whatsoever, and why should the copywriters bother when the consumer seemingly wants only to see, touch, and experience the Thunderbird?

One wonders how often consumers will continue to be confronted by this proverbial formula to get their attention. The Westwood Building Company advertised its services with the headline "One good developer is worth a million words"[41] the Brazilian Tourism Authority lured tourists with the slogan "Brazil—One visit is worth a thousand words";[42] the Angostar warmbody underwear producers claimed that "One touch is worth a thousand words";[43] the Bandido Mexican restaurant advertised its beer with the wonderful replacement of the word "picture" by its almost homonym "pitcher" in the headline "One pitcher is worth a thousand words";[44] and the American Florist Marketing Council came up with the splendid idea that "A flower is worth a thousand words."[45]

The last variant has also been used as a birthday card message above the picture of a furry cat holding a rose: ". . . They say—'One flower can speak a thousand words'. . . ." The text on the inside of the card enumerates dozens of wishes with the conclusion "in short, briefly, when it comes down to

"And I say one bomb is worth a thousand words."

Drawing by Dana Fradon; © 1980. The New Yorker Magazine, Inc.

it, at the end of the day, I really, sincerely hope that your birthday is quite nice"![46] Equally "cute" is, of course, a large poster depicting a couple of prairie dogs hugging each other with the message "A hug is worth a thousand words."[47] But such messages of friendship and love quickly disappear in such proverbial captions as "And I say one bomb is worth a thousand words"[48] underneath a caricature of two high level military officers discussing the state of the world at a cocktail party. And how unromantic is another comment by a business executive to another below a second cartoon: "One dollar is worth a thousand words."[49] Power and money have replaced the world of pictures and words, reminding us that the lack of visual and verbal communication alike endanger our very existence.

There also exist variants based on the structural formula "A (One) picture is worth a thousand y's" in which it is the usual noun "words" that has been replaced. The Business Committee for the Arts of the City of Cincinnati got Wendy's fast food franchise to promote a calendar containing pictures by local artists. A subsequent advertisement in *Time* explained this new way of selling Wendy's hamburgers; it shows one of those pictures and displays the large headline "One picture is worth a thousand hamburgers." Part of the accompanying copy reads as follows: "Wendy's has discovered there's an art to selling hamburgers. When Wendy's in Cincinnati decided to help local artists, they developed a calendar which featured paintings of scenes of the city, like the one pictured here. The calendar was sold for $1.19 in 26 of its Cincinnati restaurants. Wendy's donated 10 cents to the Cincinnati Commission on the Arts for each calendar sold . . . From Wendy's to Flanigan's Furniture Inc., the Business Committee for the Arts is helping companies of all sizes discover that supporting the arts can paint a nice picture for their business. . . . You'll find your interest repaid a thousand times."[50] This certainly represents an innovative way of joining the forces of business and art, benefiting both the sales of thousands of hamburgers and, at least equally important, the appreciation and sale of artists' works.

A second example of replacing "words" with another noun is an advertisement by the Dana Corporation of Toledo. A large headline reads "A picture is worth a thousand numbers," and the copy explains that this company does its financial reporting in a different way: "With enough numbers, you can confuse anybody. That's because very few people really understand masses of numbers and long computer printouts. But we show our finances and performance in pictures, graphs and colors. That makes them understandable."[51] This advertisement makes it clear once again that it is the image that contains the message and not complicated numbers or words; visual effects are the epitome when it comes to effective communication with non-experts. But the question remains whether smart pictures, graphs, and diagrams cannot manipulate the consumer or shareholder for that matter even more than the traditional numbers or words that are needed to authenticate the pictures.

Some copywriters have reduced the proverb "A (One) picture is worth a thousand words" even further by replacing both the nouns "picture" and "words" at the same time, the result being the structural formula "A (One) x is worth a thousand y's." In 1980 the Gulf Oil Company pushed the idea of gas economy through car pooling by showing a van that transports a number of employees to work each day with the fitting statement "Gulf is van pooling. Because one van is worth 1,000 gallons."[52] And very clever indeed was a British advertisement for Cross fountain pens based on this pattern since it included the product name in the slogan, presented a picture of such a pen, and also played on the traditional custom of placing little crosses at the end of a letter to represent love and kisses: "A Cross says more than a thousand kisses."[53] From a folkloristic point of view this can be considered a slogan masterpiece, and it is to be expected that it was a mercantile success as well. The proverbial ring of the altered proverb and the folkloric message of love must have sent plenty of consumers out on a purchasing spree, indicating once again how folklore and proverbs in particular are effective tools in modern advertising.[54]

A final group of examples illustrates yet another way that advertisers have found to manipulate this proverbial slogan. They can all be reduced to the structural formula "A (One) x is worth a thousand pictures," and they represent a fascinating reversal of the actual proverb. Of particular interest is a large advertising page from a 1980 *Fortune* magazine which in a way goes back to Fred Barnard's original advertisement of 1921. Here too there is no picture and the slogan argues provocatively "Sometimes a word is worth a thousand pictures." The adverb "provocatively" is used intentionally since the reader will obviously juxtapose this variation with the actual proverb "A picture is worth a thousand words" and wonder what has happened to this clear insight. But then follows an interesting line of argumentation by the marketing people of the James Walter Thompson advertising agency which has specialized in magazine advertisement for such publications as *Fortune:* "Whenever it's rumored that the printed word is about to disappear beneath an electronic wave, there are certain things that give us great comfort. The flourishing state of magazines—as witnessed here by *Fortune's* fiftieth anniversary—is one of them. Ultimately there is no substitute for print in the transmission of detailed information and complicated ideas. That's as true for advertising as it is for anything else."[55] It is indeed refreshing to see an advertising agency argue for once that words still count, that is, that informational advertising must rely on the spoken or written word in addition to pictures.

And yet other advertising agencies have found a way to use even the reversal formula "A (One) word is worth a thousand pictures" in a way that supports the idea that informational advertisements based on several sentences or even paragraphs are not desirable. These copywriters, if one can call them that, simply take the pronoun "a (one)" literally and print just that *one* word together with the slogan and no or only a very short explanatory comment. Thus the Meister Clothes Company printed only its name in large letters and some nondescript fabrics with the telling slogan "One word that's worth a thousand pictures."[56] The Philip Morris Company attempted a similar approach with an advertisement for its Merit filter cigarettes. The headline states "These words are worth a thousand pictures," and the short copy is composed of the following text: "Rather than a lot of interesting photos, we offer you one very interesting fact: Merit delivers the taste of cigarettes that have up to 38% more tar. The secret is Enriched Flavor. It gives Merit real, satisfying cigarette taste, but with even less tar than other leading lights. But don't take our word for it. Try one yourself. You'll get the picture."[57]

The tiny picture of a pack of cigarettes that is included is a novel way to advertise cigarettes by understatement. Supposedly the written words or, even better, the "one very interesting fact" of the low tar content should convince the consumer to make a new purchasing choice. Yet the value of informational words is immediately put into question by the proverbial statement "But don't take our word for it." Only if you "Try one yourself. You'll get

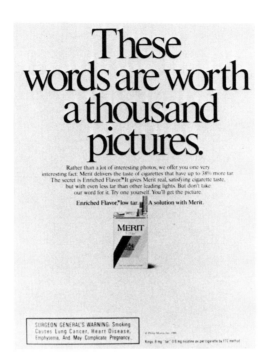

the picture" is the logical conclusion of the advertising text. Not the words but the experience will lead the consumer to the proverbial "get the picture," that is, to *see* (understand) that this is supposedly a great product.

The Howard Bank of Vermont also made effective use of this proverb reversal. Its advertisement contains an empty page with the following message on the bottom that plays beautifully on the word "Vermont" and its almost mystical qualities.[58]

> **A word that's worth a thousand pictures.**
> **Vermont.**
>
> It's more than a state in New England, it's a whole state of mind. A one-word summary of farm houses, foliage, syrup and snow that moves more people than any other word we know.
> Vermont. Whether you plow it, paint it, manufacture or market its products, being here means you're part of something very special. And we're very proud to be in the picture.
>
> The Howard Bank

As is to be expected, the proverb reversal "A (One) word is worth a thousand pictures" has become the formula "A (One) *x* is worth a thousand pictures." As early as 1957 Danish Blue Cheese was advertised with the fitting slogan

"One taste is worth a thousand pictures," for "one delicious bite reveals a new world of taste sensation—with this unique, individual flavor."[59] And a quarter century later the *Bon Appétit* magazine revived this slogan to advertise Camembert and Chevre cheese: "The Great Cheeses of Europe. One Taste is Worth a Thousand Pictures."[60] The accompanying picture of the cheese is, of course, intended to entice the consumers' tastebuds and thus get them to buy it. Again the picture and finally the true experience are what count rather than detailed verbal descriptions. An advertisement by the NBC Radio Network that obviously needs to work without pictures simply stresses the aural way of getting to the consumer. But notice that drinking sounds are being played with here while actual words once again take second stage: "Slurp . . . One sound is often worth 2,000 pictures. Do you feel you shouldn't advertise on radio because people have to see the product? Try this test. Buy your child a chocolate shake. Then cover your ears and watch him/her drink the shake. Next, treat your child to another chocolate shake. This time, close your eyes and *listen* to him/her drink the shake. . . . Hearing is believing."[61] The entire advertisement closes with yet another proverb variation that emphasizes "hearing" in this case. Both varied proverbs of this advertisement are convincing ways to indicate that radio advertisements have something new to offer that is not necessarily based on the visual sense. But the sound of "slurping" a chocolate milk shake, of course, will also bring about the mental image of that refreshing drink.

The last advertising example, one by the Irish Tourist Board, summarizes what has been said about the proverb "A (One) picture is worth a thousand words" and its use and reinterpretation in American society. Besides displaying eight colorful pictures the word "Ireland" appears in large print with the slogan "A place that's worth a thousand pictures." And part of the copy reads: "Ireland is indescribable. You've got to see it to believe it. The next best thing to being there is to picture the lush, green, rolling hills, crystal lakes and rivers, crisp fresh air and the charming friendly people who speak your language. But that's only part of the picture. Because there's much more to see and do in Ireland."[62] Yes, it's seeing, hearing, and experiencing Ireland that counts for the tourist. After all, the tourist perhaps is the perfect match for the proverb "Seeing is believing." (Maybe there will at least be some tourists who might also pay some attention to the oral folklore and the written works of James Joyce, for words ought to be part of a tourist's trying to get the complete picture as it were.)

All these examples have amply proven that "A (One) picture is worth a thousand words" has become a bona fide proverb in the Anglo-American world and through translations slowly in other countries as well. The fact that conscious variations of it occurred as early as the 1950s is yet another indication that Fred Barnard's advertising slogan reached a proverbial status in a relatively short amount of time. With such popularity it is not surprising that the proverb has now been registered as such in the third supplementary volume of the large *Oxford English Dictionary* (1982) with the wording "One picture is worth ten thousand words" and a reference to Fred Barnard's 1927 use of this version.[63] Also in 1982 John A. Simpson included the identical text in his valuable *Concise Oxford Dictionary of Proverbs.*[64] In the year 1985 the somewhat more common variant "A picture is worth a thousand words" was listed in a collection of clichés,[65] and a year later I recorded it in this form in my *Encyclopedia of World Proverbs.*[66] At that time I made the unfortunate mistake of identifying the proverb as being of English origin. It would have been better to specify it as a true American proverb that now has been disseminated throughout the English-speaking world. The proverb with its emphasis on the visual preoccupation represents the world*view* of American society in particular, and I have identified it as a unique American proverb in my *Dictionary of American Proverbs* (1992).[67] Among a population where "Seeing is believing" is a principal way of communication, the proverb "A picture is worth a thousand words" will doubtlessly retain equal importance, and it is a convincing example that new proverbs are still being coined to reflect the ever-changing value system of modern society. One thing is for certain—there is a lot of wisdom in the "new" adage "A proverb in the hand—is often worth a thousand words."[68]

Notes

This chapter was first published with different illustrations in *Southern Folklore,* 47 (1990), 207–225.

   1. Ivan Turgenev, *Otsy i deti.* Moskva: Ogonyek, 1968, p. 388. The English translation is included as a sententious remark in John Bartlett, *Familiar Quotations,* ed. by Emily Morison Beck. 15th ed. Boston: Little, Brown and Co., 1980, p. 564.
   2. F. P. Wilson, *The Oxford Dictionary of English Proverbs.* Oxford: Clarendon Press, 1970, pp. 623–624.
   3. See the detailed study of Allan Paivio, *Imagery and Verbal Processes.* New York: Holt, Rinehart and Winston, 1971.
   4. Alan Dundes, "Seeing Is Believing," *Natural History,* no. 5 (May 1972), 8–14 and 86. I am quoting from A. Dundes' more accessible essay volume *Interpreting Folklore.* Bloomington: Indiana University Press, 1980, p. 86.
   5. Dundes (note 4), pp. 90–91.
   6. See also Simon J. Bronner, "[Seeing Is Believing] . . . but 'Feeling's the Truth'," *Tennessee Folklore Society Bulletin,* 48 (1982), 117–124; and S. J. Bronner, "The Haptic Experience of Culture [Seeing Is Believing, but Feeling's the Truth]," *Anthropos,* 77 (1982), 351–362. Bronner argues that "touching" is of equally important sensory significance in American society, citing the complete proverb "Seeing is believing, but feeling is the truth" to back up his claim.
   7. For a discussion of the German translation of this proverb and its recent history see

Wolfgang Mieder, " 'Ein Bild sagt mehr als tausend Worte': Ursprung und Überlieferung eines amerikanischen Lehnsprichworts," *Proverbium: Yearbook of International Proverb Scholarship*, 6 (1989), 25–37.

8. Cited from Wolfgang Mieder, *Encyclopedia of World Proverbs*. Englewood Cliffs, N.J.: Prentice-Hall, 1986, pp. 180, 220, 329, 367, and 436.

9. Bartlett Jere Whiting, *Early American Proverbs and Proverbial Phrases*. Cambridge: Harvard University Press, 1977, p. 101.

10. Cited from Wolfgang Mieder, Stewart Kingsbury, and Kelsie Harder (eds.), *A Dictionary of American Proverbs*. New York: Oxford University Press, 1992, pp. 361, 142, 548, and 548.

11. Burton Stevenson, *The Macmillan Book of Proverbs, Maxims, and Famous Phrases*. New York: Macmillan, 1948, p. 2611.

12. *Printers' Ink* (December 8, 1921), pp. 96–97.

13. *Printers' Ink* (March 10, 1927), pp. 114–115.

14. See Barbara and Wolfgang Mieder, "Tradition and Innovation: Proverbs in Advertising," in *The Wisdom of Many. Essays on the Proverb*, ed. by W. Mieder and Alan Dundes. New York: Garland Publishing, 1981, pp. 309–322.

15. Burton Stevenson states that "It [the proverb] was immediately credited to Confucius" (see note 11), p. 2611. See also Hollis Alpert, "Movies Are Better than the Stage," *Saturday Review* (July 23, 1955), p. 6: " 'One picture is worth a thousand words'.—Fred R. Barnard, who in *Printers' Ink* credited the statement to Confucius, who, of course, said no such thing." I owe this reference to my colleague Littleton Long.

16. See John Bartlett, *Familiar Quotations*, ed. by Emily Morison Beck. 14th ed. Boston: Little, Brown and Co., 1968, p. 149.

17. Bartlett (note 1), p. 564.

18. Richard Haydn, *The Journal of Edwin Carp*. New York: Simon and Schuster, 1954, p. 84.

19. Stevenson (note 11), p. 740.

20. Stevenson (note 11), p. 740.

21. *New Yorker* (November 28, 1968), p. 19.

22. *New Yorker* (October 1, 1979), p. 93.

23. *Omni* (November 1980), back cover.

24. *New Yorker* (December 7, 1981), p. 207.

25. Quoted from *"If,"* Words and Music by David Gates, Recorded by *"Bread."* Hollywood/California: Colgems-EMI Music, 1971 (Sheet Music). I owe the reference to this song to Ann and Richard Park. My student Trinka Poppe provided me with a copy of the actual text.

26. *Fortune* (November 1934), p. 27.

27. *Fortune* (April 1944), p. 115.

28. *The Burlington Free Press* (January 18, 1982), p. 3A.

29. *The Burlington Free Press* (April 24, 1975), p. 8.

30. *New Yorker* (December 19, 1956), p. 51.

31. *The Burlington Free Press* (September 30, 1979), p. 4D.

32. *Today's Education* (September/October 1975), p. 2.

33. *New Yorker* (September 2, 1985), p. 90.

34. *People* (November 16, 1981), p. 109.

35. *New Yorker* (January 13, 1986), p. 48.

36. *New Yorker* (April 25, 1964), p. 69.

37. *The Burlington Free Press* (May 18, 1979), p. 7D.

38. *Boston Globe* (September 8, 1985), comic section.

39. *Punch* (May 10, 1972), p. 639.

40. *New Yorker* (August 20, 1984), p. 94a; and *Time* (September 3, 1984), p. 43. This

slogan is also included in Laurence Urdang and Ceila Dame Robbins (eds.), *Slogans*. Detroit: Gale Research Co., 1984, p. 44. This book presents a large collection of slogans, but it is a shame that the editors have not provided any dates whatsoever. Two similar slogans listed in this book are "One chord is worth a thousand words" (Sohner & Co. [pianos]), p. 229, and "One pictograph tells more than a thousand words" (Pictograph Corp.), p. 270.

41. *Punch* (October 31–November 6, 1973), p. iii.

42. *Saturday Review* (March 20, 1976), p. 37.

43. *Skiing Trade News* (Spring 1980), pp. 34–35. I owe this reference to my former student Marcel Schneider.

44. *Bloomington Herald Telegraph* (October 27, 1982), p. 34. I owe this reference to my former students Trixie and Eric Stinebring.

45. *Family Circle* (January 24, 1984), p. 36.

46. Greeting card from the Recycled Paper Products Co. (Chicago). Bought in February, 1989, in Burlington, Vermont. I received this card for my birthday from my colleague Helga Schreckenberger.

47. Poster from Argus Communications (Niles, Illinois). Purchased in December 1980 in Burlington, Vermont.

48. *New Yorker* (April 14, 1980), p. 52.

49. *New Yorker* (December 7, 1987), p. 52. I owe this reference to my former student Jake Barickman.

50. *Time* (July 15, 1985), p. 6.

51. *Fortune* (May 7, 1979), pp. 208–209.

52. *New Yorker* (January 21, 1980), p. 16.

53. *Punch* (December 10, 1986), p. 40.

54. See Mieder (note 14), pp. 311–314.

55. *Fortune* (February 11, 1980), p. 18. I owe this reference to my former student Marcel Schneider.

56. *Ski Business* (March 1978), p. 118.

57. *Time* (October 24, 1988), back cover. I owe this reference to my wife Barbara Mieder.

58. *The Burlington Free Press* (March 2, 1978), p. 12A.

59. *New Yorker* (February 9, 1957), p. 115.

60. *Bon Appétit* (September 1983), p. 76; and *Bon Appétit* (December 1983), p. 99. Urdang and Robbins (see note 40), p. 163, cite the same slogan for the MacFarlane Nut Co.

61. *Fortune* (November 6, 1978), p. 129.

62. *Newsweek* (March 31, 1980), p. 53.

63. R. W. Burchfield (ed.), *A Supplement to the Oxford English Dictionary*. Oxford: Clarendon Press, 1982, vol. 3, p. 476.

64. See John A. Simpson, *The Concise Oxford Dictionary of Proverbs*. Oxford: Oxford University Press, 1982, pp. 177–178.

65. James Rogers, *The Dictionary of Clichés*. New York: Facts on File Publications, 1985, pp. 196–197.

66. See Mieder (note 8), p. 373.

67. See Mieder et al. (note 10), p. 463.

68. This innovative connection of the two proverbs "A bird in the hand is worth two in the bush" and "A picture is worth a thousand words" stems from the journalist Horace Reynolds, "A Proverb in the Hand—Is Often Worth a Thousand Words. Herewith an Examination of a Much Used but Seldom Analyzed Form of Homely Literature," *New York Times Magazine* (September 13, 1959), p. 74. This is a general magazine article on proverbs drawing particular attention to Nikita S. Krushchev's (1894–1971) frequent use of Russian proverbs. Reynolds also attempts a definition of proverbs and then comments on a number of national and international proverbs.

7

" An Apple a Day Keeps the Doctor Away "

Traditional and Modern Aspects of Medical Proverbs

The health of the mind and the body has preoccupied people since the beginning of human existence. The classical Latin proverb "Mens sana in corpore sano" formulated by the satirical Roman poet Juvenal (60?–140?) and appearing in English translation as "A sound mind in a sound body"[1] for the first time in the year 1578 merely summarizes in a typically proverbial parallel structure a bit of folk wisdom based on generations of common-sense medical observation and experience that continues to be as valid a truth today as it was centuries ago. The same is true for such general health rules as "Diseases come on horseback, but go away on foot," "Health is better than wealth," "Desperate diseases must have desperate cures," "Bitter pills may have blessed effects," and of course also the Latin proverb "Similia similibus curantur" or its English translation "Like cures like" which became the underlying principle of homeopathy.[2] Such ancient medical advice in the form of folk proverbs was translated in the Middle Ages into most vernacular languages,[3] making these proverbs part of an internationally disseminated corpus.

There also exists, however, a considerable number of medical proverbs that originated and gained currency in individual ethnic or national languages.[4] There is not a proverb collection that doesn't contain some proverbs commenting on matters of health or illness, and special collections of medical proverbs have also been assembled dating back to the late Middle Ages.[5] An early specialized English collection of medical proverbs is included in John Ray's (1627–1705) *Compleat Collection of English Proverbs* (1670) with the telling title "Proverbs and Proverbial Observations belonging to Health, Diet and Physick."[6] Here we find such well-known health rules as "After dinner sit a while, after supper walk a mile," "A good surgeon must have an eagle's eye, a lion's heart, and a lady's hand," "Butter is gold in the morning, silver at noon, lead at night," "One hour's sleep before midnight is worth two hours after," and "The best physicians are Dr. Diet, Dr. Quiet, and Dr. Merryman." Vincent Stuckey Lean (1820–1899) published in 1902 dozens of English and other European medical proverbs dealing with dietary matters, drink, fruit, meats, vegetables, and food as well as health and sickness.[7] It is here where we find such everyday bits of wisdom as "Eat to live and not live to eat," "Cider on beer, never fear; beer upon cider, makes a bad rider," "The first step to health is to know that we are sick," and "Every disease will have its course." While these texts are admittedly not particularly enlightening from a scientific point of view, they nevertheless express some common-sense attitudes about basic health matters. Notice though the ironic tones of such proverbs as "Sickness soaks the purse," "God does the cure and the physician takes the fee for it," "One doctor makes work for another," and "Doctors make the very worst patients." Here the folk comments on some basic problems of the medical profession that are issues of controversy as much today as in former times.[8]

But there is no doubt that most so-called medical proverbs are rather general statements. As Russell A. Elmquist has noted in an essay on "English Medical Proverbs," proverbs hardly "give specific medical advice of a scientific nature."[9] For the modern physician, surgeon or even medical professor, these health proverbs most likely appear a bit trite and certainly unscientific. Ancient proverbs obviously cannot compete with the scientific wisdom of scholarly books and journal articles on diseases that were not even known a decade ago. We thus have no proverbs about Legionnaire's disease, organ transplants, or AIDS, but there are dozens of proverbs about general health problems, such as the common cold, normal diet, sleep, hygiene, and so on.[10]

This can be seen by the over four hundred English and German medical proverbs that Helmut A. Seidl has analyzed diachronically and medically in the most comprehensive study regarding English health proverbs to date.[11] In his book entitled *Medizinische Sprichwörter im Englischen und Deutschen* (1982) Seidl presents and discusses such dietary proverbs as "Eat when you're hungry, and drink when you're dry," "Good eating deserves good drinking," "Bread is the staff of life," and "Fresh pork and new wine kill a man before his time." Regarding the body, Seidl analyzes proverbs like "Without sleep, no health," "He that lives too fast, goes to his grave too soon," "The head and feet keep warm, the rest will take no harm," and "Hot things, sharp things, sweet things, cold things, all rot the teeth." It is interesting to note that the folk also has its proverbs that relate the so-called psychosomatic illnesses with the body, as for example "Fretting cares make grey hairs," "A merry heart makes a long life," "Laughter is the best medicine," and even "Two things do prolong your life: A quiet heart, and a loving wife." Other texts discussed by Seidl include even more general pieces of medical advice as "Little enemies and little wounds must not be despised," "Different sores must have different salves," "Desperate diseases must have desperate remedies," and "Nature, time and patience are three great physicians."[12] May these examples suffice to indicate the general nature of most English medical proverbs. There are no scientists at work in the maternity wards of proverbs, but that does not mean that some medical proverbs do not contain some very worthwhile information for everyday healthy living.

The question arises, of course, how many of these proverbs are in fact still in common use today, especially since the lay population has become much more medically aware because of the many books on health, magazine articles on diets, television reports on the newest breakthroughs in medicine, health clubs, home spas, and so on. Certainly several examples cited thus far are not used much anymore today—in fact, it could be argued that some medical proverbs are losing out to modern scientific developments much quicker than proverbs referring to other aspects of life. Proverbs like "Absence makes the heart grow fonder," "Haste makes waste," or "Too many cooks spoil the broth" are as popular as ever due to their universal appeal and solid claim to truth. In comparison, many of the old medical proverbs have already fallen out of use, for who today knows and would use proverbs like "Dine rightly and sup lightly, sleep upstairs and you'll live sprightly" or "If you would live forever, you must wash milk from your liver"? Especially the latter text is medically speaking incorrect in any case, since it is based on the old belief that the liver is a digestive organ. Milk, which today is considered one of the most nourishing drinks, was not held in particularly high esteem in earlier times. As the last proverb shows, it was believed to be necessary to drink something else after milk to cleanse the liver as it were. Realizing that this is nonsense, this proverb connecting liver and milk has obviously dropped out of use.

There are, however, a few medical proverbs in the English language that are as popular as "Out of sight, out of mind," "A rolling stone gathers no moss," "The early bird catches the worm," or any other of the truly common English proverbs. Three such health proverbs come to mind in particular, namely "Prevention is better than cure" and its longer variant "An ounce of prevention is worth a pound of cure," "Stuff (Feed) a cold and starve a fever," and the most popular medical proverb of all "An apple a day keeps the doctor away." These texts are used in their traditional wording by all of us with much frequency because they give rational medical advice using metaphors and linguistic structures that add to their memorability and reproducability by people of all strata of society. What follows will be a closer look at the origin, history, meaning, and modern use of these three medical proverbs. It will be seen that they are by no means considered sacrosanct medical advice by the folk. Exactly because these particular proverbs have been so popular, people also enjoy parodying them and adapting them to ever new contexts far removed from medical matters. To be sure, the traditional proverbs and their messages are always in the background of these innovative anti-proverbs,[13] resulting in an intriguing linguistic and semantic interplay of tradition and innovation.[14]

Prevention Is Better than Cure
An Ounce of Prevention Is Worth a Pound of Cure

In the case of "Prevention is better than cure," unsuccessful attempts have been made by several scholars to find a Latin origin or equivalent for it.[15] The earliest English variant found thus far appeared in 1618 in the religious works of Thomas Adams (fl. 1612–1653), who linked the proverb right from the start with a medical meaning: "Preuention is so much better then healing, because it saues the labour of being sicke." From 1685 dates the variant "The wisdom of prevention is better than the wisdom of remedy," while the text "Prevention is much preferable to cure" appeared for the first time in Thomas Fuller's (1654–1734) proverb collection *Gnomologia* (1732). In 1751 we find the explicit statement "Prevention is the better Cure, so says the Proverb, and 'tis sure," and finally in 1826 the standardized proverb "Prevention is better than cure" appears in one of John Pintard's (1759–1844) letters.[16] By the mid-nineteenth century this text was well established. Charles Dickens (1811–1870) employed it in 1850 in his novel *Martin Chuzzlewit*,[17] and in 1856 it is the subject of an engraving and a small didactic poem.[18]

Prevention Is Better than Cure

The child is wandering into danger great,
The mother draws it from a downward fate,
Thus stops its fall; better thus 'tis quite plain,
Than broken limbs to have, and hours of pain.
Would you prevent a man from drinking rum,
Destroy his liquor, and the work is done.

Such rigid and Victorian interpretation of this proverb brought about humorous reactions, as, for example, the proverb parody in the form of a wellerism from 1863: " 'Prevention is better than cure,' as the pig said when it ran away with all its might to escape the killing attentions of the butcher."[19] At about the same time Sir George Cornewall Lewis (1806–1863) wrote that "In my opinion, in nine cases out of ten, cure is better than prevention. . . . By looking forward to all possible evils, we waste the strength that had best be concentrated in curing the one evil which happens."[20] If this is a rather liberating reaction to the proverb during the Victorian age, the American nineteenth-century writer Henry Sedley (1835–1899) returned in 1865 to the moralistic value of the proverb by having one of his characters observe "If I was the gal's father . . . I'd think prevention was better than cure."[21] From minor novels of the twentieth century we can also cite the interesting variations "Prevention is better than a post-mortem" from 1927, and "Prevention is more important than attempting a cure—afterwards" from 1930.[22] Yet for the most part the proverb continues to be cited as "Prevention is better than cure."

But there is also the longer variant "An ounce of prevention is worth a pound of cure" that is particularly popular in the United States, giving the shorter version plenty of competition. Proverbs like "An ounce of discretion is worth a pound of wit," "An ounce of mother wit is worth a pound of learning," "An ounce of good fortune is worth a pound of forecast," "An ounce of mirth is worth a pound of sorrow," and "An ounce of practice is worth a pound of precept" for the most part predate the medical variant of this proverb pattern,[23] and even "An ounce of experience is better than a pound of science"[24] was registered already in 1748. The Quaker State Oil Company used a variant of this last text as an effective advertising slogan in 1935: "An ounce of experience is worth a pound of words."[25] Here a motorist explains that even though he knows little about engines and cars, he knows from experience that this particular brand of motor oil is worth more than words could possibly express. All these variants can clearly be reduced to the proverbial pattern "An ounce of X is worth a pound of Y," and it was most likely no one less than Benjamin Franklin (1706–1790) who took the shorter British version "Prevention is better than cure" and adapted it to this structural formula, thereby creating the variant proverb "An ounce of prevention is worth a pound of cure" in 1735.[26] His use of the proverb in a letter to Samuel Johnson (1709–1784) of September 13, 1750, is a telling document of the medical significance of the proverb.[27]

> I am sorry to hear of your Illness: If you have not been us'd to the Fever and Ague, let me give you one Caution. Don't imagine yourself thoroughly cur'd, and so omit the Use of the Bark too soon. Remember to take the preventing Doses faithfully. If you were to continue taking a Dose or two every Day for two or three Weeks after the Fits have left you, 'twould not be amiss. If you take the Powder mix'd quick in a Tea Cup of Milk, 'tis no way disagreable, but looks and even tastes like Chocolate. 'Tis an old Saying, That an Ounce of Prevention is worth a Pound of Cure, and certainly a true one, with regard to the Bark; a little

of which will do more in preventing the Fits than a great deal in removing them.

Franklin used the proverb again in 1784,[28] and because of the incredible popularity of his writings this variant soon became a proverb in its own right, being the more common version in this country.[29]

In fact, the proverb is so popular that often only the first half is cited. An advertisement by the Burroughs Company from 1952 employed the headline "An ounce of prevention"[30] to draw attention to a new way of microfilming business records as "the most effective preventive measure against the loss or destruction of vital records." Ten years later the Recordak Company advertised its microfilm service using the quite similar truncated proverb "5 ounces of prevention!"[31] as a headline. And from 1957 stems the slogan "An ounce of scientific prevention"[32] with which the Bartlett Tree Experts advertised their expertise in proper tree care. Part of the copy reads quite medically as follows: "Like the dramatic progress in medical science, modern tree care bears little resemblance to the crude methods of only fifty years ago. No longer is it enough to repair damage—to cut away a limb that has died. Today, as always, we seek the answer 'Why'—the cause of damage or disease and apply every modern technique and curative treatment . . . No one knows better than a Bartlett client, that an ounce of scientific prevention is worth many pounds of cure." It's fascinating to see how these "tree surgeons," as the expression goes, use a medical proverb to market their services. But it certainly should surprise nobody to see medical products being advertised by using part of this proverb. A magazine advertisement for Neosporin Ointment included the headline "A half-ounce of prevention."[33] The copy states in part: "Use it to prevent a topical infection. Or to treat one that's already started. In either case, it's good medicine. . . . A half-ounce of prevention. Also available in a full ounce of prevention and in convenient foil packets." With this emphasis on prevention of all sorts in our society we should not be surprised to find a cartoon depicting a consumer in a pharmacy declaring "I'll have an ounce of prevention"[34] for prophylactic purposes, whatever they might be.

The proverb or its remnants also continue to be used in a nonmedical sense. Thus the George S. May Engineering Company simply told its prospective customers that its engineers can provide prevention or cure for their problems: "An Ounce of Prevention or a Pound of Cure."[35] The caption underneath a picture depicting a backhoe operator trying to break up the ice on the Mad River in Vermont to prevent any flooding very appropriately stated "Ounce of Prevention."[36] And finally there is that newspaper article headline that employs the complete proverb "An Ounce of Prevention Is Worth a Pound of Cure."[37] The article is a review of a consumer handbook for Vermonters

"I'll have an ounce of prevention."

Drawing by Dana Fradon; © 1987. The New Yorker Magazine, Inc.

to protect them from false advertising and marketing. The booklet's title consisted of the truncated proverb *An Ounce of Prevention,* and ideally it prevented consumers from the proverbial pound of cure in the form of headache pills or more severe remedies.

Our final two references to this proverb deal with the problem that seemingly would arise if this country were ever to adapt the metric system. In a humorous magazine article on "The Metrified Forest" a journalist suggests tongue in cheek that our proverb would have to become "28 grams of prevention are worth 45/100 of a kilogram of cure,"[38] while the Canadian poet John Robert Colombo (b. 1936) came up with the variant "A milligram of prevention is worth a kilogram of cure."[39] We need not fear though, for even if we were to change over to the metric system, the proverb would easily survive the shock. It is not so much the individual word of a proverb that counts but the entire idea expressed in its metaphor. The antiquated measurements of ounce and pound would still signify figuratively that a small amount of prevention is better than a large amount of cure. This also explains why the proverb "An ounce of prevention is worth a pound of cure" can be interpreted both as a specifically medical proverb or as a more general proverb stating that paying a little attention to whatever we do or undertake in the first place will save us a lot of unnecessary bother in the future. It is this

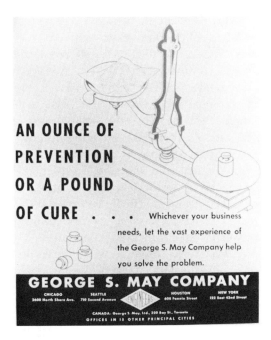
multisemanticity of proverbs that makes them so flexible and adaptable to ever new contexts and interpretations.

Stuff (Feed) a Cold and Starve a Fever

Of the three medical proverbs under discussion here the proverb "Stuff (Feed) a cold and starve a fever" gives the most precise medical advice but is at the same time also the most controversial text from a scientific point of view. It is of relative recent origin, having been recorded in print only since the middle of the nineteenth century.[40] A precursor to the second half of the proverb might have been the saying "Fasting is a great remedie in feuers" from 1574, but notice that there also existed the diametrically opposed proverb "It is better to feede a fever, then weaknesse" from 1576.[41] Concerning the first part of the proverb, we find an equally confusing statement in Henry David Thoreau's (1817–1862) account of *A Week on the Concord and Merrimack Rivers*, a report of a voyage that he undertook during August 1839 and published only in 1849. Speaking of the dichotomy of good and evil and the difficulty of knowing the difference, Thoreau also makes the following comments: "There are sure to be two prescriptions diametrically opposite. Stuff a cold and starve a cold are but two ways. They are the two practices both always in full blast. Yet you must take advice of the one school as if there was no other."[42] Our proverb "Stuff (Feed) a cold and starve a fever" presents a folk compromise of sorts concerning this confusing state of affairs. It was recorded for the first time in Edward Fitzgerald's (1809–1883) *Polonius: A Collection of Wise Saws and Modern Instances* printed in London in 1852, who points to an unfortunate misinterpretation of the meaning of this elliptical text by certain people: "Sometimes indeed our old friend the Proverb gets too much clipt in his course of circulation: as in the case of that very important business to all Englishman, a Cold—'Stuff a cold and starve a fever,' has been grievously misconstrued, so as to bring on the fever it was meant to prevent."[43] This would imply that the elliptical text actually is supposed to mean "If you stuff a cold, you will have to starve a fever later." The confusion concerning this proverb can also be seen from a conversation in Christopher Morley's (1890–1957) novel *Kitty Foyle* (1939): "I said . . . I better go downstairs and eat a square meal, 'feed a cold and starve a fever'. Then the man in the next chair pipes up. 'You misunderstand that', he says. 'It means *if* you feed a cold you'll have to starve a fever later. Subsequently. With a cold like you got it I'm prescribing Planters Punch, maybe some jelly consommé and toast Melba."[44] Even though there are some people even today who look at the meaning of the proverb in this way, this is not what the folk had in mind, as Stuart A. Gallacher has so convincingly shown in his exemplary essay on the meaning of this proverb published in the *Bulletin of the History of Medicine*.[45] Having researched various medical theories that could apply to this text, Gallacher concludes that the proverb is meant to be taken literally, that is, "a cold is to be fed, and a fever is to be starved."[46] That's also the way Mark Twain understood the proverb in his marvellous essay on "Curing a Cold" from about 1864.[47]

> The first time I began to sneeze, a friend told me to go and bathe my feet in hot water and go to bed. I did so. Shortly afterward, another friend advised me to get up and take a cold shower-bath. I did that also. Within the hour, another friend assured me that it was policy to "feed a cold and starve a fever." I had both. So I thought it best to fill myself up for the cold, and then keep dark and let the fever starve awhile.

And that's the way most of us understand the proverb today. It is even fair to assume that most people actually adhere to the two proverbs expressed in this one proverbial text. When we have a cold it makes some sense to eat in order to generate heat, while it is equally sensible to assume that if we have a fever it might be wise not to take in food so as to keep down the body heat.

So much for folk medicine. Medical science has come down quite harshly on the wisdom of our dual proverb. Two studies of the common cold state that "the old proverb 'stuff a cold and starve a fever' is unsound in that a cold should not be fed any more than is necessary" and "nothing could be farther from the right than the injunction 'Feed a cold and starve a fever'. A cold is fever . . . Overloading the stomach is directly harmful."[48] Medical accounts in newspapers also have done their part to discredit the proverb. In 1978 such an article was entitled "Don't Starve Fever," arguing against the traditional proverb and stating that "from a physiological standpoint, there appears to be little reason to restrict food when you're sniffly or with a temperature."[49] About ten years later another newspaper headline echoed the same idea with a provocative "Feed a Fever, Feed a Cold," arguing that this variant of the proverb would be more appropriate "since research indicates that the body may actually lose nutrients during an infection."[50] What the scientists and their popularizers in the media forget in their proverb bashing is perhaps that the dual proverb is not meant to be interpreted quite so directly. The verb "stuff" is quite misleading since it might imply overeating in modern language use. In this regard it would indeed be better to employ the proverb variant with the more neutral verb "feed." The verb "starve" is also not meant quite so rigidly as it might seem, but rather simply to eat a bit less than usual. Let's not forget that the common folk is quite aware of the fact that we tend to lose our appetite when we are sick, be it a cold or a fever. What the two proverb halves or even more precisely the two proverbs most likely mean to say is "Feed a cold moderately and starve a fever moderately," and that advice would in fact fit nutritional concerns during illness from a scientific point of view. As one of the newspaper articles points out at the end, "if you're ill, it's important to eat properly. Good nutrition may help your body fight off a bug."[51]

In any case, proverbs are stubborn things, and it is doubtful that this still rather young proverb will die out soon. But there is no real reason for concern, for the folk is quite aware of the shortcomings of its proverbs. They are not universal truths, and they certainly can be laughed at as well. This can be seen in modern cartoons, comic strips, and greeting cards. Realizing how much we all like to eat, a get-well card with an illustration of someone bringing goodies to the bed included the message "When you're not feeling well, Remember . . . feed a cold, feed a fever."[52] A Beetle Bailey comic strip employed the same variation of the proverb to satirize the continuous longing for food: "Is it 'Feed a cold and starve a fever' or the other way around?— You're asking old 'Feed a fever, feed a cold'?"[53] For someone who likes to drink even more than to eat, a cartoon carries the caption "Flood a cold and drown a fever,"[54] and there is even a wife who makes lightly of her husband's supposed illness and food wishes, stating ironically "Sick my eye . . . You just like the idea of 'feed a cold'."[55] Finally, there is also the wonderful

Reprinted with special permission of King Features Syndicate.

PEANUTS reprinted by permission of UFS, Inc.

Peanuts comic strip which warms any dog lover's heart. Snoopy is sitting on top of his house reading the proverb "Feed a cold and starve a fever." In the next frame he jumps off the house, and in the third frame he is seen standing in front of Charlie Brown with his food dish in his mouth reporting that "A cold just came by and said it was hungry."[56] Such verbal and visual examples are ample proof of the survival of this particular medical proverb. It is certainly also in frequent oral use, and it is doubtful that modern science will displace it soon. As much as the general population might be interested in the newest breakthroughs in medicine, people will nevertheless hold on to some notions of folk medicine, especially if it has gained great currency in the form of a popular proverb.

An Apple a Day Keeps the Doctor Away

The most often quoted medical proverb is without doubt the simple dietary advice "An apple a day keeps the doctor away." Its origin and history are still quite uncertain, but it probably gained currency in the English language toward the end of the nineteenth century.[57] An English precursor might have been the proverb "Eat an apple on going to bed, And you'll keep the doctor from earning his bread" that was registered in the journal *Notes and Queries* in 1866.[58] But strange as it might seem, the extremely popular proverb "An apple a day keeps the doctor away" has been found in print thus far for the first time only in 1913: "Ait a happle avore gwain to bed, An' you'll make the doctor beg his bread; or as the more popular version runs: An apple a day keeps the doctor away."[59] That the proverb caught on quickly can be seen by the fact that parodies of it start to appear in print as early as the 1930s, as, for example, "An onion a day keeps the world away."[60] A proverb that is quoted as often as this one, to the point perhaps that we can't look at or eat apples without thinking of it, will be subjected to parody. The truth of its wisdom, not so much that eating a daily apple will definitely prevent a serious illness but rather that it makes good nutritional sense to eat a piece of fruit every day, is so obvious that it literally beckons to be ridiculed through clever changes of its simple wording. In fact, the entire proverb has by now been reduced to the structural formula "An X a day keeps Y away," making a steady stream of puns and parodies possible.

What follows is a small florilegium of such humorous but often also satirical variations of the proverb that have been found in literary works, in advertisements, cartoons, comic strips, and on greeting cards. While many are quite funny, they still express problems and concerns of our society which unfortunately cannot heal all of its ills by simply telling people to eat an apple a day. Thus a 1940 poem by Phyllis McGinley (b. 1905) is entitled "A Hobby a Day Keeps the Doldrums Away,"[61] and a couple of detective novels include the variations "A murder a day keeps the doctor away" and "A murder a day keeps boredom away."[62] Louis Safian confronted the proverb with the antipodes "An onion a day gives your diet away" and "An onion a day keeps everybody away,"[63] of which the latter has also been registered as graffiti.[64] A sexual pun characterizes yet another graffiti text that reads "A pill a day keeps the stork away"[65] that also alludes to the folklore of the stork bringing the children. Sexual or marital politics are commented on in an Andy Capp comic strip that includes the statement that "A crisis a day keeps his lordship away,"[66] and perhaps married couples should adhere to the modern wisdom "An effort a day keeps failure away" that found its way onto a small wooden plaque sold in 1978 in a gift shop in Salt Lake City, Utah.[67] Richard Nixon, it will be recalled, made various efforts to avoid losing his presidency, which finally led to the keen observation by the national columnist James Reston (b. 1909) that seemingly "A crisis a day keeps impeachment away."[68] Finally we can also refer to a cartoon that comments in a humorous way on today's emphasis on getting proper exercise, for "A bike a day keeps the weight away."[69] Even Blue Cross, Blue Shield got in on the exercising campaign, arguing that running "5 Miles a Day Keeps the Doctor Away."[70]

The Kraft's food conglomerate used variations of the proverb "An apple a

day keeps the doctor away" for two rather large national advertising campaigns that each ran for a number of years in various magazines. In the one case the firm advertised marshmallows by depicting a cute child holding a bag of this product and including the following slogans: "A marshmallow a day makes your blue eyes bluer,"[71] "A marshmallow a day puts a twinkle in your eye,"[72] "A marshmallow a day puts a smile on your face,"[73] and "A marshmallow a day keeps your freckles on straight."[74] A similar advertising campaign was used by Kraft to market its many different types of salad dressing. This time each advertisement included a picture of the various products and always the same slogan "A flavor a day keeps temptation away."[75] The latter slogan returns to the initial intent of the medical proverb, that is, the altered proverbial slogan is also arguing for dietary awareness, albeit this time for a varied diet of salad dressings for our salads that might prevent us from eating unhealthy and heavy meals. Realizing the infatuation of our society with meals made up of salads alone, it must be assumed that these magazine advertisements were a mercantile success for the Kraft Company.

A number of allusions to our proverb can be characterized by having replaced only the noun "apple" and leaving the remainder of the proverb intact, thus following the structural formula "An X a day keeps the doctor away." A funny greeting card, for example, contains the message "If a smile a day will keep the doctor away . . . Here's Mine!"[76] Another sexually oriented card has a humorous figure dressed in a condom happily singing out

"A condom a day keeps the doctor away," while the inside message wishes the recipient of the card "A Happy Birthday and a safe New Year."[77] This makes us wonder whether one of the condom producers has not already come up with the slogan "A condom a day keeps AIDS away"? It's amazing how adaptable proverbial structures are when it comes to create new slogans for the modern age.[78] Such a condom slogan would, by the way, be strengthened by the fact that its wording and structure would also recall the old medical proverb "An apple a day keeps the doctor away," therefore reminding the consumers that condoms might be as important to their health as apples. Of course, the Gates Rubber Co. had no real apples or doctors in mind either when it advertised its various types of belts for cars and appliances with the headline "Keeps him away."[79] The truncated proverbial slogan and the illustration of two such belts in the shape of an apple simply want to convey the effective message that these superb rubber products will "keep the repairman away." The underlying metaphor of the health proverb does its part in convincing the consumer to trust and also purchase this reliable industrial product.

Quite naturally many of the modern adaptations of this proverb deal with food and dietary matters. There is even the cartoon whose caption declares that "A beer a day keeps the doctor away,"[80] a health rule I have heard many a German friend expound upon. A magazine article on food diets has also claimed that "A slice of pizza a day keeps the doctor away,"[81] whereby the emphasis is obviously on "a slice" and not the entire pizza. In this connection we can also refer to a wonderful Peanuts greeting card wishing someone well. Snoopy tells the sick Linus "Get well soon and remember: 'A pizza a day keeps the doctor away'." Linus corrects Snoopy with the answer "That's 'An apple a day keeps the doctor away." Snoopy then declares that "Actually, if the pizza has lots of garlic on it, it keeps everyone away!" To that Linus can only respond with "Good grief!"—with the final message of the card reading "Anyway, get well soon!"[82] The intent of this card is to get the patient's appetite and spirit up again, something that the thought of pizza and good times might be able to accomplish better than the idea of an apple.

What a pizza can do, a potato ought to be able to accomplish as well or even better. Already in 1974 the *Boston Globe* newspaper ran the following advertisement in a national magazine: "Can a potato a day keep the doctor away? If an apple can, a potato can, too. In fact, it can probably do it better. It has more vitamin C. More protein. And more calories. O.K., knowing this may not change your life. But it might help you plan your meals next week. Which is why we have a daily column called 'Nutrition'. It's written by Dr. Jean Mayer of Harvard. It covers all the latest findings of developments on food."[83] This altered proverb slogan in the form of a question is a most effective way to draw attention to this particular newspaper column by a Harvard

Drawing by Mankoff; © 1977. The New Yorker Magazine, Inc.

medical doctor no less. It will doubtlessly have drawn people's attention to these reports on modern insights into healthy foods. And sure enough, about ten years later we find yet another magazine article telling us about the miraculous potato, for believe it or not, "A potato a day could keep high blood pressure away."[84] If only a raw potato in our lunch bags would taste as good as a delicious apple! Oh well, we could of course also settle for a hot cup of soup for lunch to keep us fit and trim, for the advertising claim has been made that "Campbell's Soup. [is] Better than an Apple a Day."[85]

Indeed, we are obsessed with health issues and staying away from the doctor. Unfortunately life isn't always fair, and even a steady diet of apples will not assure us of avoiding illness and death. This reality is drastically illustrated in a cartoon where a bug pauses in front of an apple tree with the sign "An apple a day keeps the doctor away." As the bug decides to crawl up the tree to eat its share of this health food, an apple falls and smashes it to death: "Splat,"[86] authenticating the truth of yet another apple proverb that claims that "The apple does not fall far from the tree." That is very grim humor and awakens us to the fact that often our diseases cannot be remedied by simple dietary cures. This also appears to be the message of a *New Yorker* cartoon from 1977 that shows a man in his bathroom standing in front of his medicine cabinet filled with apples.[87] No caption is needed, for every viewer knows immediately what proverb or idea is being illustrated. But somehow we get the feeling that all these apples will not prevent this person from eventually getting cancer or any other terminal disease that neither an apple a day nor a doctor can heal. The fear of illness and perhaps the doubt that the doctor and modern medicine cannot perform miracles are verbalized in a highly pessimistic poem by Susan Fromberg Schaeffer (b. 1941), in which the mystical apple has difficulties protecting her from sickness and eventual death, symbolized by the doctor in the shape of a black crow that is ready to descend on her and declare her terminally ill.[88]

An Apple a Day Keeps the Doctor Away

Therefore, I have hung it on strong thread
In the empty space of air
That waits behind the door
Like a square mouth full of trees.

All day now, I rock my chair
And watch the doctor,
A great black crow,
Circling that red globe

Turning one cheek, then another.
O he is circling lower and lower.
His wings are drooping
Great black moth, he is wearing out!

Warm wool, I am safe now
I won't need these thick glasses again.
O he is dropping
Like a great piece of ash.

He is kept away.
I would go out now
Except for the black cloud
Like a shroud coming closer.

It is dropping down,
Already it is covering the trees
In a din of cawing,
Of cawing.

But luckily we cope, and in many cases our folk remedies, modern medicine, and the doctor can help, giving us strength and hope to live in an imperfect world. Where apples can't help, medication and advice by doctors might well heal us. This was the message on note paper distributed to doctors by the Roerig pharmaceutical company. On the top of each sheet of paper appears an advertisement for Navane medicine with a slogan including a picture of a real apple: "Navane [apple] Once a day" (c. 1975). That reminds us also of the many vitamin pills instead of apples that are being marketed to be taken "one a day" just as natural fruit products are to be consumed daily according to the proverb and nutritional rules. A humorous reaction to the fruit versus medicine conflict was well illustrated in a "B.C." cartoon stating that "An apple a day . . . could turn the A.M.A. into a fruit conglomerate."[89] Of course nobody really wants that. Folk remedies based on healthy dietary rules cannot solve serious medical problems. But it nevertheless remains a simple truth that fruit of various types is healthy for us and will help to prevent common illnesses. So let's eat our apples, as the Vermont apple growers tell us to do with a dish-towel calendar depicting apples and the proverb "An apple a day keeps the doctor away" (October 1977). There is, of course, a mercantile purpose behind this advertising scheme, but an embroidery sampler from 1977 has no such intentions but simply delights in visualizing the valid wisdom that an apple a day can keep us away from the doctor a bit longer.[90]

The three proverbs discussed in some detail in these pages represent the most popular medical wisdom expressed in folk proverbs. They do not contain scientific information based on laboratory research, but are rather common-sense expressions from generations of observation and experience. As with anything in life, their advice should be taken with moderation or *cum grano salis*. Already Hippocrates (460?–377?) argued that "Everything in excess is opposed to nature,"[91] and that is certainly also true for preventive medicine, taking care of colds and fevers, and eating apples. The fact that these proverbs give only general medical advice for healthy living will prevent them from becoming obsolete as many folk remedies have done. Our three proverbs are general enough that they have withstood the test of time and science, and it is our prognosis that they will continue to be used by people of all walks of life for generations to come. While modern medicine advances with breathtaking speed, whose intricacies are to be understood only by the experts and appreciated by those who benefit from them, traditional medical proverbs remind us of the simple pleasures of life to be enjoyed as long as we adhere to everyday health rules. As stated at the beginning of these remarks, there are dozens of other sensible medical proverbs commenting on health and illness, and there are, of course, literally hundreds of general proverbs advising us how to live properly both medically and morally. Some of these gems of wisdom continue to have significant ethical value for people of a modern society. The platitude that "An apple a day makes 365 apples a year"[92] could therefore easily be varied to read "A proverb a day makes 365 proverbs a year," and these proverbs are certainly food for thought just as apples are food for the body to assure that we continue to enjoy healthy minds in healthy bodies.

Notes

This chapter was first published in *Proverbium: Yearbook of International Proverb Scholarship,* 8 (1991), 77–106. This original essay also includes a section on the proverb "Early to bed and early to rise, makes a man healthy, wealthy and wise" (pp. 85–92). It has now become the much enlarged fifth chapter of this book.

1. See F. P. Wilson, *The Oxford Dictionary of English Proverbs.* Oxford: Clarendon Press, 1970, p. 755.

2. See the fascinating article on this proverb by Hans Trümpy, "Similia similibus," *Schweizerisches Archiv für Volkskunde,* 62 (1966), 1–6.

3. For a number of examples see Jerzy Gluski, *Proverbs, Proverbes, Sprichwörter, Proverbi, Proverbios, Poslovitsy. A Comparative Book of Proverbs with a Latin Appendix.* New York: Elsevier Publishing Co., 1971, pp. 190–193.

4. See Walter Kelly, *A Collection of the Proverbs of All Nations.* Andover, Mass.: Warren F. Draper, 1869, pp. 199–203; and Robert Christy, *Proverbs. Maxims and Phrases of All Ages.* New York: G. P. Putnam's Sons, 1887, pp. 489–492.

5. For a list see Otto Moll, *Sprichwörterbibliographie.* Frankfurt am Main: Vittorio Klostermann, 1958, pp. 534–537.

6. John Ray, *A Compleat Collection of English Proverbs.* London: W. Otridge, 1768 (1st ed. 1670), pp. 25–32.

7. For these important texts see Vincent Stuckey Lean, *Lean's Collectanea.* Bristol: J. W. Arrowsmith, 1902; rpt. Detroit: Gale Research Co., 1969, vol. 1, pp. 478–509.

8. See Renate Bebermeyer, "Ärzte im Spiegel des Sprichworts," *Sprachspiegel,* 34 (1978), 131–138; and Hans-Manfred Militz, "Vom Arzt und seinen Kranken. Der Untergang eines phraseologischen Bereichs," *Sprachpflege,* 30 (1981), 134–135.

9. Russell A. Elmquist, "English Medical Proverbs," *Modern Philology,* 32 (1934–1935), 78. See also F. H. Garrison, "Medical Proverbs, Aphorisms and Epigrams," *Bulletin of the New York Academy of Medicine,* 4 (1928), 979–1005; and Archer Taylor, *The Proverb.* Cambridge: Harvard University Press, 1931; rpt. Hatboro, Pa.: Folklore Associates, 1962; rpt. again with an introduction and bibliography by Wolfgang Mieder. Bern: Peter Lang, 1985, pp. 121–129.

10. See Françoise Loux and Philippe Richard, *Sagesses du corps. La santé et maladie dans les proverbes français.* Paris: G.-P. Maisonneuve et Larose, 1978.

11. See also Felicitas Gruttmann, *Ein Beitrag zur Kenntnis der Volksmedizin in Sprichwörtern, Redensarten und Heilsegen des englischen Volkes, mit besonderer Berücksichtigung der Zahnheilkunde.* Greifswald: L. Bamberg, 1939; Roland Rickey Woodburn, *Proverbs in Health Books of the English Renaissance.* Diss. Texas Tech University, 1975; and George Walton Williams, "Shakespeare's Metaphors of Health: Food, Sport, and Life-Preserving Rest," *Journal of Medieval and Renaissance Studies,* 14 (1984), 187–202.

12. See the comprehensive study by Helmut Seidl, *Medizinische Sprichwörter im Englischen und Deutschen. Eine diachrone Untersuchung zur vergleichenden Parömiologie.* Bern: Peter Lang, 1982.

13. For a collection of 4500 such anti-proverbs see Wolfgang Mieder, *Antisprichwörter.* 3 vols. Wiesbaden: Verlag für deutsche Sprache, 1982; Wiesbaden: Gesellschaft für deutsche Sprache, 1985; Wiesbaden: Quelle & Meyer, 1989.

14. For a discussion of the interplay of tradition and innovation in fairy tales, legends, nursery rhymes, and proverbs see Wolfgang Mieder, *Tradition and Innovation in Folk Literature.* Hanover, N.H.: University Press of New England, 1987.

15. See Seidl (note 12), pp. 257–258; and the various short notes concerning the origin of this proverb listed in Wolfgang Mieder, *Investigations of Proverbs, Proverbial Expressions, Quotations and Clichés. A Bibliography of Explanatory Essays which Appeared in "Notes and Queries" (1849–1983).* Bern: Peter Lang, 1984, p. 307.

16. For precise references see the following standard proverb dictionaries by Burton Stevenson, *The Macmillan Book of Proverbs, Maxims, and Familiar Phrases*. New York: Macmillan, 1948, p. 1877; Morris Palmer Tilley, *A Dictionary of the Proverbs in England in the Sixteenth and Seventeenth Centuries*. Ann Arbor: University of Michigan Press, 1950, p. 555; Wilson (note 1), p. 646; Bartlett Jere Whiting, *Early American Proverbs and Proverbial Phrases*. Cambridge: Harvard University Press, 1977, p. 347; John A. Simpson, *The Concise Oxford Dictionary of Proverbs*. Oxford: Oxford University Press, 1982, p. 183; and Wolfgang Mieder, Stewart Kingsbury, and Kelsie Harder (eds.), *A Dictionary of American Proverbs*. New York: Oxford University Press, 1992, pp. 482–483.

17. See Charles Dickens, *The Works of Charles Dickens*. Vol. II: *Martin Chuzzlewit*. New York: Books Inc., 1868, vol. 2, p. 785.

18. John W. Barber, *The Hand Book of Illustrated Proverbs*. New York: George F. Tuttle, 1856, p. 241.

19. Cited from Wolfgang Mieder, *American Proverbs: A Study of Texts and Contexts*. Bern: Peter Lang, 1989, p. 232.

20. Stevenson (note 16), p. 1877; and Wilson (note 1), p. 646.

21. Cited from Archer Taylor and Bartlett Jere Whiting, *A Dictionary of American Proverbs and Proverbial Phrases, 1820–1880*. Cambridge: Harvard University Press, 1958, 296.

22. Bartlett Jere Whiting, *Modern Proverbs and Proverbial Sayings*. Cambridge: Harvard University Press, 1989, p. 510.

23. See Wilson (note 1), p. 601.

24. Whiting (note 16), p. 323.

25. *Fortune* (April 1935), p. 133.

26. See Whiting (note 16), p. 323.

27. Cited from *The Papers of Benjamin Franklin*, ed. by Leonard W. Labaree. New Haven, Conn.: Yale University Press, 1961, vol. 4, p. 63.

28. See Whiting (note 16), p. 323.

29. For additional historical references see Taylor and Whiting (note 21), p. 272; and Whiting (note 22), p. 465.

30. *Fortune* (December 1952), p. 18.

31. *Fortune* (June 1962), p. 13.

32. *Fortune* (September 1957), p. 13.

33. *Alaska Medicine* (March 1975), p. 24. I owe this reference to my former student Robert Haynes.

34. *New Yorker* (November 9, 1987), p. 44.

35. *Fortune* (October 1939), p. 133.

36. *The Burlington Free Press* (February 27, 1976), p. 1A.

37. *The Burlington Free Press* (May 2, 1978), p. 5A.

38. *Family Circle* (February 1974), p. 30.

39. Cited from Mieder (note 19), p. 266.

40. See above all Seidl (note 12), pp. 282–285; and Mieder (note 15), p. 68.

41. See Wilson (note 1), p. 783; and Simpson (note 16), p. 78.

42. Henry David Thoreau, *The Writings of Henry David Thoreau*. Vol. I: *A Week on the Concord and Merrimack Rivers*. Boston: Houghton, Mifflin and Co., 1893, vol. 1, p. 338.

43. Edward Fitzgerald, *Polonius: A Collection of Wise Saws and Modern Instances*. Portland/ Maine: Thomas B. Mosher, 1901, p. xxii.

44. Christopher Morley, *Kitty Foyle*. New York: J. B. Lippincott, 1939, p. 318.

45. Stuart A. Gallacher, "Stuff a Cold and Starve a Fever," *Bulletin of the History of Medicine*, 11 (1942), 576–581; also in *The Wisdom of Many. Essays on the Proverb*, ed. by Wolfgang Mieder and Alan Dundes. New York: Garland Publishing, 1981, pp. 211–217.

46. Gallacher (note 45), p. 581. See also Archer Taylor, "Feed a Cold and Starve a Fever," *Journal of American Folklore*, 71 (1958), 190.

47. Mark Twain, *The Writings of Mark Twain*. Vol. XIX: *Sketches New and Old*. New York: Harper & Brothers, 1917, vol. 19, p. 364.

48. Gallacher (note 45), p. 579.

49. *The Burlington Free Press* (March 6, 1978), p. 2C.

50. *The Burlington Free Press* (January 28, 1987), p. 2D.

51. See note 50, p. 2D.

52. Get-well card by Hourglass Editions (1983), purchased in Burlington, Vermont, in November 1984. The artist is Linda Christensen.

53. *The Burlington Free Press* (September 22, 1983), p. 11D.

54. *St. Louis Post Dispatch* (September 13, 1974), p. 12D.

55. *St. Louis Post Dispatch* (August 22, 1974), p. 9D.

56. *The Burlington Free Press* (February 28, 1989), p. 5D.

57. See Seidl (note 12), p. 73–75; and Mieder (note 15), p. 8.

58. See John P. Phillips, ''Eat an Apple on Going to Bed, and You'll Keep the Doctor from Earning His Bread,'' *Notes and Queries*, 3rd series, 9 (1866), 153.

59. For references see Stevenson (note 16), p. 86; Wilson (note 1), p. 17; Simpson (note 16), p. 5; and Mieder et al. (note 16), p. 23.

60. See F. W. Bradley, ''South Carolina Proverbs,'' *Southern Folklore Quarterly*, 1 (1937), 60; and Bartlett Jere Whiting, ''Proverbs and Proverbial Phrases,'' in *The Frank C. Brown Collection of North Carolina Folklore*, ed. by Newman Ivey White. Durham, N.C.: Duke University Press, 1952, vol. 1, p. 362.

61. Phyllis McGinley, *A Pocketful of Wry*. New York: Grosset & Dunlap, 1959, pp. 111–112.

62. Cited from Whiting (note 22), p. 14.

63. Louis Safian, *The Book of Updated Proverbs*. New York: Abelard-Schuman, 1967, p. 30.

64. Mieder (note 19), p. 265.

65. Also cited from Mieder (note 19), p. 272.

66. *St. Louis Post Dispatch* (January 30, 1976), p. 10D.

67. Purchased in Salt Lake City, Utah, in November 1978.

68. *The Burlington Free Press* (October 30, 1973), p. 2A.

69. *San Francisco Chronicle* (February 2, 1980), comic section.

70. *Time* (November 13, 1978), p. 31.

71. *Good Housekeeping* (June 1974), p. 55.

72. *Better Homes and Gardens* (April 1976), p. 113.

73. *Family Circle* (July 14, 1976), p. 15.

74. *Family Circle* (December 13, 1977), p. 15.

75. *Better Homes and Gardens* (March 1975), p. 93; *Good Housekeeping* (July 1976), p. 22; *Good Housekeeping* (July 1977), p. 17; and *Family Circle* (July 10, 1978), p. 55.

76. Greeting card from the P. O. Drawer Card Company purchased in Burlington, Vermont, in February 1978.

77. Birthday card from the Recycled Paper Products Company (1987) purchased in Burlington, Vermont, in October 1989. The artist is John-Richard Allen.

78. See Barbara and Wolfgang Mieder, ''Tradition and Innovation: Proverbs in Advertising,'' *Journal of Popular Culture*, 11 (1977), 308–319; also in *The Wisdom of Many. Essays on the Proverb*, ed. by W. Mieder and Alan Dundes. New York: Garland Publishing, 1981, pp. 309–322.

79. *Fortune* (June 1965), p. 79.

80. *Punch* (February 13, 1985), p. 62.

81. *People* (July 27, 1981), p. 80.

82. Peanuts greeting card from the Hallmark Card Company purchased in Burlington, Vermont, in December 1977.

83. *Woman's Day* (November 1974), p. 253.

84. *Vermont* (Fall 1986), p. 12.

85. *Time* (March 7, 1983), p. 35.

86. *Boston Globe* (April 22, 1979), comic section.

87. *New Yorker* (August 22, 1977), p. 70.

88. Susan Fromberg Schaeffer, "Proverbs," *Poetry,* 120 (1972), 7–8.

89. *St. Louis Post Dispatch* (November 11, 1976), p. 10F.

90. Embroidery sampler purchased in Burlington, Vermont, in November 1977 and stitched by Dr. Barbara Mieder.

91. Stevenson (note 16), p. 719.

92. Mieder (note 19), p. 271.

8

" Good Proverbs Make Good Vermonters "

The Flavor of Regional Proverbs

Anybody trying to put together a list of American proverbs will quickly realize that this is a very problematic task indeed. Proverbs such as "Time flies," "All is not gold that glitters," "A sound mind in a sound body," "In wine there is truth," "Silence gives consent," and many others are very popular in the United States, but they are certainly not American in origin. Each of these proverbs has a long history and their origins can be traced back to classical antiquity.[1] In fact, they were already so well known over two thousand years ago that they were translated into many national languages from the Latin during the Middle Ages. Thus the Latin proverb "Manus manum lavat" appears in English as "One hand washes the other," in French as "Une main lave l'autre," in German as "Eine Hand wäscht die andere," in Italian as "Una mano lava l'altra," in Spanish as "Una mano lava a la otra," in Russian as "Ruka ruku moet," and so on. We could extend this list to include dozens of languages and many more regional dialects that would show that this is a truly international proverb that also happens to be current in the United States.[2] But an American proverb it most certainly is not.

A similar picture appears with the many Biblical proverbs which are an integral part of the proverb tradition in countries where Christianity took hold. Such common proverbs as "The love of money is the root of all evil" (1 Timothy 6:10), "Pride comes before the fall" (Proverbs 16:18), "A prophet has no honor in his own country" (Matthew 13:57), or "Man does not live by bread alone" (Deuteronomy 8:3, Matthew 4:4) exist in basically identical form in the hundreds of languages into which the Bible was translated. The

latter proverb appears in French as "L'homme ne vit pas de pain seulement," the Germans cite it as "Der Mensch lebt nicht vom Brot allein," the Italian people say "L'uomo non vive di pan solo," in the many Spanish-speaking countries one hears "El hombre no vivira de solo pan," and in the Soviet Union to this day people continue to use "Ne edinym khlebom zhiv chelovek." Not everybody thinks of the Bible when using this proverb, and only a small number of people will be able to give its precise Biblical source.[3] But again, it certainly is a very popular proverb in America, that is, one that is in use in this country but not indigenous to it.

It should be obvious by now that it is difficult to decide which proverb is peculiarly American, Chinese, German, Russian, and so on. In order to ascertain the definite origin of any given proverb, painstaking historical and comparative research must be undertaken.[4] There exist book-length studies and numerous shorter monographs or articles that trace the origin, history, and dissemination of singular proverbs, but for the great majority of proverbs we are still very much in doubt as to their time and place of origin.[5] The problem is even exacerbated by the fact that polygenesis is possible, that is, proverbs might at times have originated in separate locations at different times. It is conceivable that a proverb like "Big fish eat little fish" might have its traceable origin in Greek antiquity but that it was also created quite independently in ancient China.[6] Each and every proverb has its fascinating history, and if we want absolute certainty about the national corpus of the proverbs of a given country, a large number of individual proverb studies still need to be undertaken. In fact, this gargantuan task will never be accomplished entirely for any national proverb stock, but isolated studies of certain proverbs will help to understand certain patterns of origin and subsequent transmission.

In the case of the United States the question of what constitutes a real American proverb is especially difficult to answer.[7] This country is made up of so many groups of people with different national, ethnic, and linguistic backgrounds, and this diverse society has also brought about a proverb stock that is anything but homogenous. The many waves of immigrants have brought their popular proverbs with them, and many eventually were translated into English. Once translated, they gained greater currency in America, but their origin is definitely not American. Those proverbs brought over by the many English-speaking settlers became the basic proverbial vocabulary of this country. In fact, we can go so far as to state that for all general purposes most American proverbs have an English origin or go back even further to Biblical or classical traditions.[8]

Thus it was found, for example, that of 199 proverbs collected in the Eastern United States in 1929 only 10 texts or a mere 5% are at least with some certainty of American origin.[9]

> A sitting hen never grows fat.
>
> Don't kick a fellow when he's down.
>
> Great minds run in the same channels.
>
> It pays to advertise.
>
> Laugh and the world laughs with you, weep and you weep alone.
>
> Paddle your own canoe.
>
> The harder you fall the higher you bounce.
>
> The bigger they are the harder they fall.
>
> This won't buy the baby's shoes.
>
> This won't buy a dress for the baby or pay for the one it has on.

Such proverbs as "Don't kick a fellow when he's down," "It pays to advertise," and, of course, "Paddle your own canoe" seem to be expressions of typical aspects of American culture. It is extremely important to realize that the age of coining proverbs is obviously not over. Proverbs do come and go. Some have remained with us for centuries and have gained worldwide currency; others have disappeared since they do not fit modern mores any longer; and some proverbs have been created on American soil with regional or national distribution. For example, the proverb "It takes two to tango" originated with the song "It Takes Two to Tango" (1952), first sung by Pearl Bailey (b. 1918). It is without doubt an American proverb, but we hasten to add that it is most likely a variation of the old proverb "It takes two to quarrel." Nevertheless, it has gained great acceptance in this form not only in this country but also in translations abroad.[10] It can thus be considered as a new American proverb in its own right. Truly American proverbs of relatively recent coinage are doubtlessly "Different strokes for different folks" or "Garbage in, garbage out." The first was probably coined in the mid-twentieth century and gained much popularity through the television show that had the proverb for its title; there was also the rock song "Everyday People" (1968) sung by Sly and the Family Stone group that included the proverb as a leitmotif.[11] The second proverb is even more recent (mid 1960s) and has caught on quickly as an expression that describes perfectly the frustrations modern mankind experiences when dealing with the world of computers. We see through such examples how important modern mass media are in disseminating song lines, advertising slogans, graffiti, political maxims, and so on, which in turn might become actual proverbs.[12] But be careful—the current popularity of the proverb "No pain(s), no gain(s)" is deceiving. It dates back to at least 1648, indicating once again that the origin of each individual proverb can only be ascertained after careful historical research.

Since about the 1920s there has been a keen interest throughout the United States in collecting the proverbs in common use in the various states of this large country. Members of the American Dialect Society in 1944 even decided to create a Research Committee on Proverbial Sayings that still functions today.[13] With the help of many field workers, the incredible number of more than 250,000 proverbs and proverbial expressions was collected over a period of about forty years.[14] While some smaller regional collections have been published, Stewart Kingsbury, Kelsie Harder, and I have now finished our annotated *Dictionary of American Proverbs* (1992), which is based on these collecting efforts.[15] Although most of these texts can be traced back to English sources, some examples are clearly indigenous to the United States. Among the texts from Arkansas are "It takes a gizzard and guts to get along in the world" and "You can't run all the squirrels up the same tree." The proverb "A dollar saved is a dollar made" was collected in California and is clearly a variation of the older British original "A penny saved is a penny earned." This variant is most likely current throughout the United States. But even if we recognize such a text as a variant of an earlier proverb, that variant is ultimately accepted as a proverb in itself, that is, it in turn takes on a general currency of its own. Obviously American is the proverb "You can't steal second base while your foot is on the first," which was recorded in Illinois. We also assume that "Cigarettes are coffin nails" might well have originated in Kentucky, and this proverb has gained wide currency throughout the states. A logical variation of the traditional proverb "Take care of the pence (pennies) and the pounds will take care of themselves" was collected in the early 1930s in Nebraska as "Take care of the dimes and the dollars will take care of themselves." We also have the feeling that the two proverbs "Good liquor needs no water" and "Don't chew your tobacco twice" are of American origin, perhaps indeed from North Carolina or Kentucky. They certainly are refreshing metaphorical wisdom in comparison to such standard Anglo-American proverbs as "Honesty is the best policy," "Nothing ventured, nothing gained," or "A watched pot never boils."

The interest in the proverbs and proverbial expressions of the New England states has a considerable tradition. Already Ralph Waldo Emerson (1803–

1882), the prolific nineteenth-century American preacher, rhetorician, essayist, transcendentalist, philosopher, pragmatist, and humanist, was intrigued by proverbs throughout his long life. Not only did he assemble three small collections of proverbs, he also made much use of them in his letters, journals, sermons, lectures, and essays.[16] Interspersed in this wide range of intellectual and literary production are theoretical observations on the proverb that are as valid to proverb scholars today as they were in Emerson's time. He defines and characterizes proverbs as the "language of experience" which "gives comfort and encouragement, aid and abetting to daily action." To Emerson proverbs are "rules of good householding" whose "practical wisdom" teaches us "worldly prudence." They are "metaphor[s] of the human mind" expressing "moral truth" and transmitting "their commentary upon all parts of life." In his early lecture on "Ethics" (1837) he reduces all moral codes of conduct to proverbs, and in his significant essay on "Compensation" (1841) he makes the following acute and all-encompassing observation: "Proverbs, like the sacred books of each nation, are the sanctuary of the intuitions. That which the droning world, chained in appearances, will not allow the realist to say in his own words, it will suffer him to say in proverbs without contradiction. And this law of laws, which the pulpit, the senate and the college deny, is hourly preached in all markets and workshops by flights of proverbs, whose teaching is as true and as omnipresent as that of birds and flies."[17] Approximately one hundred years later another American author, the poet Carl Sandburg (1878–1967), echoed this high esteem for proverbs in the eleventh section of his epic poem "Good Morning, America" (1928), in which he characterizes the American melting-pot via its speech: "A code arrives; language; lingo, slang; behold the proverbs of a people, a nation."[18]

Mindful of a people's collective wisdom expressed in proverbs, and wishing to record those texts current in New England, I have recently assembled about 500 of them under the title *Yankee Wisdom: New England Proverbs* (1989).[19] Naturally it was difficult to find proverbs that are truly indigenous to this six-state region, but obviously such texts as "Hitch your wagon to a star" (coined by Emerson in 1870) and "If you don't like the weather in New England, just wait a minute and it will change" have their origin in this area of the country. As regards the small state of Vermont, some scholarly attempts at collecting its proverbial stock have been undertaken by three professors of the University of Vermont. Leon Dean (1889–1982), Vermont's renowned folklorist and former editor of the *Green Mountain Whitlin's* folklore journal, published small lists of proverbs from time to time. Muriel Hughes (b. 1903) presented her collection of "Vermont Proverbs and Proverbial Sayings" in two issues of *Vermont History* (1960),[20] and I was able to benefit from this previous work in my two collections of about 1000 sayings with the titles *Talk Less and Say More: Vermont Proverbs* (1986) and *As Sweet as Apple Cider:*

Vermont Expressions (1988).[21] My own collections are based on original field work during the past fifteen years, on the gleanings of Dean and Hughes, as well as on painstaking investigations of the regional literature of such Vermont authors as Rowland E. Robinson (1833–1900), John Godfrey Saxe (1816–1867), Dorothy Canfield Fisher (1879–1958), Walter Hard (1882–1966), Allen R. Foley (1898–1978), and others. I have concentrated on collecting primarily those proverbs that are not necessarily known throughout the United States. Most texts are hopefully current only in Vermont or on a somewhat larger scope in New England. The difficulty of deciding whether a certain proverb is in fact from Vermont can quickly be seen by such texts as "Sap runs best after a sharp frost," "The world is your cow, but you have to do the milking," and "Every cider apple has a worm." They sound as if they originated in Vermont, but why not in New Hampshire or upstate New York? Only through careful research of each individual proverb might the actual origin come to light, but for many such texts the proof of a Vermont source or any other state for that matter would be impossible. What is of importance is that the proverbs listed in my books and discussed below were in fact collected in Vermont. Most collectors of the proverb lore of a singular state preface their collections by the caveat that the title of "X (any state) Proverbs" would actually be better expressed as "The Proverbs Current in X," and that also holds true for the proverbs from Vermont we discuss here.

One additional caveat must be mentioned before looking at a number of Vermont proverbs in more detail. There is a certain danger connected with deducing national or regional characteristics from folklore in general and proverbs in particular. Obviously many of the proverbs in the various state collections do not describe the typical person or mores of a given state. However, proverbs do reflect to a certain degree the worldview of their users, and with caution one could perhaps say that a collection of proverbs from a particular state mirrors certain stereotypical values of its people. In the case of the 500 proverbs I collected from oral and written sources in Vermont, many deal with cows, maple sugaring, independence, thriftiness, and taciturnity, which all seem to be part of the Vermont scene and psyche. Others express a good dose of the dry humor Vermonters supposedly are famous for. Above all, the proverbs reflect in concise and picturesque language a way of life that appeals to both real Vermonters and so-called "flatlanders." That does not necessarily make them Vermont proverbs, but proverbs used in Vermont as expressions of traditional folk wisdom.

A good example is, of course, the appearance of the proverb "Good fences make good neighbors" in the poem "Mending Wall" (1914) by Robert Frost (1875–1963). More than one scholar has falsely concluded that this proverb originated with Frost and that it could thus be considered a Vermont or at least a New England proverb.[22] But in 1640 we find the quite similar text "A good fence helpeth to keepe peace between neighbours; but let vs take heed that we make not a high stone wall, to keepe vs from meeting,"[23] which is so reminiscent of the two men repairing the stone wall in Frost's poem. From the same year stems the similar proverb "Love your neighbor, yet pull not down your hedge,"[24] which Benjamin Franklin cited in his *Poor Richard's Almanack* for 1754.[25] There is also the medieval Spanish proverb "Una pared entre dos vecinos guarda mas (hace durar) la amistad" which Ralph Waldo Emerson recorded in English translation as "A wall between both best preserves friendship" in his journal of 1832.[26] One might well think that Frost encountered this text in Emerson and that it as well as the other English proverbs already cited inspired him to formulate the more poetic "Good fences make good neighbors." But no such luck, for the proverb in this exact wording appeared for the first time in *Blum's Farmer's and Planter's Almanac* for 1850, published annually since 1828 in Winston-Salem, North Carolina. It was cited again in Blum's almanac for 1861,[27] and the discoverer of these two early references believes that the proverb might have found its way into this southern almanac by being quoted from a New England almanac or farm journal. Be that as it may, we now know that the proverb was known on the East Coast of the United States at least six decades prior to Robert Frost's using it in one of his most famous poems.[28]

Mending Wall

Something there is that doesn't love a wall,
That sends the frozen-ground-swell under it,
And spills the upper boulders in the sun;
And makes gaps even two can pass abreast.
The work of hunters is another thing:
I have come after them and made repair
Where they have left not one stone on a stone,
But they would have the rabbit out of hiding,
To please the yelping dogs. The gaps I mean,
No one has seen them made or heard them made,
But at spring mending-time we find them there.
I let my neighbor know beyond the hill;
And on a day we meet to walk the line
And set the wall between us once again.
We keep the wall between us as we go.
To each the boulders that have fallen to each.
And some are loaves and some so nearly balls
We have to use a spell to make them balance:
'Stay where you are until our backs are turned!'
We wear our fingers rough with handling them.
Oh, just another kind of outdoor game,
One on a side. It comes to little more:
There where it is we do not need the wall:
He is all pine and I am apple orchard.
My apple trees will never get across

And eat the cones under his pines, I tell him
He only says, 'Good fences make good neighbors.'
Spring is the mischief in me, and I wonder
If I could put a notion in his head:
'Why do they make good neighbors? Isn't it
Where there are cows? But here there are no cows.
Before I built a wall I'd ask to know
What I was walling in or walling out,
And to whom I was like to give offense.
Something there is that doesn't love a wall,
That wants it down.' I could say 'Elves' to him,
But it's not elves exactly, and I'd rather
He said it for himself. I see him there
Bringing a stone grasped firmly by the top
In each hand, like an old-stone savage armed.
He moves in darkness as it seems to me,
Not of woods only and the shade of trees
He will not go behind his father's saying,
And he likes having thought of it so well
He says again, 'Good fences make good neighbors.'

We can assume that Frost must have heard the proverb in oral communication in New England, perhaps even in Vermont. But even if Frost did not coin this proverb, his poem certainly was instrumental in making it into one of the most common American proverbs. And because of Frost's fame as a New England or even Vermont poet, and the poem's preoccupation with the typical stone walls of this region, Americans have long decided to consider the proverb a New England proverb, or as we Vermonters would have it, a proverb grown on Vermont soil. As a so-called "flatlander," but one who feels positively chauvinistic about his beloved Vermont, I would give a lot to locate the proverb "Good fences make good neighbors" in a Vermont publication prior to 1850. Unfortunately I haven't had any success as yet, but "Hope springs eternal" as the proverb says.

Frost as the narrator of the poem "Mending Wall" confronts his rather taciturn neighbor during their yearly ritual of repairing their commonly held stone wall with the question of the actual need of this labor in view of the fact that in the absence of cows it serves no apparent purpose any longer. But the neighbor simply continues to labor away and responds with merely twice quoting his father's authoritative saying that "Good fences make good neighbors." In this almost noncommunicative "dialogue," if one can call it that, Frost has captured the tight-lipped taciturnity for which the stereotypical Vermonter has gained some fame throughout the United States. There must be some truth to this characterization of Vermonters, if they themselves have come up with the very short proverb "Talk less and say more." I recorded this proverb in oral use in Vermont about ten years ago, and I have not located it in any other of the dozens of Anglo-American proverb collections.

"As I see it, good fences make good neighbors."

Drawing by Kraus; © 1960. The New Yorker Magazine, Inc.

Sticking out my proverbial neck here, I am willing to declare it to be an indigenous Vermont proverb, one that encapsulates the world view of independent Vermonters. There are other proverbs that praise taciturnity current in Vermont, as, for example, "Few words are best," "Say nothing and saw wood," "He can't speak well who always talks," "Nobody ever repented holding his tongue," "Be silent or speak something worth hearing," "What you don't say won't ever hurt you," "Turn your tongue seven times before speaking," and "Never cackle unless you lay," but none of them has the paradoxical wit, the biting satire, and the linguistic pun of "Talk less and say more." I will forever be thankful to my New England Press publishers for suggesting this proverb as the title for my collection of Vermont proverbs—it certainly captures the typical Vermonter's relationship to futile oral communication.

Obviously the Vermont farmers also do not mince many words with or about their cows, but it should not be surprising to find a predominance of proverbs quoted by them that express everyday wisdom by couching it in cow metaphors. Thus the proverb "It is a lean cow that gives the milk" offers advice concerning frugality, "It isn't always the bell cow that gives the most milk" warns that appearances might be deceptive, "Don't swallow the cow and worry about the tail" reminds people not to get bogged down with minor matters, "If cows lie down before noon, it will rain soon" contains a weather prognosis based on everyday observation, "Every cow needs a tail in fly time" remarks on the usefulness of seemingly unimportant things at certain times, "A good cow may have a bad calf" shows that a good farmer may have a bad son, "The world is your cow, but you have to do the milking" expresses the need for self-reliance and serious work, and "Cursed cows have short horns" states that quarrelsome people will be controlled in a rigorous manner. Many times these "cow" proverbs are clearly regional variants of more general proverbs. Thus the farm proverb "Milk the cow which is near" probably replaces the overused and cliché-like classical proverb "Take time by the forelock," "Cows prefer the grass on the other side of the fence" is a more realistic image than the general "The grass is always greener on the other side of the fence," "You can't sell the cow and have the milk too" corresponds to "You can't have your cake and eat it too," "A man may kiss his cow" is a more drastic version of "Each to his own," and while Vermonters also use the proverb "It makes a difference whose ox is gored," they prefer the more regional variant "It makes a difference whose cow is in the well." Speaking of wells, it should not surprise us that Vermonters refer to this all-important water resource in several proverbs, for example, "It takes more than one well to make a river," "You can never tell the depth of the well from the length of the handle on the pump," and, of course, the often heard "You never miss the water till the well is dry."

Of particular interest might be how Vermonters have dealt with the very popular proverb "You can't judge a book by its cover." Over the years I have recorded such variants as "You can't judge a book by its binding," "You can't judge others by yourself," "You can't judge a man by his overcoat," and "You can't judge a horse by its harness." These texts can all be reduced to the structural formula "You can't judge X by Y," and one can quickly realize how such a proverbial pattern can yield a multitude of proverbs depending in each case on the social environment and worldview of the speaker. While I have found some references to the proverbs just cited in collections of other American regions, the uniquely Vermont text appears to be yet another "cow" proverb, namely "You can't judge a cow by her looks." What a wonderfully fitting metaphor for the rural state of Vermont to express the non-metaphorical English proverb "Never judge from appearances" from the sixteenth century.

An even more general version of this proverbial structure exists based on replacing the verb "judge" by any variable. This pattern could be summarized in the formulaic pattern of "You can't 'verb' X 'preposition' Y." Such texts express certain impossibilities and unrealistic dreams or wishes, arguing in a typically didactic fashion for the adherence to common sense in our aspirations. The following variants have been collected in Vermont: "You can't hang a man for an idea," "You can't make a whistle out of a pig's tail," "You can't get wool of a frog," "You can't swing a cat by a bull's tail," "You can't put a quart in a pint basin," "You can't build a house from the top down," and "You can't put an old head on young shoulders." The pattern can also be expanded into longer and more descriptive texts, as, for example, "You can't always tell by the looks of a toad how far he can jump," "You can't expect anything from a pig but a grunt," and "You can't mow hay where the grass doesn't grow." Important to notice with these variants is once again the explicit predominance of farm animals and rural metaphors, reflecting the traditional agricultural life of Vermont and the value system of stability, slow change, and status quo.

Farming and sugaring were a major livelihood for old-time Vermonters and to a certain degree they continue to play an important role in the state's economic structure. Little wonder that many proverbs deal with planting and harvesting, often transmitting old farming rules based on generations of experience and observation. Even though the landscape and demographic make-up of Vermont are changing toward a more urban environment, one can still hear many proverbial rules concerning farming and gardening: "If the corn has thick husks, there will be a hard winter," "Plant your corn when the leaves of the oak tree are the size of a mouse's ear," "Sow dry and set wet," "Snowy winter, plentiful harvest," "Plant cucumbers the first Sunday in June before sunrise," and "Town Meeting is time to put in the potatoes." There is even the very local planting proverb "It's time to plant corn when the icicles fall off the ledge on Snake Mountain," while others reflect more generally on the hardship and importance of farming, namely, "It's a rare farm that has no bad ground" and "If the farmer fails all will starve." But proverbs on planting and growing are not always just straightforward rules. Some contain wonderful bits of folk humor, as, for example, "Your corn will never grow until you lie naked at night" and "Time to plant beans is when it is hot enough nights so that Hannah sleeps without a sheet on her."

Maple sugaring has also resulted in the formulation of certain folk maxims based on decades of experience with this "sweet" work. Some texts refer explicitly to the hard labor involved in sugaring, namely, "A gallon of syrup is worth one day's labor" and "You boil at least thirty-two gallons of sap to make each gallon of syrup." Other proverbs contain information on when the sap runs best, as, for example, "When the sun is bright on the snow and warm on your back, the sap will be running," "Warm days, cold nights, make sap run right," "Sap runs best after a sharp frost," "Sap runs better by day than by night," and "When the wind is in the west the sap runs best." There are even proverbs that comment on the particular sweetness of the sap: "The older the tree the sweeter the sap," "Sap run during the daytime is sweeter than that run at night," "The first run of sap is the sweetest," and "The higher you tap the sweeter the sap." Regarding the scientific value of these proverbial observations, one of the leading maple syrup researchers from the University of Vermont has assured me that they do contain much truth that has been born out by years of scholarly analysis. Even the colorful and typically Vermont proverb "Trees differ as much for sugar as cows differ for butter" has plenty of scientific validity. The actual excitement of getting the sugaring started in early spring after a long Vermont winter is expressed in the poetic gem of folk wisdom "A sap-run is the sweet good-bye of winter." And finally there is the proverb "The true Vermonter never loses his taste for the sweet of the maple," which shows our personal delight about this golden product, or is it by chance a tongue-in-cheek advertisement to get people outside Vermont to buy this natural and sweet syrup that cannot possibly be touched in quality by the syrup produced in neighboring states?

In a state that depends to a large degree on agriculture there naturally exists a keen interest in the weather and the seasons. Vermonters are fond of such general weather observations as "Winter's fog will freeze a dog," "A late snowstorm is a poor man's fertilizer," "A cold wet May fills the barn with hay." "March rains serve only to fill the ditches," and "A late fall means a hard winter" which doubtlessly are applicable to other New England regions as well. However, the more general proverb "In New England we have nine months of winter and three months of damned poor sledding" also exists as a specifically Vermont variant as "Vermont has nine months of winter and three months of damned poor sledding." The same is true for the New England proverb "We have two seasons: winter and Fourth of July" which in Vermont is usually cited as "Vermont has only two seasons—winter and the Fourth of July." It is not certain whether Vermont can claim to have originated these texts, but the local weather sign "Snow on Mount Mansfield and in six weeks the valley will be white" is indigenous to Vermont without any doubt at all.

The contrast of regional flavor versus general proverbial wisdom can also be observed in the following proverb pairs. While most Americans definitely know the weather proverb "One swallow does not make a summer," which has its origin in Greek antiquity and was translated into many languages including English, the Vermonter might at times prefer to quote the regional proverb variant "It takes more than one robin to make a summer." Or rather than quoting that old standby proverb "The early bird catches the worm," a rural Vermonter might well decide to specify the generic bird and expand the standard proverb to include a farm metaphor: "The early robin looks for worms behind the early plow." Instead of the classical Latin proverb "Gutta cavat lapidem," which appeared in English translation as early as the thirteenth century as "Constant dropping wears the stone," Vermonters often cite the expanded version "Constant dripping wears away the hardest stone" or the more regional variant "The constant creeping of ants will wear away the stone" to express that important virtue of perseverance so characteristic of this area. Rather than quoting that old Biblical proverb "There is a time for all things" (Ecclesiastes 3:1) which lacks in metaphorical rhetoric, one will most likely hear a true Vermonter observe that "The time to pick berries is when they're ripe" or "Time to catch bears is when they are out." And why cite the sixteenth-century proverb "Beauty is only skin deep" as an overused cliché when the proverb "Beauty does not make the pot boil" so convincingly expresses that glamorous outside appearance does not necessarily feed the farmer and his family?

Yet it is not only by rephrasing existing proverbial structures that Vermonters have created some of their distinctively regional wisdom. There are numerous proverbs in common use in this state that commence with a traditional proverb text to which a modifying phrase beginning with the conjunction "but" is added. Such texts mirror the independent and free spirit of Vermont folks who don't just accept what everbody else says or believes. Speakers of the English language have used the proverb "A new broom sweeps clean" since the middle of the sixteenth century to indicate that a new person in control usually makes changes in personnel or procedures, often referring to this new boss simply with the shortened metaphor "new broom." Yet, in Vermont, people like to caution that the old or traditional way of conducting business is not necessarily always bad by expanding this standard proverb to "A new broom sweeps clean, but the old one finds the corners." A similar reaction can be found to the common proverb "Money makes the mare go." To Vermonters, who are known for their thriftiness, money alone does not a good life make. Too much money quickly and perhaps too easily earned brings worries and problems, a fact drastically expressed in the proverbial statement that "Money makes the mare go—but not the nightmare." The thrifty and hard-working Vermonter much prefers such proverbs as "Dirty hands make clean money" or "Take care of the dimes and the dollars will take care of themselves." All of which is not to say that Vermonters don't realize that some money is needed to overcome poverty and reach happiness of some type. With typical Vermont wit, some resident once took the proverb "Poverty is no disgrace" and changed it to "There's no disgrace in poverty, but it's damned inconvenient," while another local expanded the proverb "Money won't buy happiness" to "Money won't buy happiness, but it's nice to choose your way to be unhappy." These acute observations by some individuals have caught on, that is, they have gained currency among the people and reached a certain traditionality so that we can consider them proverbs in their own right. This is also the case with the witty elaboration of the Biblical proverb "Love your neighbor as yourself" (Matthew 22:39) to "Love your neighbor as yourself—but no more"—quite a piece of wisdom that is echoed in an even more egocentric but honest expansion of another popular proverb: "Charity begins at home and usually stays there."

Proverbs are anything but saccharine in their content. Instead they "call a spade a spade" and "let the chips fall where they may," to quote two proverbial metaphors for the honesty of proverbs as far as human behavior and relations are concerned. Observe in this regard a most telling poem the Vermont poet Tenney Call (1887–1979) wrote in about 1965 when he was almost eighty years old. He had become aware of how language was changing all around him, how ever different neologisms and euphemisms were being created to express common situations and concerns. He framed his poem entitled "Spades Ain't Spades" by two negative uses of the proverbial expression "To call a spade a spade," thereby effectively lamenting the fact that down-to-earth folk speech is unfortunately also vanishing as Vermont develops its attractive economic potential.[29]

Spades Ain't Spades

You must not call a spade a spade;
   It isn't nice to any more.
It now is termed a workman's aid,
   For spade's a word kicked out the door.
And other words are on the run,
   For instance, janitors no more.
It now is custodian
   Who vacuums or mops up the floor.
Assistant used to be the word,
   But now if you'd be up-to-date,
And not thought of as quite absurd,
   You use the word associate.
It used to be in olden days
   We simply said we had a cold,
But now a virus is the craze;
   It sounds more dignified, we're told.
It used to be when we got old
   We were referred to as old men,
But times have changed—lo and behold,
   I'm now a senior citizen!
I guess I've ranted on enough,
   And maybe I my point have made—
To be considered up to snuff
   You just don't call a spade a spade.

Proverbs clearly still call a spade a spade, and they do so with much humor or even satire by employing traditional vocabulary. Perhaps it is exactly the apparent simplicity of the proverbial language that makes them so appealing linguistically as a contrast to the sophisticated modes of expression that we are accustomed to through the mass media or at the workplace. Sure, many proverbs have become clichés because of their frequent use, and the proverb "A dog is man's best friend" is no exception in this regard. But how about the expanded variant "A dog is a man's best friend, but a good cow is more help at the table" for a revitalization of an old cliché? This is telling it straight, and the honesty of this juxtaposition of the dog as a friend and the cow as a food source expresses in plain language basic emotional, physiological, and economic needs.

Such proverbial contrasts are not always based on the structural pattern of reacting to a standard proverb with a "but"-clause. Folk speech in general delights in paradoxical statements often based on a witty wordplay or pun. These proverbs usually require a bit more mental agility than straightforward short proverbs that simply contain a topic and a comment as, for example, "A squeaking pig gets fed," "Wishes can't fill a sack," and "Mud thrown is ground lost." In contrast, the longer and more involved texts indicate the enjoyment that people find in playing with language. But while proverbs based on humorous paradoxes might lead to some laughter, they still carry a clear-cut message, especially when they appear in a communicative context. Proverbs are never a mere joke, but always a concise statement of an apparent truth, albeit couched in a humorous or playful tone.[30] Two examples of such proverbial paradoxes that concern money and thriftiness are "If you don't do any more than you are paid for, you won't get paid for any more than you do" and "He who buys what he does not need will sometimes need what he cannot buy." A particularly successful pun based on the two almost homonyms of "neat/need" and "tight/tidy" is noticable in the proverb "It is better to be neat and tidy than to be tight and needy" that also refers to the Vermonters' preoccupation with thriftiness. An anonymous folk poet of sorts certainly was at work here, basing his or her text on the standard proverbial structure of "It is better to . . . than . . . ," using parallel structure with end-rhyme in the two halves of the text, and also creating a simple word play. Proverbs are aesthetic modes of expression, and such devices as structure, rhyme, rhythm, and alliteration all increase the memorability and reproducability of the wisdom expressed in them. It must not be forgotten that proverbs to this day are primarily an oral means of communication, and they depend on poetic devices to be remembered and repeated.[31] Notice as a final paradoxical example the proverb "It won't be warm till the snow gets off the mountain, and the snow won't get off the mountain till it gets warm." Can't you just see a frustrated Vermonter stricken by cabin fever after a long winter standing in front of the house and gazing at the snow-covered mountain, wondering whether spring and warm weather will ever come. We could, of course, simply state that this is a Catch-22 situation, but this Vermont proverb expresses with much more resigned irony that the weather will still do whatever it sees fit.

Dry and witty humor, based on deep insights into the human psyche, is clearly stated in the following last few examples of Vermont-grown proverbs. What a delight it is to hear a Vermonter insist on the wisdom of such proverbs as "Keep a thing seven years and it will sort of do," "If it ain't broke don't try to fix it," and "Use it up, wear it out, make it do or do without" as the wastefulness and throwaway mentality is creeping ever more into the valleys and mountains of this state. And can't you just imagine an old-time Vermonter saying to an out-of-state person trying to argue for a new mall "There is a difference knowing how to think and what to think"? And to a fellow Vermonter who perhaps might be in favor of such mercantile change a quick witty response might well be "You can't keep trouble from coming, but you don't have to give it a chair to sit in." Seeing one of those giant new homes that some city folk are building might lead to the observation that "A small home is better than a large mortgage" or even more ironically to "Half the dwellers in glass houses don't seem to know it." The latter proverb certainly would be quite applicable to the commercial glass structures that are being built in the larger cities of Vermont, alluding perhaps to the fact that the native Vermonter is quite capable of looking through the facade of wealth of it all. In the right context we can also imagine the humor or irony of such proverbs as "Sometimes the cheese is blamed when the fault is in the ventilation," "How beautiful it is to do nothing and then rest afterwards," "It's nice to sit and think, but sometimes it's nicer just to sit," "No matter how tough the roast beef is, you can always cut the gravy with your knife," "A warm-back husband and a warm-foot wife should easily lead a compatible life," and "There's no help for misfortune but to marry again." These texts express in vivid images basic human concerns, and they are ever mindful of the human comedy that we partake in on the stage of our everyday existence.

Knowledge of and adherence to some of the proverbs discussed here might well help everyone to cope with the complex world that is changing the villages and towns of Vermont. Many of the proverbs current in Vermont reflect those old Yankee virtues of ingenuity, perseverance, independence, thriftiness, and common sense. It is this Puritan ethic that moved across the entire country as the early settlers took their value system of hard work and fair play with them. They helped to establish the foundations of the American worldview or psyche, if we can generalize in that way. In Vermont we still use such proverbs as "If you want to get to the top of the hill, you must go up it" and "Keep straight and you'll never get into trouble or grow round-shouldered" to claim that self-reliance, determination, and human decency make life worth living. Expressed directly and without any embellishment a

Vermonter might quite laconically say "Live while you live and then die and be done with it." What counts is what kind of person we are while we act as responsible citizens of one of the last rural strongholds in the United States. The wisdom and conscience contained in our regional Vermont proverbs should encourage us to maintain and treasure the uniqueness of Vermont life. Yet, while the one proverb "Good fences make good neighbors" helps us to preserve our cherished personal independence and freedom, we must be careful not to twist this proverb into the shortsighted and chauvinistic anti-proverb of "Bad neighbors make good fences"—a thought-provoking variation of that famous "Vermont" proverb that concludes the poem "Spite Fence" (c. 1980) by Richard Eberhart (b. 1904). The "Maine village" that Eberhart speaks of could, of course, just as well be located in Frost's Vermont.[32]

> **Spite Fence**
>
> After years of bickerings
>
> Family one
> Put up a spite fence
> Against family two.
>
> Cheek for cheek
> They couldn't stand it.
> The Maine village
>
> Looked so peaceful.
> We drove through yearly,
> We didn't know.
>
> Now if you drive through
> You see the split wood,
> Thin and shrill.
>
> But who's who?
> Who made it,
> One side or the other?
>
> Bad neighbors make good fences.

Many of the proverbs current or even coined in Vermont could be guiding lights of folk wisdom toward preserving traditional values in this state, while trying and needing to cope with the demands and challenges of change. They reflect life experiences and human insights that have been valid for many generations and centuries. They still contain plenty of truths, wisdom, and knowledge about what makes life so special in Vermont. It is, therefore, with legitimate justification that I conclude this chapter with a proverbial variation of Vermont's most precious proverb: "Good proverbs make good Vermonters."

Notes

A shorter version of this chapter was published in *We Vermonters: Perspectives on the Past,* ed. by Michael Sherman and Jennie Versteeg. Montpelier: Vermont Historical Society, 1992, pp. 59–69.

1. For two useful collections of such international proverbs see Jerzy Gluski, *Proverbs. A Comparative Book of English, French, German, Italian, Spanish and Russian Proverbs with a Latin Appendix.* New York: Elsevier Publishing, 1971; and Wolfgang Mieder, *Encyclopedia of World Proverbs.* Englewood Cliffs, N.J.: Prentice-Hall, 1986.

2. See again Gluski and Mieder (note 1), but also Henry G. Bohn, *A Polyglot of Foreign Proverbs Comprising French, Italian, German, Dutch, Spanish, Portuguese, and Danish, with English Translations.* London: Henry G. Bohn, 1857; rpt. Detroit: Gale Research Co., 1968; Ida von Düringsfeld and Otto von Reinsberg-Düringsfeld, *Sprichwörter der germanischen und romanischen Sprachen.* 2 vols. Leipzig: Hermann Fries, 1872 and 1875; rpt. Hildesheim: Georg Olms, 1973; Selwyn Gurney Champion, *Racial Proverbs. A Selection of the World's Proverbs arranged Linguistically.* London: George Routledge, 1938; Jens Aa. Stabell Bilgrav, *20,000 Proverbs, Sprichwörter, Proverbes, Ordspråk, Ordsprog.* Copenhagen: Hans Heide, 1985; Matti Kuusi et al., *Proverbia septentrionalia. 900 Balto-Finnic Proverb Types with Russian, Baltic, German and Scandinavian Parallels.* Helsinki: Suomalainen Tiedeakatemia, 1985; and Gyula Paczolay, *A Comparative Dictionary of Hungarian, Estonian, German, English, Finnish and Latin Proverbs with an Appendix in Cheremis and Zyryan.* Veszprém: VEAB, 1987.

3. For a comparative collection see Selwyn Gurney Champion, *The Eleven Religions and Their Proverbial Lore.* New York: E. P. Dutton, 1945. See also Carl Schulze, *Die biblischen Sprichwörter der deutschen Sprache.* Göttingen: Vandenhoeck & Ruprecht, 1860; rpt. ed. by Wolfgang Mieder. Bern: Peter Lang, 1987; and W. Mieder, *Not by Bread Alone. Proverbs of the Bible.* Shelburne, Vt.: The New England Press, 1990.

4. For a discussion of this problem see especially Archer Taylor's classical study *The Proverb.* Cambridge: Harvard University Press, 1931; rpt. Hatboro, Pa.: Folklore Associates, 1962; rpt. again with an introduction and bibliography by Wolfgang Mieder. Bern: Peter Lang, 1985, pp. 3–65.

5. For historical studies on individual proverbs see Wolfgang Mieder's bibliographical reference works: *International Bibliography of Explanatory Essays on Individual Proverbs and Proverbial Expressions.* Bern: Peter Lang, 1977; *International Proverb Scholarship: An Annotated Bibliography.* 2 vols. New York: Garland Publishing, 1982 and 1990; and *Investigations of Proverbs, Proverbial Expressions, Quotations and Clichés. A Bibliography of Explanatory Essays Which Appeared in ''Notes and Queries'' (1849–1983).* Bern: Peter Lang, 1984.

6. See Wolfgang Mieder, "History and Interpretation of a Proverb about Human Nature: 'Big Fish Eat Little Fish'," in W. Mieder, *Tradition and Innovation in Folk Literature.* Hanover, N.H.: University Press of New England, 1987, pp. 178–228 and 259–268 (notes).

7. See Frank de Caro and William K. McNeil, *American Proverb Literature: A Bibliography.* Bloomington, In.: Folklore Forum, 1971; and Wolfgang Mieder, *American Proverbs: A Study of Texts and Contexts.* Bern: Peter Lang, 1989.

8. This can readily be seen from the historical references in the following major proverb collections of the English language: Archer Taylor and Bartlett Jere Whiting, *A Dictionary of American Proverbs and Proverbial Phrases, 1820–1880.* Cambridge: Harvard University Press, 1958; F. P. Wilson, *The Oxford Dictionary of English Proverbs.* Oxford: Clarendon Press, 1970; B. J. Whiting, *Early American Proverbs and Proverbial Phrases.* Cambridge: Harvard University Press, 1977; John A. Simpson, *The Concise Oxford Dictionary of Proverbs.* Oxford: Oxford University Press, 1982; B. J. Whiting, *Modern Proverbs and Proverbial Sayings.* Cambridge: Harvard University Press, 1989; and Wolfgang Mieder, Stewart Kingsbury, and Kelsie Harder, *A Dictionary of American Proverbs.* New York: Oxford University Press, 1992.

9. See Margaret Hardie, "Proverbs and Proverbial Expressions Current in the United

States East of the Missouri and North of the Ohio Rivers," *American Speech*, 4 (1929), 461–472; and Richard Jente, "The American Proverb," *American Speech*, 7 (1931–1932), 342–348.

10. For a short history of this proverb in the United States and Germany see Wolfgang Mieder and George B. Bryan, " 'Zum Tango gehören zwei'," *Der Sprachdienst*, 27 (1983), 100–102.

11. For a detailed chapter on this proverb with illustrations see Mieder (note 7), pp. 317–332.

12. See the various chapters on these aspects in Mieder (note 7).

13. See Margaret M. Bryant, *Proverbs and How to Collect Them*. Greensboro/North Carolina: American Dialect Society, 1945.

14. For a description of this project see Stewart A. Kingsbury, "On Handling 250,000+ Citation Slips for American Dialect Society (ADS) Proverb Research," *Proverbium: Yearbook of International Proverb Scholarship*, 1 (1984), 195–205.

15. See Mieder et al. (note 8). Some of the more important regional proverb collections are Frances M. Barbour, *Proverbs and Proverbial Phrases of Illinois*. Carbondale: Southern Illinois University Press, 1963; Mac E. Barrick, "Proverbs and Sayings from Cumberland County [Pennsylvania]," *Keystone Folklore Quarterly*, 8 (1963), 139–203; F. W. Bradley, "South Carolina Proverbs," *Southern Folklore Quarterly*, 1 (1937), 57–101; Donald M. Hines, *Frontier Folksay. Proverbial Lore of the Inland Pacific Northwest Frontier*. Norwood, Pa.: Norwood Editions, 1977; Emma Louise Snapp, "Proverbial Lore in Nebraska," *University of Nebraska Studies in Language, Literature and Criticism*, 13 (1933), 51–112; Harold W. Thompson, "Proverbs and Sayings [from New York]," *New York Folklore Quarterly*, 5 (1949), 230–235 and 296–300; and Bartlett Jere Whiting, "Proverbs and Proverbial Sayings [from North Carolina]," in *The Frank C. Brown Collection of North Carolina Folklore*, ed. by Newman Ivey White. Durham, N.C.: Duke University Press, 1952, vol. 1, pp. 329–501.

16. See Ralph Charles La Rosa, *Emerson's Proverbial Rhetoric: 1818–1838*. Diss. University of Wisconsin, 1969.

17. Cited from the chapter on "Proverbs in Prose Literature [i.e., Emerson]" in Mieder (note 7), pp. 143–169.

18. The poem is included in Carl Sandburg, *The Complete Poems by Carl Sandburg*. New York: Harcourt Brace Jovanovich, 1970, pp. 328–330 (these pages refer to section 11 of the poem with numerous proverbs). For a discussion of this poem see Wolfgang Mieder, " 'Behold the Proverbs of a People': A Florilegium of Proverbs in Carl Sandburg's Poem 'Good Morning, America'," *Southern Folklore Quarterly*, 35 (1971), 160–168.

19. Wolfgang Mieder, *Yankee Wisdom: New England Proverbs*. Silhouettes by Elayne Sears. Shelburne, Vt.: The New England Press, 1989.

20. Muriel J. Hughes, "Vermont Proverbs and Proverbial Sayings," *Vermont History*, 28 (1960), 113–142 and 200–230.

21. All Vermont proverbs cited in this chapter come out of Wolfgang Mieder, *Talk Less and Say More: Vermont Proverbs*. Woodcuts by Mary Azarian. Shelburne, Vt.: The New England Press, 1986. For a collection of Vermont proverbial expressions see W. Mieder, *As Sweet as Apple Cider: Vermont Expressions*. Woodcuts by Mary Azarian. Shelburne, Vt.: The New England Press, 1988.

22. See especially George Monteiro, " 'Good Fences Make Good Neighbors'. A Proverb and a Poem," *Revista de Etnografia*, 16, no. 31 (1972), 83–88.

23. Quoted from Simpson (note 8), p. 98.

24. Wilson (note 8), p. 494.

25. See Frances M. Barbour, *A Concordance to the Sayings in Franklin's "Poor Richard."* Detroit: Gale Research Co., 1974, p. 125.

26. Quoted from Mieder (note 7), p. 160.

27. See the short note by Addison Barker, " 'Good Fences Make Good Neighbors'," *Journal of American Folklore*, 64 (1951), 421.

28. The poem is included in Robert Frost, *Complete Poems of Robert Frost.* New York: Holt, Rinehart and Winston, 1964, pp. 47–48.

29. Quoted from Tenney Call, *Rustic Rhymes by Old Scribe,* ed. by Miriam Herwig. Randolph Center, Vt.: Greenhills Book, 1979, no pp. given.

30. See, for example, A. A. Parker, *The Humour of Spanish Proverbs.* London: The Hispanic & Luso-Brazilian Councils, 1963; also in *The Wisdom of Many. Essays on the Proverb,* ed. by Wolfgang Mieder and Alan Dundes. New York: Garland Publishing, 1981, pp. 257–274.

31. For detailed discussions of these matters see Shirley L. Arora, "The Perception of Proverbiality," *Proverbium: Yearbook of International Proverb Scholarship,* 1 (1984), 1–38; and Neal R. Norrick, *How Proverbs Mean. Semantic Studies in English Proverbs.* Amsterdam: Mouton, 1985.

32. The poem is included in Richard Eberhart, *Collected Poems 1930–1986.* New York: Oxford University Press, 1988, p. 400.

9

" (Don't) Throw the Baby Out with the Bath Water "

The Americanization of a German Proverb and Proverbial Expression

When the proverb "Don't throw the baby out with the bath water" or its parallel proverbial expression "To throw the baby out with the bath water" appear today in Anglo-American oral communication or in books, magazines, newspapers, advertisements, or cartoons, hardly anybody would surmise that this common metaphorical phrase is actually of German origin and of relatively recent use in the English language. It had its first written occurrence in Thomas Murner's (1475–1537) versified satirical book *Narrenbeschwörung* (1512) which contains as its eighty-first short chapter entitled "Das kindt mit dem bad vß schitten" (To throw the baby out with the bath water) a treatise on fools who by trying to rid themselves of a bad thing succeed in destroying whatever good there was as well. In seventy-six rhymed lines the proverbial phrase is repeated three times as a folkloric leitmotif, and there is also the first illustration of the expression as a woodcut depicting quite literally a woman who is pouring her baby out with the bath water.[1] Murner also cites the phrase repeatedly in later works and this rather frequent use might be an indication that the proverbial expression was already in oral currency toward the end of the fifteenth century in Germany.

There is no doubt that the proverbial text gained rapid and universal acceptance in the satirical and polemic literature of the Age of the Reformation. Martin Luther (1483–1546), for example, changed the proverbial expression in his scholarly lecture about Salomo from 1526 to a proverb by adding the

formula "Man soll . . ." (One should, One must, or Don't) to it: "Man sol [sic] das kind nicht mit dem bad ausgiessen" (Don't throw the baby out with the bath water).[2] It is of interest to note here that Archer Taylor in an article on "The Proverbial Formula 'Man soll' . . ." (1930) takes this particular expression to point out that "the formula was used to make nonce-proverbs out of proverbial phrases. In 'Man soll das Kind nicht mit dem Bade aus-schütten,' the starting point is the phrase 'das Kind mit dem Bade ausschüt-ten' and not the proverb. It may be possible to dispute whether the phrase or the proverb was first in any particular instance, but the general method of forming nonce-proverbs from phrases remains."[3] While Taylor does not ex-plicitly refer to Luther, he certainly is correct about his statement that the formula "Man soll . . ." in general makes proverbs out of proverbial expres-sions. But even Luther preferred to use it on several occasions in its phraseo-logical form, enabling him to employ the metaphor for polemic purposes rather than as didactic wisdom that the proverb would express.

Already in 1541 the proverbial expression appears in Sebastian Franck's (1499–1542) early major proverb collection *Sprichwörter / Schöne / Weise / Herrliche Clugreden / und Hoffsprüch* as "Das kindt mit dem bad außschütten,"[4] and from there it has found its way into all German paremiographical dictio-naries. It has also been documented numerous times in the literary works of such well-known authors as Jörg Wickram (1505–1562), Johannes Nas (1534–1590), Johannes Kepler (1571–1630), Andreas Gryphius (1616–1664), Ja-kob Michael Reinhold Lenz (1751–1792), Gottfried August Bürger (1747–

1794), Johann Wolfgang von Goethe (1749–1832), Jeremias Gotthelf (1797–1854), Karl Friedrich Wilhelm Wander (1803–1879), Otto von Bismarck (1815–1898), Theodor Fontane (1819–1898), Thomas Mann (1875–1955), Heinrich Böll (1917–1985), Günter Grass (born 1927), and many others. This is not the place to comment on these interesting references, except to point out that they as well as the appearance of the proverb and the proverbial phrase in proverb collections clearly attest to their common currency among the German-speaking and writing population. In fact, judging by their frequent occurrence in modern German aphorisms, anti-proverbs, headlines, slogans, and so on, it can be stated that the two forms of this proverbial metaphor belong to the most popular examples of German folk speech.[5]

But when, how and why did this proverbial expression and proverb find their way into the English language where they are today also quite well known and often cited? Why should English speakers even consider using this somewhat grotesque image of washing a baby in a small portable tub and then throwing this human treasure out with the dirty bath water, when their language has such well-established equivalent proverbial expressions as ''To throw the helve after the hatchet,'' ''To throw away the wheat with the chaff,'' and the bland ''To throw away the good with the bad''? The major reasons surely must have been that people came in contact with the expression through a German speaker or through the written German word. The latter seems to have been the case regarding the first somewhat awkward loan translation of the proverbial phrase in English by Thomas Carlyle (1795–1881). The famous British social critic and historian was also an extreme Germanophile who studied German literature and published widely on such literary giants as Schiller and Goethe. It might well be that he found the expression in Goethe's autobiographical account *Dichtung und Wahrheit* (1811/22; *Poetry and Truth*) that he quite assuredly read in its German original and which does in fact contain the phrase. In any case, Carlyle used the phrase in an essay with the disturbing title ''The Nigger Question'' that appeared in December 1849 in *Frazer's Magazine* and as a separate pamphlet in 1853 in London. In it he argues that white people who hold black servants should make a commitment to them for life since any shorter arrangement would appear to be abuse, that is, treat the slaves kindly but don't give them their freedom:

> Servants hired for life, or by a contract for a long period, and not easily dissoluble; so and not otherwise would all reasonable mortals, Black and White, wish to hire and to be hired! I invite you to reflect on that; for you will find it true. And if true, it is important for us, in reference to this Negro Question and some others. The Germans say, ''you must empty-out the bathing-tub, but not the baby along with it.'' Fling-out your dirty water with all zeal, and set it careering down the kennels; but try if you can keep the little child!

> How to abolish the abuses of slavery, and save the precious thing in it alas, I do not pretend that this is easy, that it can be done in a day, or a single generation, or a single century: but I do surmise or perceive that it will, by straight methods or by circuitous, need to be done. . . . And truly, my friends, with regard to this world-famous Nigger Question— which perhaps is louder than it is big, after all—I would advise you to attack it on that side. Try against the dirty water, with an eye to *save* the baby! That will be a quite new point of attack; where, it seems to me, some real benefit and victory for the poor Negro, might before long be accomplished . . . .[6]

This is not only a telling account about slavery by a leading British intellectual of the nineteenth century whose reputation decreased in this century due to his love for authority and strong leaders that appears to foreshadow German Fascism. But this early English reference of the proverb is also cited with the introductory formula "The Germans say," making it absolutely clear that Carlyle was well aware of its German origin. He translates the proverb "Man soll das Kind nicht mit dem Bade ausschütten" quite clumsily as "You must empty-out the bathing-tub, but not the baby along with it" and alludes to it a bit more cleverly later on with the grotesque statement "Try against the dirty water, with an eye to save the baby!" Translated into plain and non-metaphorical English, this would mean improve and civilize the institution of slavery and the lot of the slaves themselves, but for heaven's sake don't lose the luxury of having slaves. While this is definitely a misguided argument, this passage is a fascinating indication linguistically of how an otherwise quite adept translator of German to English struggles to render a German proverb whose metaphor has struck his fancy into colloquial English, and fails miserably.

It is very doubtful that this early reference had any particular effect on spreading the expression in England. It appears to be nothing but an isolated first occurrence in awkward English which, however, does identify the phrase correctly as a translation of an originally German proverb. Lexicographers, whose business it is to find equivalents or word-for-word translations for foreign language dictionaries, continued to have the same problem with this German expression throughout the nineteenth century all the way to the mid-1950s. The following is a short historical review of how German-English dictionaries have dealt with rendering the proverbial expression "das Kind mit dem Bade ausschütten" into English.

1846:   To reject the good with the bad.[7]
1849:   To throw away the good together with the bad.[8]
1857:   To reject the good with the bad.[9]
1896:   To throw away (or to reject) the good and the bad together, to use no discrimination.[10]

1900:   To throw away (or reject) the good with the bad, to act without discrimination.[11]

1936:   Throw the child out with the bath-water, hence, act without discretion, reject the good with the bad.[12]

1941:   To throw the helve after the hatchet.[13]

1958:   Reject the good together with the bad.[14]

1965:   To cast away the good with the bad, to throw out the child with the bath-water.[15]

1972:   To throw out the child with the bath-water.[16]

1974:   To throw out the baby with the bathwater.[17]

1978:   Throw out the baby with the bathwater.[18]

1981:   To throw out the baby with the bathwater.[19]

1982:   To throw out the baby with the bathwater.[20]

As can be seen, it took until 1936 before the English version "throw the child out with the bath-water" appears in a German-English dictionary, using the direct translation of "Kind" to "child." However, this text appears to be but a precise translation without any claim on currency in the English language, since the lexicographer Karl Breul goes on to explain "hence, act without discretion, reject the good with the bad." In fact, it was not until 1965 that "to throw out the child with the bath-water" is at least given equal footing with the much older but less figurative "to cast away the good with the bad." Starting with 1974, the variant "to throw out the baby with the bathwater" finally appears and with this replacement of the noun "child" through "baby" it has become the standard lexicographical form today.

But lexicographers are a conservative breed, and an analysis of specialized phraseological dictionaries shows that the proverbial expression must certainly have been quite popular before the mid-1970s. This is clearly indicated by the following list of English equivalents for the German expression recorded by phraseologists.

1896:   To reject the good together with the bad.[21]

1897:   To kill the goose with the golden egg.[22]

1956:   To throw the baby out with the bath-water (from the German).[23]

1957:   Throw away the baby with the bath water (supersedes "to throw the helve after the hatchet"; borrowed from the German).[24]

1959:   To overdo things, to go too far, to throw out the baby with the bath water.[25]

1960:   To throw out the baby with the bath-water; to throw away the wheat with the chaff.[26]

1967:   To cast away the good with the bad; to throw out the baby with the bathwater.[27]

1968:   To throw the good out with the bad.[28]
1979:   To throw out the baby with the bathwater, be so enthusiastic in the
        rejection of the bad that the good is rejected as well.[29]
1988:   To throw the helve after the hatchet.[30]
1989:   To throw out the baby with the bathwater.[31]
1991:   To throw the baby out with the bathwater.[32]

The 1897 equivalent "To kill the goose with the golden egg" is, of course, an incorrect rendition, but since 1956 German-English phraseological dictionaries do list "To throw the baby out with the bath water" as a current English expression, that is, almost twenty years earlier than the 1974 date ascertained by the foreign language lexicographers. And Edmund P. Kremer even included for the German proverb "Man soll das Kind nicht mit dem Bad ausschütten" the precise English equivalent "Don't throw out the baby with the bathwater" in his bilingual German-English proverb collection from 1955, thus attesting to the currency of the proverb in the mid-1950s as well.[33] And I certainly did the same in 1988 in my book of *English Proverbs* by citing the very slightly different form of the proverb "Don't throw the baby out with the bathwater"[34] and referring to the fact that it is a loan translation of the German proverb.

The foreign language and phraseological dictionaries concentrated on thus far have all been concerned with the interrelationship of the German and English languages, and it is surprising not to find precise equivalencies in them of the proverb and the proverbial expression in English before the mid-1950s. Little wonder that the many translators of Goethe's aforementioned autobiography *Poetry and Truth* encountered so much difficulty for a long time in translating the passage that contains the proverbial expression. In the pertinent paragraph Goethe discusses his attempt of understanding various theories of art, declaring that he finally simply gave up on this confusing matter:

> Durch alles dieses ward ich verworrner als jemals, und nachdem ich mich lange mit diesem Hin- und Herreden, mit dieser theoretischen Saalbaderei des vorigen Jahrhunderts gequält hatte, schüttete ich das Kind mit dem Bade aus, und warf den ganzen Plunder desto entschiedener von mir . . . .[35]

In an early anonymous English rendition from 1824 the translator obviously found the proverbial expression so impossible to deal with that he decided not to employ any metaphorical phrase at all:

> All these contradictions embarrassed me excessively. I long puzzled myself with endeavouring to reconcile all the difficulties of this pedantic

theory. Wearied at length with these fruitless efforts, [missing proverbial expression] I gave up the whole system.[36]

But in the next translation from 1846 by Parke Godwin one can see at least an attempt to render the proverbial passage into some kind of metaphorical English language by using the phrase "to throw something to the dogs":

> By these means I was sorely confounded, and after having pestered myself a long time with this tittle-tattle and theoretical quackery of the previous century, threw the whole to the dogs.[37]

Two years later John Oxenford, who admits that he made use of Godwin's translation, repeats the "dog" expression but also succeeds in rendering the entire passage more authentically into English:

> Through all this I became more perplexed than ever, and after having pestered myself a long time with this talking backwards and forwards, and theoretical quackery of the previous century, threw them to the dogs, and was the more resolute in casting all the rubbish away . . . .[38]

This is in fact a rather word-for-word translation from the German, and one wonders why Oxenford did not also translate the German expression in that manner. The fact that he didn't must be seen as an indication that he felt his English readers would not comprehend or appreciate the metaphorical phrase. It is clear that the German proverbial expression could not possibly have been in use in English at that time, something that was already explained in relation to Thomas Carlyle's awkward translation attempt from 1849. Later nineteenth-century editions of the Oxenford translation maintained the expression "To throw something to the dogs,"[39] but in 1908 Minna Steele Smith published a revised version of Oxenford's translation that handles the German proverbial expression quite differently:

> Thus I became more perplexed than ever, and after tormenting myself a long time with these pros and cons, and the theoretical twaddle of the previous century, I cast away good and bad alike.[40]

The phrase "to cast away good and bad alike" is certainly close in meaning to the German original, but it took until the 1949 translation by R. O. Moon that its English proverbial equivalent "to reject the good with the bad" appears. This is quite surprising since it was considered an appropriate translation by foreign language dictionary lexicographers since 1846(!):

> Through all this I became more confused than ever, and after I had tormented myself with the controversial talk, with the twaddle of the pre-

vious century, I rejected the good with the bad and threw away all the
rubbish more decidedly from me . . . .[41]

Even more astonishing is the fact that Moon did not use the English proverbial expression "to throw the baby out with the bath-water" since it certainly
was already quite commonly known in 1949 in the Anglo-American world.
But it was not until 1987 that Robert R. Heitner took the proverbial plunge
and finally included the long overdo exact English equivalent of the German
expression in his superb translation of Goethe's autobiography:

> All of this confused me more than ever, and when I had tormented
> myself at length with the previous century's disputes and theoretical
> twaddle, I poured out the baby with the bathwater. I was that much
> more resolute about rejecting all this rubbish . . . .[42]

The appearance of "to pour (throw) out the baby with the bathwater" in this
modern translation was, of course, predictable, since all the foreign language
and phraseological dictionaries of recent publication date contain this precise
equivalent for the German original. In addition, Heitner most likely was also
aware of its common currency in oral and written German and English as
well. But this short excursus into the translation history of this passage out
of Goethe's autobiography is yet another indication that the translated German expression was not generally known among English-speaking people
until well after the turn of the twentieth century.

In fact, it took until the 1933 *Supplement* to *The Oxford English Dictionary*
that the proverbial expression appears as an English phrase in a purely English language dictionary, where its *only* historical reference is a line out of
the British newspaper *The Observer* from July 1, 1928: "There is always . . .
a risk of throwing out the baby with the bath."[43] Another fifteen years had
to pass until the phrase finally is registered in Burton Stevenson's invaluable
Book of Proverbs, Maxims, and Famous Phrases (1948), clearly identifying it as
a "German proverb" of unknown authorship: "Emptying the baby out with
the bath. (Das Kind mit dem Bade ausschütten.).[44] One would have thought
that the expression would now be on a lexicographical "roll" in English language, phraseological and proverb dictionaries, yet nothing is further from
the truth. Only with the year 1970 begins its steady inclusion in such reference books of the English language. The following list of recent dates and
references presents an overview of just how this "new" proverbial expression, and less frequently the proverb, have been treated by lexicographers,
phraseologists, and paremiographers of the English tongue.

1970:   *To empty the baby with the bath.*[45]

1970: *Throw the baby out with the bath-water.* To overdo something, carry it too far, e.g., a political measure or a commercial practice or a sociological activity, often as a warning to theorists 'Don't throw . . .': since ca. 1946. Cf. the Ger. proverbial 'Das Kind mit dem Bad ausgiessen'.[46]

1970: *To throw out the baby with the bath-water.* Overzealous reform, reorganization, or action, which in getting rid of unwanted elements casts away the essentials as well.[47]

1972: *To empty, pour,* or *throw the baby out* (or *away*) *with the bath(-water)* (cf. G. 'das Kind mit dem Bade ausschütten'), to reject the essential with the inessential, to discard what is valuable along with what is waste or useless.[48]

1975: *Throw the baby out with the bath* (or *bathwater*) v. phr. To reject all of something because part is faulty.[49]

1977: *Don't throw the baby out with the bath water* is a catch phrase—since c. 1946—addressed, in gentle warning, to theorists, esp. the theorists in politics and sociology, but also to those who carry some commercial practice beyond the bounds of good, or even of merely common, sense, and it springs immediately from the colloquialism *to throw the baby out with the bath water,* to go too far in reform-making. Cf. the Ger. proverbial *Das Kind mit dem Bad ausgiessen,* which forms the origin of *to throw* . . . . .[50]

1979: *Throw the baby out with the bath water* coll. to lose the desirable or most important part of something when getting rid of the bad part.[51]

1980: *Throw out the baby with the bath water.* To reject the essential or valuable along with the unimportant or superfluous. This graphic expression appeared in print by the turn of the century. It is frequently used in reference to proposals calling for significant change, such as political and social reforms or large-scale bureaucratic reorganization.[52]

1982: *Don't throw the baby out with the bathwater.* The proverb is often used allusively, especially in the metaphorical phrase *to throw* (or *empty*) *out the baby with the bathwater.*[53]

1983: *Throw out the baby with the bathwater,* to discard the essential along with the superfluous because of excessive zeal.[54]

1983: *Don't throw the baby out with the bath water.* This expression warns that when you are throwing anything away it is best to make sure you are not disposing of anything vital that you might need later. Alternatively, if pressure is being put on you to change your point of view, don't throw away all your ideas, stick to the ones in which you firmly believe; just make the necessary adjustments that will meet with approval, but do not abandon your ideals or main beliefs.[55]

1983:   *Throw out the baby with the bathwater.* To allow over-enthusiasm to lead one into getting rid of the essential along with the superfluous.[56]

1985:   *Throw (Empty, Pour) the Baby Out With the Bathwater.* Discard the essential with the waste; disregard the important thing. Here is George Bernard Shaw, in *Pen Portraits & Reviews* (1909): "Like all reactionists, he usually empties the baby out with the bath." Shaw used the saying on several occasions and may have originated it.[57]

1985:   *Throw the baby out with the bathwater.* To be so keen on eliminating the large-scale errors that one simultaneously tosses out the less visible but highly valuable entities hidden amongst them.[58]

1987:   *Throw the baby out with the bath water.* To lose the most important part of something when getting rid of the bad or unwanted part.[59]

1987:   *Throw away the baby with the bathwater,* reject essential with inessential.[60]

1988:   *Don't throw out the baby with the bath water.* In getting rid of waste, don't also discard what is worth keeping.[61]

1988:   *Throw out the baby with the bathwater.* This expression, suggesting that one is going a bit too far in whatever one is doing, is probably British in origin. Partridge traces it back to the mid-1940s and calls into consideration "the German proverbial *Das Kind mit dem Bade ausgiessen.*" [See notes 46 and 50 for Partridge].[62]

1989:   *Throw the baby out with the bath water.* Foolishly discard a valuable idea, plan, etc. at the same time as one is getting rid of something unpleasant or undesirable.[63]

1989:   *To throw out the Baby with the bath (water).*[64]

1991:   *Don't throw out the baby with the bath water.*[65]

What all these references show is that earlier variants that included the noun "child" have been replaced by the more appropriate "baby" that is being washed in a portable tub. For all general purposes the verbs "to empty" and "to pour" have given way to the commonly used "to throw," and there is a definite preference for the use of "bath water" rather than the less precise though shorter "bath." Only the position of the preposition "out" appears to be somewhat arbitrary, either directly following the verb or the noun "baby." We thus have today the standard form of the proverbial expression "To throw the baby out with the bath water," while the proverb is usually cited as "Don't throw the baby out with the bath water." Especially the Australian lexicographer and phraseologist Eric Partridge (see notes 46, 50, and 62) has drawn attention to the German origin of the expression, and he claims that its common currency in the English language might have started in the mid-1940s.

But as will be shown in the now following second part of this chapter by means of numerous contextualized references of the phrase throughout the twentieth century, it must have been quite solidly established at least a couple of decades earlier.

One thing is for certain, George Bernard Shaw (1856–1950) did *not* originate the expression as James Rogers (see note 57 above) would have us believe. Yet there is no doubt that Shaw was fascinated by it and at least somewhat instrumental in making it known among intellectuals. Disregarding Thomas Carlyle's somewhat clumsy and isolated use of it as a direct translation from the German for a moment, Shaw represents the starting point of its appearance in English language sources of the twentieth century. He used it for the first time in a review essay entitled "Chesterton on Shaw" that appeared in the *Nation* on August 25, 1909, as a reaction to Gilbert K. Chesterton's biography on *George Bernard Shaw*. The way Shaw employs the actual phrase together with a pun certainly indicates his obvious familiarity with it: "Mr. Chesterton is, at present, a man of vehement reactions; and, like all reactionists, he usually empties the baby out with the bath. And when he sees me nursing the collection of babies I have saved from the baths, he cannot believe that I have really emptied out their baths thoroughly."[66] This passage undoubtedly assumes that Shaw's English readers would understand the metaphor, signifying that the proverbial expression must have been somewhat current at that time. How it got to England cannot be ascertained precisely, but it is fair to assume that a German (or Germans) who might have settled there put it into circulation by translating it into English around the turn of the century. That is most likely also the way the expression traveled to the United States. Immigrants started using their German expressions as loan translations when they communicated with their English-speaking fellow citizens, and it really should be no big surprise to find it recorded in its German dialect form together with an English translation in Edwin Miller Fogel's important collection of *Proverbs of the Pennsylvania Germans* from 1929: " 'S kind mit 'm bad naus schitte. Pour out the child with its bath; to throw away the good with the bad."[67] It is, of course, of interest to note that Fogel still cites the earlier "child" variant and that he feels obliged to add the explanatory but bland phrase "to throw away the good with the bad." Might this not be taken as an indirect statement that the translated phrase had not, at least in the opinion of Fogel, quite conquered the colloquial American speech?

Two years after his first use of the proverbial expression Shaw repeats it in 1911 in his lengthy treatise on marriage that introduces his play *Getting Married*. At the end of the section on what is to become of the children of broken-up marriages and families, Shaw presents the following arguments with an effective integration of the proverbial phrase:

Means of breaking up undesirable families are as necessary to the preservation of the family as means of dissolving undesirable marriages are
to the preservation of marriage. If our domestic laws are kept so inhuman that they at last provoke a furious general insurrection against them
as they already provoke many private ones, we shall in a very literal
sense empty the baby out with the bath by abolishing an institution which needs nothing more than a little obvious and easy ration-
alizing to make it not only harmless but comfortable, honorable, and
useful.[68]

Shaw also used the expression in a letter of January 7, 1922, to his friend
Stella Tanner (Mrs. Patrick Campbell, 1865–1940), in which he discusses her
concerns about the imminent publication in book form of their long correspondence: "As to 'Relativity', I read somewhere that it is a philosophy that
'empties the baby out with the bath water'—that's what you'll do with my
book."[69] With this proverbial statement Shaw is trying to convince Stella that
even though the letters contain intimate passages that clearly were never meant
for publication, she should not fight against their publication. Just because
parts of the letters will be disturbing should be no reason to reject the entire
project. And finally there is Shaw's appropriate use of the phrase in his socio-
political volume entitled *Everybody's Political What's What* (1944). Arguing that
social life, though always changing, must be based on some civilized laws
and creeds, he comments that "When changing we must be careful not to
empty the baby out with the bath in mere reaction against the past. In Russia,
for instance, the reaction against illiteracy and tyranny of capitalist-
dominated Tsardom was so intemperate that when it was placed in power by
the revolution of 1917, it went too far."[70] Shaw thus made use of the phrase
"To empty the baby out with the bath" three times, while once also length-
ening "bath" to "bath water" which today is the preferred variant. He clearly
found the expression to be a useful metaphor to describe various types of
overreactions, and his writings might well have helped to spread this German
phrase among English and, because of his wide readership, also American
intellectuals.

Shaw certainly deserves the credit thus far for having been the first in
employing the German proverbial expression in a precise English rendition.
Whether he learned it through oral communication or perhaps even through
his German readings (he did know German very well), will most likely never
be known. But his use of the phrase in 1909, 1911, and 1922 predates all
others that have been located to this date, and while he was very consistent
in his own wording of it, subsequent references show that the standard form
of the new English expression was still in flux. This is very noticable in Henry
W. Nevinson's citation of the phrase in his discussion of Lev Tolstoy's (1828–
1910) life and thought:

> If one must find fault with such a glorified spirit, it would be in the remorseless consistency of its logic that I should seek it—a logic which, having condemned all pleasures of sense, would doom the human race to rapid extinction because life cannot be handed on without pleasure. At so ascetic a doctrine the people who profess and call themselves Christians ought not to be astonished, especially as it is practised by few. But I suppose we must still be a little careful lest, as the Germans say, we throw away the child with the bath-water in which it has been washed.[71]

This quotation establishes beyond any doubt that in 1925 Nevinson at least was very well aware that he was using an originally German expression. Just as Carlyle before him he too includes the introductory formula "as the Germans say" to draw attention to this fact, something that Shaw never did.

Three years after this telling passage the proverbial expression made its journalistic debut in a book review of *Selected Poems of Sir William Watson* that appeared on July 1, 1928, in *The Observer* (see also note 43). Commenting on the lack of interest of some modern poets in the English language while emphasizing foreign words and phrases, the reviewer J. C. Squire states that "There is always, of course, when reactions are 'on', a risk of throwing out the baby with the bath. But the bath, in the present instance, was well worth discarding."[72] This passage can be taken as yet another indication that the expression is establishing itself among British intellectuals in the 1920s.

It very definitely gained in currency in the next decade, although the three references found thus far from the 1930s do not show an overwhelming frequency. In the chapter on "New-Century Stocktaking" in her book on *Insurrection versus Resurrection* (1937) Maisie Ward states that "the Modernists saw that an enormous amount of old-fashioned apologetic had become valueless, but in their ardour to get rid of it they 'emptied out the baby with the bathwater,' losing divine truth in their dissatisfaction with its Nineteenth Century expression."[73] That this very proverbial line used by Ward in quotation marks was subsequently cited in a review of Ward's book in *The Times Literary Supplement* on January 1, 1938, shows how the phrase continued to make its rounds in intellectual circles.[74] And that it appears in the 1939 play *Pastor Hall* as "'You pour the baby out with the bath. What matters is what a man lives for and how he dies, Herr Pastor. There's the rub',"[75] should not be surprising, since its exiled author Ernst Toller (1893–1939) had written the play in New York first in German. His translators Stephen Spender and Hugh Hunt translated his native German proverbial expression quite literally from its original: "'Sie schütten das Kind mit dem Bade aus. Es kommt darauf an, wofür man lebt und wie man stirbt, Herr Pastor, das ist der Haken'."[76] But there is one major difference in comparison to the difficulties that the various translators of the phrase from Goethe's autobiography encountered. While they, with one final exception, still had to search for some kind of equivalent English expression, Spender and Hunt most likely knew that the German expression had become anglicized already, thus making their translation of it an easy task.

During the 1940s the proverbial expression must have become noticably more frequent in the oral and written language. The lexicographer and phraseologist Eric Partridge is most likely correct in stating that it gained general currency in this decade (see notes 46 and 50). Shaw's use of it in 1944 has already been discussed, but there is a second short reference from the same year by George Gordon Coulton (1858–1947). In his autobiography Coulton claims that a poem about love of humanity helped him to keep "from 'throwing out the baby with the bath' "[77] at a moment of severe self-doubt. By the time the 1950s begin, the phrase is definitely well established in England and the United States, as attested to in its appearance in various types of dictionaries, literary as well as scholarly works, and the press. By the time the American scholar Theodor Rosebury writes his book on *Microbes and Morals* in 1971, the expression is entrenched so deeply in the Anglo-American psyche that he actually could write "as the English like to say, to throw out the baby with the bathwater."[78] The introductory formula "as the Germans say" has been replaced by one that identifies the expression as being English. In a way Rosebury is, of course, partially correct in his claim since the German phrase in its translated form gained currency in England before catching on in the United States as far as can be told by the references cited in this chapter.

What follows is a list of contextualized references from 1950 to 1990 out of literary, scholarly, and journalistic writings. Together they establish the popularity of this proverbial expression and show how it is indeed an effective metaphor for the modern world despite its antiquated image. But most likely it is exactly the grotesque picture of a naked baby being thrown out with soapy and dirty water that attracts people to use it in a world of sophisticated, technological communication. The proverbial metaphor can drive an argument home as no bureaucratic jargon or cut-and-dry rationale could ever hope to do.

1950:   All scientific progress, however, has its drawbacks; no bath water is ever thrown out without some species of baby goes down the plughole with it.[79]

1955:   I said: "Don't try too hard to escape from your own faults. You know

the proverb about the baby and the bathwater?"
When I had explained it she nodded. "Already I have thrown away a great deal of my old self."[80]

1957:   We can rid ourselves of those grammarians' fetishes which make it [the English language] more difficult to be intelligible without throwing the baby away with the bathwater.[81]

1958:   The country needs protection against the aggressive tendency of the court [U.S. Supreme Court], no doubt. Unfortunately, Senate bill 2646 goes so far that its adoption would violate that ancient maxim of common sense not to throw the baby out with the bath.[82]

1958:   We repudiate this legislation as a ruthless approach which, in effect, throws out the baby with the bath.[83]

1960:   Enthusiastically despising the works of my contemporaries, I nicely evaded doing anything at all myself; the baby was well on the way out with the bath-water.[84]

1967:   Although the vagueness of our laws renders enforcement uncertain, and excessively energy-consuming when weighed against meager results, common sense does not compel the abandonment of all pornography legislation. We are not forced to throw out the baby with the bath water. There is no need for complete surrender, for the substitution in the place of poor laws of no laws at all.[85]

1971:   But to throw away all of Buret [a scholar] because of his mistakes is itself the same sort of mistake, if not quite so bad, as to throw Shakespeare away for his seacoast in Bohemia, or Beethoven for his *Battle* symphony, or, as the English like to say, to throw out the baby with the bathwater.[86]

1976:   But all of these problems are susceptible to correction and improvement—why must we throw out the baby with the bath water?[87]

1976:   The Diamond Lane will eventually work. Let's don't throw the baby out with the wash or we will have another Long Island Expressway on our hands—the world's largest parking lot.[88]

1977:   I began this book as an indulgent, antiquarian exercise in personal interest. I hoped, at best, to retrieve from its current limbo the ancient subject of parallels between ontogeny and phylogeny. And a rescue it certainly deserves, for no discarded theme more clearly merits the old metaphor about throwing the baby out with the bath water.[89]

1980:   We, the workers who were just recently told our jobs would cease at the Ford Motor Co.'s Pico Rivera on Feb. 8, builders of the larger cars, should convince state and federal legislators their demands about smog controls and mileage figures should not follow the same old adage of throwing the baby out with the bath water.[90]

1980: As the owner of a small home, I am greatly disturbed by . . . the increasing share of the real property tax being paid by homeowners. It is not the disparity that frightens me. It is the proposed remedy, which seems a classic illustration of throwing the baby out with the bath water.[91]

1982: Rather than go after inefficiency and waste in programs with surgical precision, the Reagan Administration seems to be trying to wreck the whole system—much like throwing the baby out with the dirty bath water.[92]

1982: On second thought, there's hope after all—surely lots of these [money-grubbing] kids will turn out to be smart enough, when they're a little bit older, to draw the appropriate conclusions when they see through the patently false premises [of financial success and unlimited wants] and throw out not only the bathwater, but the baby and the tub.[93]

1983: "No," Rachel replied, laughing. "But it's almost as good. Abraham and I have decided that you should keep your baby."
Now Marie laughed. "I should hope so, Mrs. Benedict. I certainly don't intend to throw it out with the bath water."[94]

1984: But the blackballing will be done verbally, and no longer by printed ballot. We have no intention of throwing out the baby with the bathwater.[95]

1988: Downey smiled, and it was a brutal little twist of his lips. "You're up shit creek, Frank. Romanenko was your baby, and you let him slip down the plughole with the bathwater. The commissioner's going to need an extra dose of the old digitals to cope with this one, chum."[96]

1990: There is a downside. In the bathwater of scientific progress, there is always the baby of second thoughts.[97]

1990: The radiation used for a skull exam is minimal, and any negative aspects are far outweighed by the very great benefits of speedy, accurate diagnosis. Let's not throw the baby out with the bath water![98]

These twenty direct references of, allusions to or even puns with the proverbial expression or the proverb show how comfortable English and American writers are with them. Even though in Dennis Barry's novel *Sea of Glass* (1955), David needs to *explain* "the proverb about the baby and the bathwater" (see note 80) to Varvara, it is basically universally known by the mid-1950s. At times such standard introductory formulas as "that ancient maxim of common sense" (see note 82), "the old metaphor" (note 89), and "the same old adage" (note 90) are employed, an old "trick" of lending even greater credence to a bit of proverbial wisdom that really is not of biblical age. The very fact that writers can "play" with the phrase is ample proof of its acceptance and knowledge. An allusion like "In the bathwater of scientific progress, there is always the baby of second thoughts" (note 97) is an effective example, drastically expressing through its very elliptic use of the proverbial metaphor how people come to regret overzealous reactions. Such expanded variants as "throw out not only the bathwater, but the baby and the tub" (note 93) and "Romanenko was your baby, and you let him slip down the plughole with the bathwater" (note 96) bring to mind the 1967 popular song "Mother's Lament" by the British group Cream. While the actual proverbial expression is never mentioned in the text, such references as "a mother was washing her baby," "your baby has rolled down the tubhole," and "he should have been washed in a jug" certainly conjure up the proverbial image.

Mother's Lament

A mother was washing her baby one night
The youngest of ten and a delicate wight.
The mother was poor and the baby thin
'Twas naught but a skeleton, covered with skin.
The mother turned 'round for the soap off the rack
She was only a moment, but when she turned back
Her baby had gone and in anguish she cried
Oh where has my baby gone! The angels replied:
Oh your baby has rolled down the tubhole,
Oh your baby has gone down the plug.
The poor little thing was so skinny and thin,
He should have been washed in a jug.
Your baby is perfectly happy,
He won't need a bath anymore.
He's amucking and about with the angels above,
Not lost but gone before.[99]

But this popular phrase has also been used quite effectively in a slightly shortened form by Christopher Durang (born 1949) as a title for his 1983 satirical play *Baby with the Bathwater.*[100] Its major theme deals with the breakdown of the family and a baby is actually involved, but the proverbial expression is not used once throughout the play. Instead, the entire drama is an enactment of the fundamental message of the phrase as it relates to the modern family, bringing to mind the vogue of so-called "proverbes dramatiques" by such playwrights as William Shakespeare (1564–1616), Thomas Middleton (1580–1627), Louis Carmontelle (1717–1806), and Alfred de Musset (1810–1857), to name a few.[101] The more or less obvious message of the proverbial title and the play's lack of success on the stage in New York prompted a rather negative review by Richard Eder that ends with a marvelous pun: "After all Durangs's gleeful banditry it seems rather a long way around to end up at a sober commonplace. Some reviewers thought it [the play] showed signs that he is maturing. But it seems a pity to throw the baby away in the bathos-water."[102]

Speaking of titles, the proverbial expression has frequently been employed as a provocative title of a journal, magazine, or newspaper article, as an advertising headline, and as a caption of a cartoon. Already in 1967 the Magazine Publishers Association placed an interesting advertisement in *Fortune* magazine that carried the slogan "Don't throw the baby out with the bathwater" while also depicting a naked baby sitting in a small portable tub. In the lengthy advertising text surrounding this center picture the reader/viewer finds out that the best thing the American economy has going for it is the principle of free competition. The copy ends with the statement that "Of course, any economy needs some regulation—*but let's be sure that we don't throw out the baby with the bath water.*"[103] It is interesting to note that the copy writer is quite unsure about the proper placement of the preposition "out" (i.e., before or after "the baby") and the proper spelling of "bath water" or "bathwater" (some use a hyphen, i.e., "bath-water", as can be seen from several references previously cited). In both instances because the standard proverb form "Don't . . ." is used instead of the proverbial expression "To throw . . ." it makes this a clear didactic message for the consumers, who must retain their capitalistic freedom of choice.

A particularly effective use of the proverbial expression as a newspaper headline appeared in the *Burlington Free Press* ten years ago. The city of Burlington in Vermont has been involved in a major development project of its shoreline at Lake Champlain, a matter of much controversy to this day. The headline of a highly politicized article read "Tossing the Waterfront Baby Out With the Bath," followed by a first paragraph that set the tone for the remainder of the report: "The tendency of some of our legislators to leap before they look almost cost Burlington its lakefront redevelopment program this week."[104] The cleverly adapted proverbial headline together with the twisted proverb "Look before you leap" help make this newspaper article an account filled with heated emotions and damaging accusations. While the journalist is not attacking the politicians directly, this proverbial language expresses the bitter satire indirectly through the innovative use of metaphors.

It is amazing to see such headlines as the following ones that are built for the most part solely on the proverb or the proverbial expression without pointing to the actual issues in a smaller explanatory secondary headline. The metaphor alone is supposed to draw the readers' attention while at the same time preparing them emotionally for a report of a controversial matter. The proverbial headline through its metaphor signals, of course, that someone has already overreacted or is about to do so by throwing out the baby, whatever that might be, with the dirty bath water.

1981: Don't toss this baby out with the dirty bath water.[105]
        (Article arguing for the continued clean up of the nation's waters)
1982: Synfuel baby is thrown out with the OPEC bathwater.[106]
        (Article about the new synfuel technologies and industries)
1983: Throwing out the Baby with the Bathwater?[107]
        (Article concerning the decision by the Russians to quit the World Psychiatric Association)
1984: The Baby and the Bathwater: Developing a Positive Socratic Method.[108]
        (Major scholarly article on new teaching strategies for American law schools)
1984: Don't Throw the Parole Baby Out With the Justice Bath Water.[109]
        (This expanded headline makes it clear that the article deals with the problem of parole)
1984: Alternatives to the Computational View of Mind: The Baby or the Bathwater?[110]
        (Article deals with various computational and information processing approaches to cognition)
1985: Baby stuff goes out with nasty bathwater.[111]
        (Article on how to deal with pornography and videos)
1985: Saving Baby from the Bath Water.[112]
        (Scholarly article on Marxist production concepts and precapitalist Africa)
1987: ''Confidentiality'': The Ethical Baby in the Legal Bathwater.[113]
        (Scholarly article on ethical and legal issues concerning confidentiality)
1987: On Babies and Bathwater: Input in Foreign Language Learning.[114]
        (Article on the monitor theory in foreign language instruction)
1987: Let's Not Throw out the Baby with the Bath Water.[115]
        (Article on getting parents involved in schools)
1988: Unbundling Natural Gas Sales Services—Is the FERC Throwing the Baby out with the Bath Water?[116]
        (Relatively clear headline signalling comments on the role of the Federal Energy Regulatory Commission in controlling natural gas companies)
1990: The Concordance of Ontogeny with Phylogeny: Putting the Baby Back into the Bath Water.[117]

(Scholarly article whose headline plays on Stephen Jay Gould's use of the expression in his famous book on *Ontogeny and Phylogeny* [see note 89])

For all their proverbial straightforwardness or punning these headlines act more as attention-getters than precise information concerning the articles' content. The communicative value of such headlines might, of course, be largely improved if the scholars or journalists would accompany their proverbial fun and games with appropriate illustrations to satisfy the visual expectations of modern readers. This was done quite successfully in a recent article on student and teacher assessment in British schools that appeared in *The Times Educational Supplement.* The journalist Caroline St John-Brooks actually used another quite popular proverbial expression as the major headline that was followed by a rather lengthy subtitle: "Testing the Water—Assessment is still generating anxiety, but resist the urge to jettison existing schemes—complex new ones may be hard to change later."[118] Above this verbal information, however, is a splendid colorful drawing of a bare-bottomed baby being poured out of a tub and just barely holding on for its life at the rim. This is indeed a marvelous juxtaposition of two proverbial expressions, the one stated explicitly and the other clearly illustrated (the verb "to jettison" also helps bring to mind the unstated expression "To throw the baby out with the bath water"), resulting in an effective proverbial introduction to the article on the problems and controversies surrounding assessment in schools.

Other pictorizations of the proverbial expression include an appropriate political cartoon from 1981 with the caption "Everybody ready for the baby-and-bathwater toss?"[119] The cartoon shows a member of the "Reagan Team" with a starter pistol lifted up high while three bureaucrats are ready and eager to toss out three babies, with the three tubs labeled "Federal Regulations," "Federal Programs," and "Federal Agencies." Quite a telling cartoon of Reagan's ideas of a decentralized government! And there was even a very early use of the expression in a *Peanuts* cartoon from 1960 attesting to the fact that Charles M. Schulz certainly assumed at that time that his readers would know it, since the cartoon would otherwise make very little sense indeed. In the first frame Linus says to Charlie Brown "I'm inclined to agree with you, Charlie Brown. . . ." Next he states "But on the other hand we must be cautious in our thinking." He continues with "We must be careful not to 'Throw out the baby with the bath'," while little Sally gets a frightened look on her face. In the fourth frame Linus turns to the bewildered Sally and says, "Please pardon the expression."[120] The little girl obviously missed the metaphorical meaning of the phrase as young children tend to do, understanding it only literally and thus as a direct threat to herself. And such a literal understanding of the proverbial expression is also involved in the wonderfully colorful poster by T.

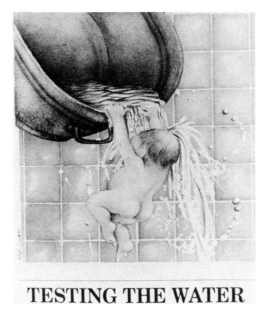

TESTING THE WATER

F. Breitenbach entitled "Proverbidioms" (1975).[121] In this obvious artistic parody of Pieter Brueghel's (c. 1520–1569) famous oil-picture "The Netherlandic Proverbs" (1559)[122] Breitenbach depicts dozens of English proverbs and proverbial expressions. In one of the many proverbial scenes someone is quite literally throwing out the baby with the bath water from a dormer window.

There is one last set of references that will help to shed additional light on the history of this proverbial expression in the United States. Gretchen Guidotti, one of the archivists of the "Folklore Archives" at the University of California at Berkeley under the directorship of Alan Dundes, provided eleven invaluable citations that were collected between 1968 and 1986 by folklore students. One of them collected the standard proverb form from an informant in 1968 at San Jose and provided the following comments: " 'Don't throw out the baby with the bath water.'—My informant can remember this proverb being used variously by different aunts and uncles while she was living in Olivet, Michigan, circa 1920. She tells me that it means not to discard the important value in a situation in your effort to get rid of unneeded, extraneous, and often distressing accompaniments (to the situation)."[123] Since the informant's name was Eleanor Vandervoort, it can safely be assumed that she was of Dutch background living in Michigan where many of the Dutch immigrants settled. The originally German proverb and proverbial expression have been current in Holland from at least the seventeenth century as "Men

Copyright 1981 by Herblock in the Washington Post.

moet het kind niet met het bad uitschudden''[124] and "Het kind met het badwater weggoien (-werpen),"[125] and the Dutch immigrants naturally brought
it with them to the United States just as their German counterparts did. The
identical texts of both language groups were subsequently translated into English, thus gaining oral currency in America in two distinct ways—a truly
fascinating way of proverb dissemination. This informant also clearly establishes the fact, of course, that the proverb was known in the English language
at least by the 1920s in oral communication.

The German side of the coin is well illustrated by texts that were actually
collected in German in 1974: The one example cites "Das Kind mit dem
Badewasser ausschütten. / To dump the child out with the bathwater," and
the student comments that he collected it from his mother who learned it
from her parents in Kronburg, Germany.[126] The other reference was collected
from a German immigrant car mechanic who had learned the proverb from
his grandfather in Darmstadt: "Man muss nicht das Kind mit dem Badewasser ausschütten. / One should not throw (pour) out the child with the bath

PEANUTS reprinted by permission of UFS, Inc.

water."[127] These relatively recent citations from the mid-1970s illustrate that the phrase is still being associated with its well-established German origin even by users in distant and modern California.

The other recordings of the expression as well as the comments by the student collectors and their informants are, however, quite unrevealing save for establishing its definite oral currency as an "American" expression.

1971:   Don't throw the baby out with the bath water.[128]
1975:   To throw out the baby with the bathwater.[129]
1979:   Don't toss the baby out with the bath water.[130]
1981:   Throw the baby out with the bathwater.[131]
        (Informant learned it in 1959 in Florida)
1983:   Threw out the baby with the bathwater.[132]
        (Informant heard it as early as 1935 in New York)
1985:   Don't throw the baby out with the bath water.[133]
        (Informant learned it in about 1947 in Boston)
1985:   Throwing the baby out with the bathwater.[134]
1986:   Don't throw out the baby with the bathwater.[135]

The reference from 1979 indicates yet another variant by changing the standard verb "to throw" to "to toss," but otherwise these texts show how standardized both the proverb and the proverbial expression have become in the English language. That this proverbial metaphor has gained general acceptance and knowledge in the American culture is also attested to by its inclusion as "Don't throw out the baby with the bath water"[136] in the chapter on "Proverbs" in E. D. Hirsch's et al. recent *Dictionary of Cultural Literacy* (1988) that supposedly lists what literate Americans know or ought to know.

Yet the German expression is by no means restricted to its successful dissemination as a loan translation in the English language. It was already pointed out that it entered the Dutch language as early as the seventeenth century, that is, much earlier than its conquest of the English-speaking world. But it is also known in other European languages, as, for example,[137]

Danish:	Man skal ikke kaste barnet ud med badevandet.
French:	Il ne faut pas jeter le bébé avec l'eau du bain.
Hungarian:	Nem kell a gyereket a fürdővizzel kiönteni.
Icelandic:	Hann steypti ut barninu i laugartroginu.
Swedish:	Man bör inte kasta ut barnet med badvattnet.

It would, of course, be interesting to study the history of this expression in these and other national languages, but this task will have to be left to linguistically better qualified scholars. The phrase has entered such diverse language groups as Finno-Ugric, Germanic, and Romance. Of speculative interest is certainly the French "Il ne faut pas jeter le bébé avec l'eau du bain" which appears to have replaced the traditional "Jeter le manche après la cognée" (To throw the helve after the hatchet) only relatively recently. Having found it in only one comparative proverb collection from 1988 thus far,[138] I will stick out my proverbial neck and venture the "scholarly" guess that it might even have been taken over into the French language from the English version and not the German original. Keep in mind that the German phrase talks of "Kind" (child) and not "Baby." Had the French taken the expression over as a direct loan translation from the German it might have done so by using "enfant"—some early English loan translations had after all also used "child" at first. The French "bébé" strikes me as an adaptation of the Anglo-American version, something not so farfetched when one considers the influence of the English and American languages on European cultures.

There is, however, some not so trivial documentation that can be cited to show that this conjecture might not be so strange after all. In this regard consider Günter Grass's well-known novel *Die Blechtrommel* (1959) in which he has little Oscar relate the following feelings and thoughts about his mother.

> Mama konnte sehr lustig sein. Mama konnte sehr ängstlich sein. Mama konnte schnell vergessen. Mama hatte dennoch ein gutes Gedächtnis. Mama schüttete mich aus und saß dennoch mit mir in einem Bade.[139]

In the last clause the acute manipulator of traditional language Günter Grass cleverly connects the shortened proverbial expression "Das Kind mit dem Bade ausschütten" with the phrase "Sie sitzen beide in einem Bade" (they are both sitting in one bath, i.e., they both have the same concerns or problems). It might even be that a third expression, namely, "Wir sitzen alle in einem Boot" (we are all in the same boat), is being alluded to as well in this pun. In any case, the experienced translator of much modern German fiction, Ralph Manheim, quite successfully translated this passage in his English rendition of *The Tin Drum* (1961).

> Mama could be very gay, she could also be very anxious. Mama could forget quickly, yet she had a good memory. Mama would throw me out with the bath water, and yet she would share my bath.[140]

While he does not do very well with the interconnection of the two if not three proverbial phrases which make up Grass's punning proverbial language, he certainly recognizes the first part to be the phrase under discussion here, rendering it very appropriately as "Mama would throw me out with the bath water." Predictably, the Swedish and Dutch translations also maintain the original German expression. The Swedish translator Nils Holmberg has for the final sentence of this passage "Mamma lät mig komma till sig i badkaret men kastade inte ut barnet med badvattnet,"[141] while the Dutch translator Koos Schuur renders it as "Mijn moeder gooide mij soms met het badwater weg en kwam toch bij mij in het bad zitten."[142] Yet the French translator Jean Amsler encountered obvious difficulty with this passage:

> Maman savait être fort gaie. Maman savait être fort anxieuse. Maman savait oublier vite. Maman avait pourtant bonne mémoire. Maman me flanquait à la porte et pourtant m'admettait dans son bain.[143]

Amsler kept the fact that Oscar's mother let him take a bath with her (i.e., she admitted him into her bath), but he replaces the German proverbial expression with the inadequate phraseological unit "flanquer quelqu'un à la porte" (i.e., to boot, throw, chuck someone out), losing the proverbial pun altogether. He also decided quite correctly that the traditional French equivalent "jeter le manche après la cognée" (to throw the helve after the hatchet) was even less fitting to translate this complex sentence. But one thing is for certain: he did *not* have at his disposal the new French proverb "Il ne faut pas jeter le bébé avec l'eau du bain" when he translated Grass's novel in 1961. The proverb and its proverbial form "jeter le bébé avec l'eau du bain" must therefore be relatively new in the French language, and that being the case, it might in fact be that the phrase entered into the French language not from the German but the English only sometime during the past two decades.

It can be assumed that the German phrase, no matter how it got into the French language, will catch on among speakers of that language just as it has done in the English tongue earlier this century. Many proverbs and proverbial expressions that are shared in common by many European languages date back to classical antiquity, the Bible, or the Middle Ages. They were usually translated word by word and gained general currency especially through widely disseminated Bible translations and also through the pioneering humanistic work of Erasmus of Rotterdam (1469–1536) whose Latin *Adagia* (1500ff.) also were translated into the vulgate languages. It is, however, of interest to note that certain indigenous proverbs or proverbial expressions of a single European national culture can still today undergo the fascinating steps to gain at least some international distribution and currency. For a long time the German proverbial expression "Das Kind mit dem Bade ausschütten" from the fifteenth century and its slightly later wording as the proverb "Man muß das Kind nicht mit dem Bade ausschütten" were pretty much restricted to the German-speaking countries. By the seventeenth century they entered the closely related Dutch language and culture and eventually spread to other Germanic languages in the North. But the successful jump across the English Channel and the Atlantic Ocean does not appear to have happened until the nineteenth century. In fact, I hope to have proven that the German phrase did not really get onto solid footing in the Anglo-American world until the early twentieth century. By now its German origin is only seldom remembered and most users think of it as an English or American expression. But appearances are deceiving, and it would surely be better to classify this old German proverbial expression and proverb as belonging at least to an impressive degree to the international stock of proverbial metaphors and wisdom. This ever-increasing internationalization is possible because the proverb and proverbial expression "(Don't) throw the baby out with the bath water" express in an easily understandable metaphor the only too human inclination toward extreme reactions. All of us, whether we like it or not, are from time to time guilty of the universally practiced act of throwing the baby out with the bath water.

Notes

1. *Thomas Murners Narrenbeschwörung*, ed. by M. Spanier. Halle: VEB Max Niemeyer, 1967, pp. 243–246.

2. Quoted from *D. Martin Luthers Werke*, ed. by Paul Pietsch. Weimar: Hermann Böhlau, 1898, vol. 20, p. 160. See also James Cornette, *Proverbs and Proverbial Expressions in the German Works of Martin Luther*. Diss. University of North Carolina, 1942, p. 157.

3. Archer Taylor, "The Proverbial Formula 'Man soll . . .'," *Zeitschrift für Volkskunde*, New Series, 2 (1930), 152–156. Also in *Selected Writings on Proverbs by Archer Taylor*, ed. by Wolfgang Mieder. Helsinki: Suomalainen Tiedeakatemia, 1975, p. 104.

4. See Sebastian Franck, *Sprichwörter / Schöne / Weise / Herrliche Clugreden / und Hoffsprüch*. Frankfurt am Main: Christian Egenolff, 1541; rpt. ed. by Wolfgang Mieder. Hildesheim: Georg Olms, 1987, p. 16[b] and p. 17[a].

5. For a detailed historical study of occurrences in German written sources of this pop-

ular proverb and proverbial expression from Thomas Murner to the present day see Wolf-gang Mieder, " 'Das Kind mit dem Bade ausschütten': Ursprung, Überlieferung und Ver-wendung einer deutschen Redensart," *Muttersprache* (in press).

6. Quoted from Thomas Carlyle, *Critical and Miscellaneous Essays*. New York: Charles Scribner's Sons, 1904, vol. 4, pp. 368–369. The entire essay on pp. 348–383.

7. Joseph Leonhard Hilpert, *Englisch-Deutsches und Deutsch-Englisches Wörterbuch*. Karls-ruhe: Braun, 1846, vol. 2, p. 118.

8. G. J. Adler, *Dictionary of the German and English Languages*. New York: Appleton, 1849, part 1, p. 77.

9. Joseph Leonhard Hilpert, *A Dictionary of the English and German, and the German and English Language*. Carlsruhe: Braun, 1857, part 1, p. 118.

10. Felix Flügel, *A Dictionary of the English and German Languages*. New York: Lemcke & Buechner, 1896, part 2, p. 130.

11. Eduard Muret and Daniel Sanders, *Encyklopädisches englisch-deutsches und deutsch-eng-lisches Wörterbuch*. Berlin: Langenscheidt, 1900, part 2, p. 1197.

12. Karl Breul, *Cassell's German and English Dictionary*. New York: Funk and Wagnalls, 1936, p. 68.

13. J. E. Wessely, *Deutsch-Englisches und Englisch-Deutsches Taschenwörterbuch*. Philadel-phia: David McKay, 1941, p. 125.

14. Harold T. Betteridge, *The New Cassell's German Dictionary*. New York: Funk & Wag-nalls, 1958, p. 261.

15. Karl Wildhagen, *The New Wildhagen German Dictionary*. Chicago: Follett, 1965, p. 670.

16. Karl Wildhagen, *English-German / German-English Dictionary*. London: George Allen, 1972, vol. 2, p. 750.

17. Otto Springer, *Langenscheidts Enzyklopädisches Wörterbuch der englischen und deutschen Sprache*. Berlin: Langenscheidt, 1974, part 2, vol. 1, p. 890.

18. Harold Betteridge, *Cassell's German-English / English-German Dictionary*. New York: Macmillan, 1978, p. 346.

19. Peter Terrell et al., *Collins German-English / English-German Dictionary*. London: Col-lins, 1981, p. 389.

20. Robin Sawers, *Harrap's Concise German and English Dictionary*. London: Harrap, 1982, p. 290.

21. John Barten, *A Select Collection of English and German Proverbs, Proverbial Expressions, and Familiar Quotations with Translations*. Hamburg: Conrad Kloss, 1896, p. 141.

22. Heinrich Loewe, *Deutsch-Englische Phraseologie*. Berlin: Langenscheidt, 1897, p. 92.

23. Wolfgang Schmidt-Hidding, "Sprichwörtliche Redensarten. Abgrenzungen—Aufga-ben der Forschung," *Rheinisches Jahrbuch für Volkskunde*, 7 (1956), 95–144. Auch in *Ergebnisse der Sprichwörterforschung*, ed. by Wolfgang Mieder. Bern: Peter Lang, 1978, p. 44.

24. W. E. Collinson, "Some German and English Idioms, with a Note on the Definition of the Term 'Idiom'," *German Life and Letters*, 11 (1957–1958), 266–269 (esp. p. 267).

25. Keith Spalding, *An Historical Dictionary of German Figurative Usage*. Oxford: Basil Blackwell, 1959, p. 154.

26. Ronald Taylor and Walter Gottschalk, *A German-English Dictionary of Idioms*. München: Max Hueber, 1960, p. 277.

27. Karl Voss, *Redensarten der englischen Sprache*. Berlin: Ullstein, 1967, p. 66.

28. Adi Andersen, *Deutsche Sprichwörter und Redensarten mit ihren englischen und franzö-sischen Gegenstücken*. Hamburg: Matari, 1968, p. 35.

29. Spalding (see note 25), p. 1466.

30. Cheri Booth, *Idioms. Lexikon der englischen Redewendungen*. Eltville am Rhein: Bechtermünz, 1988, p. 463.

31. Cheri Booth, *Slang. Lexikon der englischen Umgangssprache*. Eltville am Rhein: Bechtermünz, 1989, p. 446.

32. Wolfgang Mieder, *English Expressions*. Stuttgart: Philipp Reclam, 1992, p. 15.

33. See Edmund P. Kremer, *German Proverbs and Proverbial Phrases with Their English Counterparts*. Stanford/California: Stanford University Press, 1955, p. 61.

34. Wolfgang Mieder, *English Proverbs*. Stuttgart: Philipp Reclam, 1988, p. 26.

35. See *Goethes Werke*, ed. by order of the Großherzogin Sophie von Sachsen. Weimar: Hermann Böhlau, 1889, vol. 26, p. 170.

36. Quoted from the anonymous translation *Memoirs of Goethe Written by Himself*. New York: Collins & Hannay, 1824, p. 47.

37. *The Auto-Biography of Goethe. Truth and Poetry: From My Life*, translated and ed. by Parke Godwin. New York: Wiley and Putnam, 1846, p. 94.

38. *The Auto-Biography of Goethe. Truth and Poetry: From My Life*, translated by John Oxenford. London: Henry G. Bohn, 1848, p. 87.

39. See, for example, *The Autobiography of Goethe. Truth and Fiction: Relating to My Life*, translated by John Oxenford. New York: Lovell, Coryell & Co., 1882, vol. 1, p. 90.

40. *Poetry and Truth. From My Own Life*, a revised translation by Minna Steele Smith. London: George Bell, 1908, vol. 1, p. 92.

41. *Goethe's Autobiography. Poetry and Truth. From My Own Life*, translated by R. O. Moon. Washington/D.C.: Public Affairs Press, 1949, p. 89.

42. Johann Wolfgang von Goethe, *From My Life. Poetry and Truth*, translated by Robert R. Heitner. New York: Suhrkamp, 1987, p. 91.

43. See *The Oxford English Dictionary, Supplement*. Oxford: Clarendon Press, 1933, p. 48.

44. Burton Stevenson, *The Macmillan Book of Proverbs, Maxims, and Famous Phrases*. New York: Macmillan, 1948, p. 112 (no. 2). With a reference from 1914.

45. F. P. Wilson, *The Oxford Dictionary of English Proverbs*. Oxford: Clarendon Press, 1970, p. 220. With three references from 1911, 1937 and 1944.

46. Eric Partridge, *A Dictionary of Slang and Unconventional English*, 7th ed. New York: Macmillan, 1970, vol. 2, p. 1466.

47. Ivor H. Evans, *Brewer's Dictionary of Phrase and Fable*. New York: Harper & Row, 1970, p. 64.

48. *A Supplement to The Oxford English Dictionary*, ed. R. W. Burchfield. Oxford: Clarendon Press, 1972, vol. 1, p. 169. With five references from 1909, 1911, 1922, 1939, and 1957. The entry in the second edition of *The Oxford English Dictionary*, ed. by John A. Simpson and E. S. C. Weiner. Oxford: Clarendon Press, 1989, vol. 1, p. 851, is an exact duplicate of this statement and its five references.

49. Adam Makkai, *Handbook of Commonly Used American Idioms*. Woodbury/New York: Barron's Educational Series, 1975, p. 269.

50. Eric Partridge, *A Dictionary of Catch Phrases*. New York: Stein and Day, 1977, p. 54.

51. Laurence Urdang, *Longman Dictionary of English Idioms*. London: Longman, 1979, p. 12. With one reference from 1974.

52. Laurence Urdang and Nancy LaRoche, *Picturesque Expressions: A Thematic Dictionary*. Detroit: Gale Research Co., 1980, p. 117. With one reference from 1909. The identical entry appears in the second edition of 1985.

53. *The Concise Oxford Dictionary of Proverbs*, ed. John A. Simpson. Oxford: Oxford University Press, 1982, p. 225. With five references from 1610 (Johannes Kepler [in German]), 1853 (Thomas Carlyle), 1911, 1937, and 1979.

54. *The World Book Dictionary*, ed. by Clarence L. and Robert K. Barnhart. Chicago: World Book, 1983, vol. 1, p. 146.

55. Neil Ewart, *Everyday Phrases. Their Origins and Meanings*. Poole/Dorset: Blandford Press, 1983, p. 12.

56. *Chambers 20th Century Dictionary*, ed. by E. M. Kirkpatrick. Cambridge: Cambridge University Press, 1983, p. 88.

57. James Rogers, *The Dictionary of Cliches*. New York: Facts on File Publications, 1985, p. 263. With one reference from 1909.

58. Jonathon Green, *The Dictionary of Contemporary Slang*. New York: Stein and Day, 1985, p. 285.

59. *Longman Dictionary of Contemporary English*, ed. by Della Summers. London: Longman, 1987, p. 63.

60. *The Australian Concise Oxford Dictionary of Current English*, ed. by George W. Turner. Melbourne: Oxford University Press, 1987, p. 67.

61. E. D. Hirsch, Joseph F. Kett, and James Trefil, *The Dictionary of Cultural Literacy*. Boston: Houghton Mifflin Co., 1988, p. 56.

62. Laurence Urdang, *The Whole Ball of Wax and Other Colloquial Phrases. What They Mean & How They Started*. New York: A Perigee Book, 1988, p. 138.

63. A. P. Cowie, *Oxford Advanced Learner's Dictionary of English*. Oxford: Oxford University Press, 1989, p. 72.

64. Bartlett Jere Whiting, *Modern Proverbs and Proverbial Sayings*. Cambridge: Harvard University Press, 1989, pp. 24–25. With nine modern references from 1925, 1943, 1950, 1955, 1958 (two), 1960, 1967, and 1971. For a comparison of how the three paremiographers Wilson (see note 45), Simpson (see note 53), and Whiting have treated this proverbial expression see Wolfgang Mieder's review of Whiting's proverb collection in *Proverbium: Yearbook of International Proverb Scholarship*, 7 (1990), 287–294 (esp. 291–292).

65. *A Dictionary of American Proverbs*, ed. by Wolfgang Mieder, Stewart Kingsbury, and Kelsie Harder. New York: Oxford University Press, 1992, p. 33.

66. Quoted from George Bernard Shaw, *Pen Portraits and Reviews*. London: Constable, 1932, p. 87. My colleague Littleton Long referred me to the following passage in Shaw's essay "The Perfect Wagnerite" (1898) in which Shaw shows his distrust of violent change: "Unfortunately, human enlightenment does not progress by nicer and nicer adjustments, but by violent corrective reactions which invariably send us clean over our saddle and would bring us to the ground on the other side if the next reaction did not send us back again with equally excessive zeal." See George Bernard Shaw, *Major Critical Essays: The Quintessence of Ibsenism. The Perfect Wagnerite. The Sanity of Art*. London: Constable, 1932, p. 216. The point is that had Shaw already known the proverbial expression "To throw the baby out with the bath water" at the time of writing this essay in 1898, he would most certainly have employed it in this passage. As it is, he must have become acquainted with it only after 1898 and before 1909.

67. Edwin Miller Fogel, *Proverbs of the Pennsylvania Germans*. Lancaster: The Pennsylvania-German Society, 1929, p. 113.

68. George Bernard Shaw, *The Doctor's Dilemma, Getting Married, and The Shewing-up of Blanco Posnet*. New York: Brentano, 1920, p. 202.

69. See *Bernard Shaw and Mrs. Patrick Campbell. Their Correspondence*, ed. by Alan Dent. New York: Alfred A. Knopf, 1952, p. 273.

70. George Bernard Shaw, *Everybody's Political What's What*. London: Constable, 1944, p. 172. The chapter in which this passage occurs is entitled "The Corruptly Educated" (pp. 166–177).

71. The passage is part of the chapter entitled "Under the Tsar" (pp. 98–123) in Henry W. Nevinson, *More Changes, More Chances*. London: Nisbet, 1925, pp. 122–123.

72. *The Observer* (July 1, 1928), p. 6, col. 2. See also note 43 above.

73. See Maisie Ward, *Insurrection versus Resurrection*. New York: Sheed & Ward, 1937, p. 22.

74. See *The Times Literary Supplement* (January 1, 1938), p. 4, col. 2.

75. Ernst Toller, *Pastor Hall*, translated from the German by Stephen Spender and Hugh Hunt. New York: Random House, 1939, p. 52.

76. The German version of *Pastor Hall* is included in *Stücke gegen den Faschismus*, ed. by Christoph Trilse. Berlin: Bruno Henschel, 1970, p. 164.

77. See G. G. Coulton, *Fourscore Years. An Autobiography*. New York: Macmillan, 1944, p. 170.

78. See Theodor Rosebury, *Microbes and Morals. The Strange Story of Venereal Disease*. New York: The Viking Press, 1971, p. 60.

79. Edmund Crispin, *Sudden Vengeance*. New York: Walter J. Black, 1950, p. 124.

80. Dennis Parry, *Sea of Glass*. London: Hamish Hamilton, 1955, p. 211.

81. Sir Ernest Gowers, *H. W. Fowler: The Man and His Teaching*. Oxford: Oxford University Press, 1957, p. 14.

82. See Edward S. Corwin, "Limiting the Judiciary," *The New York Times* (March 16, 1958), p. 10E, col. 6.

83. Richard Amper, "Liberals Resent Junior High Bill," *The New York Times* (March 23, 1958), p. 61, col. 1.

84. Philip O'Connor, *The Lower View*. London: Faber and Faber, 1960, p. 93.

85. Richard H. Kuh, *Foolish Figleaves? Pornography in—and out of—Court*. New York: Macmillan, 1967, p. 228.

86. Rosebury (see note 78), p. 60.

87. Paul J. Livadary, "Santa Monica Diamond Lanes," *Los Angeles Times* (April 6, 1976), section II, p. 6. I owe all references from this newspaper to Shirley L. Arora.

88. D. E. Walz (see note 87), letter to the editor under the same heading as that of Paul Livadary.

89. Stephen Jay Gould, *Ontogeny and Phylogeny*. Cambridge: Harvard University Press, 1977, p. 2.

90. Milford C. Walker, "U.S. Auto Sales," *Los Angeles Times* (January 24, 1980), section II, p. 6.

91. David Hart, "Property Tax," *Los Angeles Times* (May 26, 1980), section II, p. 4.

92. David R. Berry, "Reagan Chainsaw," *Los Angeles Times* (June 24, 1982), section II, p. 6.

93. Lora Weinroth, "Money-grubbing Kids," *The UCLA Monthly* (December 1982), p. 14. This reference I owe to Shirley L. Arora as well.

94. Howard Frank Mosher, *Marie Blythe. A Novel*. New York: Viking, 1983, p. 139.

95. Art Buchwald, "Backlisted from Blacklist USIA Kept," *Los Angeles Times* (February 21, 1984), section V, p. 3.

96. Campbell Armstrong, *Mazurka*. New York: Harper & Row, 1988, pp. 21–22. I owe this reference to my student Eva-Maria Goy, whom I also want to thank for helping me track down some of the references discussed in this chapter.

97. Ian Shoales, "Screaming California," *California* (April 1990), p. 16. This reference I once again owe to Shirley L. Arora.

98. Alan E. Nourse, "Family Doctor," *Good Housekeeping* (July 1990), p. 78.

99. The name of the album is "Disraeli Gears" (New York: Atco Records, SD 33-232, 1967). I owe this reference to my colleague Dennis Mahoney.

100. The play is included in *Plays from Playwrights Horizons*, ed. Andre Bishop. New York: Broadway Play Publishing, 1987, pp. 47–101.

101. See Clarence D. Brenner, *The French Dramatic Proverb*. Berkeley, Calif.: Privately printed, 1977. For more references to authors of such proverb plays see Wolfgang Mieder, *International Proverb Scholarship: An Annotated Bibliography*, 2 vols. New York: Garland Publishing, 1982 and 1990.

102. Richard Eder, "Theater Reviews," *Calendar* (November 20, 1983), p. 101.

103. *Fortune* (February 1967), p. 229.

104. *The Burlington Free Press* (April 8, 1977), p. 10A.

105. Jay D. Hair in *Wildlife Digest* (September/October 1981), p. 28C.

106. See *The Economist* (March 13, 1982), p. 63.

107. Joel Greenberg in *Science News* (February 26, 1983), p. 138.

108. Steven Alan Childress in *Law Teacher,* 18 (1984), 95–109.

109. Allen F. Breed in *Federal Probation,* 48 (June 1984), 11–15.

110. Alan Allport in *Journal of Verbal Learning and Verbal Behavior,* 23 (1984), 315–324.

111. Mandy Merck in *New Statesman* (March 15, 1985), p. 17.

112. Edward A. Alpers in *Canadian Journal of African Studies,* 19 (1985), 17–18.

113. Mitchell M. Handelsman in *Journal of Applied Rehabilitation Counseling,* 18, no. 4 (1987), 33–34.

114. Bill Vanpatten in *Modern Language Journal,* 71 (1987), 156–164.

115. Dorothy Rich in *Phi Delta Kappan* (June 1987), pp. 784–785.

116. Carl W. Ulrich in *Public Utilities Fortnightly* (October 13, 1988), 19–22.

117. Lawrence W. Swan in *BioScience,* 40, no. 5 (May 1990), pp. 376–384. Swan cites Gould's use of the expression on p. 376. I owe this reference to Shirley L. Arora.

118. Caroline St John-Brooks in *The Times Educational Supplement* (September 14, 1990), p. 10. This particularly important reference I owe to Malcolm Jones.

119. *Washington Post* (February 27, 1981), p. 1A.

120. Located in Charles M. Schulz, *Go Fly a Kite, Charlie Brown. A Peanuts Book.* New York: Holt, Rinehart & Winston, 1960, no pp. given.

121. T. E. Breitenbach, "Proverbidioms" poster from 1975.

122. For a detailed discussion of this picture see Alan Dundes and Claudia A. Stibbe, *The Art of Mixing Metaphors. A Folkloristic Interpretation of the "Netherlandic Proverbs" by Pieter Bruegel the Elder.* Helsinki: Suomalainen Tiedeakatemia, 1981.

123. The student collector was Linda M. Scott, who recorded the information from Eleanor Vandervoort on February 18, 1968, in San Jose, California. I would like to thank Gretchen Guidotti and Alan Dundes for making these archival materials available to me.

124. See P. J. Harrebomée, *Spreekwoordenboek der nederlandsche taal.* Utrecht: Kemink, 1858, vol. 1, p. 27.

125. See F. A. Stoett, *Nederlandsche spreekwoorden, uitdrukkingen en gezegden,* 4th ed. Zutphen: Thieme, 1923, p. 451 (no. 1143).

126. Henry Sanguinetti collected this text from his German-born mother Hilda Sanguinetti (née Haessler) on November 25, 1974, in Lodi, California.

127. Judith Greenberg collected this text from Conrad Blaschezyk on February 27, 1974, in Fairfax, California.

128. Collected by Denyse Goff from Pat Laffin on November 12, 1971, in Berkeley, California.

129. Recorded by Aleta Grabbe herself on November 23, 1975, at Walnut Creek, California.

130. Collected by Bruce Friedman from Vivian Altmann on November 20, 1979, in San Francisco.

131. Collected by Peter Jacobs from Mary Phillips on December 4, 1981, in San Francisco.

132. Collected by Suzanne Harvey from her father Wilson Harvey on December 1, 1983, in Berkeley, California.

133. Collected by Jill Kauffman from her mother Edie Kauffman on September 23, 1985, in Sacramento, California.

134. Collected by Kathryn Winogura from David Longerbeam on November 5, 1985, in Oakland, California.

135. Collected by Jennie Tollenaere from Jim Shea on November 12, 1986, in Berkeley, California.

136. Hirsch (see note 61), p. 56. See also Wolfgang Mieder, "Paremiological Minimum and Cultural Literacy," in *Creativity and Tradition in Folklore: Essays in Honor of Wilhelm Nicolaisen*, ed. by Simon J. Bronner. Logan: Utah State University Press, 1992, pp. 185–203.

137. See especially Ida von Düringsfeld and Otto von Reinsberg-Düringsfeld, *Sprichwörter der germanischen und romanischen Sprachen*. Leipzig: Hermann Fries, 1872; rpt. Hildesheim: Georg Olms, 1973, vol. 1, p. 488 (no. 898); Jens Aa. Stabell Bilgrav, *20,000 Proverbs, Sprichwörter, Proverbes, Ordspråk, Ordsprog*. Copenhagen: Hans Heide, 1985, pp. 247–248 (no. 346); and Gyula Paczolay, *A Comparative Dictionary of Hungarian, Estonian, German, English, Finnish and Latin Proverbs*. Veszprém: VEAB, 1987, pp. 78–79 (no. 177).

138. H. L. Cox, *Spreekwoordenboek in vier talen: Nederlands, Frans, Duits, Engels*. Utrecht: Van Dale, 1988, p. 187 (no. 861).

139. Günter Grass, *Die Blechtrommel*. Neuwied am Rhein: Hermann Luchterhand, 1959, pp. 193–194.

140. Günter Grass, *The Tin Drum*, translated by Ralph Manheim. London: Secker and Warburg, 1961, p. 163.

141. Günter Grass, *Blecktrumman*, translated by Nils Holmberg. Stockholm: Albert Bonniers Förlag, 1961, p. 124.

142. Günter Grass, *De blikken trommel*, translated by Koos Schuur. Amsterdam: Meulenhoff, 1964, p. 173.

143. Günter Grass, *Le Tambour*, translated by Jean Amsler. Paris: Éditions du Seuil, 1961, p. 171.

10

❝ Proverbs in Nazi Germany ❞
The Promulgation of Anti-Semitism and Stereotypes Through Folklore

Historians of German folklore have begun to examine carefully the role that this science played during the period of National Socialism. Adolf Bach includes a detailed chapter on "Die deutsche Volkskunde 1933/45" in the third edition of his monumental study *Deutsche Volkskunde* (1960),[1] and Hermann Bausinger analyzes these dark years of German folklore scholarship in his significant article on "Volksideologie und Volksforschung: Zur nationalsozialistischen Volkskunde."[2] There is also Christa Kamenetsky's study of "Folklore as a Political Tool in Nazi Germany,"[3] which summarizes the manipulation of folklore studies in Germany for the English reader. The three surveys explain that the study of folklore, just like everything else, was subjected to the misconceived racial theories of National Socialism. Folklore was not to be considered an international and objective science any longer, but rather a means to an end, namely, the proof of racial supremacy of the Aryans. Folklore became politicized, and the guiding principles were the chauvinistic and anti-Semitic policies that governed Germany during this time. Obviously, not every German folklorist participated in this scholarly perversion, but the ones who did were published extensively. The titles of these publications alone bear witness to the *Gleichschaltung* ("political coordination") of folklore and National Socialism.

Shortly after Hitler's ascent to power, Matthes Ziegler published a short but programmatic article on "Volkskunde auf rassischer Grundlage,"[4] which states that German folklore must be based on the racial theories of National Socialism. Similar views were held by Walther Steller in his *Volkskunde als nationalsozialistische Wissenschaft* (1935); he declared that folklore had to be a National Socialist science, one based on political ideas more than on cultural or ethnic considerations.[5] Max Hildebert Boehm added the anti-Semitic component to this stance by characterizing the Jews as racial parasites who must not be allowed to infiltrate and destroy the Nordic race.[6] In such statements one can see how folklore became misused to deepen and broaden anti-Semitism among the German people. Jews were shown not to be part of the allegedly racially pure German folklore tradition. Verbal folklore forms especially, such as fairy tales, tall tales, legends, jokes, wellerisms, and proverbs, were analyzed and quoted to prove that the "healthy" folk mind had long recognized the negative qualities of Jews who threatened the racial purity of the Aryans as well as the National Socialist regime.

Even though folklorists have been slow in turning to the study of this area of German folklore scholarship, philologists have studied the language of National Socialism in considerable detail. Realizing that language usage does allow us to make certain deductions concerning the psychological makeup of the users, Heinz Paechter published in 1944 in the United States a treatise on *Nazi-Deutsch,* in which he emphasized the use of slogans by the Nazis.[7] But also in Germany, Victor Klemperer, a Jewish professor of Romance Philology at Dresden who survived Nazi Germany, kept a philological diary during those years, which he published as a shocking document shortly after the end of the Third Reich. In this courageous book Klemperer analyzes the brutal and anti-Semitic jargon of the Nazis as he was forced to witness it while suffering humiliation and persecution.[8] In the meantime, many more studies have appeared which investigate the specific vocabulary of the Nazis,[9] the propagandistic perversion of language,[10] and various other aspects such as syntax, foreign words, and sport terms[11] of the German language during this period. All these studies show that the Nazis used language consciously to manipulate and appeal to the masses. As the propaganda minister Joseph Goebbels formulated it in a speech in 1934: "Wir müssen die Sprache sprechen, die das Volk versteht, wer zum Volke reden will, muss, wie Luther sagt, dem Volke aufs Maul sehen"[12] ("We must speak the language which the folk understands, whoever wants to speak to the folk must, as Luther says, pay heed to folk speech").

This interest in what the folk says was of particular importance to the National Socialists in their attempt to discredit the Jewish population. If they could find quotations, slogans, phrases, and proverbs that were clearly anti-Semitic in nature, they could use them to spread stereotypical views of the Jews. Neither folklorists nor philologists have hitherto studied the use of proverbial expressions and proverbs by the Nazis for this purpose, even though proverbial slurs and stereotypes played a major role in Nazi propaganda, be it in political speeches by Hitler, Goebbels, and others, or in official press releases, newspapers, popular proverb collections, "scholarly" articles, dissertations, or books. Accordingly, an analysis of what was done to and with proverbs during the Nazi period will exemplify how supposedly simple pieces of traditional wisdom can become dangerous weapons when used to poison people's feelings, thoughts, and actions.

Before considering the use and function of proverbs during Nazi Germany, a short review of nineteenth-century proverb scholarship as it pertains to Yiddish proverbs and the image of the Jew in German proverbs is necessary. The nineteenth century was an extremely active time for the national proverb collectors throughout Europe and resulted in dozens of large proverb collections. This interest in recording proverbs also extended to the large number of Yiddish proverbs used across Europe and particularly in Germany. An excellent collection entitled *Sprichwörter und Redensarten deutsch-jüdischer Vorzeit* (1860) was published by Abraham Moses Tendlau. It contains 1070 German-Jewish proverbs and proverbial expressions, and each text is supplemented by detailed linguistic and cultural annotations. In his introduction, Tendlau explains that for many of the texts it was impossible to determine whether they were of Yiddish or German origin. As long as the proverbs were current among German Jews, they were included in the collection. When the Nazi proverb manipulators later used proverbs to prove Aryan supremacy, they quickly forgot the important fact that the same proverbs had been used by the Jewish population for centuries—another proof that the German Jewish population had long accepted much of German folklore. Yet these same proverbs were used to argue that only the Germans were interested in heredity, hygiene, proper marriage, or the family. Befitting the honesty and integrity of a true scholar, Tendlau included expressions that were not complimentary toward the Jews. He did not share the concern of some of his fellow Jews that "irgend ein Uebelwollender das Buch benutzen möchte, um daraus judenfeindliche Pfeile zu schmieden"[13] ("some ill-willed person might use the book in order to fashion arrows hostile to the Jews out of them [the proverbs]"). There is a tragic irony in this sentence when one considers that several decades later the Nazis would indeed use these uncomplimentary proverbs as destructive weapons against the Jews.

A second major collection of Yiddish proverbs with Hebrew translations and German annotations is Ignaz Bernstein's *Jüdische Sprichwörter und Redensarten* (1908). Bernstein presents 3993 texts current primarily among the Ashkenazic Jews of Eastern Europe; but he includes only very short linguistic, and occasionally cultural, notes. Interestingly enough, the Nazi proverb collections do not refer to either Bernstein's or Tendlau's superb works, since they would have shown clearly that purely nationalistic interpretations of proverbs are utterly absurd when one deals with proverbs that are of international currency due to their Greek or Roman and Biblical origin. Valuable scholarship was certainly ignored by the Nazi propaganda machine when it stood in the way of advancing preconceived theories and stereotypical views.

These collections notwithstanding, there was considerable anti-Semitism in German scholarship in the latter part of the nineteenth century. This prompted Ad. Jellinek to compile two monographs on *Der jüdische Stamm in nichtjüdischen Sprichwörtern* (1881–82), in which he attempted to explain the views of Jews expressed in non-Jewish proverbs from various national cultures. Jellinek's book is not intended to popularize anti-Semitic proverbs; instead the author asks "wann werden die scharfen, schneidenden, und scheelsüchtigen Verdikte über die Juden zum Abschlusse kommen?"[14] ("When will the sharp, cutting and jealous verdicts on the Jews come to an end?"). And he rightfully warned against the danger of national slurs dressed in proverbial form:

> So wenig Sprichwörter von Franzosen über Engländer, oder von Deutschen über Franzosen immer der unbedingten Wahrheit entsprechen, ebensowenig dürfen wir die Sprichwörter der Völker über die Juden ohne Unterschied als unerschütterliche Erfahrungssätze gelten lassen.[15]

> (The French proverbs about the English or the German proverbs about the French do not correspond to absolute truths; neither do the proverbs of any people about the Jews represent unshakable reflections of experience.)

He then proceeds to interpret and explain a relatively small number of proverbs about Jews in two- to four-page sections, showing that many of the proverbs are only true in limited cases and equally applicable to non-Jewish people. For example, Jellinek cites the Prussian dialect proverb "Fert Gewesene gofft de Jud nüscht" ("For lost property the Jew gives nothing") and comments correctly:

> Und die Nichtjuden? Geben sie auf gewesenen Besitz? Creditieren sie heute Jemandem eine Summe Geldes, der gestern sein Vermögen verloren hat? Öffnen sie ihre Cassen bereitwillig einem Manne, der früher zu den Reichen gezählt hatte? Gewiss nicht! In ihren Augen hat das Gewesene denselben Wert, wie in denen der Juden, und wenn sie sich in unserem Sprichworte auf den Juden berufen, so ist dieses gleichsam das Feigenblatt, mit welchem sie sich bedecken oder ein Euphemismus für die ganz prosaische Antwort: Ich borge Ihnen nichts, mein Herr; denn Sie waren einst vermögend, besitzen aber jetzt gar nichts.[16]

> (And the non-Jews? Do they give anything for lost property? Do they give a sum of money as credit to someone who has lost his fortune yesterday? Will they willingly open their accounts to a man who once upon a time was rich? Certainly not! In their eyes the lost property has the same value as in those of the Jews, and if they refer to Jews in our proverb, then this [the proverb] is actually the fig leaf with which they are covering themselves or a euphemism for the simple prosaic answer:

I will not lend you anything, Sir; for although you were once wealthy, you do not own anything now.)

Jellinek also gives a splendid analysis of the German proverb "Man darff keiner Jüden mehr, es sind andere, die wuchern können." ("One doesn't need Jews anymore, there are others who can practice usury"). Part of his commentary reads: "In der That ist der Wucher weder jüdisch noch christlich, weder national, noch confessionell, sondern ein Produkt gesellschaftlichen [sic!] Verhältnisse."[17] ("Indeed, usury is neither Jewish nor Christian, neither national nor religious, but rather a product of societal conditions"). He continues to argue that Jews are not as greedy as anti-Semitic politicians and businessmen were claiming in the 1880s. Hitler and his supporters nevertheless branded the Jews for their monetary expertise; if the Nazis ever heard of the proverb quoted above, they certainly did not use it or include it in their lists of proverbs against the Jews.

While Jellinek presented humane and objective analyses of seemingly anti-Semitic proverbs, Sally Simon Tilles counteracted this voice of reason with the deliberate collection of anti-Semitic quotations and proverbs entitled *Der Jude im Citat und im Sprichwort* (1892). The texts are divided into chapters entitled "Was ist Antisemitismus," "Was ist der Jude," "Wie ist der Jude," "Was treibt der Jude," "Wohin mit den Juden," etc. ("What is anti-Semitism," "what is the Jew," "what is the Jew like," "what does the Jew do," "where to go with the Jews," etc.). One anti-Semitic quotation or proverb is quoted after another. There are statements by Goethe, Richard Wagner, and others, but some of the quotations from Martin Luther, especially, show how rampant anti-Jewish sentiments were throughout Germany's history. From Luther's essay "Von den Juden und ihren Lügen" (1541), Tilles quotes the following apocalyptic sentences.

Ins Feuer, ins Feuer mit den Synagogen! In die Ställe mit den Juden! Man verwende ihr Hab' und Gut für die Neubekehrten; alle rüstigen Juden und Jüdinnen treibe man zu harter Arbeit, man nehme ihnen den Talmud und die Bibel weg, verbiete ihnen bei Todesstrafe, den Namen Gottes auszusprechen.
Keine Nachsicht, kein Mitleid mit den Juden! Möchten die Fürsten dieselben ohne weitere Umstände verjagen![18]

(Into the fire, into the fire with the synagogues! Into the stables with the Jews! Let one use their goods and chattels for the newly converted people; let one drive all vigorous male and female Jews to hard labor, let one take away from them the Talmud and the Bible, [and] forbid them on pain of death to speak the name of God.
No indulgence, no sympathy for the Jews! May the princes drive them away without further ado!)

Interspersed with such slurs, the context of which is purposely not explained since their anti-Semitism might thereby be weakened, are such proverbs as:

> Der Jude hat wohl des Menschen Gestalt,
> Doch fehlt ihm des Menschen inn'rer Gehalt.[19]
> (Even though the Jew has a human body,
> he is lacking the inner character of humans.)

> Judentrug und Judenplag'
> Währet bis zum jüngsten Tag.[20]
> (Jewish deception and Jewish vexation
> will last to the Judgement Day.)

> Der Jude so zum Menschen steht,
> Wie ein Wolf, der in der Herde geht.[21]
> (The Jew corresponds to the human
> as the wolf to the flock.)

The Jew is characterized as an evil person, a cheater, an animal. Obviously, such a book did its part in spreading and deepening anti-Semitic sentiments, by demonstrating to German readers that their literary giants as well as their traditional proverbs were of the same opinion.

Such direct printed attacks against the Jewish population were more the exception than the rule, at least until the rise of National Socialism. But anti-Semitism continued to be present, and as part of the official Nazi doctrine it was increased to the level of a grotesque hate campaign against every Jew. Adolf Hitler had made no secret of his anti-Semitism in his programmatic book *Mein Kampf* (1925–27), and the proclamation of a "Boykott gegen die Juden" ("Boycott against the Jews") on March 28, 1933, set into motion the deliberate exclusion of the Jews from normal life in Germany, leading ultimately to their final destruction. Hitler seems to have believed that this boycott against Jews from all walks of life would suffice to make them leave Germany; he even went so far as to declare: "Krümmt auch weiterhin keinem Juden auch nur ein Haar!"[22] ("Continue not to harm a single hair on a Jew's head!"). Here Hitler used the proverbial expression "jdm. kein Haar krümmen" ("not to harm a hair on someone's head") in its literal meaning, but later he went beyond the mere negation of the expression and ordered the bodily torture and destruction of the Jews. One cannot help but feel that Hitler used this proverbial expression with devilish irony, knowing all along that he would finally go much further than harming the hair of Jews.

The National Socialists, particularly Adolf Hitler and Joseph Goebbels, used a considerable amount of folk language in their speeches and proclamations, so that all the people could follow their arguments. Hitler stated in *Mein Kampf* that "Die Rede eines Staatsmannes zu seinem Volk habe ich nicht zu messen nach dem Eindruck, den sie bei einem Universitätsprofessor hinterlässt, sondern an der Wirkung, die sie auf das Volk ausübt"[23] ("I must not measure the speech of a statesman to his people by the impression it makes on a university professor but rather by the effect that it has on the folk"). And concerning the language of propaganda, Hitler stated quite similarly:

> Jede Propaganda hat volkstümlich zu sein und ihr geistiges Niveau einzustellen nach der Aufnahmefähigkeit des Beschränktesten unter denen, an die sie sich zu richten gedenkt. Verzichtet die Propaganda auf die Urwüchsigkeit der Ausdrucksweise, findet sie nicht den Weg zum Empfinden der breiten Masse.[24]

> (All propaganda must be popular and must tune its intellectual level to the comprehension capacity of the most limited mind among those to whom it is being directed. If propaganda renounces earthiness of expression, then it will not find the way to the feeling of the broad masses.)

In addition to assuring effective communication with the largest number of people, Hitler also wanted to emotionalize and educate the crowds; thus, he frequently used proverbs and proverbial expressions, as Otto von Bismarck, Vladimir Ilich Lenin, and others had done before him and as Winston Churchill and Franklin D. Roosevelt also did during his time.[25]

It is not surprising that Hitler particularly liked the expression "jdm. in Fleisch und Blut übergehen"[26] ("to become second nature to somebody, to become ingrained in somebody"), in light of his ideas on racial purity. He often used folk expressions to argue a certain point, as when he explained his actions against plotters against his regime, "die man endlich nicht mehr auf die leichte Schulter nehmen konnte"[27] ("whom one finally could not shrug off any longer"). He even went so far as to use the Biblical proverb "Der Mensch lebt nicht vom Brot allein"[28] ("Man does not live by bread alone") in a speech during 1933 concerning the revitalization of German culture and art under the auspices of National Socialism. He also praised the German industrialists of the time, because they had the courage, "die Flinte nicht ins Korn zu werfen"[29] ("not to throw in the towel"). Such expressions add familiarity and imagery to his lengthy and verbose speeches; they also helped to increase the efficacy of the communication. Hitler was even capable of creating his own triad of comparisons in his vision of the German male youth that became proverbial in Nazi Germany: "In unseren Augen, da muss der deutsche Junge der Zukunft schlank und rank sein, flink wie Windhunde, zäh wie Leder, und hart wie Kruppstahl"[30] ("In our eyes the young German male of the future must be slender and slim, quick as a greyhound, tough as leather, and hard as Krupp steel").

Of course there were also those instances in Hitler's speeches where he used proverbs and proverbial expressions during his tirades against the Jewish people. After blaming them once again for all of Germany's misfortunes, and after threatening to destroy the Jewish people all over Europe, he declared in a speech of January 30, 1939: "Man bleibe uns also vom Leib mit Humanität. Das deutsche Volk wünscht nicht, dass seine Belange von einem fremden Volk bestimmt und regiert werden"[31] ("Don't you saddle us with humanity. The German folk does not want its concerns to be determined and governed by an alien race"). And on January 30, 1942, he showed that he was not susceptible to any feelings of humanity himself, when he stated that "das Ergebnis dieses Krieges die Vernichtung des Judentums sein wird. Zum erstenmal wird diesmal das echt altjüdische Gesetz angewendet: 'Aug' um Aug', Zahn um Zahn'!"[32] ("the result of this war will be the destruction of Jewry. This time, for the first time, the authentic old Jewish law will be applied: 'An eye for an eye, a tooth for a tooth' "). Hitler and his comrades did not take this old proverb figuratively, but they applied it literally and acted it out, one gruesome and inhuman step after another. The proverb was no longer a metaphor under the Nazis, but rather became crude reality.[33]

Most Germans did not notice how Hitler and his propaganda machinery manipulated them with such popular expressions. But the Austrian cultural critic, Karl Kraus, had already analyzed the Nazis through their language in 1933 and attempted to show through satirical analysis that Hitler was in fact negating the metaphorical nature of proverbs and proverbial expressions. The expressions that refer to parts of the body especially were interpreted not metaphorically, but realistically. The result was a brutality and inhumanity of language that became progressively worse as time went on:

> Wenn diese Politiker der Gewalt noch davon sprechen, dass dem Gegner "das Messer an die Kehle zu setzen", "der Mund zu stopfen" sei, oder "die Faust zu zeigen"; wenn sie überall "mit harter Faust durchgreifen" wollen oder mit "Aktionen auf eigene Faust" drohen: so bleibt nur erstaunlich, dass sie noch Redensarten gebrauchen, die sie nicht mehr machen. . . . Vollends erfolgt die Absage an das Bildliche in dem Versprechen eines Staatspräsidenten:
>> Wir sagen nicht: Auge um Auge, Zahn um Zahn, nein, wer uns ein Auge ausschlägt, dem werden wir den Kopf abschlagen, und wer uns einen Zahn ausschlägt, dem werden wir den Kiefer einschlagen.
> Und diese Revindikation des Phraseninhalts geht durch alle Wendungen, in denen ein ursprünglich blutiger oder handgreiflicher Inhalt sich längst zum Sinn einer geistigen Offensive abgeklärt hat. Keine noch so raffinierte Spielart könnte sich dem Prozess entziehen—selbst nicht das entsetzliche: "Salz in offene Wunden streuen". Einmal muss es geschehen sein, aber man hatte es vergessen bis zum Verzicht auf jede Vorstellung eines Tätlichen, bis zur völligen Unmöglichkeit des Bewusstwerdens. Man wandte es an, um die grausame Erinnerung an einen Verlust, die Berührung eines Seelenleids zu bezeichnen: das gibt's immer; die Handlung, von der's bezogen war, blieb ungedacht. Hier ist sie:
>> Als sich der alte Genosse beim Kartoffelschälen einen tiefen Schnitt in die Hand zufügte, zwang ihn eine hohnlachende Gesellschaft von

Nazi, die stark blutende Hand in einen Sack mit Salz hineinzuhalten. Das Jammergeschrei des alten Mannes machte ihnen grossen Spass. Es bleibt unvorstellbar; doch da es geschah, ist das Wort nicht mehr brauchbar. . . . Es war eine Metapher gewesen. . . . In allen Gebieten sozialer und kultureller Erneuerung gewahren wir diesen Aufbruch der Phrase zur Tat.[34]

(If these politicians of violence still talk about "putting the knife at the throat" of the enemy, "of gagging his mouth" and "showing him the fist," if they want "to come at him with a clenched fist" or if they threaten him "with actions off their own bat": then it is astonishing that they are still only using these expressions but not acting them out. . . . The renunciation of the metaphorical is complete in the promise of a certain president:

> We don't say: An eye for an eye, a tooth for a tooth, no, he who knocks out our eye will have his head cut off, and he who knocks out our tooth will have his jaws smashed.

And this revindication of the content of such phrases permeates all expressions in which the originally bloody and corporeal content has long since been filtered into a mere metaphorical attack. No matter how crafty the metaphor is it couldn't possibly avoid this process—not even the terrible expression: "To rub salt into the open wound." It must have happened once upon a time, but one repressed all visions of the concrete action until such a point that one couldn't possibly consciously conceive of it. One used it in order to refer to the gruesome memory of a personal loss or to the contact with a particular anguish. Such cases always existed; the action from which the phrase stems remained unthought. Here it is:

> When the old comrade cut his hand deeply while peeling potatoes, a sneering group of Nazis forced him to hold his profusely bleeding hand in a sack of salt. The painful screaming of the old man gave them great pleasure.

One can't imagine this; but since it happened the expression is no longer usable. . . . It had been a metaphor. . . . In all areas of social and cultural renewal we notice this metamorphosis from a mere phrase to the action.)

Another German author, Bertolt Brecht, also had the courage in the 1930s to show how the Nazis misused proverbs. In his essay "Über den Satz 'Gemeinnutz geht vor Eigennutz,' " Brecht argued that this proverb, which became a favorite Nazi slogan, is not at all a socialist statement, as the Nazis claimed:

Viele halten den Satz *Gemeinnutz geht vor Eigennutz*, den die Nationalsozialisten auf ihre Fahne geschrieben haben, für einen sozialistischen Satz. . . .

Unsere Meinung ist es, dass es kein sozialistischer Satz ist. Wie das? Was haben wir denn jetzt wieder gegen diesen Satz? Wir sind doch zu unzufriedene Leute. Sicher passt es uns nicht, dass Hitler diesen schönen Satz hat, und da wollen wir ihn schnell schlechtmachen. . . .

In einem sozialistischen Gemeinwesen besteht kein Gegensatz zwischen dem Nutzen des einzelnen und dem Nutzen der Allgemeinheit. Es ist keine grundsätzliche Verschiedenheit der Interessen vorhanden. Es gibt keine Gruppen, die sich mit dem Messer bekämpfen, weil eine Gruppe nur gut leben kann, wenn die andere Gruppe schlecht lebt. Im sozialistischen Gemeinwesen werden nicht Autostrassen gebaut von der Allgemeinheit, auf denen nur einzelne fahren können, so dass die teuren Autostrassen fertig werden, aber die billigen Autos werden nicht fertig. Und es fährt auch nicht eines Tages die Allgemeinheit doch auf diesen Autostrassen, nämlich in Tanks, damit einzelne ihre Kriegsprofite machen können. Im sozialistischen Gemeinwesen nützt der einzelne durch seine Arbeit sich selber und zugleich der Allgemeinheit, er nützt ihr gerade dadurch, dass er sich selber nützt. Weil das Gemeinwesen so eingerichtet ist, dass jeder, der sich selber nützt, auch der Allgemeinheit nützt, und die Allgemeinheit sich nützt, wenn sie dem einzelnen nützt, ist es eben ein sozialistisches Gemeinwesen. Im sozialistischen Gemeinwesen ist der Satz *Gemeinnutz geht vor Eigennutz* also überflüssig und arbeitslos und ein anderer Satz gilt, nämlich der Satz *Eigennutz ist Gemeinnutz.*[35]

(Many consider the phrase *The common good takes precedence over self-interest* which the National Socialists have written on their banners as a socialist phrase. . . .

Our opinion is that it is not a socialist phrase. How so? Now what do we have against this phrase? We are really too dissatisfied. It's because we don't like the fact that Hitler has this beautiful phrase and that's why we want to speak ill of it. . . .

In a socialist community there is no opposition between the good of the individual and the good of the general public. There is no basic difference between the various interests. There are no groups which fight against each other with knives because one group can live well only if the other group lives poorly. In the socialist community roads on which only a few can travel are not built by the general public. Likewise expensive roads will not be completed when cheap cars are not being made. And the general public would not one day find itself traveling on these roads, in tanks, just so that a few can make their war profits. In the socialist community the individual helps himself through his work and at the same time helps the general public; he helps it precisely because he helps himself. Because the community is established in such a fashion that each person who helps himself also helps the general public and because the general public helps itself when it helps the individual it is a socialist community. In the socialist community the sentence *The common good takes precedence over self-interest* is therefore superfluous and unemployed and another phrase is valid, namely the phrase *Self-interest is common good.*)

But those were small voices in the darkness and heard by only a few. Many more people listened to the multitude of speeches and proclamations over the Nazi-controlled radio or read the by now completely Nazi-run newspapers. German mass media were completely in the hands of the Nazis, and that was the case with almost all book publishers. It appears almost incredible that the famous Jewish Schocken publishing house was still able to bring out a shortened version of Abraham Tendlau's German-Jewish proverb collection discussed above in 1934 in Berlin.[36] Only one year later a shortened edition of the well-known German equivalent of *Bartlett's Quotations* came out in a "purified" edition, meaning that literary quotations from Jewish authors were no longer included: "in Übereinstimmung mit den kulturpolitischen Richtlinien der Gegenwart [wurden] die im Umlauf befindlichen Aussprüche nichtarischer Schriftsteller im Textteil ausgeschaltet"[37] ("in agreement with the cultural-political guidelines of the day the quotations of non-Aryan authors which are current were excluded from the text"). Instead the editor added many new Nazi slogans, some of which were proverbs or varied proverbs, as, for example, "Gemeinnutz [geht] vor Eigennutz" ("The common good takes precedence over self-interest") and "Wissen ist Blei, Charakter ist Gold" ("Knowledge is lead, character is gold"), which was based on the proverb "Reden ist Silber, Schweigen ist Gold"[38] ("Speech is silver, silence is golden").

The 28th edition of the large German quotation and proverb collection *Geflügelte Worte* (1937) retained Jewish authors, but

> selbstverständlich sind die jüdischen Autoren als solche gekennzeichnet worden, und es wird auch ausdrücklich darauf hingewiesen, dass etwa das Verbleiben Heinrich Heines in dem Kapitel 'Aus deutschen Schriftstellern' nicht besagen soll, dass die Herausgeber ihn dem deutschen Schrifttum zurechnen.[39]

> (obviously the Jewish authors have been marked as such, and special attention is drawn to the fact that the retention of Heinrich Heine, for example, in the chapter on "From German authors" does not signify that the editors count him in the German literary world.)

Such identification of Jewish writers did its part in putting a stigma on Jewish intellectual thought, and this anti-Semitic campaign went so far as no longer to consider Heinrich Heine, one of Germany's great poets, as a German author. Throughout the book, references are made to Hitler's use of famous literary quotations, probably to impress the intelligent readers with Hitler's knowledge of German intellectual thought. A whole new section (pp. 641–650) is dedicated to "quotable" Nazi phrases by Adolf Hitler, Joseph Goebbels, Hermann Göring, Alfred Rosenberg, and Horst Wessel, which indicates how the Nazis created new slogans or manipulated old ones. Thus, Goebbels used a proverb to present his new definition of socialism in a speech of May 11, 1930: "Wahrer Sozialismus heisst nicht: allen das Gleiche, sondern: jedem das Seine"[40] ("True socialism does not mean to all the same, but to each his own"). "To all the same" would have meant that the Jewish population might be treated the same as the Aryans, but the proverb "To each his own" gave the National Socialists proverbial strength to separate the Jewish people. The editors also proudly include a large paragraph on the proverbial slogan "Gemeinnutz [geht] vor Eigennutz" ("The common good takes precedence over self-interest"), which goes back to old German legal codes. Hitler had used the old proverb on February 24, 1920, at a large party rally in the Munich Hofbräuhaus beer hall, claiming that the National Socialist Party "bekämpft den jüdisch-materialistischen Geist in und ausser uns und ist überzeugt, dass eine dauernde Genesung unseres Volkes nur erfolgen kann von innen heraus auf der Grundlage: Gemeinnutz vor Eigennutz"[41] ("fights against the Jewish-materialistic spirit in and outside of us and it is convinced that a lasting recovery of our folk can come only from the inside on the basis of: The common good takes precedence over self-interest").

It has already been shown through Bertolt Brecht's courageous essay about this proverb how the Nazis used it for their own gains. The old proverb was used to arouse the German people's collective spirit to work for the common good, that is, for war preparation and the establishment of German supremacy at the expense of the Jewish population by the Nazis. The Germans did not improve their personal lot, but rather were misled to work toward final destruction of the Jews and Germany itself.

In 1943, one of the editors, Werner Rust, brought out an even more perverted edition of *Geflügelte Worte* as a "Volksausgabe" ("popular edition").[42] And this time the editor even came up with the grotesque idea of attaching an asterisk to non-Aryan names, that is, a "star" just like the Jews were forced to wear in the street:

> Hinsichtlich der Behandlung jüdischer und nichtarischer Urheber "geflügelter Worte" wird ausdrücklich darauf verwiesen, dass diese im Namenregister mit einem Stern besonders gekennzeichnet wurden, denn es ist nicht zweckmässig, solche "geflügelten Worte" kurzweg aus dem Büchmann zu streichen. Gerade, *weil* es heute wichtig ist, feststellen zu können, ob eine Redensart jüdischer Herkunft ist oder nicht, will der Büchmann auch fernerhin über solche Worte Auskunft geben.[43]

> (As regards the treatment of Jewish and non-Aryan coiners of "winged words" [sententious remarks], special attention is drawn to the fact that these have been marked with a star in the name index because it is not appropriate simply to cross out such "winged words" from the Büchmann. Exactly *because* it is important today to be able to ascertain whether an expression is of Jewish origin or not, the Büchmann is continuing to give information about such words.)

Thus, Jewish authors were retained not because of their cultural importance in Germany, but solely to identify them as Jews and thereby to urge people to discontinue quoting them. In practice this was handled in the following manner: quotations from the German Jew Heinrich Heine are listed, but only with a special reference to the statement in the foreword mentioned above: "Von Heinrich Heine (1797–1856) [vgl. das Vorwort, S. VI] wird heute deshalb noch vieles zitiert, weil man beim Gebrauch dieser Worte leider nicht an den Urheber denkt"[44] ("People still quote Heinrich Heine [1797–1856] a great deal today [see the foreword, p. VI] because they unfortunately do not think of the coiner when using these words"). Implied, of course, is that one ought not to quote Jews and other non-Aryans at all. It is incredible to see how such standard reference works became perverted in the hands of the Nazis.

What all of this added up to was linguistic censorship by the Nazis. As if one could prevent people from remembering classical quotations and proverbs! But the Nazis could control their use in open speech and writing and they succeeded in doing so. The absurdity of this chauvinistic program can be seen in a fascinating brief satirical essay by Paul Elbogen that appeared in 1932 (a few years later this could never have been published!).

Was der Nazi nicht darf . . .

Im Parteiprogramm und in den zahllosen Enzykliken des Osaf steht genau zu lesen, wie es der Pg. anfängt, ein hitlergefälliges Leben zu führen. Er darf nichts Jüdisches berühren, keine Nichtarierin heiraten, nicht in Kaufhäusern kaufen—die Mönchsregel ist lang. Aber doch enthält sie kein Wort der zahllosen Verbote, die sie konsequenterweise aufzählen müsste. Wir haben im Folgenden versucht, sie zusammenzustellen—leider gibt es keine Exekutive, um die orthodoxen Hitleranbeter zu zwingen, sie wirklich einzuhalten.

Verboten ist—um eine kleine Auswahl aufzuzählen—der Gebrauch der folgenden, aus der jüdischen Bibel stammenden Phrasen und Zitate: Kein Nazi ist "ein gewaltiger Jäger vor dem Herrn," keiner ein "Kopfhänger" (Jes. 58, 5), keiner ein "Lästermaul" (Salom. 4, 24). . . . Sie dürfen ihren Führer nicht "wie den Augapfel hüten" (5. Mos. 32, 10), nicht "auf der Bank der Spötter sitzen" (Psalm 1, 1), nicht "ihr Herz ausschütten" (1. Sam. 1, 15), sich nicht "mit Füssen treten" lassen (Jes. 10, 24). Keiner darf ein Deutscher sein "vom Scheitel bis zur Sohle" (5. Mos. 28, 35), keiner "sich gütlich tun" (Kohel. 3, 12), keiner "ums goldene Kalb tanzen", keinem dürfen "die Haare zu Berge stehen" (Hiob 4, 15), keiner darf "auf Herz und Nieren geprüft werden" (Ps. 7, 10), niemand darf ihm "ein Dorn im Auge" sein (4. Mose 33, 55). . . .

Verboten [sind] die aus dem Talmud herrührenden Sprichworte: "Im Hause des Gehenkten spricht man nicht vom Strick (Talmud Baba mezia 57b), Gedanken sind zollfrei (Kiddusch 49b), Jeder ist sich selbst der Nächste (Sanh. 9b), Einem Lügner glaubt man nicht und wenn er auch die Wahrheit spricht (Sanheddrin 89b), Schmiede das Eisen solange es heiss ist, Unter Blinden ist der Einäugige König (Ber. r. 30), Not kennt kein Gebot (Erub 27a), Gleich und gleich gesellt sich gern" (Baba R 92b)—und andre, die alle auf die Parteigenossen (siehe das letzte und das erste) so gut passen. . . .

Aber verboten sind leider auch viel näher ans Herz gehende Dinge: verboten ist—ach, man kann keine Rheinfahrt mehr machen!—das deutscheste aller deutschen Lieder: "Die Lorelei" des Juden Heine. . . .

"Schwer zu sein ein Nationalsozialist!"[45]

(What the Nazi is not allowed to do. . . .

In the party program and in numerous encyclicals of the Osaf [Supreme Commander of the SA] one can read precisely how a party member goes about leading a life which is pleasing to Hitler. He is not allowed to touch anything Jewish, marry a non-Aryan, buy in department stores [Jewish owned]—the list of vows is large. And yet it contains no word of the countless prohibitions which for the sake of consistency it should have enumerated. We have attempted to assemble them in the following list—unfortunately there is no executive power to force the orthodox Hitler worshippers to adhere to them.

Forbidden is—just to give a small selection—the use of the following phrases and quotations out of the Jewish Bible: No Nazi is "a mighty hunter before the Lord," no one "bows down his head" (Jes. 58, 5), no one has "crooked speech" (Salom. 4, 24). . . . They are not allowed "to keep their 'Führer' as the apple of their eye" (5. Mos. 32, 10), not "to sit in the seat of scoffers" (Psalm 1, 1), not "to pour out their soul" (1. Sam. 1, 15), not "to let themselves be smitten with the rod" (Jes. 10, 24). No one may be a German "from the sole of his foot to the crown of his head" (5. Mos. 28, 35), no one [may] "enjoy himself" (Kohel. 3, 12), no one "dance around the golden calf," [no] one's "hair is allowed to stand on end" (Hiob 4, 15), no one may "be put through his paces" (Ps. 7, 10), nobody may be "a thorn in someone's side" (4. Mos. 33, 55). . . .

Forbidden are proverbs from the Talmud such as: "Name not a rope in the house of him that was hanged (Talmud Baba mezia 57b), Thoughts are free from toll (Kiddush 49b), Charity begins at home (Sanh. 9b), One doesn't believe a liar even if he speaks the truth (Sanheddrin 89b), Strike while the iron is hot, In the kingdom of blind men the one-eyed is king (Ber. r. 30), Necessity knows no law (Erub 27a), Like will to like" (Baba R 92b)—and others which all fit so well for party comrades (see the last and the first text). . . .

But things much closer to our hearts are unfortunately also forbidden: forbidden is—what a pity, one can't take a steamboat ride on the Rhine any longer!—the most German of all German songs: "The Lorelei" of the Jew Heine. . . .

"It is difficult to be a Nazi!")

This enlightening essay shows only too clearly the absurdity of Hitler's theory of racial and linguistic purity.[46] Obviously, such old proverbs continued to be used since they had long been a part of the German stock of proverbs. No anti-Semitic language purification program could have stopped the German population from using such texts, many of which are known in most Western languages through biblical tradition.

But the National Socialists tried by whatever means available to show how German culture and life had become infected by alien Jewish thought. If it was difficult to stop people from using Jewish vocabulary, quotations, and proverbs, they could always attempt to use proverbs to prove the supremacy of the Aryan race and discredit the Jews through proverbial invective. This politicized and perverted use of proverbs was by no means an isolated phenomenon, but a well-orchestrated defamation process. A number of publications concentrated on proving Nazi racial theories through proverbs, while others assembled dozens of anti-Semitic proverbs to add to the racial hatred already rampant in Germany. The proverb texts were usually taken at their literal level without any contextual consideration, and they were amassed blindly to convince the reader by mere saturation. They were intended to be accepted without any thought or analysis, just as Nazi doctrine demanded and expected a blind and nonanalytical following. It was here that proverbs played directly into the propagandistic hands of the Nazis, since proverbs are usually used to spread insights and wisdom in an authoritative and generalized fashion. The danger of accepting proverbs at face value is best illustrated in the use the Nazis made of them as ready-made weapons against the Jewish population. They became convincing formulaic statements of Nazi ideology, and because of their traditional ring were accepted only too quickly as another proof of Hitler's reactionary racial theory.[47]

Such intentional misuse of proverbs to spread racism was especially marked in the work of Professor Karl Bergmann, a philologist from Darmstadt, who sought to teach racial purity to his countrymen through deliberately selected proverbs. For a large exhibition entitled "Rasse, Volk, Familie" ("Race, Folk, Family") which opened at the Institute of Education in Mainz on September 17, 1934, Bergmann put together posters with approximately 250 proverbs that showed "Das deutsche Sprichwort als Künder völkischen Gedankengutes"[48] ("The German proverb as bearer of pure German thought"). The proverbs were intended to instruct people in problems of heredity, proper marriage partners, hygiene, children, and related matters. They were meant to show that there was a long tradition of proverbs that stress mental and physical health, love of country, and, above all, the fight against alien elements. Some of these proverbs were published by Bergmann as a small collection in the Nazi folklore journal *Volk und Rasse* in 1936 under the title "Lebendige Rassenhygiene im deutschen Sprichwort" ("Living racial hygiene in the German proverb"). A few examples show how proverbs became guiding slogans for a pure German race.[49]

> Kein besser Heiratsgut als gesunder Leib und Mut.
> (There is no better dowry than a healthy body and mind.)
>
> Heiraten ins Blut tut selten gut.
> (To marry into the blood [close relatives] is seldom good.)
>
> Nur die sich gleichen, sollen sich die Hände reichen.
> (Only those who are similar should marry.)
>
> Ledig, sündlich.
> (Single, sinful.)
>
> Kinder sind der Eltern grösster Reichtum.
> (Children are the greatest riches of parents.)
>
> Der Apfel fällt nicht weit vom Stamm, wie das Schaf, so das Lamm.

(The apple does not fall far from the tree, as the sheep so the lamb.)

Art lässt nicht von Art.
(Race sticks to race.)

Some of the texts merely stressed the need for healthy marriage partners and the joy of children. But in view of Nazi doctrine even these proverbs took on new meanings, that is, purity in reproduction and the need for more Aryans! Texts such as "Nur die sich gleichen, sollen sich die Hände reichen" and "Art lässt nicht von Art" were cited to emphasize Nazi hereditary principles. Only Germans should marry Germans, and there should not be any intermarriage whatsoever with Jews. Without mentioning Jews at all, these isolated texts became dangerous slogans of confrontation and their harmless general meaning of "Like father, like son" became one of racial discrimination.

In more "scholarly" articles, Bergmann was much more explicit. In 1934, he started one of his proverb-perverting papers with the announcement: "Erst Adolf Hitler musste kommen, um die Gewissen aufzurütteln und durch gesetzgeberische Massnahmen das deutsche Volk von der 'Sünde wider Blut und Rasse als der Erbsünde dieser Welt' zu erlösen"[50] ("Adolf Hitler had to appear in order to shake up the conscience and to redeem the German folk through legal measures from the 'sin against blood and race as the original sin of this world' "). By this "sin against the blood," Bergmann meant once again racial purity in marriage, and he cited one proverb after another to prove the wisdom of the folk in these matters, culminating in the proverb: "Drei Dinge machen die besten Paare: gleich Blut, gleich Glut und gleiche Jahre" ("Three things make the best couples: same blood, same passion and same age"). And another essay in which Bergmann stressed German love for the homeland and the danger of longing for distant lands was summarized by a proverb dealing with racial purity at home.

> Der an und für sich gesunde Trieb in die Ferne wird aber krankhaft, wenn er zu einer Überschätzung des Fremden und zur Geringschätzung, ja Verachtung des Einheimischen führt. . . . Es ist . . . [die] Stimme des Blutes, die den Menschen immer zur gleichen oder gleichartigen Rasse sich gesellen lässt, vom Andersartigen aber abstösst. Es liegt ein tiefer Sinn im Sprichwort: *Gleich und gleich gesellt sich gern.* Zwar gebrauchen wir dieses Sprichwort häufig in wegwerfend/humoristischem Sinn, aber es enthält bei richtiger Auffassung eine tiefere Lebensweisheit, die um die unselige, unheimliche Wirkung des Andersartigen wohl weiss.[51]

> (The drive to go abroad, healthy in and of itself, does however get perverted when it leads to an overestimation of the foreign and to the contempt or even disdain of the native. . . . It is the voice of the blood which allows people the desire to be part of the same or similar race, but which repels them from the alien. There is a deeper meaning in the proverb: *Like will to like.* To be sure, we use this proverb frequently in a downgrading/humorous sense, but when looked at objectively it con-

tains a deeper worldly wisdom that is well aware of the wretched, sinister effect of the alien.)

Bergmann the scholar seemed to know only too well that the proverb, "Gleich und gleich gesellt sich gern" ("Like will to like") was usually used as a humorous comment, but his own Nazi indoctrination forced him to interpret it racially.

In 1936, Bergmann published his longest paper on proverbs as reflections of Nazi ideology, and by this time he had become so convinced of his argumentation via proverbs that he closed a section on "heredity" proverbs with the statement:

> Solche Sprichwörter reden eine andere Sprache als wissenschaftliche Zahlennachweise. Sie ist deshalb aber nicht weniger eindringlich. Nur muss man sie zu lesen verstehen und sich davor hüten, über der humorvollen Einkleidung den Ernst des zum Ausdruck kommenden Gedankens zu übersehen.[52]

> (Such proverbs speak a different language than scientific statistics. Nevertheless it is no less convincing. One must simply understand how to read it and take heed not to miss the seriousness of the thought expressed because of its humorous guise.)

Scientific study had given way to emotion and irrationality; proverbs were used to prove preconceived notions. Bergmann argued, "Wir wollen wieder ein erbgesundes Volk werden" ("We want to become an hereditarily healthy folk again"), and he sought to advance this racial doctrine by searching for proverbs which dealt with "Arbeit, Ehe, Vererbung, Volksgesundheit, Erziehung, Ehre, Freiheit, Volksgemeinschaft"[53] ("Work, marriage, heredity, folk hygiene, education and upbringing, honor, freedom, folk community").

For each of these concepts Bergmann listed numerous examples which supposedly promoted Nazi policy in traditional language. Under "Arbeit" ("work"), one finds, for example, "Arbeit schändet nicht" ("Work does no harm"), an old German proverb that encourages solid work ethics. But if Bergmann had bothered to open Tendlau's collection of German-Jewish proverbs, he would have discovered that German Jews knew the same proverb as "Arbeit is kaan Charpe [cherpah, hebr. Schande (shame)]"[54] Proverbs on the "Ehe" ("marriage") are interpreted as "Gesetz(e) zum Schutz der Erbgesundheit des deutschen Volkes"[55] ("laws for the protection of the hereditary health of the German folk"), as the racial interpretation of the following proverb shows: "Erst gesundes Blut, dann grosses Gut und schöner Hut"[56] ("First healthy blood, then large property and a pretty hat").

Interesting also are the proverbs that Bergmann listed under aspects of "Erziehung" ("education and upbringing") of young children. Just like Hitler, he emphasized commands and obedience in the following examples: "Wer wohl befiehlt, dem wird wohl gehorcht" ("He who commands well, is well obeyed"), and "Gehorsam ist die Grundfeste aller Ordnung"[57] ("Obedience is the foundation of all order"). Little wonder that people trained in such blind obedience were quick to accept the Nazi slogan "Führer befiehl, wir folgen dir!" ("Führer command, we will follow you!"). This was indeed "Erziehung zur Unterordnung" ("training for subordination") as Bergmann called it. And on the economic side of Nazi propaganda, Bergmann too quoted the familiar proverb "Gemeinnutz geht vor Eigennutz"[58] ("The common good takes precedence over self-interest"), which was blatantly misinterpreted by the Nazis as Bertolt Brecht showed in his satirical essay quoted above. Bergmann even cited the politicized variation "Gemeiner Nutz ist des Vaterlandes Schutz" ("Common good is the protection of the fatherland"), that is, everyone had better work together to build the war machinery as a defense of the fatherland against outside aggression. Bergmann closed his article by prophesying a renaissance of proverbs: "Im Dritten Reich, das vom 'klügelnden Verstand' wieder zum 'instinktsicheren Empfinden' des unverdorbenen Menschen zurückführen will, werden diese [alten] Wahrheiten wieder lebendig und mit ihnen das deutsche Sprichwort"[59] ("In the Third Reich, which wants to lead one back from 'overwise reason' to the 'instinctive feeling' of unspoiled people, these [old] truths, and with them the German proverb, will be revitalized"). Proverbs took on mythological characteristics that were to be followed as blindly and irrationally as every other slogan and command.

There is no doubt that Bergmann enlisted proverbs in the service of Nazi propaganda. He interpreted them as authoritative proof of Nazi doctrine, and quoted them to spread racial discrimination dressed in easily remembered and recognizable formulaic patterns. In 1939, he went so far as to publish a 455-page proverb collection entitled *Deutsche Ahnenweisheit,* which assembled dozens of proverbs viewed as comments on racial purity. Bergmann called them "Vererbungssprichwörter" ("hereditary proverbs"), "Arbeitssprichwörter" ("work proverbs"), "Erziehungssprichwörter" ("education and upbringing proverbs"), and "Gesundheitssprichwörter" ("hygiene proverbs").[60] One proverb followed the other, but this time Bergmann included some anti-Semitic proverbs as well.[61]

> Ebenso wie die Eule das Licht, verträgt der Jude die Wahrheit nicht.
> (Just as the owl can not bear the light so the Jew can not bear the truth.)
>
> Dem Juden sind alle Wege recht, führt's nur zu Geld, ist keiner zu schlecht.
> (All ways are acceptable to the Jew; as long as it leads to money, no way is too bad.)
>
> Der Jude ist der Selbstsucht Kind,

er tut nichts, wo er nichts gewinnt.
(The Jew is the child of selfishness,
he does nothing where he gains nothing.)

Der Juden liebste Farbe ist gelb.
(The Jews' favorite color is yellow [i.e., gold, money].)

Der Jude weiss sich zu nähren und andre zu scheren.
(The Jew knows how to support himself and how to clip others.)

All texts were cited without any context or explanation, and their only purpose was to spread stereotypical views of the Jews. They were meant to be taken at face value without any objective historical and societal analysis. Their cumulative existence was thought of as proof of the inferiority and criminality of Jews.

Unfortunately, Karl Bergmann was no isolated phenomenon. Two years prior to the publication of his large collection, there appeared a similar work by the medical doctor Julius Schwab, *Rassenpflege im Sprichwort* (1937). Schwab argued from a medical "scientific" point of view that "in unseren deutschen Sprichwörtern ein reicher Schatz rassenhygienischer Weisheit verborgen ist"[62] ("a rich treasure of racially hygienic wisdom is concealed in our German proverbs"). He was much more explicit in his racism than Bergmann, and declared openly: "Die liberalistische These von der Gleichheit alles dessen, was Menschenantlitz trägt, stimmt nicht. Unser Herrgott hat die Menschen nicht als einen einzigen grossen Rassenbrei geschaffen. . . . Gott kennt Unterschiede des Blutes und der Rasse"[63] ("The liberal thesis of the equality of everything which has a human face is not correct. Our Lord has not created the humans as a single large racial mush. . . . God is aware of differences of blood and race"). Proverbs that supposedly supported such racial statements were "Gott hat nicht alle Finger gleich lang gemacht" ("God has not created all fingers of the same length"), "Ungleich kommen wir auf die Welt, ungleich scheiden wir davon" ("Unequal we arrive in the world, unequal we leave it"), "Jeder zeugt seinesgleichen" ("Everyone creates his own equal"), "Ein jeder niest nach seiner Nase" ("Everyone sneezes according to his own nose"), "Kein Mohr wird weiss" ("No Moor turns white"), etc.[64] Schwab continued with proverbs that reflected on Nordic ideals of beauty, heredity, proper marriage, children, and other moral issues just as Bergmann did, but with more explicit racial explanations.

This is painfully evident in the absurd section entitled "Rassengegensätze" ("racial opposites"), in which Schwab argued against intermarriage of Germans and Jews.

Die Juden sind ein vorderasiatisch-orientalisches Mischvolk mit negroidem Einschlag und Einschlag von ihren Wirtsvölkern, bei denen sie wie Parasiten seit Jahrhunderten wohnen. Sie bringen uns in dieser Blutzusammensetzung eine unserer nordischen Aufgabe durchaus schädigende Rassenmischung entgegen. Aus dieser Erkenntnis hat der nationalsozialistische Staat das Gesetz zum Schutz des deutschen Blutes und der deutschen Ehre geschaffen, das einmal die Mischung mit jüdischem Blut verbietet und weiterhin verhindern will, dass der deutsche Blutanteil im deutschjüdischen Mischlingsblut als Wertreservoir für das jüdische Volk aufgeht.[65]

(The Jews are a Near Eastern, Oriental mixed race with Negroid influence and influence from their host peoples with whom they have lived like parasites for centuries. Through this blood composition they bring a damaging racial mixture to our Nordic mission. Recognizing this, the National Socialist state has created the law for the protection of German blood and German honor which on the one hand forbids the mixture with Jewish blood and which on the other hand wants to prevent the German blood stock from dissipating its value in the German-Jewish blood mixture.)

After this tirade, many German proverbs are listed that were supposed to show how evil, greedy, and criminal Jews were, as, for example, the following:[66]

Trau keinem Juden bei seinem Eid
und keinem Wolf auf grüner Heid.
(Don't trust a Jew's oath
or a wolf on the green heath.)

Wer einen Juden betrügt, bekommt einen ersten Platz im Himmel.
(Whoever betrays a Jew gets a preferred place in heaven.)

Wo viele Juden sind, da sind viele Diebe.
(Wherever there are many Jews, there are many thieves.)

Juden seid ihr, Juden bleibt ihr.
(Jews you are and Jews you will remain.)

Die Juden seynd einem Land so nutz, als die Mäuss auf dem Getreideboden und die Motten einem Kleid.
(The Jews are as much use to a country as mice are on the threshing floor and moths on a dress.)

Beim Juden und beim Raben ist alles Baden umsonst.
(For Jews and ravens all bathing is in vain.)

Such manipulated and unscientific compilations are ample proof of how Nazism had poisoned the minds of intelligent people. If these collections did not deserve the paper on which they were printed, then dissertations that tried to give them credence deserve still less consideration, except as examples of what can happen to scholarship when it is guided by political fervor. The "scholarly" counterpart to Schwab's and Bergmann's proverb collections is Helene Heger's study, *Das deutsche Idealbild im Sprichwörterschatz des Volkes* (1939). In this dissertation, Heger attempted to reconstruct the ideal

German type by studying German proverbs from all walks of life. The tall, blond, blue-eyed Nordic type was pieced together through selected proverbs, and much care was taken not to use proverbs of international distribution. Heger deliberately concentrated on regional and dialect proverbs in the hope of citing only "German" proverbs. These she felt she could easily differentiate from German-Jewish proverbs since the latter are characterized by "Phantasielosigkeit und Bildermangel"[67] ("lack of imagination and absence of imagery"). This assertion, of course, is easily belied by one glance into Tendlau's and Bernstein's collections and Beatrice Silverman-Weinreich's more recent research.[68] Heger also argued against scholars, who "im Anschluss an das Vorhandensein einer mehr oder minder grossen Anzahl von gleich- oder ähnlichlautenden Sprichwörtern bei verschiedenen Völkern und Sprachen die kühne Behauptung aufstellten, diese Gleichheit der Sprichwörter sei ein Beweis für die Gleichheit der Menschen[69] ("[who,] because of the existence of a more or less large number of equal or similar-sounding proverbs among different peoples and languages, boldly declared that this equality of proverbs is a proof of the equality of people"). Every proverb scholar knows that equal experiences can lead to textually similar proverbs in parts of the world that have had no prior contact. This, of course, is also the reason why proverbs are borrowed and translated from one language group to another. Many human experiences are the same, and the assertion that humans are equal is "kühn" ("bold") only to one who wants to differentiate according to race and blood. Heger stressed national proverbs and brushed aside international proverbs as signs of the internationalism of the Jewish people. She called for a chauvinistic and racially oriented paremiography in Germany: "Die Aufgabe einer künftigen deutschen Sprichwörtersammlung wird es sein, den deutschen Sprichwörterschatz von dieser Überdeckung 'internationaler Kultur' wieder zu befreien, soweit dies heute noch möglich ist"[70] ("The task of a future German proverb collection will be to liberate the treasury of German proverbs from the influence of 'international culture' in as far as this is still possible today"). In other words, the German proverb stock had to be purified of foreign and possibly Jewish elements.

As the open campaign against the Jewish population became more intense, the anti-Semitic proverb publications also took on a more aggressive nature. In 1940, Hartmann Schiffer published yet another article on the theme of "Rasse und Erbe im Sprichwort" ("Race and Heredity in Proverbs") in the Nazi magazine *Neues Volk*.[71] Once again, he dealt with proverbs on heredity, race, marriage, and children, but he also attacked intermarriage between Germans and Jews. He even went so far as to speak of an "Abscheu der breiten Volksmasse vor dem Juden" ("disgust of the folk masses for the Jew"), and quoted such proverbial expressions as "Ear stinkt wia a Zwiflijud" ("He stinks like an onion Jew"), and "Ear sicht aus wia a ghengter Jud" ("He looks like a hanged Jew, i.e., a deceiver"). Finally, Schiffer stated that the inner and outer impurity of the Jews was reflected in the following widely known folk verse.

> Nichts auf Erden dauert ewig,
> Nur der Jud bleibt immer schäbig![72]
> (Nothing on earth lasts forever,
> only the Jew will always remain shabby!)

Yet the most gruesome publication of anti-Semitic proverbs was *Der Jude im Sprichwort der Völker* (1942) by Ernst Hiemer. In 210 pages Hiemer divided his materials and comments into 25 chapters, the titles of which alone are repugnant: "Die geborenen Verbrecher" ("The born criminals"), "Ungeziefer der Menschheit" ("Vermin of humanity"), "Meister der Lüge" ("Masters of deception"), "Das Diebesgesindel" ("Gang of thieves"), "Die Erzbetrüger" ("The arch deceivers"), "Ihr Gott ist das Geld" ("Their God is money"), "Die Rassenschänder" ("The racial defilers"), "Menschenmörder von Anfang an" ("Human murderers from the very beginning"), "Das Teufelsvolk" ("The folk of the devil"), "Hinaus mit den Juden" ("Out with the Jews"), and others in this vein. The book was issued by the Nazi publishing house, "Der Stürmer," and included a request to readers for additional anti-Semitic proverbs to bolster the 1200 texts already included in the book: "Jene Leser, die antijüdische Sprichwörter, Redensarten, Sinnsprüche und Reime kennen, die in diesem Buche noch nicht aufgeführt sind, werden gebeten, uns dieselben mitteilen zu wollen"[73] ("Those readers who know anti-Semitic proverbs, proverbial expressions, maxims, and rhymes that are not listed in this book are asked to be kind enough to communicate them to us").

As the title of the book indicates, this was an international proverb campaign against the Jews. One slur was followed by another, and Hiemer even perverted the international proverb "Vox populi, vox dei" to give credibility to his undertaking: " 'Volkes Stimme ist Gottes Stimme.' Seit die Welt besteht, hat die gesunde Meinung gesunder Völker immer das Richtige getroffen und mit prophetischer Sicherheit die Wahrheit gefunden"[74] (" 'The voice of the people, the voice of God.' Since the world has existed, the healthy opinion of healthy peoples has always hit the mark and has found the truth with prophetic certainty"). These unfortunate slurs had been formulated by "healthy" people, as Hiemer argued, but they certainly did not amass them into a heap of invective as this book did. It is true that unflattering proverbs exist about other nationalities and races, but they certainly were never meant to be directed against every member of a group.[75] Proverbs are oversimplifications and generalizations, they are not universal truths and certainly not God's voice. Besides, one could compile similar collections of proverbs against the

Germans, French, English, and so on. One of the best international collections of such slurs was published by Abraham Aaron Roback only two years after Hiemer's work with the title *A Dictionary of International Slurs* (1944). This book is ample proof that one can discredit any group of people through proverbs. But Roback researches these verbal prejudices in order to shed light on their dangers and misconceptions, while Hiemer used anti-Semitic slurs to deepen the hatred against the Jews and deliver Jews to their destruction. Hiemer's work shows only too clearly the ultimate danger of proverbial stereotypes when they are collected and placed in the hands of criminals.

A few examples of Hiemer's methods must follow here to show how this misuse of proverbs played its part in the annihilation of the Jewish population in Germany. By also quoting texts from other countries, Hiemer was able to increase his effectiveness since the German reader soon became convinced that the whole world looked down on the Jews. Take, for example, just the section on "Ungeziefer der Menschheit" ("Vermin of humanity"). Hiemer stated in his introduction: "Der Jude ist seelisch völlig verderbt und fühlt sich daher auch körperlich nur im Pfuhle wohl. So ist denn der Jude für die nichtjüdische Welt die Verkörperung des Ungeziefers in Menschengestalt geworden"[76] ("The Jew is spiritually completely corrupt and therefore he feels physically well only in the cesspit. Thus the Jew has become the embodiment of vermin in human shape for the non-Jewish world"). And this was followed by dozens of proverbs that linked Jews with lower animals.[77]

> Juden im Haus
> Sind schlimmer als Wanze und Laus. (Mitteldeutschland)
> (Jews in the house
> are worse than bedbug and louse.) (Middle Germany)
>
> Juden sind schlimmer als Filzläuse. (Schwaben)
> (Jews are worse than lice.) (Swabia)
>
> Een Jood en een luis is de pest in je huis. (Niederlande)
> (A Jew and a louse is the plague in every house.) (Netherlands)
>
> Jud, Jud, du Natternbrut! (Franken)
> (Jew, Jew, you brood of vipers!) (Franconia)

And in the chapter entitled "Hinaus mit den Juden" ("Out with the Jews") Hiemer quoted many proverbs to back up the expulsion of the Jews because they were "geborene Verbrecher" ("born criminals"): "Erst wenn sie aus dem Volkskörper ausgeschieden werden, sind die Nichtjuden vor weiterem Schaden durch jüdische Lügner, Betrüger, Wucherer, Meineidige, Rassenschänder und Mörder bewahrt"[78] ("Only when they [the Jews] are eliminated from the populace are the non-Jews safe from further damage by Jewish liars, deceivers, usurers, perjurers, racial defilers and murderers"). A few of Hiemer's examples are the following:[79]

Solange Juden auf dieser Welt,
solange ist kein Frieden. (Sudetenland)
(As long as there are Jews on this earth,
there will be no peace.) (Sudetenland)

Gäb's kein Judengeschmiss,
Wär die Welt ein Paradies! (Oberdonau)
(If there were no Jewish scum,
The world would be a paradise!) (Upper Danube)

Die Juden gehören nicht in unsere Zeit. (Sudetenland)
(The Jews don't belong in our time.) (Sudetenland)

Schlag drauf, es ist ein Jud'! (Westmark)
(Beat on him, it is a Jew!) (Westmark)

Bei Juden und Läusen hilft nur eine Radikalkur. (Süddeutschland)
(In the case of Jews and lice only a radical cure helps.) (Southern Germany)

Schneidet ihm die Hälse ab,
Dem verdammten Judenpack. (Sachsen)
(Cut the throats
of the damned Jewish pack.) (Saxony)

Jud' spei Blut,
Spei! in eine Ecken,
Morgen sollst verrecken. (Oberfranken)
(Spit blood, Jew,
Spit! into a corner with you,
Tomorrow you shall croak.) (Upper Franconia)

Erst wenn der letzte Jude ist verschwunden,
Hat das Volk seine Erlösung gefunden. (Deutschland)
(Only when the last Jew has disappeared,
Will the folk find its salvation.) (Germany)

It is important to point out here that not a single one of these gruesome texts appears in Karl Friedrich Wilhelm Wander's *Deutsches Sprichwörter-Lexikon* (1867–80). This liberal German folklorist lists many proverbs about Jews, but he adds many explanatory notes to put these slurs into proper historical perspective and warn against them. Following the proverb "Ein Jüd steckt so voll Abgötterey vnd Zauberey als neun Kühe Haare haben" ("A Jew is as full of idolatry and sorcery as nine cows have hairs"), he adds that this text stems

aus den finstern Jahrhunderten mit ihren Judenverfolgungen. In unsern Tagen ist es kaum begreiflich, mit welchem Fanatismus die Juden einst verfolgt worden sind und in welcher Weise man sie geschmäht hat. Selbstredend hat dieser Judenhass auch in den Sprichwörten seinen Ausdruck gefunden, und ich werde keine derselben unterdrücken, denn die Schmähungen, die sie enthalten, fallen auf die zurück, die sie ausgesprochen haben, und auf das Zeitalter, in dem ein fanatisches Pfaffentum den blinden Glauben an die Stelle der humanen Grundsätze des Weisen aus Nazareth gesetzt hatte, der selbst ein Jude war.[80]

(from the dark ages with its persecutions of the Jews. In our day it is hardly comprehensible with what kind of fanaticism the Jews were once persecuted and the ways in which they have been insulted. Obviously this hatred of the Jews has also found its expression in the proverbs, and I shall not suppress any of them, for the insults contained in them fall back on those who have voiced them and on the age in which a fanatic clericalism mobilized blind belief in place of the humane principles of the wise man from Nazareth who himself was a Jew.)

Blind belief in Adolf Hitler and sick anti-Semitism resulted in publications by people such as Hiemer who, as far as one can tell, even invented anti-Semitic proverbs to support the Nazi drive to exterminate the Jews. Many of his texts such as "Erst wenn der letzte Jude ist verschwunden, / Hat das Volk seine Erlösung gefunden" ("Only when the last Jew has disappeared, / Will the folk find its salvation") are, in fact, invented Nazi slogans of the "Endlösung" ("final solution") dressed in the formulaic and rhymed pattern of proverb structures. They are sick reminders of the perversion of thought and language of which Nazi propaganda was capable when it came to manipulating aggression and hate.

In addition to such pernicious publications, there were also minor references and allusions to Nazi doctrine in proverb publications of the 1930s and early 1940s. An article on "Deutsches Recht im deutschen Sprichwort" ("German law in German proverbs"), for example, placed some German legal proverbs into the service of "Rasse- und Blutbewusstsein" ("consciousness of race and blood"). Such proverbs as "Art lässt nicht von Art" ("Race sticks to race"), and "Keine Atzel (Elster) heckt eine Taube" ("No magpie breeds a pigeon") were seen as expressions of racial, biological heredity laws.[81] And Alarich Mahler referred specifically once again to the Nazi proverb slogan "Gemeinnutz geht vor Eigennutz" ("The common good takes precedence over self-interest") in the introduction to his book on property laws expressed in legal proverbs. He was convinced that the old German proverb "Gemeiner nutz gehet vor sonderlichen nutz" ("The common good takes precedence over special interest") summarized "anschaulich und einprägsam das Wesen sozialistischen Wollens" ("clearly and impressively the essence of socialist intentions") and that it was a proper statement for the programs of National Socialism.[82] Thus, even lawyers tried to support the Nazis by quoting old legal proverbs that were supposed to lend historical authority and credibility to the movement. Against such propagandistic use of proverbs, Bertolt Brecht's analysis of the proverb "Gemeinnutz geht vor Eigennutz" had little influence. Instead, critical minds like Brecht were driven out of Germany, and the misuse of proverbs was extended to all walks of life.

The question arises whether there were any proverb publications during the Nazi period that were not infected by party doctrines. The famous literary historian and folklorist, Robert Petsch, published his book *Spruchdichtung des Volkes* (1938) during that time and included an important chapter on proverbs in which he gives a short historical survey of German proverbs and also analyzes the content of proverbs with special emphasis on humor and parody. There is also a section on wellerisms and a good discussion of the form of proverbs, including metaphor, rhyme, rhythm, and alliteration. Above all, he warns against the "Erklärung der Art eines Volkes aus seinen Sprichwörtern"[83] ("interpretation of the character of a people by means of its proverbs"), a caution often repeated by other folklorists.[84] Nevertheless, even Petsch refers once to the Germans as an "echter Leistungsmensch nordischer Art"[85] ("a true realization of the Nordic type"), which shows that Nazi racial vocabulary had become part of everyday vocabulary in the late 1930s. However, in his 1936 essay on literary quotations, he certainly did not include Nazi quotations together with Goethe and Schiller as the editors of Büchmann's *Geflügelte Worte* were doing at the same time.[86]

A solid philological, folkloric, and cultural essay on German proverbial expressions appeared in 1931 by Fritz Rahn in which the author showed how their content reflects the language of occupations and concerns of everyday life.[87] He also discussed their metaphorical nature and their importance as a stylistic element in various types of writing. This article is so sound from a scholarly point of view that it was republished in a slightly expanded version after the war in 1948–49, in order to point out the continued usefulness of proverbial expressions as instructional tools in German classrooms.[88] A perfectly legitimate article was also published in 1931 by Wilhelm Schwer on the sociology of proverbs. The author treats the social function of proverbs especially in the Middle Ages and discusses their importance in various social groups. Like Robert Petsch, he too warns against national stereotyping through proverbs: "Versuche, aus einer Vergleichung des Sprichwortschatzes der verschiedenen Völker zu besonderen völkerkundlichen und völkerpsychologischen Ergebnissen zu gelangen, sind im allgemeinen gescheitert"[89] ("Attempts to reach special ethnographic and ethnopsychological conclusions by means of comparing the proverbs of different peoples have generally failed"). And finally there is a short article by Eilert Pastor with the simple and straightforward title "Das deutsche Sprichwort" ("The German Proverb") that appeared in 1941 in a regional German folklore journal.[90] Here, in the midst of racist and anti-Semitic proverb publications, there is finally a voice of reason. Pastor alludes briefly to the general claim that some proverbs reflect national character, but his general article deals primarily with problems of definition, form, and content of the proverb. He also includes a short discussion of weather and legal proverbs, a survey of major German proverb collections, and an analysis of Pieter Brueghel's 1559 proverb picture *Netherlandic Proverbs*. In other words, one could still publish honest, humane, and objective research, and this small article on German proverbs is like a glimmer of hope and reason among the flood of slanderous proverb publications of the Nazi period.[91]

With the end of the dark ages of German National Socialism, such appalling publications ceased immediately, but they are painful reminders of how proverbs and folklore can be used to influence, manipulate, and poison people's feelings, thoughts, and actions. Proverbs in themselves might be harmless pieces of folk wisdom, but when they become propagandistic tools in the hands of malicious persons, they can take on unexpected powers of authority and persuasion. The publications analyzed here are extremely rare today and virtually unknown, but the two truly scholarly Yiddish proverb collections from the nineteenth and early twentieth century by Abraham Tendlau and Ignaz Bernstein have been reprinted in Germany and contain rich treasures of Jewish proverbial wisdom untouched by perverted Nazi theories. In 1965, there even appeared in Germany a popular paperback book on Jewish anecdotes and proverbs,[92] and Abraham Roback's *Dictionary of International Slurs* was republished in 1979.[93] There is today a healthy interest in studying proverbs as expressions of worldview[94] in order to understand the psychology behind the many proverbial stereotypes and slurs that exist around the world. Folklorists and scholars from other disciplines must study them in the hope that proverbs will never again be used to assist in bringing death to millions of innocent people.

Notes

This chapter was first published in the *Journal of American Folklore*, 95 (1982), 435–464.

I would like to thank Prof. David Scrase for his help with the translations and Dr. Barbara Mieder for her stylistic assistance. This chapter is dedicated to Prof. and Mrs. Harry Kahn who had to flee Nazi Germany to find a more humane life in the United States.

1. See Adolf Bach, *Deutsche Volkskunde* (Heidelberg: Quelle & Meyer, 1960), pp. 89–108. Bach provides a critical review of folklore scholarship under National Socialism with extensive bibliographical references.

2. Hermann Bausinger, "Volksideologie und Volksforschung. Zur nationalsozialistischen Volkskunde," *Zeitschrift für Volkskunde*, 61 (1965), 177–204.

3. Christa Kamenetsky, "Folklore as a Political Tool in Nazi Germany," *Journal of American Folklore*, 85 (1972), 221–235. See also her more specific study on "Folktale and Ideology in the Third Reich," *Journal of American Folklore*, 90 (1977), 168–178.

4. Matthes Ziegler, "Volkskunde auf rassischer Grundlage," *NS-Monatshefte*, 5 (1934), 711–717.

5. See Walther Steller, *Volkskunde als nationalsozialistische Wissenschaft* (Breslau: Ostdeutsche Verlagswissenschaft, 1935), p. 31 and pp. 38–39. It is particularly painful to read the introduction to Hans Naumann's third edition of his significant book *Deutsche Volkskunde*

in Grundzügen (Leipzig: Quelle & Meyer, 1935), pp. 7–11, in which this scholar places his research in the service of National Socialism.

6. See Max Hildebert Boehm, *Volkskunde* (Berlin: Weidmann, 1937), pp. 48–51.

7. See Heinz Paechter, *Nazi-Deutsch. A Glossary of Contemporary German Usage* (New York: Frederick Ungar, 1944), pp. 6–7.

8. Victor Klemperer, *LTI [Lingua Tertii Imperii, Sprache des Dritten Reiches]. Notizbuch eines Philologen* (Berlin: Aufbau, 1947). See as an opposing view the following dissertation written by the Nazi Manfred Pechau, *Nationalsozialismus und deutsche Sprache* (Diss. Greifswald, 1934; Greifswald: Hans Adler, 1935).

9. See Cornelia Berning, *Vom Abstammungsnachweis zum Zuchtwort. Vokabular des Nationalsozialismus* (Berlin: Walter de Gruyter, 1964) and Dolf Sternberger, Gerhard Storz and W. E. Süsskind, *Aus dem Wörterbuch des Unmenschen* (Hamburg: Claassen, 1957).

10. See Sigrid Frind, *Die Sprache als Propagandainstrument in der Publizistik des Dritten Reiches* (Diss. Freie Universität Berlin, 1964) and Lutz Winckler, *Studie zur gesellschaftlichen Funktion faschistischer Sprache* (Frankfurt: Suhrkamp, 1970.)

11. See Eugen and Ingeborg Seidel, *Sprachwandel im Dritten Reich* (Halle: Verlag Sprache und Literatur, 1961) and Siegfried Bork, *Mißbrauch der Sprache. Tendenzen nationalsozialistischer Sprachregelung* (Bern: Francke, 1970).

12. See Cornelia Berning, "Die Sprache des Nationalsozialismus," *Zeitschrift für deutsche Wortforschung*, 18 (1962), 109. The long article can be found in that journal in the following volumes: 16 (1960), 71–149, 178–188; 17 (1961), 83–121, 171–182; 18 (1962), 108–118, 160–172; 19 (1963), 92–112. Berning's book mentioned in note 9 contains primarily only the lexicographical items of this long article.

13. Abraham Moses Tendlau, *Sprichwörter und Redensarten deutsch-jüdischer Vorzeit* (Frankfurt: J. Kauffmann, 1860; rpt. Hildesheim: Georg Olms, 1980), p. viii.

14. Ad. Jellinek, *Der jüdische Stamm in nichtjüdischen Sprichwörtern* (Wien: M. Walzner, 1881), p. 5.

15. Jellinek, p. 7.

16. Ad. Jellinek, *Der jüdische Stamm in nichtjüdischen Sprichwörtern* (Wien: M. Walzner, 1882), p. 93.

17. Jellinek (1881), p. 27. In this regard see also Abraham Aaron Roback, "The Yiddish Proverb—A Study in Folk Psychology," *The Jewish Forum*, 1 (1918), 331–338 and 418–426.

18. Sally Simon Tilles, *Der Jude im Citat und im Sprichwort* (Berlin: Paul Huchen, 1892), p. 52.

19. Tilles, p. 16.

20. Tilles, p. 28.

21. Tilles, p. 29.

22. See Max Domarus, *Hitler—Reden und Proklamationen 1932–1945* (Neustadt a. d. Aisch: Schmidt, 1962), vol. I, p. 251. The entire proclamation against the Jewish population is printed on pp. 248–251.

23. Domarus, vol. I, p. 45.

24. Frind, pp. 41–42.

25. For a discussion of proverb usage in politics see Joseph Raymond, "Tensions in Proverbs: More Light on International Understanding," *Western Folklore*, 15 (1956), 153–158; also reprinted in Wolfgang Mieder and Alan Dundes (eds.), *The Wisdom of Many: Essays on the Proverb* (New York: Garland, 1981), pp. 300–308. There is also a chapter on "Das Sprichwort und die politische Sprache" in Wolfgang Mieder, *Das Sprichwort in unserer Zeit* (Frauenfeld: Huber, 1975), pp. 14–22. For more specific studies see also Hugo Blümmer, *Der bildliche Ausdruck in den Reden des Fürsten Bismarck* (Leipzig: S. Hirzel, 1891), pp. 182–186; L. A. Morozova, "Upotreblenic V. I. Leninym poslovits," *Russkaia Rech'*, no. vol., no. 2 (1979), 10–14; and Edd Miller and Jesse J. Villarreal, "The Use of Clichés by Four Con-

temporary Speakers," *Quarterly Journal of Speech*, 31 (1945), 151–155 (the four speakers are Winston Churchill, Anthony Eden, Franklin D. Roosevelt and Henry Wallace).

26. Domarus, vol. I, p. 86 and p. 205.

27. Domarus, vol. I, p. 413.

28. Domarus, vol. I, p. 316.

29. Domarus, vol. I, p. 209.

30. Domarus, vol. I, p. 533.

31. Domarus, vol. II, p. 1057.

32. Domarus, vol. II, p. 1829.

33. For some additional examples of proverbial expressions used by the Nazis see Frind, pp. 21–23.

34. Karl Kraus, *Die dritte Walpurgisnacht*, ed. Heinrich Fischer (München: Kösel, 1952), pp. 122–123. See also Wolfgang Mieder, "Karl Kraus und der sprichwörtliche Aphorismus," *Muttersprache*, 89 (1979), 97–115. Concerning the brutality of language see Hans Winterfeldt, "Elemente der Brutalität im nationalsozialistischen Sprachgebrauch," *Muttersprache*, 75 (1965), 231–236.

35. Bertolt Brecht, *Gesammelte Werke in 20 Bänden*, ed. Elisabeth Hauptmann (Frankfurt: Suhrkamp, 1967), vol. 20, pp. 230–233. The modern Austrian author Peter Handke also refers to this proverb and how it was already expanded during Nazi times to "Gemeinnutz geht vor Eigennutz, Gemeinnutz geht vor Eigensinn" (Common good precedes self-interest, common good precedes self-will) in his short novel *Wunschloses Unglück* (Frankfurt: Suhrkamp, 1974), p. 24.

36. See Abraham Tendlau, *Sprichwörter und Redensarten deutsch-jüdischer Vorzeit* [gekürzte Ausgabe] (Berlin: Schocken, 1934).

37. See Georg Büchmann, *Geflügelte Worte*, ed. Valerian Tornius (Leipzig: Philipp Reclam, 1935), p. 6.

38. Tornius, p. 263.

39. Georg Büchmann, *Geflügelte Worte. Der Zitatenschatz des deutschen Volkes*, eds. Gunther Haupt and Werner Rust (Berlin: Haude & Spener, 1937), p. vii. The 29th edition published in 1942 by the same editors is identical.

40. Büchmann (eds. Haupt and Rust), p. 646.

41. Büchmann (eds. Haupt and Rust), p. 648.

42. Georg Büchmann, *Geflügelte Worte. Der Zitatenschatz des deutschen Volkes. Volksausgabe*, ed. Werner Rust (Berlin: Haude & Spener, 1943).

43. Büchmann (ed. Rust), p. vi. In case a researcher might not have read the preface, there is another very noticable statement about the Jewish star at the end of the table of contents (p. viii): "Zur Beachtung! Jüdische und nichtarische Urheber geflügelter Worte sind im Namensverzeichnis durch * besonders gekennzeichnet" (Notice! Jewish and non-Aryan authors of sententious remarks are specially marked through an * in the name index).

44. Büchmann (ed. Rust), p. 203.

45. Paul Elbogen, "Was der Nazi nicht darf . . . ," *Die Weltbühne*, 28 (1932), 493–494. I owe this reference to Helmut Walther from the "Gesellschaft für deutsche Sprache" (Society of the German Language) in Wiesbaden, Germany.

46. For an intriguing essay on linguistic purification attempts in Germany see Peter von Polenz, "Sprachpurismus und Nationalsozialismus," in *Germanistik—eine deutsche Wissenschaft*, eds. Eberhard Lämmert, Walther Killy, Karl Otto Conrady and Peter von Polenz (Frankfurt: Suhrkamp, 1967), pp. 111–165.

47. The only short reference to this misuse of proverbs during the German fascist period is made by Friedrich Redlich in his essay "Sprichwort" in *Deutsche Volksdichtung. Eine Einführung*, ed. Hermann Strobach (Leipzig: Philipp Reclam, 1979), p. 238 (the entire essay on pp. 221–240 and pp. 392–393).

48. This is the title of a short statement (pp. 28–29) that Bergmann published in the 31-page catalogue *Rasse, Volk, Familie* that accompanied this exhibition by the Rhein-Mainische Stätte für Erziehung (Rhine-Main Institute for Education). I would like to thank Helmut Walther for obtaining a copy of this catalogue for me.

49. See Karl Bergmann, "Lebendige Rassenhygiene im deutschen Sprichwort," *Volk und Rasse,* 11 (1936), 296–297.

50. Karl Bergmann, "Das deutsche Sprichwort als Künder völkischen Gedankengutes," *Volk und Scholle,* 12 (1934), 325 (the whole article on pp. 325–328).

51. Karl Bergmann, "Deutsche Heimatliebe und Wandersehnsucht in Sprache und Sprichwort," *Zeitschrift für Deutschkunde,* 50 (1936), 340 (the entire article on pp. 337–343).

52. Karl Bergmann, "Völkisches Gedankengut im deutschen Sprichwort," *Zeitschrift für deutsche Bildung,* 12 (1936), 368 (the entire article on pp. 363–373).

53. Bergmann, "Völkisches Gedankengut," p. 364.

54. Tendlau, pp. 263–264. Note the German proverb "Arbeit ist keine Schande" (Work is no disgrace), which is the precise equivalent.

55. Bergmann, "Völkisches Gedankengut," p. 367.

56. Bergmann, p. 367.

57. Bergmann, p. 371.

58. Bergmann, p. 372.

59. Bergmann, p. 373.

60. See Karl Bergmann, *Deutsche Ahnenweisheit. Ein verpflichtendes Erbe* (Stuttgart: Verlag für nationale Literatur Gebrüder Rath, 1939), p. 7.

61. Bergmann, *Deutsche Ahnenweisheit,* pp. 338–339.

62. Julius Schwab, *Rassenpflege im Sprichwort. Eine volkstümliche Sammlung* (Leipzig: Alwin Fröhlich, 1937), p. 5.

63. Schwab, p. 6.

64. Schwab, pp. 7–9.

65. Schwab, pp. 19–20.

66. Schwab, pp. 20–21.

67. See Helene Heger, *Das deutsche Idealbild im Sprichwörterschatz des Volkes* (Diss. Wien, 1939), p. 15.

68. See Beatrice Silverman-Weinreich, "Towards a Structural Analysis of Yiddish Proverbs," *Yivo Annual of Jewish Social Science,* 17 (1978), 1–20; also reprinted in Wolfgang Mieder and Alan Dundes (eds.), *The Wisdom of Many: Essays on the Proverb* (New York: Garland, 1981), pp. 65–85.

69. Heger, p. 22.

70. Heger, p. 24.

71. Hartmann Schiffer, "Rasse und Erbe im Sprichwort," *Neues Volk,* 8, no. 3 (1940), 25–27; no. 4, pp. 27–28; no. 5, p. 28.

72. Schiffer, no. 4, p. 28.

73. Ernst Hiemer, *Der Jude im Sprichwort der Völker* (Nürnberg: Der Stürmer, 1942), p. 210.

74. Hiemer, p. 8.

75. See Alan Dundes, "Slurs International: Folk Comparisons of Ethnicity and National Character," *Southern Folklore Quarterly,* 39 (1975), 15–38.

76. Hiemer, p. 34.

77. Hiemer, pp. 34–36.

78. Hiemer, p. 164.

79. Hiemer, pp. 164–168.

80. See Karl Friedrich Wilhelm Wander, *Deutsches Sprichwörter-Lexikon* (Leipzig: Brockhaus, 1870; rpt. Darmstadt: Wissenschaftliche Buchgesellschaft, 1964); vol. II, col. 1034, no. 29. Wander lists 143 proverbs dealing with Jews, cols. 1031–1040. Notice also Wan-

der's irate remark concerning the proverb "Wo viele Juden sind, da sind viel Diebe" (Where there are many Jews, there are many thieves): "Diesen ziemlich allgemein gehaltenen Aussprüchen gegenüber möchte ich die Bemerkung beifügen, dass ich zwar schon verschiedenemal von Christen, aber noch nie von einem Juden betrogen worden bin" (To these rather generalized expressions I would like to add the statement that I have been cheated on various occasions by Christians but never by a Jew), see col. 1038, no. 94.

81. See Otto Urbach, "Deutsches Recht im deutschen Sprichwort," *Muttersprache*, 52 (1937), col. 232 (the entire article on cols. 230–234).

82. See Alarich Mahler, *Bäuerliches Bodenrecht in Rechtssprichwörtern* (Berlin: C. V. Engelhard, 1943), p. 15. The book itself is a scholarly treatise without obvious Nazi orientation.

83. Robert Petsch, *Spruchdichtung des Volkes. Vor- und Frühformen der Volksdichtung* (Halle: Max Niemeyer, 1938), p. 111 (the entire chapter on pp. 103–125). Another short chapter on proverbs is included in Hans Naumann, *Deutsche Volkskunde in Grundzügen* (Leipzig: Quelle & Meyer, 1935), pp. 130–133. Even though Naumann became a declared Nazi, these few pages are identical to those of the first edition (1922) and second edition (1929) of this book and are free from Nazi doctrine. Equally free from anti-Semitism and Nazi propaganda is Naumann's collection of old literary verse quotations and proverbs entitled *Germanische Spruchweisheit* (Jena: Eugen Diederich, 1935).

84. For references see Lutz Röhrich and Wolfgang Mieder, *Sprichwort* (Stuttgart: Metzler, 1977), pp. 70–72.

85. Petsch, p. 112.

86. See Robert Petsch, " 'Geflügelte Worte' und Verwandtes. Aus der Formenwelt der menschlichen Rede," in R. Petsch, *Deutsche Literaturwissenschaft. Aufsätze zur Begründung der Methode* (Berlin: Emil Ebering, 1940), pp. 230–238.

87. See Fritz Rahn, "Die Redensart. Ein Stück Sprachkunde," *Die Volksschule*, 26 (1931), 970–980.

88. Fritz Rahn, "Die Redensart—ein Kapitel Sprachkunde," *Deutschunterricht*, 1, no. 4 (1948–1949), 22–38.

89. See Wilhelm Schwer, "Zur Soziologie des Sprichwortes," *Bonner Mitteilungen*, 5 (1931), 9 (the entire article on pp. 8–14). I would like to thank Dr. Gerda Grober-Glück (University of Bonn) for obtaining this article for me.

90. Eilert Pastor, "Das deutsche Sprichwort," *Die Heimat. Zeitschrift für niederrheinische Heimatpflege*, 20, nos. 1–2 (1941), 3–7.

91. See the following publications from this time that are *not* influenced by Nazi ideology: Ludwig Meyn, "Germanische Wesensart in altisländischen Sprichwörtern und Sprüchen," *Zeitschrift für deutsche Bildung*, 11 (1935), 566–574; Willy Kramp, "Sind Sprichwörter wahr?" *Die Furche*, 23 (1937), 135–140; Gisela Linder, *Zahnheilkundliches in deutschen Sprichwörtern und Redensarten*. Diss. Universität Köln, 1938; Karl Helm, "Bauernregeln," *Hessische Blätter für Volkskunde*, 38 (1939), 114–132; and Lutz Mackensen, "Deutschland in niederländischen Sprichwörtern und Redensarten," *Oostvlaamsche Zanten*, 16 (1941), 131–156.

92. See Salcia Landmann (ed.), *Jüdische Anekdoten und Sprichwörter* (München: Deutscher Taschenbuchverlag, 1965, 1974).

93. Abraham Aaron Roback, *Dictionary of International Slurs* (Cambridge, Mass.: Sci-Art, 1944; rpt. Waukesha, Wis.: Maledicta, 1979).

94. See Wolfgang Mieder and Alan Dundes (eds.), *The Wisdom of Many. Essays on the Proverb.* New York: Garland Publishing, 1981.

BIBLIOGRAPHY

This bibliography lists only those studies referred to in the individual chapters that have a clear relevance to paremiology and paremiography. For additional references to folkloric, historical, cultural, philological, and historical sources please see the detailed notes of the individual chapters. For easy reference, the bibliography is divided into four parts: bibliographies, proverb journals, collections of proverbs and quotations, and scholarly studies on the proverb.

Bibliographies

Bonser, Wilfrid. *Proverb Literature. A Bibliography of Works Relating to Proverbs.* London: William Glaisher, 1930; rpt. Nendeln, Liechtenstein: Kraus Reprint, 1967.
De Caro, Francis A., and William K. McNeil. *American Proverb Literature: A Bibliography.* Bloomington: Folklore Forum, Indiana University, 1971.
Mieder, Wolfgang. "International Bibliography of Explanatory Essays on Proverbs and Proverbial Expressions Containing Names." *Names,* 24 (1976), 253–304.
Mieder, Wolfgang. "Bibliographischer Abriß zur bildlichen Darstellung von Sprichwörtern und Redensarten." In *Forschungen und Berichte zur Volkskunde in Baden-Württemberg 1974–1977,* ed. by Irmgard Hampp and Peter Assion. Stuttgart: Müller & Gräff, 1977, vol. 3, pp. 229–239.
Mieder, Wolfgang. *International Bibliography of Explanatory Essays on Individual Proverbs and Proverbial Expressions.* Bern: Peter Lang, 1977.
Mieder, Wolfgang. *Proverbs in Literature: An International Bibliography.* Bern: Peter Lang, 1978.
Mieder, Wolfgang. *International Proverb Scholarship: An Annotated Bibliography.* New York: Garland Publishing, 1982.
Mieder, Wolfgang. "International Bibliography of New and Reprinted Proverb Collections." Annual bibliography in *Proverbium: Yearbook of International Proverb Scholarship,* 1984ff.
Mieder, Wolfgang. "International Proverb Scholarship: An Updated Bibliography." Annual bibliography in *Proverbium: Yearbook of International Proverb Scholarship,* 1984ff.
Mieder, Wolfgang. *Investigations of Proverbs, Proverbial Expressions, Quotations and Clichés. A Bibliography of Explanatory Essays which Appeared in "Notes and Queries" (1849–1983).* Bern: Peter Lang, 1984.
Mieder, Wolfgang. *International Proverb Scholarship: An Annotated Bibliography. Supplement I (1800–1981).* New York: Garland Publishing, 1990.
Moll, Otto. *Sprichwörterbibliographie.* Frankfurt am Main: Vittorio Klostermann, 1958.
Urdang, Laurence, and Frank R. Abate. *Idioms and Phrases Index.* 3 vols. Detroit: Gale Research Co., 1983.

Proverb Journals

Proverbium: Bulletin d'information sur les recherches parémiologiques, nos. 1–25 (1965–1975), 1–1008. Ed. by Matti Kuusi et al. (Helsinki). Reprint (2 vols.). Ed. by Wolfgang Mieder. Bern: Peter Lang, 1987.
Proverbium Paratum: Bulletin d'information sur les recherches parémiologiques, 1–4 (1980–1989), 1–460. Ed. by Vilmos Voigt et al. (Budapest).
Proverbium: Yearbook of International Proverb Scholarship, 1984ff. Ed. by Wolfgang Mieder et al. (Burlington, Vt.).

Collections of Proverbs and Quotations

Adams, A. K. *The House Book of Humorous Quotations.* New York: Dodd, Mead & Co., 1969.
Adams, Franklin Pierce. *Book of Quotations.* New York: Funk & Wagnalls, 1952.
Aik, Kam Chuan. *Dictionary of Proverbs.* Singapore: Federal Publications, 1988.
Andersen, Adi. *Deutsche Sprichwörter und Redensarten mit ihren englischen und französischen Gegenstücken.* Hamburg: Matari Verlag, 1968.
Anonymous. *Ben Franklin's Wit & Wisdom.* White Plains, N.Y.: Peter Pauper Press, 1960.
Apperson, G. L. *English Proverbs and Proverbial Phrases. A Historical Dictionary.* London: J. M. Dent, 1929; rpt. Detroit: Gale Research Co., 1969.
Backer, Theodore B. *A Compact Anthology of Bartlett's Quotations.* Middle Village, N.Y.: Jonathan David Publishers, 1974.
Barber, John W. *The Hand Book of Illustrated Proverbs: Comprising also a Selection of Approved Proverbs of Various Nations and Languages, Ancient and Modern. Interspersed with Numerous Engravings and Descriptions.* New York: George F. Tuttle, 1856.
Barbour, Frances M. *Proverbs and Proverbial Phrases of Illinois.* Carbondale: Southern Illinois University Press, 1963.
Barbour, Frances M. *A Concordance to the Sayings in Franklin's "Poor Richard."* Detroit: Gale Research Co., 1974.
Barrick, Mac E. "Proverbs and Sayings from Cumberland County [Pennsylvania]." *Keystone Folklore Quarterly,* 8 (1963), 139–203.
Barten, John. *A Select Collection of English and German Proverbs, Proverbial Expressions, and Familiar Quotations with Translations.* Hamburg: Conrad Kloss, 1896.
Bartlett, John. *Familiar Quotations.* 15th ed. by Emily Morison Beck. Boston: Little, Brown and Co., 1980 (various other editions since 1855 are also cited).
Benham, William Gurney. *Putnam's Complete Book of Quotations, Proverbs and Household Words.* New York: G. P. Putnam's Sons, 1926.
Bergmann, Karl. *Deutsche Ahnenweisheit. Ein verpflichtendes Erbe.* Stuttgart: Rath, 1939 (emphasizing Nazi ideology).
Bilgrav, Jens Aage Stabell. *20.000 Proverbs, Sprichwörter, Proverbes, Ordspråk, Ordsprog.* Copenhagen: Hans Heide, 1985.
Bohn, Henry G. *A Hand-Book of Proverbs Comprising an Entire Republication of Ray's Collection of English Proverbs, with his Additions from Foreign Languages.* London: Henry G. Bohn, 1855.
Bohn, Henry G. *A Polyglot of Foreign Proverbs, Comprising French, Italian, German, Dutch, Spanish, Portuguese, and Danish, with English Translations & a General Index.* London: Henry G. Bohn, 1857; rpt. Detroit: Gale Research Co., 1968.
Bradley, F. W. "South Carolina Proverbs." *Southern Folklore Quarterly,* 1 (1937), 57–101.
Booth, Cheri. *Idioms. Lexikon der englischen Redewendungen.* Eltville am Rhein: Bechtermünz, 1988.
Booth, Cheri, and Christian Gerritzen. *Slang. Lexikon der englischen Umgangssprache.* Eltville am Rhein: Bechtermünz, 1989.

Brewer, Ebenezer Cobham. *Dictionary of Phrase and Fable.* New York: Harper & Row, 1870. Centenary edition revised by Ivor H. Evans. New York: Harper & Row, 1970.

Brown, Marshall. *Sayings that Never Grow Old. Wit and Humor of Well-Known Quotations.* Boston: Small, Maynard & Co., 1918.

Browning, David C. *Dictionary of Quotations and Proverbs.* London: Dent, 1951; rpt. London: Octopus Books, 1982.

Büchmann, Georg. *Geflügelte Worte.* 33rd ed. by Winfried Hofmann. Berlin: Ullstein, 1986 (various other editions since 1864 are also cited).

Carruth, Gorton, and Eugene Ehrlich. *The Harper Book of American Quotations.* New York: Harper & Row, 1988.

Champion, Selwyn Gurney. *Racial Proverbs. A Selection of the World's Proverbs Arranged Linguistically with Authoritative Introductions to the Proverbs of 27 Countries and Races.* London: George Routledge, 1938; rpt. London: Routledge & Kegan, 1963.

Champion, Selwyn Gurney. *The Eleven Religions and Their Proverbial Lore.* New York: E. P. Dutton, 1945.

Christy, Robert. *Proverbs, Maxims and Phrases of All Ages.* New York: G. P. Putnam's Sons, 1887; rpt. Norwood, Pa.: Norwood Editions, 1977.

Clarke, John. *Paroemiologia Anglo-Latina in usum scholarum concinnata. Or Proverbs English, and Latine.* London: Felix Kyngston, 1639.

Codrington, Robert. *A Collection of Many Select, and Excellent Proverbs out of Several Languages.* London: W. Lee, 1664; 2nd ed. London: S. Griffin, 1672.

Cox, H. L. et al. *Spreekwoordenboek in vier talen. Nederlands, Frans, Duits, Engels.* Utrecht: Van Dale Lexicografie, 1988.

Daintith, John et al. *The Macmillan Dictionary of Quotations.* New York: Macmillan, 1987.

Darwin, Bernard. *The Oxford Dictionary of Quotations.* Oxford: Oxford University Press, 1953.

Draxe, Thomas. *Bibliotheca Scholastica Instructissima.* London: Ioann Billius, 1616; rpt. Norwood, N.J.: Walter J. Johnson, 1976.

Düringsfeld, Ida von, and Otto von Reinsberg-Düringsfeld. *Sprichwörter der germanischen und romanischen Sprachen vergleichend zusammengestellt.* 2 vols. Leipzig: Hermann Fries, 1872 and 1875; rpt. Hildesheim: Georg Olms, 1973.

Edwards, Tryon. *Useful Quotations. A Cyclopedia of Quotations.* New York: Grosset & Dunlap, 1936.

Evans, Bergen. *Dictionary of Quotations.* New York: Avenel Books, 1968 (2nd ed. 1978).

Ewart, Neil. *Everyday Phrases. Their Origins and Meanings.* Poole, Dorset: Blandford Press, 1983.

Farmer, John S. (ed.). *The Proverbs, Epigrams, and Miscellanies of John Heywood.* London: Early English Drama Society, 1906; rpt. New York: Barnes & Noble, 1966.

Fogel, Edwin Miller. *Proverbs of the Pennsylvania Germans.* Lancaster: The Pennsylvania-German Society, 1929.

Franck, Sebastian. *Sprichwörter / Schöne / Weise / Herrliche Clugreden / vnnd Hoffsprüch.* Frankfurt am Meyn: Christian Egenolff, 1541; rpt. ed. by Wolfgang Mieder. Hildesheim: Georg Olms, 1987.

Fuller, Thomas. *Gnomologia; Adagies and Proverbs; Wise Sentences and Witty Sayings, Ancient and Modern, Foreign and British.* London: B. Baker, 1732.

Gluski, Jerzy. *Proverbs. A Comparative Book of English, French, German, Italian, Spanish and Russian Proverbs with a Latin Appendix.* New York: Elsevier Publishing Co., 1971.

Green, Jonathon. *The Dictionary of Contemporary Slang.* New York: Stein and Day, 1985.

Guinzbourg, Lt. Colonel Victor S. M. de. *Wit and Wisdom of the United Nations. Proverbs and Apothegms on Diplomacy.* New York: Privately printed, 1961.

Hardie, Margaret. "Proverbs and Proverbial Expressions Current in the United States East of the Missouri and North of the Ohio Rivers." *American Speech,* 4 (1929), 461–472.

Harrebomée, Pieter Jacob. *Spreekwoordenboek der Nederlandsche Taal.* 3 vols. Utrecht: Kenink, 1858–1870; rpt. Amsterdam: Van Hoeve, 1980.

Hazlitt, W. Carew. *English Proverbs and Proverbial Phrases.* London: Reeves and Turner, 1869; rpt. Detroit: Gale Research Co., 1969.

Henderson, Alfred. *Latin Proverbs and Quotations with Translations and Parallel Passages.* London: Sampson Low, 1869.

Hiemer, Ernst. *Der Jude im Sprichwort der Völker.* Nürnberg: Der Stürmer Buchverlag, 1942 (dangerous anti-Semitic collection).

Hines, Donald M. *Frontier Folksay. Proverbial Lore of the Inland Pacific Northwest Frontier.* Norwood, Pa.: Norwood Editions, 1977.

Hirsch, E. D., Joseph Kett, and James Trefil. *The Dictionary of Cultural Literacy: What Every American Needs to Know.* Boston: Houghton Mifflin Co., 1988 ("Proverbs" on pp. 46–57).

Howell, James. *Paroimiografia. Proverbs, or, Old Sayed Savves & Adages in English (or the Saxon Toung), Italian, French and Spanish, whereunto the British, for their great Antiquity, and Weight are added.* London: J.G., 1659.

Hughes, Muriel J. "Vermont Proverbs and Proverbial Sayings." *Vermont History,* 28 (1960), 113–142 and 200–230.

Jellinek, Ad. *Der jüdische Stamm in nichtjüdischen Sprichwörtern.* 2 vols. Wien: Löwy's Buchhandlung, 1881 and 1882.

Keitges, John. *Proverbs and Quotations for School and Home.* Chicago: A. Flanagan, 1905.

Kelly, Walter K. *A Collection of the Proverbs of all Nations. Compared, Explained, and Illustrated.* Andover, Mass.: Warren F. Draper, 1869.

Körte, Wilhelm. *Die Sprichwörter und sprichwörtlichen Redensarten der Deutschen.* Leipzig: F. A. Brockhaus, 1837; rpt. Hildesheim: Georg Olms, 1974.

Kremer, Edmund Philipp. *German Proverbs and Proverbial Phrases with Their English Counterparts.* Stanford, Calif.: Stanford University Press, 1955.

Kuusi, Matti et al. *Proverbia septentrionalia. 900 Balto-Finnic Proverb Types with Russian, Baltic, German and Scandinavian Parallels.* Helsinki: Suomalainen Tiedeakatemia, 1985.

Landmann, Salcia. *Jüdische Anekdoten und Sprichwörter.* München: Deutscher Taschenbuchverlag, 1965 (7th ed. 1974).

Lawson, James Gilchrist. *The World's Best Proverbs and Maxims.* New York: Grosset & Dunlap, 1926.

Lean, Vincent Stuckey. *Lean's Collectanea. Collections of Proverbs (English and Foreign), Folklore, and Superstitions, also Compilations Towards Dictionaries of Proverbial Phrases and Words, Old and Disused.* Ed. by T. W. Williams. 4 vols. Bristol/England: J. W. Arrowsmith, 1902–1904; rpt. Detroit: Gale Research Co., 1969.

Loewe, Heinrich. *Deutsch-Englische Phraseologie in systematischer Ordnung.* Berlin-Schöneberg: Langenscheidt, 1877.

Makkai, Adam. *Handbook of Commonly Used American Idioms.* Woodbury, N.Y.: Barron's Educational Series, 1984.

Marvin, Dwight Edwards. *Curiosities in Proverbs. A Collection of Unusual Adages, Maxims, Aphorisms, Phrases and Other Dicta from Many Lands.* New York: G. P. Putnam's Sons, 1916; rpt. Darby, Pa.: Folcroft Library Editions, 1980.

McKenzie, E. C. *Mac's Giant Book of Quips & Quotes.* Grand Rapids, Mich.: Baker Book House, 1980.

Mencken, H. L. *A New Dictionary of Quotations on Historical Principles from Ancient and Modern Sources.* New York: Alfred A. Knopf, 1942 (2nd ed. 1960).

Mieder, Wolfgang. *Antisprichwörter.* 3 vols. Wiesbaden: Verlag für deutsche Sprache, 1982; Wiesbaden: Gesellschaft für deutsche Sprache, 1985; Wiesbaden: Quelle & Meyer, 1989.

Mieder, Wolfgang. *Talk Less and Say More: Vermont Proverbs.* Shelburne, Vt.: The New England Press, 1986.

Mieder, Wolfgang. *The Prentice-Hall Encyclopedia of World Proverbs.* Englewood Cliffs, N.J.: Prentice-Hall, 1986.

Mieder, Wolfgang. *As Sweet as Apple Cider: Vermont Expressions.* Shelburne, Vt.: The New England Press, 1988.

Mieder, Wolfgang. *English Proverbs.* Stuttgart: Philipp Reclam, 1988.

Mieder, Wolfgang. *Yankee Wisdom: New England Proverbs.* Shelburne, Vt.: The New England Press, 1989.

Mieder, Wolfgang. *Not By Bread Alone: Proverbs of the Bible.* Shelburne, Vt.: The New England Press, 1990.

Mieder, Wolfgang. *English Expressions.* Stuttgart: Philipp Reclam, 1992.

Mieder, Wolfgang, Stewart Kingsbury, and Kelsie Harder (eds.). *A Dictionary of American Proverbs.* New York: Oxford University Press, 1992.

Otto, August. *Die Sprichwörter und sprichwörtlichen Redensarten der Römer.* Leipzig: Teubner, 1890; rpt. Hildesheim: Georg Olms, 1971.

Paczolay, Gyula. *A Comparative Dictionary of Hungarian, Estonian, German, English, Finnish and Latin Proverbs with an Appendix in Cheremis and Zyryan.* Veszprém: VEAB, 1987.

Partridge, Eric. *A Dictionary of Slang and Unconventional English.* New York: Macmillan, 1937 (7th ed. 1970).

Partridge, Eric. *A Dictionary of Catch Phrases.* New York: Stein and Day, 1977.

Permiakov, Grigorii L'vovich. *300 obshcheupotrebitel'nykh russkikh poslovits i pogovorok (dlia govoriashchikh na nemetskom iazyke).* Moskva: Russkii iazyk, 1985.

Permiakov, Grigorii L'vovich. *300 allgemeingebräuchliche russische Sprichwörter und sprichwörtliche Redensarten. Ein illustriertes Nachschlagewerk für Deutschsprechende.* Leipzig: VEB Verlag Enzyklopädie, 1985.

Permiakov, Grigorii L'vovich. *300 obshcheupotrebitel'nykh russkikh poslovits i pogovorok (dlia govoriashchikh na bolgarskom iazyke).* Sofiia: Narodna prosveta, 1986.

Ray, John. *A Compleat Collection of English Proverbs.* Cambridge: W. Morden, 1670; 4th ed. London: W. Ortidge, 1678.

Reinsberg, Düringsfeld, Otto von. *Internationale Titulaturen.* 2 vols. Leipzig: Hermann Fries, 1863; rpt. ed. by Wolfgang Mieder. Hildesheim: Georg Olms, 1992.

Ridout, Ronald, and Clifford Witting. *English Proverbs Explained.* London: Pan Books, 1967.

Roback, Abraham Aaron. *A Dictionary of International Slurs.* Cambridge, Mass.: Sci-Art Publishers, 1944; rpt. Waukesha, Wis.: Maledicta Press, 1979.

Rogers, James. *The Dictionary of Clichés.* New York: Facts on File Publications, 1985.

Röhrich, Lutz. *Lexikon der sprichwörtlichen Redensarten.* 2 Bde. Freiburg: Herder, 1973.

Rosten, Leo. *Infinite Riches. Gems from a Lifetime of Reading.* New York: McGraw-Hill, 1979.

Russell, Thomas Herbert (ed.). *The Sayings of Poor Richard: Wit, Wisdom and Humor of Benjamin Franklin in the Proverbs and Maxims of Poor Richard's Almanacks from 1733 to 1758.* Chicago: Veterans of Foreign Wars of the United States, 1926.

Safian, Louis A. *The Book of Updated Proverbs.* New York: Abelard-Schuman, 1967.

Schulze, Carl. *Die biblischen Sprichwörter der deutschen Sprache.* Göttingen: Vandenhoeck & Ruprecht, 1860; rpt. ed. by Wolfgang Mieder. Bern: Peter Lang, 1987.

Schwab, Julius. *Rassenpflege im Sprichwort. Eine volkstümliche Sammlung.* Leipzig: Alwin Fröhlich, 1937 (dangerous anti-Semitic collection).

Simpson, John A. *The Concise Oxford Dictionary of Proverbs.* Oxford: Oxford University Press, 1982.

Snapp, Emma Louise. "Proverbial Lore in Nebraska." *University of Nebraska Studies in Language, Literature and Criticism,* 13 (1933), 51–112.

Spalding, Keith. *An Historical Dictionary of German Figurative Usage.* Fascicles 1–49. Oxford: Blackwell, 1952–1991.

Stevenson, Burton. *The Macmillan (Home) Book of Proverbs, Maxims and Familiar Phrases.* New York: Macmillan, 1948.

Stoett, F. A. *Nederlandsche spreekwoorden, uitdrukken en gezegden.* Zutphen: Thieme, 1901 (4th ed. 1923).

Taylor, Archer, and Bartlett Jere Whiting. *A Dictionary of American Proverbs and Proverbial Phrases, 1820–1880.* Cambridge, Mass.: Harvard University Press, 1958.

Taylor, Ronald, and Walter Gottschalk. *A German-English Dictionary of Idioms.* München: Max Hueber, 1960 (4th ed. 1973).

Tendlau, Abraham Moses. *Sprichwörter und Redensarten deutschjüdischer Vorzeit.* Frankfurt am Main: J. Kauffmann, 1860; rpt. Hildesheim: Georg Olms, 1980; shortened ed. Berlin: Schocken Verlag, 1934.

Thiele, Ernst (ed.). *Luthers Sprichwörtersammlung.* Weimar: Hermann Böhlau, 1900.

Tilles, Sally Simon. *Der Jude im Citat und im Sprichwort. Ein Bädeker für Anti- und Philo-Semiten.* Berlin: Paul Heichen, 1892.

Tilley, Morris Palmer. *A Dictionary of the Proverbs in England in the Sixteenth and Seventeenth Centuries.* Ann Arbor: University of Michigan Press, 1950.

Tonn, Maryjane Hooper. *Proverbs to Live By.* Milwaukee, Wis.: Ideals Publishing, 1977.

Urdang, Laurence. *Longman Dictionary of English Idioms.* London: Longman, 1979.

Urdang, Laurence. "The Whole Ball of Wax" and Other Colloquial Phrases. What They Mean & How They Started. New York: Perigee Books, 1988.

Urdang, Laurence, and Nancy LaRoche. *Picturesque Expressions: A Thematic Dictionary.* Detroit: Gale Research Co., 1980; rpt. enlarged with the help of Walter W. Hunsinger. Detroit: Gale Research Co., 1985.

Urdang, Laurence, and Ceila Dame Robbins. *Slogans.* Detroit: Gale Research Co., 1984.

Voss, Karl. *Redensarten der englischen Sprache.* Frankfurt am Main: Ullstein, 1967 (2nd ed. 1975).

Walther, Hans. *Proverbia sententiaque latinitatis medii aevi. Lateinische Sprichwörter und Sentenzen des Mittelalters in alphabetischer Anordnung.* 9 vols. Göttingen: Vandenhoeck & Ruprecht, 1963–1986.

Wander, Karl Friedrich Wilhelm. *Deutsches Sprichwörter-Lexikon.* 5 vols. Leipzig: F. A. Brockhaus, 1867–1880; rpt. Darmstadt: Wissenschaftliche Buchgesellschaft, 1964.

Whiting, Bartlett Jere. "Proverbs and Proverbial Sayings [from North Carolina]." In *The Frank C. Brown Collection of North Carolina Folklore,* ed. Newman Ivey White. Durham, N.C.: Duke University Press, 1952, vol. 1, pp. 329–501.

Whiting, Bartlett Jere. *Proverbs, Sentences, and Proverbial Phrases from English Writings Mainly Before 1500.* Cambridge: Harvard University Press, 1968.

Whiting, Bartlett Jere. *Early American Proverbs and Proverbial Phrases.* Cambridge: Harvard University Press, 1977.

Whiting, Bartlett Jere. *Modern Proverbs and Proverbial Sayings.* Cambridge: Harvard University Press, 1989.

Wilson, F. P. *The Oxford Dictionary of English Proverbs.* Oxford: Clarendon Press, 1970.

Studies on the Proverb

Albig, William. "Proverbs and Social Control." *Sociology and Social Research,* 15 (1931), 527–535.

Anonymous. "The Influence of Proverbs." *The New York Times* (April 29, 1877), p. 6, cols. 5–6.

Anonymous. "Proverbs as Literature." *The Living Age,* 226 (September 22, 1900), 785–787.

Anonymous. "Twilight of the Proverbs." *The New York Times* (May 3, 1930), p. 18, col. 6.

Anonymous. "Can Anybody Compose a Proverb?' *The New York Times* (November 12, 1961), sect. IV, p. 8, col. 3.

Anonymous. "The Wild Flowers of Thought." *Time* (March 14, 1969), pp. 74–75.

Arora, Shirley L. "The Perception of Proverbiality." *Proverbium: Yearbook of International Proverb Scholarship*, 1 (1984), 1–38.

Arora, Shirley L. "Weather Proverbs: Some 'Folk' Views." *Proverbium: Yearbook of International Proverb Scholarship*, 8 (1991), 1–17.

Bain, Read. "Verbal Stereotypes and Social Control." *Sociology and Social Research*, 23 (1939), 431–446.

Barker, Addison. " 'Good Fences Make Good Neighbors'." *Journal of American Folklore*, 64 (1951), 421.

Barley, Nigel. "A Structural Approach to the Proverb and Maxim with Special Reference to the Anglo-Saxon Corpus." *Proverbium*, no. 20 (1972), 737–750.

Barley, Nigel. " 'The Proverb' and Related Problems of Genre-Definition." *Proverbium*, no. 23 (1974), 880–884.

Barulin, A. "Russkii paremiologicheskii minimum i ego rol' prepodavanii russkogo iazyka." In *Paremiologicheskie issledovaniia*, ed. by Grigorii L'vovich Permiakov. Moskva: Nauka, 1984, pp. 264–265.

Bebermeyer, Renate. "Ärzte im Spiegel des Sprichworts." *Sprachspiegel*, 34 (1978), 131–138.

Bergmann, Karl. "Das deutsche Sprichwort als Künder völkischen Gedankengutes." *Volk und Scholle*, 12 (1934), 325–328 (all of the following publications by Bergmann are based on Nazi doctrine).

Bergmann, Karl. "Deutsche Heimatliebe und Wandersehnsucht in Sprache und Sprichwort." *Zeitschrift für Deutschkunde*, 50 (1936), 337–343.

Bergmann, Karl. "Lebendige Rassenhygiene im deutschen Sprichwort." *Volk und Rasse*, 11 (1936), 296–297.

Bergmann, Karl. "Völkisches Gedankengut in deutschen Sprichwörtern." *Zeitschrift für deutsche Bildung*, 12 (1936), 363–373.

Berneker, Erich. "Das russische Volk in seinen Sprichwörtern." *Zeitschrift des Vereins für Volkskunde*, 14 (1904), 75–87 and 179–191.

Blehr, Otto. "What Is a Proverb?" *Fabula*, 14 (1973), 243–246.

Blümmer, Hugo. *Der bildliche Ausdruck in den Reden des Fürsten Bismarck.* Leipzig: S. Hirzel, 1891 (proverbs esp. pp. 182–186).

Bock, J. Kathryn, and William F. Brewer. "Comprehension and Memory of the Literal and Figurative Meaning of Proverbs." *Journal of Psycholinguistic Research*, 9 (1980), 59–72.

Bond, Donald. "English Legal Proverbs." *Publications of the Modern Language Association*, 51 (1936), 921–935.

Brenner, Clarence D. *The French Dramatic Proverb.* Berkeley, Calif.: Privately printed, 1977.

Bronner, Simon J. "[Seeing is Believing] . . . but 'Feeling's the Truth'." *Tennessee Folklore Society Bulletin*, 48, no. 4 (1982), 117–124.

Bronner, Simon J. "The Haptic Experience of Culture ['Seeing is Believing, but Feeling's the Truth']." *Anthropos*, 77 (1982), 351–362.

Browne, Ray B. " 'The Wisdom of Many': Proverbs and Proverbial Expressions." In *Our Living Traditions. An Introduction to American Folklore*, ed. by Tristram Potter Coffin. New York: Basic Books, 1968, pp. 192–203.

Bryant, Margaret M. *Proverbs and How to Collect Them.* Greensboro, N.C.: American Dialect Society, 1945.

Burke, Kenneth. "Literature as Equipment for Living." In K. Burke. *The Philosophy of Literary Form: Studies in Symbolic Action.* Baton Rouge: Louisiana University Press, 1941, pp. 253–262.

Bushui, Anatolii Mikhailovich. "Paremiologicheskii minimum po nemetskomu iazyku dlia srednei shkoly." In *Problemy metodiki prepodavaniia razlichnykh distsiplin v shkole i vuze*, ed. by Kh. M. Ikramova. Samarkand: Samarkandskii gosudarstvennyi universitet, 1979, pp. 4–28.

Collinson, W. E. "Some German and English Idioms, with a Note on the Definition of the Term 'Idiom'." *German Life and Letters*, 11 (1957–1958), 266–269.

Coo, Jozef de. "Twaalf spreuken op borden van Pieter Bruegel de Oude." *Bulletin des Musées royaux des Beaux-Arts*, 14 (1965), 83–104.

Corbett, Scott. "Our Toothless Old Saws." *Atlantic Monthly*, 193 (March 1954), 92.

Cornette, James C. *Proverbs and Proverbial Expressions in the German Works of Luther*. Diss. University of North Carolina, 1942.

Cöster, Oskar. "Maulschellen für den 'Volksmund'. Epigramme zur Dialektik des Sprichworts." In *Projekt Deutschunterricht 12. Kommunikationsanalyse II—Sprachkritik*, ed. by Bodo Lecke. Stuttgart: Metzler, 1977, pp. 131–147 and 168*–175*.

Cram, David. "The Linguistic Status of the Proverb." *Cahiers de Lexicologie*, 43 (1983), 53–71.

Cram, David. "Argumentum ad lunam: On the Folk Fallacy and the Nature of the Proverb." *Proverbium: Yearbook of International Proverb Scholarship*, 3 (1986), 9–31.

Daniels, Karlheinz. " 'Idiomatische Kompetenz' in der Zielsprache Deutsch. Voraussetzungen, Möglichkeiten, Folgerungen." *Wirkendes Wort*, 35 (1985), 145–157.

Doyle, Charles Clay. "On Some Paremiological Verses." *Proverbium*, no. 25 (1975), 979–982.

Dundes, Alan. " 'Seeing Is Believing'." *Natural History*, no. 5 (May 1972), 8–14 and 86; also in A. Dundes. *Interpreting Folklore*. Bloomington: Indiana University Press, 1980, pp. 86–92.

Dundes, Alan. "On the Structure of the Proverb." *Proverbium*, no. 25 (1975), 961–973; also in Wolfgang Mieder and A. Dundes (eds.). *The Wisdom of Many. Essays on the Proverb*. New York: Garland Publishing, 1981, pp. 43–64.

Dundes, Alan. "Slurs International: Folk Comparisons of Ethnicity and National Character." *Southern Folklore Quarterly*, 39 (1975), 15–38.

Dundes, Alan. *Life Is Like a Chicken Coop Ladder. A Portrait of German Culture Through Folklore*. New York: Columbia University Press, 1984.

Dundes, Alan. "On Whether Weather 'Proverbs' are Proverbs." *Proverbium: Yearbook of International Proverb Scholarship*, 1 (1984), 39–46; also in A. Dundes. *Folklore Matters*. Knoxville: University of Tennessee Press, 1989, pp. 92–97.

Dundes, Alan, and Claudia A. Stibbe. *The Art of Mixing Metaphors. A Folkloristic Interpretation of the "Netherlandish Proverbs" by Pieter Bruegel the Elder*. Helsinki: Suomalainen Tiedeakatemia, 1981.

Elmquist, Russell A. "English Medical Proverbs." *Modern Philology*, 32 (1934–1935), 75–84.

Fraenger, Wilhelm. *Der Bauern-Bruegel und das deutsche Sprichwort*. Erlenbach-Zürich: Eugen Rentsch, 1923.

Frank, Grace, and Dorothy Miner. *Proverbes en rimes. Text and Illustrations of the Fifteenth Century from a French Manuscript in the Walters Art Gallery, Baltimore*. Baltimore, Md.: The Johns Hopkins Press, 1937.

Gallacher, Stuart A. " 'Stuff a Cold and Starve a Fever'." *Bulletin of the History of Medicine*, 11 (1942), 576–581.

Gallacher, Stuart A. "Franklin's Way to Wealth: A Florilegium of Proverbs and Wise Sayings." *Journal of English and Germanic Philology*, 48 (1949), 229–251.

Gallacher, Stuart A. "Frauenlob's Bits of Wisdom: Fruits of His Environment." In *Middle Ages, Reformation, Volkskunde. Festschrift for John G. Kunstmann*, no editor given. Chapel Hill: University of North Carolina Press, 1959, pp. 45–58.

Garrison, F. H. "Medical Proverbs, Aphorisms and Epigrams." *Bulletin of the New York Academy of Medicine*, 4 (1928), 979–1005.

Goodwin, Paul D., and Joseph W. Wenzel. "Proverbs and Practical Reasoning: A Study in Socio-Logic." *Quarterly Journal of Speech*, 65 (1979), 289–302; also in Wolfgang Mieder and Alan Dundes (eds.). *The Wisdom of Many. Essays on the Proverb.* New York: Garland Publishing, 1981, pp. 140–160.

Grambo, Ronald. "Paremiological Aspects." *Folklore Forum,* 5 (1972), 100–105.

Grauls, Jan. *Volkstaal en volksleven in het werk van Pieter Bruegel.* Antwerpen: N. V. Standaard-Boekhandel, 1957.

Gruttmann, Felicitas. *Ein Beitrag zur Kenntnis der Volksmedizin in Sprichwörtern, Redensarten und Heilsegen des englischen Volkes, mit besonderer Berücksichtigung der Zahnheilkunde.* Greifswald: L. Bamberg, 1939.

Grzybek, Peter. "Foundations of Semiotic Proverb Study." *Proverbium: Yearbook of International Proverb Scholarship,* 4 (1987), 39–85.

Grzybek, Peter, and Wolfgang Eismann (eds.). *Semiotische Studien zum Sprichwort. Simple Forms Reconsidered I.* Tübingen: Gunter Narr, 1984.

Hasan-Rokem, Galit. *Proverbs in Israeli Folk Narratives: A Structural Semantic Analysis.* Helsinki: Suomalainen Tiedeakatemia, 1982.

Hasan-Rokem, Galit. "The Pragmatics of Proverbs: How the Proverb Gets Its Meaning." In *Exceptional Language and Linguistics,* ed. by Loraine K. Obler and Lise Menn. New York: Academic Press, 1982, pp. 169–173.

Hattemer, K., and E. K. Scheuch. *Sprichwörter. Einstellung und Verwendung.* Düsseldorf: Intermarket. Gesellschaft für internationale Markt- und Meinungsforschung, 1983.

Heger, Helene. *Das deutsche Idealbild im Sprichwortschatz des Volkes.* Diss. Wien, 1939 (emphasizing Nazi ideology).

Helm, Karl. "Bauernregeln." *Hessische Blätter für Volkskunde,* 38 (1939), 114–132.

Higbee, Kenneth L., and Richard J. Millard. "Visual Imagery and Familiarity Ratings for 203 Sayings." *American Journal of Psychology,* 96 (1983), 211–222.

Hogg, R. D. "Proverbs." *Secretariat News,* 14 (1960), 5–7.

Holbek, Bengt. "Proverb Style." *Proverbium,* no. 15 (1970), 470–472.

Honeck, Richard P., and Clare T. Kibler. "The Role of Imagery, Analogy, and Instantiation in Proverb Comprehension." *Journal of Psycholinguistic Research,* 13 (1984), 393–414.

Hulme, F. Edward. *Proverb Lore; Being a Historical Study of the Similarities, Contrasts, Topics, Meanings, and Other Facets of Proverbs, Truisms, and Pithy Sayings, as Expressed by the Peoples of Many Lands and Times.* London: Elliot Stock, 1902; rpt. Detroit: Gale Research Co., 1968.

Jente, Richard. " 'A Woman Conceals What She Knows Not'." *Modern Language Notes,* 41 (1926), 253–254.

Jente, Richard. " 'Morgenstunde hat Gold im Munde'." *Publications of the Modern Language Association,* 42 (1927), 865–872.

Jente, Richard. "The American Proverb." *American Speech,* 7 (1931–1932), 342–348.

Jente, Richard. "The Untilled Field of Proverbs." In *Studies in Language and Literature,* ed. by George R. Coffman. Chapel Hill: University of North Carolina Press, 1945, pp. 112–119.

Kanfer, Stefan. "Proverbs or Aphorisms?" *Time* (July 11, 1983), 74.

Kanyo, Zoltan. *Sprichwörter—Analyse einer Einfachen Form. Ein Beitrag zur generativen Poetik.* The Hague: Mouton, 1981.

Keene, H. G. "Conflicts of Experience [in Proverbs]." *The Living Age,* 185 (May 24, 1890), 483–486.

Kemper, Susan. "Comprehension and Interpretation of Proverbs." *Journal of Psycholinguistic Research,* 10 (1981), 179–198.

Kenner, Hugh. "Wisdom of the Tribe. Why Proverbs Are Better than Aphorisms." *Harper's,* 266, no. 1596 (May 6, 1983), 84–86.

Kindstrand, Jan Fredrik. "The Greek Concept of Proverbs." *Eranos,* 76 (1978), 71–85.

Kingsbury, Stewart A. "On Handling 250,000+ Citation Slips for American Dialect Society

(ADS) Proverb Research." *Proverbium: Yearbook of International Proverb Scholarship*, 1 (1984), 195–205.

Kirshenblatt-Gimblett, Barbara. "Toward a Theory of Proverb Meaning." *Proverbium*, no. 22 (1973), 821–827; also in Wolfgang Mieder and Alan Dundes (eds.). *The Wisdom of Many. Essays on the Proverb*. New York: Garland Publishing, 1981, pp. 111–121.

Kramp, Willy. "Sind Sprichwörter wahr?" *Die Furche*, 23 (1937), 135–140.

Krikmann, Arvo. *On Denotative Indefiniteness of Proverbs*. Tallinn: Academy of Sciences of the Estonian SSR, Institute of Language and Literature, 1974; also in *Proverbium: Yearbook of International Proverb Scholarship*, 1 (1984), 47–91.

Krikmann, Arvo. *Some Additional Aspects of Semantic Indefiniteness of Proverbs*. Tallinn: Academy of Sciences of the Estonian SSR, Institute of Language and Literature, 1974; also in *Proverbium: Yearbook of International Proverb Scholarship*, 2 (1985), 58–85.

Kuusi, Matti. *Parömiologische Betrachtungen*. Helsinki: Suomalainen Tiedeakatemia, 1957.

Kuusi, Matti. *Towards an International Type-System of Proverbs*. Helsinki: Suomalainen Tiedeakatemia, 1972; also in *Proverbium*, no. 19 (1972), 699–736.

Kuusi, Matti. "Nachtrag [zu Permiakovs 75 sprichwörtlichen Vergleichen]." *Proverbium*, no. 25 (1975), 975–978.

Kuusi, Matti. "Zur Frequenzanalyse." *Proverbium Paratum*, no. 2 (1981), 119–120.

Lane, Earl. "A Proverbial Quest that Intrigues Scholars." *Newsday* (June 27, 1975), part II, 4A–5A. Rpt. numerous times with different titles, for example, as "In the Proverbial Stew." *Boston Globe* (July 6, 1975), 1B; "Probing Perennial Proverbs." *The Montreal Star* (July 19, 1975), 1C; and "Hot on the Trail of a Proverb." *San Francisco Sunday Examiner and Chronicle* (August 10, 1975), 5.

La Rosa, Ralph Charles. *Emerson's Proverbial Rhetoric: 1818–1838*. Diss. University of Wisconsin, 1969.

Lebeer, Louis. " 'De blauwe huyck'." *Gentsche Bijdragen tot de Kunstgeschiedenes*, 6 (1939–1940), 161–229.

Levin, Isidor. "Überlegungen zur demoskopischen Parömiologie." *Proverbium*, no. 11 (1968), 289–293; and no. 13 (1969), 361–366.

Lieber, Michael D. "Analogic Ambiguity: A Paradox of Proverb Usage." *Journal of American Folklore*, 97 (1984), 423–441.

Linder, Gisela. *Zahnheilkundliches in deutschen Sprichwörtern und Redensarten*. Diss. Köln, 1938.

Loomis, C. Grant. "Traditional American Wordplay: The Epigram and Perverted Proverbs." *Western Folklore*, 8 (1949), 348–357.

Loux, Françoise, and Philippe Richard. *Sagesses du corps. La santé et la maladie dans les proverbes français*. Paris: G.-P. Maisonneuve et Larose, 1978.

Lucas, F. L. "The Art of Proverbs." *Holiday*, 38 (September 1965), 8 and 10–13.

Mackensen, Lutz. "Deutschland in niederländischen Sprichwörtern und Redensarten." *Oostvlaamsche Zanten*, 16 (1941), 131–156.

Mahler, Alarich. *Bäuerliches Bodenrecht in Rechtssprichwörtern*. Berlin: Engelhard, 1943.

Marzolf, Stanley. "Common Sayings and 16PF [Personality Factor] Traits." *Journal of Clinical Psychology*, 30 (1974), 202–204.

Maw, Wallace H. and Ethel. "Contrasting Proverbs as a Measure of Attitudes of College Students Toward Curiosity-Related Behaviors." *Psychological Reports*, 37 (1975), 1085–1086.

Meister, Charles W. "Franklin as a Proverb Stylist." *American Literature*, 24 (1952–1953), 157–166.

Meyer, Maurits de. " 'De Blauwe Huyck' van Jan van Doetinchem, 1577." *Volkskunde*, 71 (1970), 334–343. Also in French translation as " 'De Blauwe Huyck', La Cape Bleue de Jean van Doetinchem, datée 1577." *Proverbium*, no. 16 (1971), 564–575.

Meyn, Ludwig. "Germanische Wesensart in altisländischen Sprichwörtern und Sprüchen." *Zeitschrift für deutsche Bildung*, 11 (1935), 566–574.

Mieder, Barbara and Wolfgang. "Tradition and Innovation: Proverbs in Advertising." *Journal of Popular Culture*, 11 (1977), 308–319; also in W. Mieder and Alan Dundes (eds.). *The Wisdom of Many. Essays on the Proverb*. New York: Garland Publishing, 1981, pp. 309–322.

Mieder, Wolfgang. " 'Behold the Proverbs of a People': A Florilegium of Proverbs in Carl Sandburg's Poem 'Good Morning, America'." *Southern Folklore Quarterly*, 35 (1971), 160–168.

Mieder, Wolfgang. *Das Sprichwort in unserer Zeit*. Frauenfeld: Huber, 1975.

Mieder, Wolfgang (ed.). *Ergebnisse der Sprichwörterforschung*. Bern: Peter Lang, 1978.

Mieder, Wolfgang. "Proverbial Slogans are the Name of the Game." *Kentucky Folklore Record*, 24 (1978), 49–53.

Mieder, Wolfgang. "Rund um das Sprichwort 'Morgenstunde hat Gold im Munde'." *Muttersprache*, 88 (1978), 378–385.

Mieder, Wolfgang. "The Use of Proverbs in Psychological Testing." *Journal of the Folklore Institute*, 15 (1978), 45–55.

Mieder, Wolfgang. *Deutsche Sprichwörter und Redensarten*. Stuttgart: Philipp Reclam, 1979.

Mieder, Wolfgang. "Karl Kraus und der sprichwörtliche Aphorismus." *Muttersprache*, 89 (1979), 97–115.

Mieder, Wolfgang. "A Samplar of Anglo-American Proverb Poetry." *Folklore Forum*, 13 (1980), 39–53.

Mieder, Wolfgang. "Moderne deutsche Sprichwortgedichte." *Fabula*, 21 (1980), 247–260.

Mieder, Wolfgang. "Traditional and Innovative Proverb Use in Lyric Poetry." *Proverbium Paratum*, no. 1 (1980), 16–27.

Mieder, Wolfgang. " 'Der Apfel fällt weit von Deutschland'. Zur amerikanischen Entlehnung eines deutschen Sprichwortes." *Der Sprachdienst*, 25 (1981), 89–93.

Mieder, Wolfgang. " 'Eine Frau ohne Mann ist wie ein Fisch ohne Velo'!" *Sprachspiegel*, 38 (1982), 141–142.

Mieder, Wolfgang. "Sexual Content of German Wellerisms." *Maledicta*, 6 (1982), 215–223.

Mieder, Wolfgang. *Deutsche Sprichwörter in Literatur, Politik, Presse und Werbung*. Hamburg: Helmut Buske, 1983.

Mieder, Wolfgang. "Sprichwörter unterm Hakenkreuz." *Muttersprache*, 93 (1983), 1–30.

Mieder, Wolfgang. " 'Wine, Women and Song': From Martin Luther to American T-Shirts." *Kentucky Folklore Record*, 29 (1983), 89–101.

Mieder, Wolfgang. " 'Wer nicht liebt Wein, Weib und Gesang, der bleibt ein Narr sein Leben lang'. Zur Herkunft, Überlieferung und Verwendung eines angeblichen Luther-Spruches." *Muttersprache*, 94 (1983–1984), 68–103.

Mieder, Wolfgang. " 'Wine, Women and Song': Zur anglo-amerikanischen Überlieferung eines angeblichen Lutherspruches." *Germanisch-Romanische Monatsschrift*, 65, new series 34 (1984), 385–403.

Mieder, Wolfgang. "A Proverb a Day Keeps no Chauvinism Away." *Proverbium: Yearbook of International Proverb Scholarship*, 2 (1985), 273–277.

Mieder, Wolfgang. "Neues zur demoskopischen Sprichwörterkunde." *Proverbium: Yearbook of International Proverb Scholarship*, 2 (1985), 307–328.

Mieder, Wolfgang. *Sprichwort, Redensart, Zitat. Tradierte Formelsprache in der Moderne*. Bern: Peter Lang, 1985.

Mieder, Wolfgang. "History and Interpretation of a Proverb about Human Nature: 'Big Fish Eat Little Fish'." In W. Mieder. *Tradition and Innovation in Folk Literature*. Hanover, N.H.: University Press of New England, 1987, pp. 178–228 and pp. 259–268 (notes).

Mieder, Wolfgang. *Tradition and Innovation in Folk Literature*. Hanover, N.H.: University Press of New England, 1987.

Mieder, Wolfgang. *American Proverbs: A Study of Texts and Contexts*. Bern: Peter Lang, 1989.

Mieder, Wolfgang. " 'Ein Bild sagt mehr als tausend Worte'. Ursprung und Überlieferung eines amerikanischen Lehnsprichworts." *Proverbium: Yearbook of International Proverb Scholarship*, 6 (1989), 25–37.

Mieder, Wolfgang. "Moderne Sprichwörterforschung zwischen Mündlichkeit und Schriftlichkeit." In *Volksdichtung zwischen Mündlichkeit und Schriftlichkeit*, ed. by Lutz Röhrich and Erika Lindig. Tübingen: Gunter Narr, 1989, pp. 187–208.

Mieder, Wolfgang. " 'Das Kind mit dem Bade ausschütten': Ursprung, Überlieferung und Verwendung einer deutschen Redensart." *Muttersprache*, 102 (1992), in press.

Mieder, Wolfgang, and George B. Bryan. " 'Zum Tango gehören zwei'." *Der Sprachdienst*, 27 (1983), 100–102.

Mieder, Wolfgang, and Alan Dundes (eds.). *The Wisdom of Many. Essays on the Proverb*. New York: Garland Publishing, 1981.

Militz, Hans-Manfred. "Vom Arzt und seinen Kranken: Der Untergang eines phraseologischen Bereichs." *Sprachpflege*, 30 (1981), 134–135.

Miller, Edd, and Jesse J. Villarreal. "The Use of Clichés by Four Contemporary Speakers [Winston Churchill, Anthony Eden, Franklin Roosevelt, and Henry Wallace]." *Quarterly Journal of Speech*, 31 (1945), 151–155.

Milner, George B. "De l'armature des locutions proverbiales: Essai de taxonomie sémantique." *L'Homme*, 9 (1969), 49–70.

Milner, George B. "What Is a Proverb?" *New Society*, 332 (February 6, 1969), 199–202.

Milner, George B. "The Quartered Shield: Outline of a Semantic Taxonomy." In *Social Anthropology and Language*, ed. by Edson Ardener. London: Tavistock, 1971, pp. 243–269.

Monteiro, George. "Proverbs in the Re-Making." *Western Folklore*, 27 (1968), 128.

Monteiro, George. " 'Good Fences Make Good Neighbors': A Proverb and a Poem." *Revista de Etnografia*, 16, no. 31 (1972), 83–88.

Morozova, L. A. "Upotreblenie V. I. Leninym poslovits." *Russkaia rech'*, no. 2 (1979), 10–14.

Muller, Henri F. "The French Seen Through Their Proverbs and Proverbial Expressions." *French Review*, 17 (1943–1944), 4–8.

Naumann, Hans. *Germanische Spruchweisheit*. Jena: Diederichs, 1935.

Newcomb, Robert. *The Sources of Benjamin Franklin's Sayings of Poor Richard*. Diss. University of Maryland, 1957.

Nierenberg, Jess. "Proverbs in Graffitti. Taunting Traditional Wisdom." *Maledicta*, 7 (1983), 41–58.

Norrick, Neal R. *How Proverbs Mean. Semantic Studies in English Proverbs*. Amsterdam: Mouton, 1985.

Parker, A. A. *The Humour of Spanish Proverbs*. London: The Hispanic & Luso-Brazilian Councils, 1963; also in Wolfgang Mieder and Alan Dundes (eds.). *The Wisdom of Many. Essays on the Proverb*. New York: Garland Publishing, 1981, pp. 257–274.

Pasamanick, Judy. "Watched Pots Do Boil: Proverb Interpretation through Contextual Illustration." *Proverbium: Yearbook of International Proverb Scholarship*, 2 (1985), 145–183.

Pastor, Eilert. "Das deutsche Sprichwort." *Die Heimat*, 20, nos. 1–2 (1941), 3–7.

Pei, Mario. "Parallel Proverbs." *Saturday Review*, 47 (May 2, 1964), 16–17 and 53.

Penn, Nolan F., Teresa C. Jacob, and Malrie Brown. "Familiarity with Proverbs and Performance of a Black Population on Gorham's Proverbs Test." *Perceptual and Motor Skills*, 66 (1988), 847–854.

Permiakov, Grigorii L'vovich. *Ot pogovorki do skazki (Zametki po obshchei teorii klishe)*. Moskva: Nauka, 1970. Also published in English as *From Proverb to Folk-Tale. Notes on the General Theory of Cliché*. Translated by Y. N. Filippov. Moscow: Nauka, 1979.

Permiakov, Grigorii L'vovich. *Paremiologicheskie eksperiment. Materialy dlia paremiologicheskogo minimuma*. Moskva: Nauka, 1971.

Permiakov, Grigorii L'vovich. "On the Paremiological Level and Paremiological Minimum of Language." *Proverbium*, no. 22 (1973), 862–863.

Permiakov, Grigorii L'vovich. "75 naibolee upotrebitel'nykh russkikh sravnimel'nykh oboromov." *Proverbium*, no. 25 (1975), 974–975.

Permiakov, Grigorii L'vovich. "K voprosu o russkom paremiologicheskom minimume." In *Slovari i lingvostranovedenie*, ed. by E. M. Vereshchagina. Moskva: Russkii iazyk, 1982, pp. 131–137. Translated into English by Kevin J. McKenna as "On the Question of a Russian Paremiological Minimum." *Proverbium: Yearbook of International Proverb Scholarship*, 6 (1989), 91–102.

Permiakov, Grigorii L'vovich (ed.). *Paremiologicheskie issledovaniia. Sbornik statei.* Moskva: Nauka, 1984.

Permiakov, Grigorii L'vovich. *Osnovy strukturnoi paremiologii*, ed. by G. L. Kapchits. Moskva: Nauka, 1988.

Petsch, Robert. *Spruchdichtung des Volkes. Vor- und Frühformen der Volksdichtung.* Halle: Max Niemeyer, 1938.

Petsch, Robert. " 'Geflügelte Worte' und Verwandtes. Aus der Formenwelt der menschlichen Rede." In R. Petsch. *Deutsche Literaturwissenschaft. Aufsätze zur Begründung der Methode.* Berlin: Emil Ebering, 1940, pp. 230–238.

Priebe, Richard. "The Horses of Speech: A Structural Analysis of the Proverb." *Folklore Annual of the University [of Texas] Folklore Association*, no. 3 (1971), 26–32.

Rahn, Fritz. "Die Redensart. Ein Stück Sprachkunde." *Die Volksschule*, 26 (1931), 970–980. Also published with slight changes as "Die Redensart—ein Kapitel Sprachkunde." *Deutschunterricht*, 1, no. 4 (1948–1949), 22–38.

Raymond, Joseph B. *Attitudes and Cultural Patterns in Spanish Proverbs.* Diss. Columbia University, 1951.

Raymond, Joseph B. "Tensions in Proverbs: More Light on International Understanding." *Western Folklore*, 15 (1956), 153–158; also in Wolfgang Mieder and Alan Dundes (eds.). *The Wisdom of Many. Essays on the Proverb.* New York: Garland Publishing, 1981, pp. 300–308.

Redlich, Friedrich. "Sprichwort." In *Deutsche Volksdichtung. Eine Einführung*, ed. by Hermann Strobach. Leipzig: Reclam, 1979, pp. 221–240 and pp. 392–393 (notes).

Rendall, Vernon. "Proverbs and Popular Similes." *The Saturday Review*, 148 (October 19, 1929), 443.

Reynolds, Horace. "A Proverb in the Hand—Is Often Worth a Thousand Words. Herewith an Examination of a Much Used but Seldom Analyzed Form of Homely Literature." *New York Times Magazine* (September 13, 1959), 74.

Robinson, F. N. "Irish Proverbs and Irish National Character." *Modern Philology*, 43 (1945), 1–10; also in Wolfgang Mieder and Alan Dundes (eds.). *The Wisdom of Many. Essays on the Proverb.* New York: Garland Publishing, 1981, pp. 284–299.

Roh, Franz. *Pieter Bruegel d. Ä. "Die niederländischen Sprichwörter."* Stuttgart: Philipp Reclam, 1960 (2nd ed. 1967).

Röhrich, Lutz. "Die Bildwelt von Sprichwort und Redensart in der Sprache der politischen Karikatur." In *Kontakte und Grenzen: Probleme der Volks-, Kultur- und Sozialforschung. Festschrift für Gerhard Heilfurth*, ed. by Hans Friedrich Foltin. Göttingen: Otto Schwarz, 1969, pp. 175–207.

Röhrich, Lutz, and Wolfgang Mieder. *Sprichwort.* Stuttgart: Metzler, 1977.

Rothstein, Robert A. "The Poetics of Proverbs." In *Studies Presented to Professor Roman Jakobson by His Students*, ed. by Charles Gribble. Cambridge, Mass.: Slavica Publications, 1969, pp. 265–274.

Ruef, Hans. "Zusatzsprichwörter und das Problem des parömischen Minimums." In *Europhras 88. Phraséologie contrastive. Actes du colloque international Klingenthal-Strasbourg, 12–16 mai 1988*, ed. by Gertrud Gréciano. Strasbourg: Université des Sciences Humaines, 1989, pp. 379–385.

Salamone, Frank A. "The Arrow and the Bird: Proverbs in the Solution of Hausa Conjugal Conflicts." *Journal of Anthropological Research*, 32 (1976), 358–371.

Schellbach-Kopra, Ingrid. "Parömisches Minimum und Phraseodidaktik im finnisch-deutschen Bereich." In *Beiträge zur allgemeinen und germanistischen Phraseologieforschung*, ed. by Jarmo Korhonen. Oulu: Oulun Yliopisto, 1987, pp. 245–255.

Schiffer, Hartmann. "Rasse und Erbe im Sprichwort." *Neues Volk*, 8, no. 3 (March 1940), 25–27; no. 4 (April 1940), 27–28; and no. 5 (May 1940), 28 (based on Nazi ideology).

Schmidt-Hidding, Wolfgang. "Sprichwörtliche Redensarten. Abgrenzungen—Aufgaben der Forschung." *Rheinisches Jahrbuch für Volkskunde*, 7 (1956), 95–144; also in *Ergebnisse der Sprichwörterforschung*, ed. by Wolfgang Mieder. Bern: Peter Lang, 1978, pp. 27–65.

Schoeps, Hans-Joachim. "Völkerpsychologie im Sprichwort." In H.-J. Schoeps. *Ungeflügelte Worte. Was nicht im Büchmann stehen kann*. Berlin: Haude und Spener, 1971, pp. 162–171.

Schwer, Wilhelm. "Zur Soziologie des Sprichworts." *Bonner Mitteilungen*, 5 (1931), 8–14.

Segalen, Martine. "Le mariage, l'amour et les femmes dans les proverbes populaires français." *Ethnologie Française*, 5 (1975), 119–160; and 6 (1976), 33–88.

Seidl, Helmut A. "Health Proverbs in Britain and Bavaria. A Sampling of Parallels." In *Bavarica Anglica. A Cross-Cultural Miscellany Presented to Tom Fletcher*, ed. by Otto Hietsch. Bern: Peter Lang, 1979, pp. 71–97.

Seidl, Helmut A. *Medizinische Sprichwörter im Englischen und Deutschen. Eine diachrone Untersuchung zur vergleichenden Parömiologie*. Bern: Peter Lang, 1982.

Seitel, Peter. "Proverbs: A Social Use of Metaphor." *Genre*, 2 (1969), 143–161; also in Wolfgang Mieder and Alan Dundes (eds.). *The Wisdom of Many. Essays on the Proverb*. New York: Garland Publishing, 1981, pp. 122–139.

Silverman-Weinreich, Beatrice. "Towards a Structural Analysis of Yiddish Proverbs." *Yivo Annual of Jewish Social Science*, 17 (1978), 1–20; also in Wolfgang Mieder and Alan Dundes (eds.). *The Wisdom of Many. Essays on the Proverb*. New York: Garland Publishing, 1981, pp. 65–85.

Suard, François, and Claude Buridant (eds.). *Richesse du proverbe*. Vol. I: *Le proverbe au Moyen Age*. Vol. II: *Typologie et fonctions*. Lille: Université de Lille, 1984.

Szemerkényi, Agnes, and Vilmos Voigt. "The Connection of Theme and Language in Proverb Transformations." *Acta Ethnographica Academiae Scientiarum Hungaricae*, 21 (1972), 95–108.

Taylor, Archer. " 'Sunt tria damna domus'." *Hessische Blätter für Volkskunde*, 24 (1926), 130–146; also in A. Taylor, *Selected Writings on Proverbs*, ed. by Wolfgang Mieder. Helsinki: Suomalainen Tiedeakatemia, 1975, pp. 133–151.

Taylor, Archer. "The Proverbial Formula 'Man soll'." *Zeitschrift für Volkskunde*, new series 2 (1930), 152–156; also in A. Taylor. *Selected Writings on Proverbs*, ed. by Wolfgang Mieder. Helsinki: Suomalainen Tiedeakatemia, 1975, pp. 101–105.

Taylor, Archer. *The Proverb*. Cambridge: Harvard University Press, 1931; rpt. Hatboro, Pa.: Folklore Associates, 1962; rpt. again with an introduction and bibliography by Wolfgang Mieder. Bern: Peter Lang, 1985.

Taylor, Archer. " 'Feed a Cold and Starve a Fever'." *Journal of American Folklore*, 71 (1958), 190.

Taylor, Archer. *Selected Writings on Proverbs*, ed. by Wolfgang Mieder. Helsinki: Suomalainen Tiedeakatemia, 1975.

Thierfelder, Franz. "Sprich- und Schlagwörter zwischen den Völkern." *Welt und Wort*, 11 (1956), 369–370 and 373.

Thompson, Harold W. "Proverbs and Sayings." *New York Folklore Quarterly*, 5 (1949), 230–235 and 296–300.

Tilley, Morris Palmer. *Elizabethan Proverb Lore in Lyly's "Euphues" and in Pettie's "Petite Pallace" with Parallels from Shakespeare*. New York: Macmillan, 1926.

Tillhagen, Carl-Herman. "Die Sprichwörterfrequenz in einigen nordschwedischen Dörfern." *Proverbium,* no. 15 (1970), 538–540.

Trench, Richard Chenevix. *On the Lessons in Proverbs.* New York: Redfield, 1853 (later editions also with the title *Proverbs and Their Lessons*).

Trümpy, Hans. " 'Similia similibus'." *Schweizerisches Archiv für Volkskunde,* 62 (1966), 1–6.

Urbach, Otto. "Deutsches Recht im deutschen Sprichwort." *Muttersprache,* 52 (1937), cols. 230–234.

Weekley, Ernest. "Proverbs Considered." *Atlantic Monthly,* 145 (April 1930), 504–512.

Whiting, Bartlett Jere. "The Origin of the Proverb." *Harvard Studies and Notes in Philology and Literature,* 13 (1931), 47–80.

Whiting, Bartlett Jere. "The Nature of the Proverb." *Harvard Studies and Notes in Philology and Literature,* 14 (1932), 273–307.

Williams, George Walton. "Shakespeare Metaphors of Health, Food, Sport, and Life-Preserving Rest." *Journal of Medieval and Renaissance Studies,* 14 (1984), 187–202.

Woodburn, Roland Rickey. *Proverbs in Health Books of the English Renaissance.* Diss. Texas Technical University, 1975.

Yankah, Kwesi. "Toward a Performance-Centered Theory of the Proverb." *Critical Arts,* 3, no. 1 (1983), 29–43.

Zholkovskii, Aleksandr K. "At the Intersection of Linguistics, Paremiology and Poetics: On the Literary Structure of Proverbs." *Poetics,* 7 (1978), 309–332.

Zinnecker, Jürgen. "Wandsprüche." In *Jugend '81. Lebensentwürfe, Alltagskulturen, Zukunftsbilder,* ed. by Arthur Fischer. Hamburg: Jugendwerk der Deutschen Shell, 1981, vol. 1, pp. 430–476.

ART CREDITS

Page 9. *The Burlington Free Press* (February 9, 1974), p. 17.

Page 10. Grace Frank and Dorothy Miner, *Proverbes en rimes. Text and Illustrations of the Fifteenth Century from a French Manuscript in the Walters Art Gallery, Baltimore.* Baltimore: The Johns Hopkins Press, 1937, plate XXXIV.

Page 14. Charles de Tolnay, *The Drawings of Pieter Bruegel the Elder. With a Critical Catalogue.* New York: The Twin Editions, 1953, plate XXIV.

Page 15. *The Burlington Free Press* (July 1, 1985), p. 14A.

Page 26. Lisle de Vaux Matthewman, *Completed Proverbs. Uniform with Crankisms, Brevities, Whimlets.* Pictured by Clare Victor Dwiggins. Philadelphia: Henry T. Coates & Co., 1904, plate 31.

Page 30. Charles H. Bennet, *Proverbs with Pictures.* London: Chapman and Hall, 1859, plate 2.

Page 31. *Playboy* (May 1969), p. 245.

Page 37. *The New York Times Magazine* (January 2, 1977), p. 35.

Page 43. John W. Barber, *The Hand Book of Illustrated Proverbs.* New York: George F. Tuttle, 1858, p. 83.

Page 48. *National Lampoon* (March 1976), p. 97.

Page 49. *Omni* (August 1983), p. 29.

Page 54. Lizzie Lawson and Clara L. Mateaux, *Old Proverbs with New Pictures.* London: Cassell, Petter, Calpin & Co., 1881, p. 48.

Page 60. Christopher Brown, *Bruegel.* New York: Crescent Books, 1975, p. 11.

Page 62. Jacques Lavalleye, *Pieter Bruegel the Elder and Lucas van Leyden. The Complete Engravings, Etchings, and Woodcuts.* New York: Harry N. Abrams, 1967, plate 158.

Page 64. Michael Wynn Jones, *The Cartoon History of Britain.* New York: The Macmillan Co., 1971, p. 270.

Page 67. *New Yorker* (August 27, 1960), p. 45.

Page 72. Bob Abel (ed.), *The American Cartoon Album.* New York: Dodd, Mead & Co., 1974, no pp. given.

Page 89. *New Yorker* (February 4, 1980), p. 58.

Page 123. *Punch* (January 13, 1989), p. 15.

Page 125. Birthday card by Mark I Inc. (Chicago), purchased in November 1980 in Chicago.

Page 125. *The Burlington Free Press* (June 9, 1985), comics section, no pp. given.

Page 127. The embroidery sampler is on the cover of my book *American Proverbs: A Study of Texts and Contexts* (Bern: Peter Lang, 1989) and was made by my wife Barbara Mieder in 1977.

Page 141. *The Burlington Free Press* (April 24, 1975), p. 8.

Page 143. *The Burlington Free Press* (May 18, 1979), p. 7D.

Page 144. *New Yorker* (April 14, 1980), p. 52.

Page 147. *Time* (October 24, 1988), outside back cover.

Page 158. *New Yorker* (November 9, 1987), p. 44.

Page 159. *Fortune* (October 1939), p. 133.

Page 162. *The Burlington Free Press* (September 22, 1983), p. 11D.

Page 162. *The Burlington Free Press* (February 28, 1989), p. 5D.

Page 164. Birthday card by Recycled Paper Products, purchased in October 1989 in Burlington, Vermont. The artist is John-Richard Allen (1987).

Page 166. *New Yorker* (August 22, 1977), p. 70.

Page 174. *International Herald Tribune* (June 13, 1980), p. 20.

Page 181. *New Yorker* (March 5, 1960), p. 38.

Page 194 M. Spanier (ed.), *Thomas Murners Narrenbeschwörung*. Halle: VEB Max Niemeyer, 1967 (1st ed. 1894), p. 244.

Page 213. *The Times (London) Educational Supplement* (September 14, 1990), p. 10.

Page 214. *The Washington Post* (February 27, 1981), p. 1A.

Page 215. Charles M. Schulz, *Go Fly a Kite, Charlie Brown. A Peanuts Book*. New York: Holt, Rinehart & Winston, 1960, no pp. given.

INDEXES

The indexes include references only to the text and do not include names, subjects, and proverbs mentioned in the extensive notes and bibliography.

Names

Subjects

Proverbs